ANTI-SLAVERY,
RELIGION,
AND REFORM

Roger Thomas Anstey (1927–79)

Professor of Modern History, University of Kent at Canterbury, 1968–79

ANTI-SLAVERY, RELIGION, AND REFORM:
Essays in Memory of Roger Anstey

Edited by

CHRISTINE BOLT
SEYMOUR DRESCHER

LIBRARY ST. MARY'S COLLEGE
DAWSON · ARCHON

First published in 1980
© Wm Dawson & Sons Ltd, 1980

Wm Dawson & Sons Ltd, Cannon House
Folkestone, Kent, England

Archon Books, 995 Sherman Avenue,
Hamden, Connecticut, USA

British Library Cataloguing in Publication Data

Anti-slavery, religion and reform.
1. Slavery – Emancipation – Congresses
2. Abolitionists – Congresses
I. Anstey, Roger   II. Bolt, Christine
III. Drescher, Seymour
322.4′4′09033   HT1025   79-41532

Dawson ISBN 0–7129–0945–1

Archon ISBN 0–208–01783–6

Printed and bound in Great Britain
by W & J Mackay Limited, Chatham

CONTENTS

CONTRIBUTORS

Roger Anstey. *Educated:* Shrewsbury School; St Johns College, Cambridge, M.A., 1952; Ph.D., London, 1957. *Appointments:* Lecturer in History, University of Ibadan, Nigeria, 1952–7; Lecturer, University of Durham, 1958–66; Visiting Professor, University of British Columbia, 1966–7; Reader, University of Durham, 1967–8; Professor of Modern History, University of Kent at Canterbury, 1968–79. *Publications:* these include *Britain and the Congo in the Nineteenth Century* (1962); *King Leopold's Legacy: The Congo Under Belgian Rule* (1966); *The Atlantic Slave Trade and British Abolition, 1760–1810* (1975); editor (with P. E. H. Hair), *Liverpool, the African Slave Trade, and Abolition* (Historic Society of Lancashire and Cheshire, 1976); and contributions to *African Historical Studies*, *Economic History Review*, *English Historical Review*.

Professor Anstey will be fondly remembered by his colleagues at the University of Kent, to which he contributed so much, and by the local community, in which he was known as a devout and active Methodist, and as a Governor of Kent College and Christ Church College. We hope to remember him formally through the establishment at the University of Kent of a regular series of Anstey Lectures, designed to reflect Professor Anstey's wide-ranging intellectual interests and to be published by Macmillan.

Christine Bolt is Reader in American History at the University of Kent at Canterbury, where she has taught since 1966, with visiting teaching appointments at American universities, 1969–71. Her publications include *The Anti-Slavery Movement and Reconstruction* (1969); *Victorian Attitudes to Race* (1971); *A History of the USA* (1974); and articles in academic publications. She is the co-author of a book on pressure groups in nineteenth- and twentieth-century America to be published by Martin Robertson in 1980, and is currently working on a book for Allen & Unwin on aspects of Indian–White relations in the USA.

Serge Daget has been a Professor of History at the Université Nationale de Côte d'Ivoire since 1972. His doctorate from the Sorbonne was on the French abolition of the slave trade, on which subject he has published many articles in various reviews, the principal ones being: 'La France et l'abolition de la traite des Noirs, 1814–31', *Cahiers d'Etudes Africaines* (1971); 'Le trafic négrier illégal français: historiographie et sources', *Annales de l'Universite d'Abidjan* (1975); 'Long cours et négriers nantais du trafic illégal', in *La Traite des Noirs par l'Atlantique: Nouvelle approches* (Paris, 1976); 'British repression of the illegal French slave trade: some considerations', in *The Uncommon Market* (New York, 1979).

David Brion Davis is Sterling Professor of History at Yale University. From 1955 to 1969 he taught at Cornell University, and in 1969–70 was Harmsworth Professor at Oxford. His books include *The Problem of Slavery in Western Culture* (Cornell, 1966), which won the Pulitzer Prize for non-fiction; and *The Problem of Slavery in the Age of Revolution, 1770–1823* (Cornell, 1975), which won the National Book Award for history and biography, the Bancroft Prize, and the Beveridge Award of the American Historical Association. His most recent book is *Antebellum American Culture*. He is now completing a work, *Slavery and Human Progress*, and is working on the final volume of a trilogy: *The Problem of Slavery in the Age of Emancipation*.

G. M. Ditchfield, F.R.Hist.S., was educated at Durham and Cambridge Universities; was Leverhulme Fellow, University of Liverpool, 1968–70; and has been Lecturer in History, University of Kent at Canterbury, since 1970. His publications include articles in *Journal of Ecclesiastical History*, *English Historical Review*, *Bulletin of the Institute of Historical Research* and other journals. He is currently engaged on a study of nonconformity and the Test laws in late eighteenth-century Britain.

Seymour Drescher has been Professor of History at the University of Pittsburgh since 1969, where he has taught since 1962, after two years teaching at Harvard. In addition to his books on Tocqueville, he has published *Econocide: British Slavery and the Slave Trade in the Era of Abolition* (Pittsburgh, 1977); and his articles include: 'Le "déclin" du système esclavagiste brittannique et l'abolition de la traite', *Annales: Economies, Societés, Civilisations* 31 (Mars–Avril 1976); 'Capitalism and abolition: values and forces in Britain, 1783–1814', in *Liverpool, the Slave Trade, and Abolition,* ed. Anstey and Hair (The Historic Society of Lancashire and Cheshire, 1976); and 'Capitalism and the decline of slavery: the British case in comparative perspective', in *Comparative Perspectives on Slavery in New World Plantation Societies, Annals of the New York Academy of Sciences,* 292 (1977).

David Eltis has taught history and economics at Algonquin College, Ottawa, for several years. He is the author of several articles on the slave trade and abolition and is currently co-editing a volume of essays on these subjects in addition to writing a book on the nineteenth-century slave trade.

Pieter C. Emmer has been Senior Lecturer, Department of History, University of Leiden and Secretary, Centre for the History of European Expansion, since 1975. He was Curator, Dutch Economic History Archive, 1969–74, and Fellow Commoner, Churchill College, Cambridge, 1978–9. He is the author of *Engeland, Nederland, Afrika en de slavenhandel in de negentiende eeuw* (Leiden, 1974); and editor, with Jean Mettas and J. C. Nardin of *The Atlantic Slave Trade: New Approaches* (Paris, 1976). His present research concerns immigration into the Dutch possessions in the Caribbean during the second half of the nineteenth century.

Stanley L. Engerman is Professor of Economics and History at the University of Rochester. He is co-author of *Time on the Cross: The Economics of American Negro Slavery* (1974) and co-editor of *The Reinterpretation of American Economic History* (1971), and *Race and Slavery in the Western Hemisphere: Quantitative Studies* (Princeton, 1975).

Eric Foner is Professor of History, City College, City University of New York; Pitt Professor of American History, Cambridge University, 1980–1. His publications include *Free Soil, Free Labor, Free Men: The Ideology of the Republican Party Before the Civil War* (New York, 1970), *Tom Paine and Revolutionary America* (New York, 1976), numerous articles and reviews in *Journal of American History, Civil War History, New York Review of Books,* and others. He is currently working on the volume on Reconstruction for the 'New American Nation Series' (Harper & Row).

x   Contributors

Brian Harrison has been Fellow and Tutor in Modern History and
Politics at Corpus Christi College, Oxford, since 1967. He was
visiting professor at the University of Michigan (1970) and Harvard
University (1973), and visiting fellow at the University of Mel-
bourne, Australia (1975). He has published *Drink and the Victorians. The Temperance Question in England 1815–1872* (1971),
Separate Spheres. The Opposition to Women's Suffrage in Britain
(1978) and several articles on social and political history in col-
laborative volumes and academic journals. He has edited (with
Patricia Hollis) *Robert Lowery. Radical and Chartist* (1979) and is
now studying the history of British women's organizations since the
1840s.

Patricia Hollis is Senior Lecturer in nineteenth-century history,
University of East Anglia. She took her first degree at Cambridge
followed by graduate work at Berkeley, California; Columbia, New
York; and Nuffield College, Oxford. Her publications include *The
Pauper Press* (1970); *Class and Conflict in Nineteenth Century
England* (1973); *Pressure from Without* (editor, 1974); *Women in
Public 1850–1900* (1979); *Robert Lowery. Radical and Chartist*
(1979, with Brian Harrison).

Donald G. Mathews is Professor of History at the University of
North Carolina at Chapel Hill, where he has taught since 1968, after
teaching at Princeton and Duke universities. He is the author of
*Slavery and Methodism: A Chapter in American Morality,
1780–1845* (Princeton, 1965); *Religion in the Old South* (Chicago,
1977); editor of *Agitation for Freedom: The Abolitionists* (1971);
and has published various articles on related themes in academic
journals and collections. He is currently writing a study of opposition to the Equal Rights Amendment in North Carolina (with Jane
D. Hart Mathews) and working on a study of society and religion in
the South, 1846–1956.

C. Duncan Rice is Dean of the College and Professor of History at
Hamilton College, New York, having previously taught at the university of Aberdeen and at Yale. His publications include *The Rise
and Fall of Black Slavery* (1975); *The Scots Abolitionists, 1831–61*
(forthcoming); and articles on related subjects in journals and
collections. He is now working on Anglo-American middle-class
reform, 1770–1860, and on the response of the Scottish Enlightenment to slavery and savagery.

Howard Temperley is Reader in American History at the University of East Anglia, where he is currently Dean of the School of English and American Studies. He previously taught at the universities of Wales and Manchester. Since 1977 he has been Editor of the *Journal of American Studies*. His publications include *British Anti-slavery, 1833–1870* (1972) and 'Capitalism, Slavery and Ideology', *Past and Present*, May 1977.

David M. Turley has been Lecturer in History at the University of Kent at Canterbury since 1968, having previously taught at the University of Sheffield, and as a visiting professor at universities in Pennsylvania and Colorado. He has contributed text and maps on slave economies and transatlantic connections to a historical atlas; is completing a book on *The Culture of British Anti-Slavery, 1780–1860*; and is collecting material for a study of the impact of the slave revolution in Haiti, both internally and externally. He has also written on cartoons as social and political commentary.

James Walvin is Senior Lecturer in the Department of History, University of York. His publications include *Black and White: The Negro and English Society, 1555–1945* (1973); *The Black Presence* (1972); *A Jamaican Plantation: Worthy Park, 1670–1970* (with M. Craton, 1970); and *Slavery, Abolition and Emancipation* (with M. Craton and D. Wright, 1976). He is now working, with M. Craton, on a book to be called *Freeing the Slaves: Emancipation of Slaves in the British Caribbean*.

Bertram Wyatt-Brown is Professor of History at Case Western Reserve University, where he has taught since 1966, and has previously taught at Colorado State University, the University of Colorado, and the University of Wisconsin (visiting appointment). He is the author of *Lewis Tappan and the Evangelical War Against Slavery* (Cleveland, 1969); editor of *The American People in the Antebellum South* (1973); and has contributed articles to anthologies, books, and such journals as *American Quarterly*, *Journal of American History*, *Journal of Southern History*, *Soundings* and *Societas*. He is now preparing a study of 'The Southern ethic: cultural foundations of the antebellum South'.

ACKNOWLEDGEMENTS

The essays published here were originally presented as papers at a conference on religion, anti-slavery and reform, held in the Rockefeller centre at Bellagio, Italy, in July 1978. We should like to express warm thanks to the Rockefeller Foundation, whose generosity made the conference possible, and to the staff at the Bellagio Centre, who made it a memorable experience. The conference was organized with great efficiency by the late Professor Roger Anstey and Professor Donald Read, both of the University of Kent at Canterbury; they were helped by the secretarial staff of Eliot College, who have subsequently given willing assistance in the preparation of this volume. Our thanks must go to them and to participants at the conference whose comments at the sessions and on the essays collected here were invaluable: Professor Read, Mr Fred Mather of the University of Southampton, Dr John Walsh of Jesus College, Oxford, and Professor Lewis Perry of the University of Indiana at Bloomington.

Publisher's Note
Place of publication of books cited is London unless otherwise stated.

INTRODUCTION

by Christine Bolt and Seymour Drescher

Fields of knowledge, like fields of enterprise, seldom expand in perfect symmetry. In the past generation there has been an enormous upsurge of interest in European-sponsored slavery. During this period, the major focus of scholarly research has been on the establishment and internal dynamics of a system of human relations which deeply affected the social and economic development of Africa and the Americas. Scholars have opened up vast new sources of data and evolved new analytical techniques. The aspects of society to be examined have been expanded and the range of comparative regional analysis broadened.

Relatively less attention has been devoted to the demise of chattel slavery. A little over two centuries ago the institution existed as a virtually unchallenged, if not ubiquitous, element of the international economic network. The trans-oceanic slave trade not only constituted one of the great diasporas of world history, but was based on one of the most complex, dynamic and technologically advanced enterprises ever developed by European capitalism. Yet in less than half the time they took to unfold, transatlantic slavery and the slave trade had disappeared from all European-linked societies and were rapidly eroding at their African core. By the beginning of the twentieth century, slavery was becoming just another part of the dismantled 'old orders' which were fast converging on a single progressive system of individual rights and contractual reciprocity.

As long as this process of emancipation endured, the British part in it seemed to historians to be a fairly straightforward business, underwritten by assumptions of providential design and material progress. One had to account for its momentum and direction no more than one has to account for the direction and flow of a river system, the metaphor graphically used by Thomas Clarkson, the first historian of abolition, in 1808. Even Eric Williams's challenge to the humanitarian school of moral progress in *Capitalism and Slavery* (1944) was written within the framework of a dialectical evolutionary theory of material progress. In his schema, economic interests rather than moral aversion fueled the movement towards abolition. But regardless of the subsequent fate of Williams's specific analysis, his attempt to link the source and timing of abolition to events outside the abolition campaign was crucial in stimulating scholars to broaden their horizons and re-examine old assumptions, in a way not unlike the Tannenbaum thesis in the history of slavery itself.

The first estimations of abolition in the United States were, of course, less simple. Just as sectional loyalties, in which economic interests played a large part, came to dominate the responses of Americans to anti-slavery activities by the 1850s, so the pioneering historical assessments of that movement were complicated by memories of the bloody Civil War which ended with both abolition and the destruction of southern prosperity. In time, the bitter personal recollections faded and the sectional apologetics dwindled. However, anti-slavery remained something less than the triumph of complete moral rectitude over the forces of evil. Thus scholars in the 1930s, notably Gilbert H. Barnes and Dwight L. Dumond, though they emphasized the inspiration abolitionists drew from evangelical religion, revived the initial nineteenth-century view, which was not confined to southerners, that at least some organized abolitionists were disruptive, impractical fanatics. Nonetheless it is still true to say that until comparatively recently, American commentators, like their British counterparts, have generally been content to present anti-slavery – as did the abolitionists themselves – in terms of great moral forces, with only secondary reference to economic or social influences. And what was thought to be true of anti-slavery was applied to reform as a whole, whose chroniclers once explained it with too emphatic a focus on the impact of romantic faith in human perfectibility; on the explosive blending of Jeffersonian rationalism with democratic optimism.

I

The essays in this collection attempt to explore some of the relations of the process of abolition to the broader social, political, and cultural development of North Atlantic metropolises which were anti-slavery's main areas of strength. Although the essays are not based upon, nor do they address themselves to, any single theory of social evolution or historical explanation, for the most part they investigate the putative relationship between the topics indicated in the title. A number of questions appear to have emerged from the various contributions. To what extent was the connection between anti-slavery, religion, and reform confined to certain political or cultural regions, to certain social classes or races, to certain points in time? To what extent can one speak of a convergent development of anti-slavery, religion, and reform in terms of motivation, tactics and ideas, and in what ways do they diverge? Finally, does concentration on these particular relationships obscure other patterns of social, economic, or cultural linkage in the countries studied?

The first question raises the issue of the comparative strength of the phenomena in different non-slave centres. It is entirely fitting that a project initiated by Roger Anstey should have taken as one of its basic themes the stimulus given to individual self-mastery and social improvement by Protestant evangelicalism in the eighteenth and nineteenth centuries. By looking at the experiences of Britain, France, the Netherlands, and the United States, it has been possible to construct what Seymour Drescher in his essay calls an Anglo-American and a Continental model of anti-slavery, with popular mobilization and the related evangelical impulse being of fundamental importance in the former but not in the latter. In France, because of the dominating position of the Catholic church, numerically and in every other way, evangelicals were obviously not well placed to exercise a guiding influence over reform, notwithstanding the disproportionate participation of French Protestants in anti-slavery organizations. But the situation was similar in such predominantly Protestant countries as Holland, a fact which helps to remind us that comparative studies tend to bring out what is distinctive in the communities being compared. Thus, despite changes in *international* attitudes toward blacks and slavery from the eighteenth century, and toward what constituted or retarded progress, local political and economic considerations still largely determined how far and how fast these changes would be acted upon.

In Britain, as Roger Anstey shows, while the pattern of anti-slavery efforts altered during the eighteenth and nineteenth centuries, later successes followed naturally from and consolidated earlier ideological shifts, organizational experiments, and political manoeuvres. Yet, Serge Daget relates, the achievements of the 1790s in France were actually followed by the re-imposition of slavery, and the formation of a series of anti-slavery societies of limited scope and fluctuating idealism. And in Holland, Pieter Emmer suggests, the path to abolition was impeded before the 1850s by a degree of economic and intellectual stagnation, despite occasional miniscule protests against the institution from the eighteenth century onwards. Nor did evangelical religion elsewhere on the Continent propel its adherents either within or without the political arena, into the host of reforms that clustered about anti-slavery in Britain and the United States. It is unlikely that this contrast between the Anglo-American and Continental models of abolition, as they apply to the period before slavery's extinction in the Americas, will be much altered by extending the Continental survey to include the Danish, Swedish, German, Spanish, or Portuguese cases. The slave societies themselves may provide a different set of relationships between popular activism, religious mobilization, and reform. Indeed, from the evidence presented by Donald Mathews, one might infer that there was more popular discussion of slavery in the evangelicizing slave South, at one critical moment, than in the whole European Continent over three-quarters of a century.

A number of contributors have also indicated some of the differences as well as similarities which existed between the British and American reform experiences. There were reformers on both sides of the Atlantic who felt ambivalent about engaging in the corrupt world of politics and found bi-partisanship both morally attractive – in its appeal to the higher public good – and a wise means of addressing potential supporters who might already be politically committed. But British activists were distinctive in their focus on the national legislature, in their realization that no campaign could succeed which failed to enlist the sympathy of that body, and in being able to address themselves to a party, the Whig/Liberal coalition, which as the party of progress had no similarly consistent American counterpart. Equally there are no sectional divisions in British reform comparable to that between the ante-bellum South and the rest of the United States, though it is possible to exaggerate southern separateness before the 1850s and to undervalue regional variations within Britain.

Another point of Anglo-American divergence would seem to be the deliberate way in which middle-class British reformers – except at times on the vexed question of anti-slavery – appealed for working-class backing, thereby linking their causes to the 'dangerous' elements for long excluded from political participation. Consequently the 'watersheds' for British reformers occur fairly frequently, often coinciding with various suffrage extensions. In the United States, the Civil War is plainly the great divide for humanitarians, albeit it administered no fatal blow and its impact is of a substantially different kind, while a host of factors reduced the distinctiveness of the working-class constituency for agitators. Moreover, there has been less debate among British than American scholars about a proper definition of reform, perhaps because of its clearer political connotations and the clearer definition of political 'outsider' groups in the British context. And neither contemporaries nor historians in Britain have struggled as much as Americans have to pinpoint the precise role of the abolitionists. In fact anti-slavery is often seen by the latter as undermining, even as it epitomized, aspects of ante-bellum reform. This is hardly surprising. The British anti-slavery movement enjoyed comparatively swift success and was an acknowledged inspiration to subsequent reformers, whereas organized abolitionism peaked in the United States before having achieved its primary purpose. Thereafter, having alienated a large section of American public opinion from anti-slavery and associated good causes, it endured in an increasingly complex and fragmented state. Yet, when all these differences between the two countries have been acknowledged, the central validity of the Anglo-American model and the basic distinction between it and the Continental model of reform remains.

II

On the question of the relationship of anti-slavery to religion and reform within the 'core' Anglo-American area, the essays appear to fall within two broad categories. Roger Anstey, Brian Harrison, G. M. Ditchfield, David Turley, James Walvin and Bertram Wyatt-Brown would seem to stress the positive correlation between at least two of the three phenomena under consideration. Ditchfield's use of Parliamentary voting lists on three representative issues during the course of a single Parliament allows him to establish comparative overlap and divergence with enviable precision. Brian Harrison draws from an enormous range of documentation over a century of British reform activity to show how closely interwoven was the pattern of reform in matters of personnel, ideology, techniques, and the institutions of religion, family and politics. He traces the evolution of a large view of moral progress which, supplemented by mutual reproaches about neglected evils and the stimulus provided by success and failure alike, could lead reformers into innumerable good causes. Along the way women – in the United States as well as Britain – found new opportunities for employment and self-expression, just as their horizons had been initially broadened by the enlargment of prospects for working outside the home. Harrison's notion of 'reciprocal rebuke' also presents a way of fitting dissident elements among reformers into a fundamental unity of ideas and behaviour. Furthermore, it illuminates the tension between reformer and statesman which David Turley elaborates in connection with the issue of fugitive slaves. Abolitionists might be uneasy about the British government's slipping from the ground of moral principle, but in 1840 it was the only government they had. Bertram Wyatt-Brown likewise delves more precisely into the connection which Harrison notes between family, religion and career choice. While emphasizing the common evangelical background from which American abolitionists and missionaries emerged, his essay reminds us that evangelicalism was a source for far more than anti-slavery or indeed domestic political activism. Given Donald Mathews's conclusion that abolition may demonstrate the failure of evangelicalism as much as its success, it is important to note that the virtually total convergence of anti-slavery with evangelicalism may be confined to the English case alone at the national level. James Walvin picks up another major theme: the congruence of anti-slavery and popular mobilization noted in Part I of this volume. Walvin traces a community of interest, and a cross-over of both techniques and ideology between anti-slavery and agitation for political reform out-of-doors.

III

Another set of essays probe somewhat more dysfunctional aspects of the connection between anti-slavery, religion, and reform. Christine Bolt, Donald Mathews, Eric Foner and Patricia Hollis illustrate the difficulties of reciprocal reinforcement models when they traverse boundaries of race and class. Christine Bolt's essay exemplifies a parting of pro-black and pro-Indian activity in the age of abolition. This shift in priorities reflected the weight of numbers, the contrasting images of the two races, and the factor of black slavery among the southern Indian tribes. Donald Mathews's article demonstrates the bifurcation of the evangelical experience along racial lines in the South, with dire consequences for the evangelical abolitionist connection. Patricia Hollis and Eric Foner examine the confrontation between evangelical abolitionism and working-class radicalism in England and America respectively. The authors present parallel evidence for a confrontation between anti-slavery leadership and ideology and working-class radicals c. 1830, although

Foner's perspective on the anti-slavery commitment of the working-class constituency, as opposed to that of its leaders, comes closer to other essays than does Hollis's.

All four of these articles, however, allow for the implication that the breaches they describe were deviations from the norm. For Bolt, Hollis, and Foner they were departures which constituted only an intermediate phase in the linkage between anti-slavery and reformism. Thus after seeking to explain why the eradication of black slavery was given priority by humanitarians, and why neither working men nor Indians could co-operate effectively with them, Bolt and Foner point out that the connection between anti-slavery, the labour movement, and other reforms was renewed in the 1850s and sustained after 1865, when slavery itself had been destroyed. For Mathews, the evangelical abandonment of anti-slavery was a departure from the logically revolutionary implications of the evangelical experience. But one cannot simply decide that evangelicalism was 'not itself' in the South – just another victim of the slave-holding ethos. Rather, so Mathews argues, 'the logic of slavery reinforced and was in turn reinforced by evangelical emphasis on the holy life as an orderly, disciplined struggle to subdue the unruly self', even if black evangelicals managed to shape out of their religion 'a history which acknowledged the injustice of their bondage and promised freedom'. On the other hand, one might wish to stress the still longer-range fissures which have developed between the libertarian outlook of abolitionism and the group-centred ideologies of socialism noted in Harrison's essay, or the imperialist potential of anti-slavery noted by David Davis. Whether the overlap of anti-slavery, religion, and reform looks full or empty depends to an extent on when one chooses to turn the hour-glass.

IV

The traditional paradigms have not been overlooked altogether. Stanley Engerman and David Eltis address themselves to the ongoing debate over the relative roles of economics and humanitarianism as both sources of abolitionism and as the basis of its success. Their analysis indicates that the causal inquiry has shifted from the search for a direct confrontation of economic interests towards ideological assumptions and the indirect working of economic forces. This essay introduces us to those articles in the collection which concentrate on the broad cultural and ideological dimensions of the relationship between abolition and evolving European society. Duncan Rice attempts to move far beyond the network of social activity which constitutes the focus of the essays in Part 2, by sampling changes in British public opinion over a century of imaginative literature. He emphasises both the revolutionary transformation in attitudes towards slavery coincident with the rise of popular abolitionism and the emergence of an outlook which was simultaneously anti-slavery and anti-abolitionist, an attitude apparently not confined to some of the working-class. Howard Temperley's article seeks to ground the emergence of anti-slavery ideology in the general development of the North Atlantic area, and in so doing provides the most detailed examination in this volume of the recent literature on the causes of the rise of abolitionism.

The discussion of the economic implications of slavery and anti-slavery by a number of contributors – including Engerman and Eltis, Hollis, Temperley, and Davis – also has the effect of bringing together what has often been separated in the past and by modern scholars. Instead of seeing economic and moral reasons for abolishing slavery as largely separate and conflicting entities, in the manner of Eric Williams, they show quite plainly that these distinctions are frequently meaningless when applied to the nineteenth century. They argue that for most Anglo-American reformers no crude distinctions existed between material and spiritual objectives, between the struggle for self-control and the good society – that is, an economically expansive and strictly regulated society in which the virtuous individual could flourish. This is not to say that reformers did not generally prefer to stress the moral aspects of their case; that we now have fully satisfying answers to reformer motives; or that being moved by complex considerations caused the reformers to describe accurately the complex systems they attacked. Rather we are reminded that if we have demolished the old, simple explanations for the ending of slavery, especially those connected with its alleged debility, we have not yet agreed upon a new, universally applicable one. The inadequacy of individualistic abolitionist debates on the nature and potential of free labour is well brought out, together with the different part it played in British and American calculations. We are further reminded that the reformist impulse was as aggressive in its attitude towards the periphery as it was towards its own society. Indeed, seen from this vantage, the apolitical missionaries of Wyatt-Brown's essay turn out to be only the outer edge of a vast secular process of European-sponsored transformation.

The paradoxes of abolitionist ideology, touched on elsewhere, form the core of the concluding article by David Davis. His purpose is to demonstrate that the link of North Atlantic dynamism to anti-slavery is only a phase of a symmetrical cycle beginning with a Europe whose progress was tied to slavery and completed by connecting the advance of anti-slavery to imperialism. Regardless of the significance attached by reformers to the idea that they lived in a progressive world, whose further improvement they were obliged to advance, we learn how perceptions of slavery, as much as of anti-slavery, have ironically been yoked, 'over a broad sweep of time, to notions of human progress'. Davis also emphasises the erosion of progress as well as chattel slavery, and the emergence of new forms of coercion as cruel and even more extensive than that which was destroyed in the age of abolition.

Some attention has been given throughout the collection to the opponents of reform and the contentious question of why, among people of similar backgrounds, some chose to take up the cause while others chose alternative paths to virtue or rejected their duty altogether. But the motives and attitudes of rank-and-file supporters of reform still need more investigation, and due note has been taken here that a distinctly partial view is obtained by scanning reform only through the medium of reformer literature. There are no easy explanations to be derived for a phenomenon so intricately rooted and multi-faceted as nineteenth-century reform, when nearly all articulate men and women might express a desire to improve society in some respect, whether or not they organized to that end. And as Ralph Waldo Emerson observed in his 1841 lecture *The Conservative*, in most Americans at least there struggled twin desires for change and stability; a belief that in 'a true society, in a true man, both must combine'.

Yet as European hegemony and the idea of moral progress clearly join slavery in the twilight of history, our senses about the age we have lost are sharpened. It becomes more important to probe the precise relationships of ideas and institutions which once seemed to dovetail automatically and logically. We may hope that the scholarship of this volume, dedicated to the friend we have lost, is a stirring of the owl of Minerva at dusk.

September 1979   C.B.
                                                           S.D.

AN APPRECIATION OF ROGER ANSTEY

by David Brion Davis

For all students of slavery and anti-slavery, Roger Anstey's death is an incalculable loss. No other historian on either side of the Atlantic has acquired a comparable mastery of such diverse subjects as the Congo under Belgian rule, the profitability of the African slave trade, the politics of British abolition and emancipation, the role of Wesleyan Methodism in British reform, and the diplomacy of slave-trade suppression. Like a Thomas Clarkson or Zachary Macaulay, Roger sought out co-workers of different faiths, ideologies, and nationalities, and became a kind of nerve center and organizational impetus for international and comparative scholarship. These efforts culminated in the conference on Religion, Anti-Slavery and Reform, held in July 1978 at the Villa Serbelloni in Bellagio, Italy. From its inception to its successful completion, this international gathering was one of the crowning achievements of Roger's career.

Like most of the British abolitionists, he was more centrally concerned with the African slave trade than with New World slavery, but he closely followed the work being done in virtually every aspect of the subject. A list of the scholars Roger has aided, befriended, and counseled would include a sizable proportion of our international brotherhood and sisterhood of slavery historians. I was fortunate in having opportunities for prolonged discussions with him in several states and countries, and was privileged to count him as a faithful and always informative correspondent from 1966 until 25 January 1979, the day before he died. The profound and universal respect with which Roger was regarded by those who knew him can be attributed to his native generosity, good humor, and kindness, and to the fact that he incarnated the disciplined zeal of a man who knows that he has enlisted in a lifetime's campaign.

Much of Roger Anstey's recent work had been concerned with religion and anti-slavery, and at the outset I want to say something about his own religious perspective. Because historical scholarship has become so thoroughly secularized, we generally consider it bad taste to discuss private and supposedly irrelevant religious beliefs, though of course we attach considerable significance to a historian's political ideology. Thus Roger's last book, *The Atlantic Slave Trade and British Abolition*, was generally interpreted as an anti-Marxist work because it demolished many of the premises of Eric Williams' *Capitalism and Slavery*. No-one could deny Anstey's desire to discredit economic determinism and to counter Williams' contention that humanitarianism became convincing in Britain only when it served material interests. But it is a serious mistake, I think, to translate Anstey's arguments into political terms, for he was, as he once referred to himself, a 'working historian who is also a believer'. He scrupulously avoided sermonizing, being convinced that the truth, if once uncovered, would in the long run speak for itself. But if his professional writings seem to conform to the standards of secular history, every work reflects the world view of a devout Christian who literally *lived* the Protestant ethic.

Roger candidly affirmed his belief in history as the Providence of God under the lordship of Christ, observing that modern pretensions to 'objective history' only conceal unconscious presuppositions which, 'since we are all in some measure children of our age, usually consist of a varying mish-mash of woolly liberal, neo-Marxian, vaguely Weberian or vulgar Freudian ideas'. Inspired particularly by the works of Oscar Cullman, Roger Anstey drew a sharp distinction between conventional historical theology and the theology of history, or 'the place of historical development in Christian theology'. More concretely, this means that he believed in the integrity and unity of historical time between the resurrection of Christ and the Second Coming, a stream of intermediate time characterized both by contingency and the constancy of a divine plan, by incompleteness and even disaster as well as by the unfolding of a 'saving process'. As one begins to discern 'a religious dynamic in mundane events', Roger once wrote, 'the whole of History associated with Max Weber lends itself to this, even constitutes it. . . .'

For non-Christians like myself, it is extremely difficult to understand a perspective from which the Church's role in abolition is viewed as a 'saving event' within the context of salvation history. What Anstey's perspective does suggest to me, with a certain shock of self-recognition, is that we have uncritically tended to assume that anti-slavery can be understood as part of an irreversible process of secularization. In other words, we have assumed that Christianity was somehow diluted and secularized as religious men and women became preoccupied with social problems. The reform movements of the early nineteenth century were thus, to use Emerson's phrase, 'a falling from the church nominal' and a bridge to the social gospel, to pragmatic or utilitarian reform or to socialism itself. Such assumptions lead easily to a crude reductionism in which 'sin', for example, means something other than sin and in which religious motivation is explained in terms of various secular 'interests'.

What Roger Anstey has done is to turn such assumptions upside down. The key argument of his last book is that in 1806 'an unpredictable and fortuitous conjunction of politico-economic circumstances' enabled the British abolitionists to suppress their religious and humanitarian goals and appeal entirely to national interest in order to secure passage of a law which effectively abolished about two-thirds of the British slave trade. This tactical victory opened the way for the breakthrough of 1807, when the abolitionists ran up the flag of moral principle and killed off the remnant. In his more recent papers he pointed to a somewhat similar but even more complex conjunction of expediency and moral principle in the enactment of West Indian emancipation. 'The great importance of the anti-slavery lobby', he writes, which exploited '"the popular feeling excited by religious principle"', was 'that by its constant pressure on the Government it ensured a tolerable solution'. The point I want to emphasize here is that as an alternative to the theme of secularization, Anstey pictured anti-slavery as a means of sanctifying or in effect *sacralizing* the cause of social justice, in the sense of extending the line of demarkation between sacred and profane. Thus the significance of abolitionism was not that evangelicals, Quakers, and Methodists became preoccupied with secular affairs, but that they defined slavery as a moral and religious rather than as a political issue. While Roger recognized that the abolitionist crusade created 'a precedent for agitation about, and state intervention in, an expanding range of evils', he seemed less certain about the role of such agitation and state intervention in the history of human salvation. Like the abolitionists themselves, he believed that 'no status to be reformed could have such basic importance as that of slavery and no evil to be ended could be as fundamental as the enslavement and transhipment of the free. After all, the issue as between slave and free underlies all questions of improvement in human status'.

One reason for this centrality of slavery, as Roger well knew, is that the Judeo–Christian tradition begins with a great myth of

14   David Brion Davis

slavery and human redemption – the Mosaic account of Hebrew slaves being delivered from Egyptian bondage, of their transferring their ultimate allegiance from worldly masters to a supreme God, and of their struggles to preserve their freedom and historic mission by faithful observance of God's law and remembrance of their former slavery. This was the 'overarching typology' of bondage and redemption which Christianity inherited. If early Christians essentially accepted the Roman social order, it was at a price of extending, in the expectation of the imminent Kingdom of God, the Stoics' topsy-turvy perspective from which a great king might be a slave and a man in chains a freeman. There was more than verbal play to Jesus' announcement that 'he that was called in the Lord being a bondservant, is the Lord's freeman: likewise he that was called being free, is Christ's bondservant'.

For the most part, Roger avoided the suggestion that the Judeo–Christian tradition contained latent seeds of anti-slavery predestined for future fruition. Yet he also insisted, correctly I think, that the relations between spiritual and physical slavery were more than metaphorical – at least as we generally understand metaphor. We may not accept Roger's own belief in progressive revelation under the sustaining power of Providence, but it is important to understand the implications of this belief for Christian abolitionists, especially evangelicals. As Roger makes clear in his book, according to the evangelical reading of the Old Testament, 'God's whole redemptive purpose is placed firmly in the context of physical slavery and liberation'. And when one moves from Old Testament typology to the evangelical quest for salvation, 'the bedrock concept is of redemption as the quintessential blessing which is made possible by the atoning work of Christ'. To complete the dialectic, if I may use a term rather alien to Roger Anstey, he shows with illuminating clarity how the yearning for redemption surges back from the particular Providence directing individual lives to the general Providence giving moral coherence to history. The evangelical abolitionist, being assured that his sin is forgiven through the grace of God and that he can overcome the evil in his own heart, is both freed and compelled to conquer the physical embodiment of sin in human history. As Anstey puts it in his paper, as evangelicals 'related the idea of redemption, in its existential, individual application, to God's great redemptive purpose as made known in the Old Testament, they saw that, historically, redemption was a redemption from physical bondage'.

Roger Anstey lived in the same spiritual world as the evangelical abolitionists. If this meant that he lacked some of the detachment of secular historians, it also gave him unrivaled insights into the historical meaning of sin, redemption, Providence, and retribution. As a mediator and interpreter, with one foot in the world of James Stephen and Wilberforce and the other foot in the world of modern academia, he has enriched our understanding of the abolitionists' motives, perceptions, strategies, and contradictions. At times, this straddling of worlds led to certain strains and inconsistencies. For example, I think he became unduly preoccupied with a rather simplistic view of economic interest, which he continued to see as a rival threat to religion in explaining British abolition and emancipation. In this respect he shared with many secular historians what can only be termed a Williams Complex. Yet in the abolitionists' own world view, as Anstey at times realized, Providence virtually guaranteed that religious duty and true economic interest would coincide.

In other ways, however, Roger's straddling of two worlds has been extraordinarily rewarding. His work successfully obliterates the conventional dualism between ethereal religious values and the hard-nosed realm of political action. Again and again he has shown how devout reformers, who confined their piety to the most private modes of expression, became seasoned experts at political maneuver and even at 'guile of a high order'. While I would not accuse Roger of even the highest order of guile, he clearly shared with the British abolitionists a delight in pragmatic detail. With unflagging enthusiasm he accumulated data and compiled charts on the volume and profitability of various branches of the slave trade. With no less devotion he analyzed the constituency and voting patterns of various Parliaments; calculated the growing strength of Nonconformist voters and petitioners; and mastered the labyrinths of the Foreign Office's 'Official Mind'. For Roger Anstey, as for the British abolitionists, there was nothing vague or sentimental about the holy cause. The stakes were too high for careless or slipshod research, or for missing a scrap of evidence which might illuminate the truth.

Throughout these comments I have pictured Roger as a kind of reborn abolitionist. Assuming that at least some of the abolitionists were as kind, generous, and warmly human as Roger Anstey, I shall always regard them, as a result of knowing him, with a higher degree of respect.

Part One
INTERNATIONAL PATTERNS

1

THE PATTERN OF BRITISH ABOLITIONISM IN THE EIGHTEENTH AND NINETEENTH CENTURIES*

by Roger Anstey

The theme of this paper is the way in which an essentially eighteenth-century impulse in Britain – anti-slavery – develops and mutates in the nineteenth. I hope to contribute in a modest way to the analysis of the reform process, by relating British abolitionism to Oliver Macdonagh's model of administrative reform and then by tentatively suggesting a model of my own.

It is not my purpose here to comment directly on the various interpretations of British abolition – especially as I offered a critique of Williams some years ago.[1] I am concerned only to outline a thesis on the origins and development of British anti-slavery in the eighteenth century, its two triumphs of 1807 and 1833 respectively, and not least interesting, the paradox that the yet later triumphs of British abolitionism took place precisely when popular enthusiasm for the cause had largely disappeared. It is that four-fold task which I wish to attempt.

First, then, there are the eighteenth-century intellectual and religious origins of anti-slavery in Britain (and here I briefly trench on the ground of a recent book of my own). It would be foolish to assert that the major significance of all eighteenth-century British philosophers, still less of the French *philosophes*, was that they demanded the abolition of slavery. It would be no less foolish to claim that I have studied in depth the development of their individual thought and the interconnections between their philosophies. For that I refer you to David Brion Davis' outstanding *The Problem of Slavery in Western Culture*[2] and, more generally, to studies of the Enlightenment. What I believe one can demonstrate is that, however much the thinkers of the century differed amongst themselves, there was much common ground between them in what, in both a general and a particular sense, pertained to anti-slavery. It can be shown that they attached much importance to liberty and tended to extend the definition of it; that a belief in benevolence, in its eighteenth-century sense, was general among them; that happiness as the particular expression of the principle of utility was frequently invoked as a criterion; that in Britain there was much more often than not, or was felt to be, a compatibility between the teachings of moral philosophy and of revealed religion; and that one believed in a moral order, the other in a compatible idea of a providential order. One significance of all this is that the more emphasis was given to liberty and happiness, the more condemned and isolated did the slave system appear. Moreover, slavery was specifically condemned with near unanimity by the leading moral philosophers of the day.

A further significance of eighteenth century thought that is highly relevant to our theme is that the emphasis on benevolence and the invoking of the principles of nature and utility were themselves marks of a growing disposition to effect change in the area of natural, civil, and political liberty, by legislative action – a noteworthy development. And the trend was furthered by the development of a dynamic out of a static concept of the Chain of Being.

The relevance of mainstream theological developments to anti-slavery reform lay in the theological origins and religious dimension of the powerful idea of benevolence; in the reinforcement of belief in a providential moral order as a sanction on conduct; and in that important root of the idea of progress which consisted in the belief in revelation as progressive, with the necessary corollary that the Christian was called to new commitment, as he received new revelation. Eighteenth-century literature (and regrettably there is no time to elaborate upon this) mainly through the anti-slavery implications of the noble savage theme, and through its reflexion – appropriation even – of ideas of liberty and benevolence, sharpened and extended awareness of the problem of slavery, and made its own contribution to the emergence of anti-slavery conviction.

In essence, then, little serious intellectual defence of slavery was being offered by about the end of the third quarter of the eighteenth century. The next stage of our argument will seek to demonstrate that it was mainly religious conviction, insight and zeal, which made it possible for anti-slavery feeling to be subsumed in a crusade against the slave trade and slavery. But there *was* nevertheless profound significance in the way in which intellectual attitudes to slavery and change had altered, both in itself and because abolitionists thereby had a complex of ideas to which to appeal, and because, being children of their age, it was part of their own thinking.

For the dynamic of change, in the eighteenth and earlier part of the nineteenth century at any rate, we have to look to Quakerism and evangelicalism. We look to Quakerism because it was in the bosom of the Anglo-American Quaker community that ever-hardening anti-slavery resolve was fashioned as a result of a transatlantic dialogue in which first the pressure for action came from one side of the Atlantic and then from the other. What this suggests is the important role of a denominational community in which sharpening conviction and growing consensus can develop side by side until commitment and action resulted. The contribution of evangelicalism was rather different. In assessing the importance of the mainly evangelical abolitionist leadership one must keep in tension that they did share many of their age's assumptions *and* that they had an extraordinary and positive dynamic of their own. They accepted much of the moral philosophy of their day, the emphasis on liberty, benevolence, and happiness, but transposed them into a religious key; from the assurance that their sin was forgiven through the grace of God in the redemptive work of Christ, they knew not only that they could overcome the evil in their own hearts but also that they could conquer those evils in the world which they felt called to combat. They believed especially powerfully in Providence as the sustaining power in the moral order and this belief gave them a satisfactory and coherent, albeit disturbing, philosophy of history. Equally their lively sense of a particular Providence directing their own lives was also their inescapable summons to mould the world to a righteousness which would avert national catastrophe, relieve the earthly sufferings of men and pave the way for the salvation of men's eternal souls. Finally, in the very warp and woof of evangelical faith, slavery, of all social evils, stood particularly condemned. This was because evangelicals apprehended salvation primarily through the concept of redemption and when they related the idea of redemption, in its existential, individual application, to God's great redemptive purpose as made known in the Old Testament they saw that, historically, redemption was not least a redemption from physical bondage. Moreover, two abolitionist evangelicals, Granville Sharp and Rev. Thomas Scott, so interpreted scriptural passages on the treatment and emancipation of slaves owned by the

Hebrews that the hesitancy and ambivalence of Scripture about slavery was cut through and virtually all forms of slavery condemned at the bar of the law of love. All in all the evangelical was likely to be a formidable force if he turned to political action against the slave trade.

In analysing what happened when evangelicals did turn to political action we must be even more summary than we have already been. Admittedly they were unsuccessful in their first great campaign for nigh on twenty years – explicable in terms of the limits on Pitt's abolitionism imposed by contemporary conventions of the narrowness of the claims on Cabinet unanimity, a generalized fear (stemming from the French Revolution) of *all* reform, and a widely disseminated sense amongst the political nation that the West Indies, and hence the slave trade which supplied them, were a vital imperial interest with which one would tamper at the nation's peril. The decisive change came when a fortuitous combination of circumstances permitted abolitionists to present the supply of enemy, other foreign, and captured territories with slaves by British slave ships as simple foolishness on the grounds that those self-same slaves were then used to grow sugar which undercut, or would undercut, British grown sugar on the all-important Continental market – whither it was carried in neutral ships. In other words the abolitionists, in 1806, inspired by James Stephen the elder, had the wit to see that abolition of about two-thirds of the British slave trade could be procured by disguising their own humanitarian motivation as elementary national interest in time of war, and were able to secure the vital support of the leading men in the Ministry of all the Talents, that of prime minister Grenville being especially important. A commentator of 1806, probably Stephen himself, aptly put it 'that moral reformation might reasonably be deferred, till the extent of the sacrifice involved in it, was first reduced to its true value by the application of a merely political retrenchment'.[3] Apt though these comments are, and important as it is to see the vital role of the neglected 1806 Foreign Slave Trade Bill in abolitionist strategy, it is no less important to see that the 1807 measure of abolition, whose actual effect, given the Foreign Slave Trade Bill of the previous year, was to end the slave trade to the older British West Indian islands, and which was overtly based on justice and humanity, served no national interest but in fact ran starkly counter to it. The manifest interest of Britain, by 1806–7 was to maintain and even augment her own slave trade and deny slaves to her rivals.[4] Seymour Drescher's recent work, subsumed in his *Econocide:*

Economic Development and the Abolition of the British Slave Trade, has shown that

> over the whole period from 1783–1807, the British slave system enlarged its frontier, its supply of virgin soil, its relative proportion of British trade, its imports and exports, its share of world sugar and coffee production . . . and the slave trade was, of course, a major ingredient in the continuing expansion of the slave system. . . . Abolitionism came not on the heels of trends adverse to slavery but in the face of propitious ones.[5]

Thus far in our analysis of British anti-slavery we have seen intellectual and theological change, religious dynamism, the political weight of ministers of the Talents Government, the brilliant stroke of taking advantage of a fortuitous politico-economic conjuncture in 1806 to abolish two-thirds of the British slave trade, and action manifestly against the national interest in the 1807 measure. To these one should add the establishment of a grass-roots national anti-slavery organization and a considerable appeal to public opinion, especially in 1792.

For sixteen years after 1807 the British anti-slavery movement was dominated by a concern to end the continued participation of foreigners in the slave trade as this was confidently expected to lead to the speedy amelioration of slave conditions.[6] The only significant variation from this approach, apart from protesting at cruelties inflicted on slaves, was to urge slave registration, formally a device for preventing the illicit importation of slaves but which also enshrined the principle of statutory intervention in slave conditions.[7]

It was in 1821–2 that a concern to act against slavery itself emerged. Probably it was James Cropper, a Liverpool Quaker, who initiated action. With men like William Roscoe, William Rathbone IV and William Rathbone V, Cropper was a member of a small liberal–radical, nonconformist group which had been important in Liverpool's earlier exertions against the British slave trade. Now in 1821, whether consciously or not, Cropper showed himself in an earlier tradition by concentrating on the impolicy of slavery. In a series of letters to Wilberforce, published in the *Liverpool Mercury*, he took for granted the inhumanity of slavery and argued that the key to the abolition of slavery lay in the equalization of duties on East and West Indian sugar, for once free-grown East India sugar competed on equal terms the old West India system would be doomed and the way be paved for slave emancipation.[8] Cropper also urged this course on Zachary Macaulay and it was probably due to one or both of them that that polymath of benevolence, the

London Quaker, William Allen obtained from the Yearly Meeting of 1822 authorization for the Meeting for Sufferings 'to take any measures for the gradual abolition of slavery' pending the next Yearly Meeting.[9]

At this same time the ageing Wilberforce was in process of handing over the parliamentary leadership of the abolitionist party to T. F. Buxton, a fellow evangelical, and it was as a result of discussions between Buxton, Wilberforce, Macaulay, Stephen, Cropper, Allen, Dr Lushington (a lawyer and MP), Samuel Hoare (a London Quaker), and Lord Suffield (an evangelical), and probably others that the Society for the Mitigation and Gradual Abolition of Slavery throughout the British Dominions was founded in January 1823.[10] In mid-May Buxton moved in the Commons that 'the state of slavery is repugnant to the principles of the British Constitution and of the Christian Religion; and that it ought to be gradually abolished throughout the British Colonies with as much expedition as may be found consistent with a due regard to the well-being of the parties concerned'.[11] Hardly a radical proposal, yet only a much watered down version expressed in three resolutions was acceptable to Canning and the Ministry. The essence of Government policy was now amelioration with a view to eventual freedom – though the word itself was carefully eschewed. Government would leave the colonies themselves to enact the necessary measures, save where it could act by order-in-council, but the imperial Parliament would step in if the colonial response was insufficient.

In the next ten years little effective action was in fact taken. How do we explain this? It is, firstly, the case that the West Indian representation in the Commons was significantly stronger in the three parliaments of the 1820s than it had been in the eve of the 1806/7 abolition. Barry Higman, using G. P. Judd's figures and supplementary evidence, finds, on a restrained definition of West Indian, 19 West Indians in the 1806 parliament, 39 in 1820, 40 in 1826, and 36 in 1830.[12] Lushington, who had family connections in the West Indies, using an extended definition, arrived at a figure of 56 in 1825, which is also broadly supported by P. F. Dixon. This is certainly to be preferred to the wild figure of about 200 cited by Buxton and Stephen – though that figure is significant[13] as suggesting that the abolitionist leadership may have been unnecessarily overawed. We have no figure for peers with West Indian connections in 1806 but Dixon has identified thirty-three in the upper house between 1821 and 1833.[14]

If the West Indians in the Commons were more numerous than at the beginning of the century it would appear that committed abolitionists were fewer. Dixon's researches,[15] together with supplementary enquiry, suggest a maximum of thirty-one and a minimum of fifteen. In the Lords there just was no visible abolitionist group. There is also an interesting qualitative contrast with the situation three decades earlier. Whereas Tories constituted the largest single faction in the abolitionist group in 1796,[16] only five certainly, plus two more possibly, out of the maximum size group of thirty-one, were not liberals in the 1820s. The abolitionist party, especially after Wilberforce's retirement in 1825, had become predominantly liberal, and in this connection it is of some significance that the Whigs were out of office until 1830.

Finally, we may invoke as a cause of failure the inability to harness free trade to the cause of emancipation, as Cropper had urged and as the Anti-Slavery Society had accepted. Essentially this was because the East India merchants did not see on which side, in the Cropperian dispensation, their bread was buttered and because the mercantile community generally could not be brought to link the cause of emancipation to that of free trade. 'Our E.I. merchants have many of them opposing interests and will not contribute [to Anti-Slavery Society funds]', lamented Cropper, himself an East Indian, in 1822;[17] 'I wish', sighed Macaulay six years later, 'I could . . . see our commercial and manufacturing bodies duly affected with the evil effects of monopoly, and with a sense of the extensive benefits which cannot fail to result from its complete extinction'.[18] To lend a statistical undergirding, Dixon has conclusively demonstrated that the 130 East Indians in the Commons between 1823 and 1830 provided a mere 19 of the 198 speakers or voters on the abolition side during the period.[19]

Finally, public opinion, though fully seized of the horrors of the slave trade was seemingly not aware of the actual evils of plantation slavery. As Burn has shown, the abolitionist newspapers and periodicals were counterbalanced by others with more cautious views and the former were too often of limited circulation, or featured emancipation only infrequently.[20]

With the resulting conjecture that the abolition campaign in the years 1823–30 had achieved nothing significant we must agree: yet there was a longer term significance in the abolitionist activity of the period. The Anti-Slavery Society had not only come into being but was quite effectively organized; the tried devices of the provincial tour and of petitioning Parliament were again resorted to, and with more effect in terms of the number of petitions instigated and local associations formed. More use was made of the large public meeting and one important departure made (not without fears that it would involve the fair sex in an unwomanly role) – the foundation of numerous Ladies Anti-Slavery Associations.[21] At least as important as this last development was the forgoing of much stronger links with nonconformity, and especially Wesleyans and Baptists. This was because the principal location of the missionary work which was one of the fruits of the evangelical revival, was, as far as these two denominations were concerned, the West Indies, and the intermittent persecution of slave converts and missionaries by West Indian whites began to lead these two denominations in particular to couple a Pauline injunction to the slaves to render obedience to their masters with an anti-slavery testimony at home. One of the fruits of this development was the particularly active involvement first of the Rev. Jabez Bunting, the Methodist 'Pope', in the Anti-Slavery Committee, and later of the only less influential Rev. Richard Watson and of a leading Wesleyan barrister, Richard Matthews, who for good measure became secretary of the Society.[22]

In October 1829 an editorial in the *Anti-Slavery Reporter* referred to the 'torpor' on the slavery question which had 'seized, with a few rare exceptions, on all classes'.[23] In the following February, however, largely as a result of an interview with the Colonial Secretary in the Duke of Wellington's government, the Anti-Slavery Society Committee, at least, had been brought to a sense that more urgent action was needed than Government had in contemplation if slavery was not to continue 'for ages yet to come'.[24] The next three and a half years saw a rising tempo of anti-slavery agitation with five main characteristics. Firstly, traditional tactics were pressed forward with more vigour and success, especially the large public meeting and petitioning. The meeting convened by the Anti-Slavery Committee in the Freemason's Hall in April 1830, for instance, attracted an audience of 3000 with several hundred more unable to gain admission.[25] Petitioning, too, reached new heights of success with no less than 5020 petitions against slavery presented to the first reformed Parliament in the opening months of 1833, and with the total number of anti-slavery petitions in this period far outstripping the number urging political reform.[26] Secondly, provincial support was canvassed by methods quite novel. The inspiration behind this departure was a group of radical abolitionists grouped round George Stephen, a younger son of James Stephen the elder. They conceived the idea of appointing paid anti-slavery agents, or lecturers, who would the more effectively arouse anti-slavery feeling in the country. Originally, if somewhat guardedly, accepted by the Anti-Slavery Society Committee, the more radically inclined group around Stephen broke away in 1832 to form the Agency Anti-Slavery Society. The new approach was most effective, leading to the formation of up to 1300 provincial anti-slavery associations.[27] Thirdly, and constituting an important inspiration of this last development, was the growth of immediatism in the British (as in the American) anti-slavery movement. David Davis has traced the origins of this with particular reference to the pamphlet of the Quakeress, Mrs Elizabeth Heyrick, *Immediate not Gradual Abolition* (1824) which asserted that since anti-slavery was a war against the powers of darkness there could be no delay and no compromise – no gradualism.[28] The opening paragraph of the instructions to the stipendiary agents makes the point with total clarity: 'the system of colonial slavery is a crime in the sight of God, and ought to be immediately and for ever abolished.'[29] Fourthly, due to the initiatives particularly of Lushington in the Anti-Slavery Society and of Watson both in the Society and in the Wesleyan Methodist Conference, voters in parliamentary elections were urged to pledge their votes only to candidates who would agree to support immediate abolition if returned.[30] Although used as an electioneering device on previous occasions it seems not previously to have been used on the scale it was used in the December 1832 elections. Moreover it was regarded as a politically radical device and it is very interesting that the most conservative of all nonconformist denominations, the Wesleyans, should actively promote this technique. A fifth development was the forging of closer ties between the two Anti-Slavery societies and nonconformity, particularly the Wesleyan and Baptists, especially in the singular political atmosphere of mid-1832 to mid-1833.

Not only from mid-1832 to mid-1833 but from 1830 onwards the political atmosphere of Britain had been dominated by the reform question.[31] That question had complex interactions with the achievement of emancipation. One clear effect of the preoccupation with reform was to inhibit anti-slavery activity. It is clear that during the reform crisis even ardent anti-slavery men soft-pedalled emancipation.[32] This was in part because, as the reformers that most of them were, they feared that to pursue both objects simultaneously would prejudice reform, and as abolitionists, they believed that emancipation was most likely to be attained on the flood tide of achieved political reform. This holding back, however, did not prevent the building up of anti-slavery organization and sentiment – just the inception of a full-blooded Westminster campaign. As for the ministry, its role was indeed modest: Howick, under-secretary in the Colonial Office made very clear in private letters to his father, the prime minister, that no serious thought was given to a policy on slavery either by the ineffective colonial secretary, Goderich, or by a Cabinet distracted by reform and many other pressing problems.[33] With the virtual safe arrival in port of the Reform Bill in June 1832, however, the political situation for emancipation changed greatly, especially as a dissolution of parliament soon followed, and because nonconformist anti-slavery feeling reached a new pitch of intensity in the aftermath of the Jamaica slave rising of December 1831. This rising – the result of injudicious planter conduct, of some slaves seeing in the idea of Christian freedom a physical dimension, and of frustrated slave coloured expectations resulting from demographic 'imbalance' caused by the cessation of slave imports since 1807[34] – has as one characteristic of an altogether vicious aftermath the persecution of missionaries and slave converts alike. Buxton believed that nothing did more to arouse the religious public[35] and so did Macaulay. 'The religious persecutions in Jamaica', the latter wrote to Brougham, 'however have aroused them [the Methodists and Dissenters] to a feeling of intense interest in the matter and they have not only caught fire themselves but have succeeded in igniting the whole country'.[36] So strong was the feeling that the abolitionist leaders, in May 1832, were alarmed at the militancy of their cohorts[37] but a dissolution of parliament in August shifted attention to influencing the forthcoming elections – the first under the reformed franchise.

The striking feature of abolitionist exertions here – and it was the Agency Committee who did most by publishing nationally lists of 'pledged' and 'irredeemable' candidates in a popular anti-slavery journal, *The Tourist*[38] – was their success in gaining pledges. In the event a bloc of some 140–200 pledged candidates was actually returned, and of the 134 precisely identified all save eight were liberals, thus underlining the liberal basis of abolition support.[39] It may therefore seem surprising, when one recalls both the return of a Whig government with an increased majority, and the sharp drop in West Indian representation in the Commons,[40] that the swift passage of emancipation was not a foregone conclusion. At first indeed, and even before Parliament met, the framing of an emancipation bill by a Cabinet Committee made good progress.[41] But by the end of March Grey was persuaded that the Colonial Office (in fact, his son's) plan of emancipation was impracticable and would harm the West Indies and the mother country, and he would not approve it.[42] Buxton's pressure in the Commons, however, compelled Althorp, the leader of government business in the Commons, to name a day when the Government would bring forward a scheme[43] – at which point further confusion supervened on Goderich's enforced resignation and the succession to the seals of the Colonial Department of Edward Stanley.

Stanley immediately began work on an emancipation scheme and what had for some weeks been increasingly evident now became crystal clear – that it was with the West Indians that the real haggling – essentially over the amount and form of compensation and over the terms of apprenticeship[44] – would have to take place. Here was a paradox. Feeling in the country was strongly in favour of emancipation and in the Commons there was a very large bloc of support. Yet the Lords, in the aftermath of the humiliation of the 'die hards' over the Reform Bill, were now determining the limits within which the Government might act. Time and time again ministers attested the need to secure West Indian co-operation in emancipation[45] and it soon became clear, that Government felt abolitionist pressure to be certainly such that a measure *must* be enacted, but that there was even more danger in affronting the West Indian view of their minimum requirements than there was in presenting to the abolitionist an insufficiently thoroughgoing measure. Why? Both because the West Indians were a powerful and undiminished group in the Lords – some thirty strong in what was effectively quite a small house – and because the Duke of Wellington and the party which he led were prepared to oppose any measure of emancipation which the West Indians, as an important interest group, would not accept. It is highly significant that Grey would only take up to the Lords the six resolutions on emancipation, passed by the Commons, when the Duke had written to the Earl of Harewood saying that he would offer no substantive opposition because the Commons had passed the resolution *and* because the West Indians were satisfied.[46]

Eventually the act drawn by James Stephen the younger on the bases of the Resolution – his most important contribution to emancipation – was passed: the issue was decided by the end of July. The emancipation campaign had clear affinities with the earlier campaign for the abolition of the slave trade but became more of a popular movement and used more popular, even radical methods. In the emancipation movement the role of Quakers paralleled that of their fathers a quarter of a century earlier but on this later occasion the evangelicals in the ranks of active abolitionist sympathizers were overshadowed by nonconformists, especially Wesleyans and Baptists.[47] The generalized pressure of popular opinion was much more effective in 1832–3 than in 1806–7. The earlier occasion was still the era of what George Stephen called 'sagacious manoeuvring within' whereas in 1833 only a massive, organized 'pressure from without', exerted through Buxton the parliamentary leader, brought the ministry to a commitment which they then had to honour. As in 1806–7 the Lords still played a key part but, whereas in these years Fox and Grenville had used all the political leverage they possessed to induce compliance in measures which they were determined to further, Grey and his colleagues in 1833 merely acted as brokers though they did prevent a fatal junction between West Indians and Tory opposition Peers.

The West Indians in Parliament – paradoxically, because the importance of the Caribbean in the imperial economy was declining – had more weight and were more effective in checking anti-slavery in 1823–33 than twenty-five years earlier. In the earlier case they had been spared abolition for two decades because of the conviction of independent men of the importance of the West Indies; in the later case their politically stronger position ensured for them terms of compensation which the Tory party believed such an established interest deserved. We have seen that in 1806–7 the adroit use of politico-economic conjuncture was of great importance in the passage of abolition. In the case of emancipation, politico-economic considerations had only a negative influence. There is a most illuminating minute by the younger Stephen on this: in March 1832, in reference to a recent West Indian deputation, he observed that it was remarkable that the Secretary of State, in his proposed answer, had adverted so little to the effect of an emancipation measure upon the commerce of Britain. 'It can however be scarcely necessary to deny that the bearings of the proposed law on the commercial interest of Great Britain have been really unheeded'. Nor is there any need 'for embarking on such a discussion'. Suffice it to say that no lasting harm would be done to the industry and trade of this country if sugar were obtained from other parts of the world.[48] There was another negative sense in which the politico-economic situation in 1833 was propitious for emancipation. Such was the depression in West Indian agriculture that the proprietors were prepared to grasp at an emancipation measure which included generous compensation. Rather as the Balkan peasant in a bad year must eat his seed corn, so the West Indian proprietor saw the lure of escaping from present insolvency by yielding up a long term asset. Of economic forces positively demanding abolition there are none.[49] Just as the East Indians, right through from the 1790s to the 1830s, failed to act as an interest group using anti-slavery as the cloak for free trade, so any group of emerging capitalists has left, in the mountains of literature and documentation, not a trace of its activities.

But how – and here we come to a pivotal point in the paper – are we to explain the continuance, nay strengthening of measures against the slave trade when popular support fell away, when political support was much reduced and when the principal branch of the official anti-slavery movement opposed the Government in its policy of forcibly suppressing the continuing slave trade?

Everything seemed to go wrong for the abolition cause in the 1840s. As late as 1838 the diarist Greville commented that 'the Anti-Slavery question . . . is a favourite topic in the country'[50] but the failure of the abolitionist inspired and Government supported Niger expedition in 1841–2 seems to have brought a dramatic change. Public support for the policy, begun in 1808, of diplomatic and naval action against the foreign slave trade weakened sharply. Not only this, the British anti-slave trade lobby was in disarray: firstly the British and Foreign Anti-Slavery Society had, from 1839, increasingly followed the pacifism of leading lights like Joseph Sturge;[51] secondly, the British anti-slavery movement came both to reflect the divisions in the American anti-slavery movement *and* to preoccupy itself at worst with the politics of that rivalry and at best with a problem – slavery in the United States[52] – about which it could do nothing effective; thirdly, there was some division within the anti-slavery movement over the pressure in the 1840s to equalize the sugar duties, that is progressively to end the preference on imperial (now free-grown) sugar, admit the cheaper Brazilian and Cuban slave-grown sugar and thus encourage these two lusty surviving branches of the slave trade.[53] At least as importantly, the Whig Government of 1841 seemed to have fatally compromised with slavery by attempting sugar equalization in 1841 and achieving it in 1846, whilst the continued existence of the West African squadron and of the whole diplomatic campaign against the slave trade seemed seriously threatened by William Hutt's Commons Committee of enquiry into the effectiveness of the coercion policy.

Yet by 1851 the major branch of the Atlantic slave trade, that to Brazil, was ended, and though the Cuban trade lasted another decade, imports, compared with the 34,000 p.a. to Brazil in the 1840s, averaged only about 12,000 a year.[54] How is this seeming contradiction to be explained? We must remember, firstly, that the intensifying process of diplomatic and naval action against slave trading powers, which had begun as early as 1808, had *always* rested on humble addresses to the Crown, supported by other parliamentary representations. This procedure had first been adopted even before the completion of the British abolition in 1807 when, as a related move, taken both for its own sake and to reduce the domestic opposition to British abolition, an humble address had been voted requesting that steps be taken to persuade foreign powers to cease slave trading. In the years that followed abolitionists maintained the pressure. Between February 1808 and May 1814 there were eleven such addresses or kindred interventions[55] and, to take a subsequent random period, nineteen between 1816 and 1822, the object being both to keep up pressure on the ministry and to strengthen its hands, both aims being served by the virtually complete unanimity of parliamentary opinion. It is important in this context to remember that those who opposed British abolition in 1806–7, because of the advantage abolition would afford to foreign competitors, were consequently now as enthusiastic as convinced abolitionists for the suppression of the foreign slave trade. In short, within a very few years of 1807 parliamentary opinion had crystallized as solidly behind the suppression of the foreign slave trade. Drawing out one of the implications of this brings us to an important truth. It is that parliamentary support for the diplomatic and naval action had become institutionalized, a part of received tradition, an attitude which scarcely needed to be argued from parliament to parliament. W. E. Gladstone saw this very clearly when in 1850, as Leslie Bethell points out, 'he warned the House that the slave trade preventive system was in danger of being perpetuated unquestioningly on a permanent basis, thereby becoming "one of the institutions of the country", and beyond rational criticism'.[56] Furthermore, Palmerston was a conspicuous case of a minister who was conscious of the need to keep the support of Parliament – over suppression as other matters – as numerous references in his private correspondence attest.[57]

If the institutionalization of suppression was important so also was what I will term the bureaucratization of the preventive policy within the Foreign Office. This process began with the creation of a separate Slave Trade Department in 1819. As is the way with such agencies its business steadily increased over the years and although by 1850 its staff consisted only of a superintendent and four clerks,[58] remember that the total Foreign Office strength in 1853, including the housekeeper, 'Chamber keepers', porters and doorkeepers was only fifty-three.[59] In short two vital conditions existed for a policy to go rumbling on, namely the institutionalization of legislative backing and the bureaucratization of executive action.

Together these are a striking exemplification of something akin to what Robinson and Gallagher in their study of imperialism call 'the official mind'.[60] But if what we have been saying about institutionalization may explain why the coercion policy continued through the 1840s, it can not really explain why the policy prevailed against an attempt in the Commons to overset it, and why it had a signal triumph, resulting from a new initiative, in 1850–1.

The answer, in three words, is 'Russell and Palmerston'. Palmerston, particularly, had earlier been active against the slave trade. When he went out with the Whigs in 1841 he had had an almost unbroken decade at the Foreign Office, over a period which had seen some real triumphs against the slave trade, especially effective action against Portugal in 1839.[61] Moreover Palmerston believed that his support of equalization was compatible with effective action against the slave trade. 'If we had thought' he said in Parliament in 1841, 'that this measure would give to the slave trade any encouragement, which we should not be able by other means amply to counterbalance, we would not have proposed the measure to Parliament'.[62] The problem in 1846 as regards the Brazilian slave trade was that, despite a strong treaty concluded by Aberdeen with Brazil in 1845, Palmerston was not immediately able to get Cabinet backing for really forceful action against Brazil,[63] whilst British naval power in South America was anyway mainly taken up with the intervention on the River Plate. A further obstacle to effective action might well have been the proceedings of the Commons Select Committee which, by intimating its support for negotiations with Brazil, was implicitly against strong action. Palmerston, however, saw the Committee's threat differently: strong action must be shown to work in order to get the traditional policy continued.[64] In the event it was the local naval commander, backed or inspired by the British minister in Rio who, significantly, was in extended private correspondence with Palmerston on the suppression question,[65] who forged the winning tactic. This was to cut out slavers within Brazilian territorial waters,[66] a tactic which involved the owners in crippling losses. Now was the time to give full backing to the squadron in the use of this tactic, urged Hudson. In one of the many private letters[67] sent at this time Hudson makes clear the argument he had been putting forward:

> I beg also to point out to your Lordship that another so favourable opportunity for acting against slave trade may not occur again for years to come. The relations of Brazil with Buenos Ayres are assuming a very threatening attitude – this Government cannot successfully resist our attempts against the slave dealers and their ships here, and meet General Rosas and tribe in the field at the same moment: they must, to save Rio Granda de Sul and Paraguay, abandon the slave dealers to our tender mercies.

Significantly the whole of the second sentence is scored – presumably by Palmerston.[68]

Meanwhile Palmerston and Russell faced up to the clear threat from the Commons Select Committee to the continuance of the suppression policy. A meeting of their parliamentary supporters was summoned on 19 March 1850 and Palmerston and Russell threatened resignation if a sufficient number of their party did not support the squadron on a vote.[69] This threat made the policy safe but, again, Palmerston and Russell interpreted success not as an inducement to complacency but as a summons to make the traditional policy more effective.[70] Very clear instructions to the naval commander were authorised on 22 April confirming the line he had recently adopted.[71] Within months the Brazilian slave trade was at an end. Of decisive importance was the exertion of political will by Palmerston and Russell and the complementary perceptions and initiatives of the men on the spot and the taking advantage of the varied embarrassments of the Brazilian Government. Less visible but significant was the role of Lushington. Here was the committed abolitionist who was also the influential expert. Instigator of the highly significant definition of Brazilian slavery as piracy in the 1826 Anglo-Brazilian treaty, he was the extremely influential adviser who urged a strong line with Portugal in 1839, who was heavily involved in the negotiations with Brazil in 1845 (as well as those with France in the same year) and thus fashioned the instrument Britain was eventually to wield in 1850. Altogether he fulfilled a role somewhat similar to that of James Stephen the younger in 1833 and of the elder Stephen in 1806–7.

Before we ask whether any contribution to a model of the reforming impulse and its development emerges, we ought to notice that, as far as suppression is concerned, coercion, used particularly against Portugal and Brazil, was neither the only method used nor the only one to succeed. There was in fact another strand of British anti-slavery endeavour. The fascinating tale has yet to be told of the 'Evangelical International', of how the tender plant of French anti-slavery zeal was nurtured by British abolitionists for three decades from 1814 – a relationship hard to disentangle from the reinforcement which British and French evangelicalism offered each other, for Protestants, including some influenced by the French evangelical revival, were disproportionately active in the French anti-slavery movement.[72] An unpredictable fruit of this closer association was garnered in the early 1830s, for such was the importance of French abolitionists in the ranks of the men who wrought the July Revolution that the prized mutual right of search treaties were able to be negotiated in 1831 and 1833. These seem at least to have been successful in sealing the end of the French slave trade and even when internal political hostility to the exercise by Britain of the right of search forced prime minister – and abolitionist – Guizot to jettison these agreements, they were immediately replaced by a new Anglo-French treaty, negotiated by the ubiquitous Lushington and by the Duc de Broglie, minister, abolitionist, and correspondent of British evangelicals and abolitionists, which was envisaged as a major joint effort to prevent slavers from clearing from the African coast.[73] Such a development wholly cohered with Aberdeen's strong desire for friendly relations with France as the corner stone of his foreign policy and with his wish to emphasize co-operation between the powers in suppressing the slave trade rather than to rest only on the right of search. One might conclude that the few months remaining to Peel's ministry were insufficient for the system of joint cruising by a total of fifty-two warships to produce decisive results – Palmerston in 1846 reverted to a wary rivalry with France[74] and in any event the July Monarchy fell in 1848 – but events could well have turned out otherwise. In the same vein one can argue that since there was manifestly no possibility of Britain successfully coercing the United States, the conciliatory policy enshrined in the Webster-Ashburton treaty of 1842, and misliked by Palmerston, should have been persisted in, despite the failure of the United States to fulfil its obligations under it. After all, the United States, paradoxically, accepted the practice of visits by British warships to check the identity of suspected slavers wearing the US flag, once Malmesbury, in 1858, abandoned the principle of the right of visit.[75]

I believe that some contribution to a model of the reforming impulse does emerge from the foregoing.

Firstly, we can see *some* similarities to Oliver Macdonagh's model of the 'legislative-cum-administrative process'. We may recognize his 'intolerability' principle in the resolve to end the slave trade and slavery; we may see the same stages of legislation, the slow realization that it is insufficient, and consequential further legislation; we may observe (in the Slave Trade Department of the Foreign Office) the accumulation of 'evidence of the extent and nature of the evils' (of the slave trade); and we may discern that same Department coming to see that suppression was indeed 'a slow, uncertain process of closing loopholes and tightening the screw ring by ring'. But the similarities, if real, are limited and in any event our concern – a model of the reforming impulse – is not the same as Macdonagh's. What seem to me to be the key ingredients of the former are the preparation of the ground by changes in philosophical and theological ideas; the slow germination of reform in the bosom of a denominational community; the impetus for reform coming from a new, or newly rediscovered, religious dynamism; the decisive seizure by the reformers of opportunities (in 1806 and 1807, and in 1833);[76] the institutionalization and bureaucratization of the reforming impulse in the legislature and executive respectively, so that impulse outlasts the weakening of the forces which gave it life; and the periodic and sometimes complex interventions of the committed expert and of 'great men', especially Fox and Grenville in 1806–7 and Palmerston and Russell four decades later.

How wide is the application of this very tentative model? I will answer that, still tentatively, by quoting Bentham: 'We have begun by attending to the condition of slaves, we shall finish by softening that of all the animals which assist our labours or supply our wants'.[77] The establishment of the essential links between the initial and the later movement remains to be effected. But that Bentham's prediction was good prophecy is not open to doubt.[78]

Notes

* I am grateful for comments on the original version of this paper made in general discussion at the American Society for Eighteenth-Century Studies 1976 Conference, and at a seminar at the University of Pittsburgh, as well as for comments on subsequent drafts, especially those of Dr Seymour Drescher, Mr David Eltis, Dr Stanley Engerman and Dr Oliver Macdonagh.
(Professor Anstey unfortunately died before he was able to revise his

article, but the editors have felt it best to reproduce it as nearly as possible in its original form.)

1 Roger Anstey, 'Capitalism and slavery: a critique', *Economic History Review*, 2nd ser. xxi (1968), 2, pp. 307–20.

2 (Ithaca, 1966).

3 Duke University, Grenville/W. B. Hamilton Microfilm Collection, Reel 17 f. 189, Memo., probably by Stephen, on abolitionist tactics, 19 May 1806, The Dropmore MSS have now been accessioned in the British Museum.

4 Unless otherwise indicated the source for the foregoing paragraphs is Roger Anstey, *The Atlantic Slave Trade and British Abolition, 1760–1810* (1975), *passim*.

5 This convenient quotation is a summary in English of Seymour Drescher, 'Le "Declin" du Systeme Esclavagiste Britannique et l'Abolition de la Traite', *Annales ESC* (Mars–Avril 1976), pp. 414–35, contained in the same author's 'Abolition and the Historians', in Roger Anstey and P. E. H. Hair (eds.), *Liverpool, the African Slave Trade, and Abolition* (Liverpool, 1976), pp. 170–1. See note 49 for particulars of Drescher's major work.

6 See e.g. *Parliamentary Debates*, 1st ser., xxviii, 803, also quoted in B. W. Higman, *Slave Population and Economy in Jamaica, 1807–34* (Cambridge, 1976), p. 231.

7 For a summary of the Registration campaign see Sir George Stephen, *Anti-Slavery Recollections* (1854) (2nd edn., 1971, with new introduction by Howard Temperley), pp. 20–38. A government-sponsored slave registry bill was eventually enacted in 1819 with an ease which prefigured its subsequent ineffectiveness.

8 K. Charlton, 'James Cropper and Liverpool's contribution to the anti-slavery movement', *Trans. Hist. Soc. Lancs. and Cheshire*, cxiii (1971), 57–9. It was the subsequent view of the Anti-Slavery Society itself that the initiative was Cropper's (*Anti-Slavery Reporter*, 11 Mar. 1840, quoted in G. R. Mellor, *British Imperial Trusteeship, 1783–1850* (1951), p. 125n.)

9 BM Add MSS 41267A (Clarkson MSS), ff. 102–3, 104–6, Cropper to Z. Macaulay, 2 May 1822 and 8 May 1822; Allen, diary, 27 May 1822, quoted in William Allen, *Life with Selections from his Correspondence* (1847), ii, p. 230; *Friends House, London Yearly Meeting*, Minute Book, 22, 382, 27 May 1822; for testimony to Quaker initiative in the matter see also BM Add MSS 51820 (Holland House MSS), Wilberforce to Lord Holland, 25 Feb. 1823.

10 Charles Buxton (ed.), *The Memoirs of Sir Thomas Fowell Buxton* (1925; 1st edn., 1849), pp. 125–35; Allen, diary, 5 Sep. 1822, 13 and 28 Jan. 1823 in *Life*, ii, pp. 245, 326; Rand S. Wilberforce, *The Life of William Wilberforce* (1835), v, pp. 160–7; *Friends House, Meetings for Sufferings, Minutes*, 42, p. 628, 3 Jan. 1823.

11 P.D.; Buxton, *Memoirs*, pp. 136–43; W. L. Burn, *Emancipation and Apprenticeship in the British West Indies* (1937), pp. 80–1.

12 B. W. Higman, 'The West India "Interest" in Parliament, 1807–33', *Historical Studies*, xiii (Oct. 1967), 49, 1–5. Note Higman's definition of three levels of West Indian support.

13 *Ibid.*, pp. 2–3; P. F. Dixon, 'The politics of emancipation: the move-ment for the abolition of slavery in the British West Indies, 1807–33', Oxford D.Phil thesis (1970), p. 41 and Appendix B.

14 Dixon, 'Politics of emancipation', p. 42 and Appendix B.

15 *Ibid.*, pp. 234, 336–74.

16 Anstey, *Atlantic Slave Trade*, pp. 283, 343–402 *passim*.

17 Add MS 41267A, ff. 112–13, Cropper to Macaulay, 5 Aug. 1822.

18 UCL, Brougham MSS 10275, Macaulay to 'My dear Friend', 16 Feb. 1828; see also Ian Rennie, 'Evangelicalism and English public life, 1823–50', University of Toronto Ph.D. thesis (1962), p. 178.

19 Dixon, 'Politics of emancipation', pp. 61–2 and Appendix C. Cf. Anstey, *Atlantic Slave Trade*, p. 307. As Dixon says, the figures almost suggest an inverse correlation between East Indians and abolitionists.

20 Burn, *Emancipation and Apprenticeship*, p. 84 and n.; see also Stephen, *Anti-Slavery Recollections*, esp. pp. 17, 43 and 69.

21 For the Anti-Slavery Society's work see *Anti-Slavery Reporter*, *passim* and Rhodes House, Anti-Slavery MSS E2/1–3, Minute Books, *passim*. For the importance of Ladies Associations see Brougham MSS, 10275, Macaulay to 'My dear Friend', 16 Feb. 1828.

22 For the evolution of the Wesleyan anti-slavery testimony, including its notable re-statement in 1825 and the encouragement of petitioning see especially *Wesleyan Methodist Magazine*, 3rd ser., II, 461–5, Jul. 1823; III, 49–53, Jan. 1824; III, 618, 687–92, Oct. 1824; IV, 115–19, Feb. 1825 and 628–43, Nov. 1825; V, 121–5, Feb. 1826; IX, 435, June 1830 and 608–10, Sept. 1830; *Minutes of the Wesleyan Methodist Conference*, 1825, 1829 and 1830; *Anti-Slavery Reporter*, 65, 349ff., 20 Aug. 1830.

23 *Anti-Slavery Reporter*, 53, Oct. 1829; See also *Eclectic Review*, 3rd ser., III (Apr. 1830), 352, quoted in Burn, *Emancipation and Apprentice-ship*, p. 84 n.

24 Anti-Slavery MSS, E2/3, Minutes, 9 Feb. 1830, see also *Anti-Slavery Reporter*, 13 Feb. and 2 Mar. 1830.

25 *Anti-Slavery Reporter*, 61, June 1830. Report of Brougham's speech; Stephen, *Anti-Slavery Recollections*, p. 120.

26 Total of slavery petitions to Reformed Parliament is in the *Methodist Magazine*, 3rd ser., XIII (1834), 229. Compare the 5484 anti-slavery petitions between October 1830 and April 1831 with the 3000 reform petitions in the same period (*Anti-Slavery MSS* E2/3, Minutes, 1 Sep. 1830, 16 Sep. 1830, 17 Nov. 1830, 1 Dec. 1830; *Anti-Slavery Reporter*, 74, 5 Jan. 1831, 75 and 80, 9 May, 1831, 252n.; John Cannon, *Parliamentary Reform, 1640–1832* (Cambridge, 1973), p. 252n.)

27 Stephen, *Anti-Slavery Recollections*, pp. 127–31, 143–53, 158. For the split see Anti-Slavery MSS, E2/3, Minutes, 1 and 25 June 1831, 22 Feb., 7 Mar., 6 June and 4 Jul. 1832; *Agency Committee Report*, 1832; *The Tourist*, I, no. 11 (26 Nov. 1832), 94; David B. Davis, 'The emergence of immediatism in British and American anti-slavery thought', *The Mississippi Valley Historical Review*, 49 (1962–3), p. 222n.

28 Davis, 'Emergence of immediatism', 219–21.

29 Quoted in Stephen, *Anti-Slavery Recollections*, p. 136, and also in *Agency Committee Report*, 1832, 1ff. See also the analysis of George

Thompson's (an Agent) Dover lecture in Dixon, 'Politics of emancipation', p. 286.

30 *Anti-Slavery Reporter*, 61, June 1830, Report of May Meeting; 65, 20 Aug. 1830, 349ff. *Minutes of the Wesleyan Methodist Conference*, VI, 1830; *Methodist Magazine*, 3rd ser., IX (Sep. 1830), 608–10; B. Gregory, *Side Lights on the Conflicts of Methodism 1827–52* (1898), p. 550.

31 For the reform question see especially Cannon, *Parliamentary Reform* and Michael Brock, *The Great Reform Act* (1973).

32 For the views of Cropper and Joseph Sturge see H. Richard *Memoirs of Joseph Sturge* (1864), p. 33, and of Allen see Allen, diary entry, May 1832 n.d., in *Life*, III, p. 36.

33 Grey Papers, 2nd Earl, Box 24, Howick to Grey, 29 May 1832 and 1 Dec. 1832.

34 Mary Reckord, 'The Jamaica slave rebellion of 1831', *Past and Present*, 40 (Jul. 1969), 108–25; Higman, *Slave Population and Economy*, pp. 231–2.

35 Buxton, *Memoirs*, p. 306.

36 Brougham MSS, 10544. Macaulay to Brougham, 13 May 1833, Private. Reprinted in Viscountess Knutsford, *The Life and Times of Zachary Macaulay* (1900), p. 470, but wrongly attributed to 1832.

37 Brougham MSS, 10376, Lushington, memo., n.d. (between 17 Apr. and 12 May 1832).

38 *The Tourist*, Sep.–Dec. 1832 and especially 24 Sep., 10; 3 Dec., 104 and 17 Dec., 126.

39 For party affiliation and electoral information see F. W. S. Craig, *British Parliamentary Election Results 1832–85* (1977) and Charles R. Dod, *Electoral Facts 1832–53 impartially stated* (1973 edn., with introduction by H. J. Hanham). *The Parliamentary Pocket Companion, 1833* gives biographical and political information about most candidates and it may be significant that the clearly well informed compiler could find no more than eight pledged Scottish and Irish members. On the other hand the Agency Committee List is in general likely to be more accurate as regards English and Welsh members and is therefore to be preferred.

40 Reduced to 19 (Higman, 'West India Interest', 3). Note George Stephen's conclusion that 'an Anti-Slavery House was for the first time returned by an Anti-Slavery public' (*Anti-Slavery Recollections*, p. 168).

41 Grey Papers, 3rd Earl, Slavery Papers 66, Howick, minute of discussions on slavery, 1833; Hobhouse, diary, 12 Jan. 1833, quoted in Lord Broughton, *Recollections of a Long Life* (1909), IV, pp. 268–9.

42 Grey Papers, 3rd Earl, Howick, MS Journal, 16 Mar. 1833 ff.

43 *Parl. Debates*, 3rd ser., XVI, 826–7; Buxton, *Memoirs*, pp. 312–20. See also Anti-Slavery Papers, E2/4, Minutes, 6 and 9 Mar. 1833.

44 See CO318/116 for voluminous file on the discussions between the Government and the West Indians, Jan.–Sept. 1833. The file is partly duplicated and complemented by Grey Papers, 3rd Earl, Box 147, Item 53. Printed Minutes of proceedings between Government and West Indians, 16 Jan.–2 May 1833.

45 See e.g. Grey Papers, 3rd Earl, Slavery Papers No. 56, Howick, memo.,

1 Dec. 1832; *ibid.*, Howick MS Journal; CO318/116, Stanley to West Indians, copy, 29 Apr. 1833; *Parl. Debates*, 3rd ser. xvi, 1188–9, Grey; xviii, 547–50, Stanley and *ibid.*, 1201–11, Grey; Lord Holland, diary, 27 and 29 May 1833 in E. D. Kriegel (ed.) *The Holland House Papers* (1976), pp. 212–13.

46 Lord Ellenborough, diary, 23 June 1833 in A. Aspinall, *Three Early Nineteenth Century Diaries* (1952). See also *Parl. Debates*, xviii, 1180–94, 25 June 1833, Duke of Wellington.

47 Rennie, 'Evangelicalism', chap. 3. 'Recordite' was the name given to the (millenarian) Evangelicals groups round *The Record*.

48 Grey Papers, 3rd Earl, Colonial Papers, Slavery, Item 6, Stephen, Draft of an Answer, n.d. [March 1832], 105–6.

49 As both Seymour Drescher, *Econocide: British Slavery in the Era of Abolition* (Pittsburgh, 1977), pp. 177–83 and my own *Atlantic Slave Trade*, *passim*, also show for their respective periods.

50 P. W. Wilson (ed.), *Greville Diary* (1927 edn.), ii, pp. 59–60.

51 Howard Temperley, *British Anti-Slavery 1833–1870* (1972), pp. 168–83.

52 *Ibid.*, pp. 184–220; Betty Fladeland, *Men and Brothers: Anglo-American Anti-Slavery Co-operation* (Urbana, 1972), pp. 257–301. For divisions amongst anti-slavery activists in Scotland see C. Duncan Rice's forthcoming, *The Scots Abolitionists, 1833–1861*, kindly lent to me in typescript. For a helpful introduction as well as 493 letters see Clare Taylor, *British and American Abolitionists* (Edinburgh, 1974).

53 C. Duncan Rice, 'Humanity sold for Sugar: the anti-slavery interest and the sugar duties', *Historical Journal*, xiii (1970), 402–18, has demonstrated that most British abolitionists, though for the most part also free traders, believed that there should *not* be free trade in slave grown sugar.

54 P. Curtin, *The Atlantic Slave Trade: a Census* (Madison, 1969), pp. 36–234. Contemporaries mostly believed the Brazilian trade to be much larger.

55 See e.g. Humble Addresses of 15 June 1810 (*Parl. Debates*, xvii, 658–89), 14 Jul. 1813 (*P.D.*, xxvi, 1211–15), 2 May 1814 (*P.D.*, xxvii) and 5 May 1814 (*P.D.*, xxvii, 656–62).

56 Bethell, *The Abolition of the Brazilian Slave Trade* (Cambridge, 1970), p. 323, quoting *Hansard*, cix, 1160–70.

57 For instances of Palmerston's keen awareness of the importance of parliamentary backing for suppression see Broadlands MSS, GC/HO/827, Palmerston to Howard de Walden, 12 & 19 May 1838 (Copies); National Maritime Museum, Minto MSS, ELL/218, Palmerston to Minto, 13 Nov. 1838, 9 Sep., 17 Oct. and 29 Dec. 1839.

58 FO84/818, Memo on business of Slave Trade Dept., n.d.

59 *Foreign Office List, 1853* (1853), 9 and 11. See also *ibid.*, 1852, the first to be published. The Slave Trade Dept. was one of five geographical divisions, each with a strength of four or five.

60 R. E. Robinson and J. Gallagher, *Africa and the Victorians; the Official Mind of Imperialism* (1960). Note that only the English edition has this sub-title.

61 Also agreements on suppression with France in 1831 and 1833 and the

addition of the so-called Equipment Clause to the Spanish slave trade treaty in 1835.

62 *Parl. Debates*, 3rd ser., LVII, 648. The sentiment was repeated in a Cabinet minute in 1841 (F097/430, Cabinet minute, 23 Jul. 1846, quoted in Bethell, *Abolition*, p. 274).

63 PRO30/22/10G (Russell MSS) ff. 174–78; Palmerston to Russell, 19 Jan. 1853, PRO30/22/9B, f.252; Palmerston to Russell, 15 Mar. 1851.

64 Broadlands MSS, GC/HU/45, Palmerston to Hudson, 4 Aug. 1848 (copy); GC/RU/306, Russell to Palmerston, 24 Nov. 1849.

65 Note *ibid.*, GC/HU/39, Hudson to Palmerston, 10 Oct. 1851, in reply to Palmerston's intimation that Hudson was to be transferred on promotion.

66 F084/765, Hudson to F.O., 24 Mar. 1849 and Encl., Cdr. Skipwith to Hudson, 5 Mar. 1849 (copy), Hudson to F.O., 13 Aug. 1849 and Encls; F084/802, Hudson to F.O., 20 Feb. 1850 (Nos. 8, 9 and 10).

67 Broadlands MSS, GC/HU/14/4, Hudson to Palmerston, 10 Jul. 1849; *ibid.*, GC/HU/15, Hudson to Palmerston, 15 Aug. 1849; *ibid.*, GC/HU/18, Hudson to Palmerston, 10 Oct. 1849; ibid., GC/HU/20, Hudson to Palmerston, 17 Jan. 1850, (? rec'd 23 Feb. 1850); GC/HU/21, Hudson to Palmerston 21 Feb. 1850, (rec'd 5 Apr. 1850), Copy in F084/801; GC/HU/26, Hudson to Palmerston, 2 Sep. 1850.

68 *Ibid.*, GC/HU/26, Hudson to Palmerston, 2 Sep. 1850.

69 Text of Russell's speech, 19 Mar. 1850 is in PR030/22/8D; Bethell, *Abolition*, 323–24.

70 'The House of Commons have given us another year's trial of the African Squadron, but if we are not able at the end of that time to show that we have made some considerable progress, they will be much tempted to withhold the means which they at present afford us' (Broadlands MSS, GC/HU/49, Palmerston to Hudson, 4 Jun. 1850 (Copy).) See also GC/HU/48, Palmerston to Hudson, 31 Mar. 1850 (copy) and GC/HU/50, Palmerston to Hudson, 6 Nov. 1850 (Copy) and GC/HU/26, Hudson to Palmerston, 2 Sep. 1850: 'The "Ides of March" . . . are rapidly approaching'.

71 F084/825, Palmerston, minute, 12 Apr. 1850 on Ad. to F.O., 6 Apr. 1850 and Encls. F084/823, F.O., to Ad. 22 Apr. 1850.

72 Serge Daget, 'L'Abolition de la traite des noires en France de 1814 a 1831', *Cahiers d'Etudes Africaines*, No. 41, Tome XI (1971), 1er Cahier, *passim*.

73 See especially Aberdeen MSS, B.M. Add MSS 43357, Confidential Print of minutes of evidence taken before de Broglie and Lushington, 31 Mar.–4 Apr. 1845; and *ibid*. 43125, ff.319–39, Lushington's commentary on the Anglo-French treaty of 29 May 1845, n.d. That, during the year 1846, the French fully carried out their commitment to keep twenty-six ships on the station has been confirmed to me by the kindness of M. le Professeur Serge Daget on the basis of his very close archival knowledge. For Lushington's role in the campaign for emancipation see especially David Eltis, 'Dr Stephen Lushington and the campaign to abolish slavery in the British Empire', *Journal of Caribbean History*, I, 41–56.

74 Roger Anstey, *Britain and the Congo in the Nineteenth Century* (Oxford, 1962), pp. 38–9.

75 See H. G. Soulsby, *The Right of Search and the Slave Trade in Anglo-American Relations, 1814–1862* (Baltimore, 1933), passim and A. Taylor Milne, 'The Slave Trade and Anglo-American Relations, 1807–62', University of London unpublished M.A. thesis (1930), passim.

76 See Oliver Macdonagh, *A Pattern of Government Growth, 1800–60* (1961), especially pp. 320–36, and Oliver Macdonagh, 'The nineteenth century revolution in government: a re-appraisal', *The Historical Journal*, 1 (1958), 1, 52–67 and especially 58–61.

77 Cf. Cobden's comment on the anti-Corn Law campaign: 'Ultimate victory would depend upon accident or upon further political changes. But our only chance is the enlightenment of the public mind, so as to prepare it to take advantage of such an accident when it arises' (quoted in Donald Read, *Cobden and Bright* (1967), 45).

78 Brian Harrison in P. Hollis (ed.), *Pressure From Without* (1974), 292–3.

2

TWO VARIANTS OF ANTI-SLAVERY: RELIGIOUS ORGANIZATION AND SOCIAL MOBILIZATION IN BRITAIN AND FRANCE, 1780–1870

by Seymour Drescher

Dealing with its international aspects, histories of abolition tend to concentrate primarily on its Anglo–American dimension as a mutually reinforcing 'connection', rather than as a subject for comparative national analysis.[1] In this context other European colonial powers are treated as peripheral. French anti-slavery is duly accorded recognition in the intellectual history of pre-abolitionism, and a brief dramatic role in the French Revolutionary era. Thereafter French abolitionists disappear into oblivion, or remain in the unfolding drama as modest members of the chorus.

One might begin by broadly contrasting an 'Anglo–American' and a 'Continental' model of abolitionism. The distinguishing characteristic of the Anglo–American variant was its relatively broad appeal. It had the characteristics of what we think of as a social movement.[2] It attempted to bring public pressure to bear on reluctant or hostile economic interests and agencies of government. At critical moments it used mass propaganda, petitions, public meetings, lawsuits and boycotts, presenting anti-slavery action as a moral and political imperative. Its adherents achieved, at least occasionally, a reputation for fanaticism. Organizationally, it tended to be decentralized in structure and rooted in local communities. It usually aimed at inclusiveness, welcoming participants who were otherwise excluded by sex, religion, race, class or locality, from the ordinary political process. Europe had one example of this variant – Britain.

The 'Continental' variants generally had the opposite characteristics. They were usually confined to a very small political or cultural elite. They generally were reluctant or unable to seek mass recruitment. Efforts were concentrated on plans of abolition submitted to government, and on elaborate post-emancipation social control. They often attempted to act as brokers between governments and external pressure groups, including British abolitionists and their own colonial interests. Debate was confined to one or two localities, the capital, and/or the chief commercial center. Continental abolitionism, in other words, preferred to work quietly from within. It rarely achieved the status of fanaticism, even in the eyes of enemies. The 'Continental' variant tended to be not only limited in participation but enjoyed a brief existence. A movement would typically emerge in response to external pressures and last only until the abolition of a single slave trade or slave system. With the partial exception of France, Continental abolitionist societies remained satellites of their British counterpart, and failed to capture any mass following on their own soil.

French abolition is a particularly interesting and partly anomalous case of the Continental variety. At the outset it looked very much like its British counterpart. The abolitionist climate of philosophical opinion which inclined heavily against colonial slavery from 1760 to 1790 was as much a Franco–Anglo–American enterprise, as the subsequent movement was predominantly Anglo–American. If only momentarily, France was the first metropolitan nation to declare slavery abolished throughout its sphere of influence in 1794. But after 1800 abolitionism either lacked formal organization, or was confined to a small group in the capital.[3] It had become a 'Continental' movement. For the next three-quarters of a century French manifestations of popular support for anti-slavery were either aborted by larger revolutionary events, or nipped in the bud by repression. France also had the unenviable distinction of having restored slavery and the slave trade in 1802. Her later abolitionist acts were, like the original, always decreed in the wake of political revolution, and without reference to organized domestic pressure.

The primary purpose of this essay is to broadly compare the relation of religious activity in Britain and France in regard to political abolition. Our hypothesis is that such religious activity was decisively bounded by more general political and social developments. It explicitly does not assume that the particular theological stance of specific religious groups made the critical difference in the timing or intensity of the abolitionist movements at a national level, although the possibility of such a correlation is by no means ruled out. Predominantly Protestant Holland, Denmark and Sweden, for example, were even more clearly Continental cases than was predominantly Catholic France. Nor do we assume that religious networks were the only channels for social change. The press, itinerant propagandists, public meetings at taverns and halls, and the petition were effective alternative or complementary means of mobilizing communal opinion. Over the period 1780–1870 as a whole, however, religious organization remained a primary form of cosmopolitan social organization, linking communities to the larger national and international world. Thus, the response of religious organizations of each society to the social potential of abolitionism seems an excellent place to study metropolitan association for overseas reform.

I

Religious networks were especially significant in the development of British abolitionism. Interlocking specialized anti-slavery societies did not appear until late in the history of anti-slavery. Other institutions which were important in political mobilization, such as newspapers and public houses, could not match religious institutions in ubiquity and international connections. Once launched by the resources and personnel of the Quaker international, Anglo–American abolitionism was quickly identified with the evangelical wing of Protestantism, even in institutions where it was not dominant, as in the Anglican church, or regions where anti-slavery was soon overwhelmed by a powerful countervailing force, as in the American South.[4]

English anti-slavery and evangelical non-conformity seem to have peaked together (see Figure 1). The most dynamic period of nonconformist growth coincides almost exactly with the dynamic period of anti-slavery. In strictly institutional terms, however, evangelical nonconformity latched on to, rather than independently launched the anti-slavery movement. In its formative period, abolition appealed to a broad spectrum among the politically mobilized, ranging from theological rationalists and Unitarians to Quakers and artisanal radicals. If evangelicals participated actively in the earlier petition campaigns they participated as members of geographical rather than religious communities. Table 1 shows that it was only toward the climax of anti-slavery in 1830–3, that denominationalism

Figure 1

Methodist and New Dissenting Membership, and Abolitionist Petitions

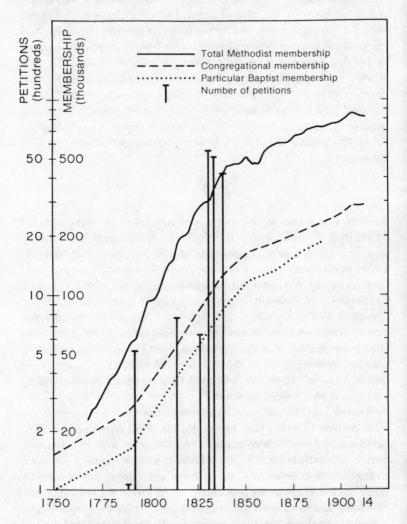

SOURCES: Nonconformist membership, A. D. Gilbert, *Religion and Society in Industrial England: Church, Chapel and Social Change, 1740–1914* (1976), p. 38, Figure 2.1; abolitionist petitions *The House of Commons Journals*, 1788–1838.

Table 1

Anti-slavery petitions and religious affiliation, 1788–1833

Date	Total petitions	Established churches*(%)	Dissent (%)
1788	108	23	2
1792	509	14	1
1814	774	1	3
1824	509	3	6
1826	634	7	7
1831	5484	3	72
1833	5020	N.A.	56

Date	Total signatures		
1833	1,309,931	N.A.	27

* Including all petitions in which ministers of the Established churches appear as sponsors of petitions, but not in petitions indicating only that the document originated in a particular parish.

Sources: *Journals of the House of Commons*, 1788–1831; *Anti-slavery Reporter*, 1831; *First Report from the Select Committee on Public Petitions* (1833). N.B. the percentage for 1831 is uncertain owing to obscurities in the classification of petitions in the House Journal that year.

rivaled location as an indicator of the origin of such petitions.

The relevant parliamentary committee was so impressed with the nonconformist component of the climactic anti-slavery petition, that it published a unique appendix to its report in 1833, aggregating the signatures of nonconformity by denomination (Table 2). Earlier, evangelical identity apparently merged sufficiently with community affiliation to lend a peculiarly pan-denominational image to anti-slavery. Moreover, although well over half of the petitions of 1833 were explicitly affiliated with non-denominational organizations, Table 1 shows that only 27 per cent of the total signatures were submitted under specifically nonconformist banners.

Another aspect of British religious development is salient in accounting for the sustained strength of programs for overseas social change. The peak period of mass abolitionism in Britain also coincided with an expansion of the Anglo–American religious network to full planetary dimensions. The take-off of British abolitionism coincided almost exactly with the revival of the British missionary movement. After 1790, the British-sponsored religious networks in Africa and the West Indies were responsive to

Table 2

Anti-slavery and English Evangelical Denominations c. 1833

Denomination	(1)* Estimated membership	(2) Anti-slavery petition signatures (1832–3)	(3) percentage of (2) in (1)
Wesleyan Methodist	(1831/36) 241,000	229,426	95.2
Other Methodist	(1831/36) 62,500	7166	11.5
Congregational	(1800/38) 112,500	26,430	23.5
Baptist, Particular, General, and New connexion	(1800/30/38) 87,800	34,650	39.5
Total	503,800	297,672	59.1

* Column 1 is calculated on the basis of enclosed estimates

Sources: Column (1), A. D. Gilbert, *Religion and Society in Industrial England: Church, Chapel and Social Change 1740–1914* (1976), pp. 31, 37; (2), *First Report from the Select Committee on Public Petitions* (1833).

increasingly abolitionist pressures at home.[5] Missionaries could appeal more directly to their metropolitan sources of support than ever before. This linkage also allowed the development of a religious relationship between slaves and missionaries well before emancipation. Conversely British missionaries after 1790 were less dependent upon the metropolitan state church or on the colonial elite for financial support than their predecessors.

In the first half-century of abolitionism the British dominated the Protestant missionary movement as thoroughly as its imperial navy dominated the oceans, and far more thoroughly than its trade dominated the world's commercial networks. Of the missionary establishments created outside the United States by European Protestants or their descendants in the formative generation (1790–1820), 22 were British, 5 were American, and 1 was Dutch. During the next thirty years, of 72 new missions, 26 were British, 28 were American and 17 were Continental. (America's great surge came in the 1820s, as her abolitionist movement was entering a new phase.) Of the Continental establishments, only the two sponsored by French Protestants came from nations with slave colonies, and none originated in the Netherlands.[6]

This is not to say that evangelical expansion automatically entailed a resolutely abolitionist posture. Before 1790 the fate of religious missions to slave colonies demonstrated the opposite. Until the fate of American slavery was decided, evangelical Christianity temporized with slavery. The history of the international 'Evangelical Alliance' abundantly illustrated this. But if slaveholding American Protestants were long powerful enough to prevent international movements for evangelical unity from becoming organs of abolitionism, the thickening network of religious communication kept the question at the forefront of Protestant politics. Anti-slavery advocates clearly played a role in evangelical ideology and organization, sometimes to the disadvantage of British religious initiatives (the international Evangelical Alliance controversy, for example), which was absent from other religious organizations with similar international dimensions.[7]

Religious organizations in France never achieved the same prominence in anti-slavery. If the dynamism of missionary activism may be taken as an indicator of the potential linkage of overseas to domestic change, French activity indicates a low level of metropolitan interest both before and after the Great Revolution of 1789. For more than sixty years, coinciding with the development of Anglo–American anti-slavery, the whole European Catholic missionary enterprise was virtually paralyzed. The monarchical attack on the Jesuits in the 1760s and 1770s entailed the recall or displacement of hundreds of French colonial missionaries. The French Revolution shattered the resources of the Church. The old French empire and the broader missionary effort disintegrated together. In many areas the entire Catholic overseas network was abandoned for decades. In others, such as the French Antilles, with only one priest to 10,000 souls, only the free population received the attentions of the clergy. Effectively, until the second third of the nineteenth century, Catholic mobilization for abolitionist or missionary enterprise moved in the opposite direction from Anglo–American development, and until the last third, lagged far behind.[8]

From its foundation in 1788 to its demise in the early 1790s, the French antislavery society, the *Amis des Noirs*, did not seek to use religious organizations or their personnel to mobilize French opinion. The French Revolution shook the Catholic Church to its roots, and it had to make its peace with a post-revolutionary government which had already restored slavery and required civil subservience in exchange for its protection. A restored Church, which identified the abolitionist Abbé Grégoire with all the sufferings and apostacies of its revolutionary martyrdom, was unlikely to raise another abolitionist to take up the mantel of the Constitutional Bishop of Blois. The first concern of the Church was its own survival in a post-revolutionary society where the trauma of the Jacobin terror at home had been re-inforced by the trauma of the Haitian revolution overseas.

In addition to its obligations as a state-supported religion, Catholicism was also deeply embedded in the colonial status quo.[9] Its clerical training center, Saint-Sulpice, maintained the accommodating doctrine of the legitimacy of slavery, and a passive role towards the issue of emancipation. Equally, those Catholic periodicals most clearly subordinated to the hierarchy also tended to defend a passive and pastoral role for the clergy in the colonies.[10]

The embryonic theological hostility to slavery which appeared in France at the outbreak of the French Revolution appears to have found no sequel in nineteenth century France. Like the Protestant denominations which established deep roots in slave systems, French Catholicism continued to maintain its traditional compromise with the institution.[11] Hesitant to embrace anti-slavery because of its linkage with an anticlerical revolution, the French Church found its performance measured against more a progressive Protestantism in Britain and a more radical secularism in France. Until the eve of the second emancipation in 1848, calls for clerical participation in the movement received little encouragement from the French hierarchy.

If the clergy hesitated to become identified with the French campaign for emancipation from a general wariness of political agitation, nineteenth-century conditions offered few incentives for international Catholic pressures in favor of anti-slavery. Catholicism was linked to an institutional network which discouraged any radical transformations in attitudes or in social structures. In the first half of the nineteenth century the Papacy was closely bound to metropolitan forces of order which sanctioned various forms of bound labor within and without Europe. Neither the Central Europe of the Holy Alliance, nor Iberia were likely sources of pressure against the status quo. Indeed, Rome was busily restricting attempts to atune theology to libertarian values.[12] Even in the Americas the balance of social pressures and immigration patterns weighed against an anti-slavery stance by Catholics. The largest concentration of Catholics in the South, the French of Louisiana, adhered to the slave system. In the North, the bulk of the burgeoning Irish Catholic immigration before the Civil War was not mobilized for anti-slavery.[13]

One major campaign with a highly visible, if quantitively indeterminate, Catholic presence, was the Antislavery Address to Irish Americans, signed by 60,000–70,000 people in Ireland in 1841–2. Neither the intended recipients, nor the American Catholic hierarchy gave the Address a favorable reception, despite the well-publicized adhesion of Daniel O'Connell, Father Theodore Mathews, and many Irish priests. Equally significant, this attempt by Irish abolitionists to convert their fellow countrymen was not repeated with coreligionists on the Continent. When an appeal was addressed to the French clergy very shortly after the Irish Address, it took the form of a private letter by a Catholic abolitionist to the archbishop of Paris. The potential of massive international pressure was never realized.

One cannot, however, explain the relative quietism of French Catholicism towards abolition simply in terms of French Revolutionary demoralization, or international affiliation. French Catholicism had certainly achieved some internal stability as early as the First Empire, and despite occasional threats was not again subjected to a sustained institutional attack before 1870. Moreover, in its broader context, European Catholicism did renew its overseas mission, especially after 1830. France again became Europe's principal Catholic exponent of overseas religious, as well as economic and political expansion. The central Catholic missionary periodical, the *Annales de la propagation de la foi*, was founded in France in 1825. In 1847, on the eve of the second French emancipation, 178,000 copies circulated, of which 55 per cent went to French subscribers alone. By contrast, the other Catholic slave powers accounted for less than 2 per cent of the subscribers.[14]

Therefore, while France lagged behind Britain in its depth of international penetration and religious investment in overseas activity, there was no lack of means in France for converting concern with religious conversion abroad into a concern for overseas social transformation. There are other, more proximate, indicators that French Catholicism was becoming available for political mobilization, especially after 1830. In the absence of a Catholic religious organization dedicated to popular mobilization, it was still possible to use other means to galvanize religious support for anti-slavery.

The July Monarchy witnssed an enormous expansion of newspaper circulation. Like its secular counterparts, the Catholic lay press began to demand a role in the articulation of opinion, breaking with the accommodating posture of the hierarchy *vis-à-vis* the state. The most successful example was Louis Veuillot's *L'Univers*.[15] Veuillot was eager to employ the technique of the mass petition as well as of popular journalism. In 1847, while a handful of French abolitionists were accumulating less than 11,000 signatures for emancipation, Veuillot was able to elicit almost 90,000 in favor of proclerical legislation. *L'Univers* was also the most anti-slavery Catholic newspaper in France. By the end of the year it was clear that *L'Univers* would support plans for a new, broadly based campaign.[16] There were equally obvious signs that the French clergy could be drawn into the anti-slavery network. In the petition campaign of 1846–7, during an assembly of the clergy of Paris, a French abolitionist collected 800 signatures, the first substantial intrusion of the Catholic clergy into the anti-slavery cause. For a few months before the February Revolution of 1848 it appeared as though splintered groups of abolitionists were on the verge of forming a national movement. Notables, urban radicals, metropolitan *hommes de couleur*, and men identified with religious opinion began to co-ordinate their efforts for the first time. Catholics figured prominently in abolitionist plans. The Archbishop of Paris indicated his approval of Catholic involvement. Abbé Dupanloup, a leader of liberal Catholicism, promised to help gather 20,000 clerical signatures. *L'Univers* publicized the activities of the special bureau created to launch the 1848 campaign and to create pressure 'from below'.[17]

The events of February 1848 snapped the still frail abolitionist alliance. Once again emancipation became the work of Parisian revolutionaries acting by decree. At the popular level the only abolitionist group visible was the radical *Club des Amis des Noirs*, formed in Paris in the wake of the revolution.[18] The only petitions on slavery which reached the Emancipation Committee from beyond the capital were those of Chambers of Commerce, pleading for compensation, delay, or guarantees of order and labor.[19] Emancipation was decreed in the name of the Provisional Government, before it handed over power to the socially and fiscally more conservative Constituent Assembly. Despite flickerings of a national appeal, abolitionism never became linked with mass Catholic support or organization.

Before assessing the historical context of this disjuncture, it may be useful to consider the role of Protestants in French abolitionism. The Protestant clergy were excluded from the state-supported French missionary enterprise both before and after the Revolution. A minor branch of world Protestantism, its overseas missionary effort was meager. The Paris Evangelical Mission Society succeeded in establishing only one overseas post before 1845, and only in a British sphere of influence.[20] In terms of its own economic resources and the persistent policy of subordination to the French state, on which it was heavily dependent, French Protestantism had little of the dynamic which made slavery so significant an organizational issue in Britain.

French Protestants were more visibly involved in abolitionism than their French Catholic counterparts during the Constitutional Monarchy in France (1815–48). The *Société de la Morale Chrétienne*, the only French organization with an abolitionist committee during the Bourbon restoration, was disproportionately Protestant. For most of the period of July Monarchy, however, independent Protestant involvement in abolition leaned heavily on English information and initiatives. The July Monarchy was especially receptive to the integration of the French Protestant elite into the highest echelons of power and respectability. It was relatively cautious about the opportunity to organize a mass appeal around the question of abolition.[21] At least one section of French Protestant journalism consistently urged British-style abolitionism campaigns throughout the July Monarchy, a suggestion just as consistently ignored by abolitionist notables.[22]

On the eve of the Revolution of 1848, and encouraged by the British, French Protestants showed clear signs of becoming activists. The campaign was, in fact, initiated by a provincial Protestant and a mulatto from the Antilles.[23] Some communities began to submit abolitionist petitions to the Chamber of Deputies, with their pastors heading the lists.[24] In relative terms, French Protestants were therefore probably over-represented among the provincial localities which responded to the campaign. Constituting about 2 per cent of the French population, they accounted for about 10 per cent of the abolitionist petition in 1847. Protestant ministers also made up about 10 per cent of the total clerical support.[25]

French Protestant anti-slavery, like all other varieties, disappeared in the wake of the February Revolution. Protestants were probably always represented among the abolitionists, but French Protestants were closer to their Catholic and Protestant counterparts on the Continent than to the British in terms of broad involvement in abolitionist activity. Given the inhibitions of a small, minority sect, it is the situation of French Catholicism which was the more significant determinant of the national pattern.

II

In all metropolitan countries abolitionism declined as a popular issue following the elimination of the institution in their respective colonial areas. Yet, here too, we have British and Continental variants. British anti-slavery remained a relatively salient issue for a generation after emancipation. It was manifested not only in the continuance of specialized organizations for international abolition, but in the continuance of institutional involvement with freedmen. A large scale metropolitan religious and educational effort continued in the British colonies and the African continent, and issues raised by slavery in the United States were continuously debated before interested and contributing British audiences. The British post-emancipation movement was also still capable of launching campaigns which involved tens and hundreds of thousands of signatories.

In France, emancipation was equivalent to the total suspension of abolitionism as an organized movement. The radical Parisian *Amis des Noirs* of 1848 was a victim of the general reaction against associations. The elite anti-slavery society looked forward to its own demise even before the emancipation decree.[26] The combination of apathy and governmental hostility to political associations after the presidential coup of December 1851 discouraged even a nominal institutional revival until the imperial liberalization of the mid-1860s.[27]

The religious shoots that had appeared towards the end of the July Monarchy withered. The ties between popular Catholic journalism and anti-slavery seem to have disappeared. Veuillot swung sharply over to the traditional view that abolitionism was the tool of British liberalism. When Imperial France embarked on a barely disguised renewal of the African slave trade in the late 1850s, *L'Univers* was as vitriolic as the conservative French press in denouncing British abolitionist complaints as the Anglo-Protestant complement to revolutionary subversion in Europe. Imperial policy was defended against 'comedies of philanthropism' and 'Negrophilia'.[28]

The American Civil War produced a final opportunity to arouse flagging European concern with the question of slavery in the

Americas. Interest was heightened and vastly complicated by the high stakes of international power politics, and the acute suffering which prevailed in the textile districts of both France and Britain.[29] In Britain this took the form of a vigorous press war, public meetings, and petitions on behalf of both belligerents.[30] In the British political campaign revolving around the American conflict, the division between the Establishment and nonconformity was even more striking than in the previous generation. Of ninety-four petitions submitted to Parliament against recognition of Confederate independence in 1863, twenty (21 per cent) were sent in on behalf of nonconforming congregations. None were headed up by the Anglican clergy. On the opposite side during the following year, seventeen (21 per cent) of the eighty petitions in favour of British action to terminate hostilities were presented on behalf of the 'Clergy and Laity' of various communities. No nonconformist congregation subscribed to what would have amounted to *de facto* recognition of Southern independence, with slavery. More significantly, however, the combined number of signatures accumulated in both campaigns amounted to less than 30,000. The conflict over slavery had ceased to be a major concern of either the religious or the political community.

In France, because of the imperial restrictions, journalistic commentary was more muted, and public activity almost nonexistent. On this occasion, even so, there were signs of attempts to use the religious network to increase the domestic salience of the struggle. After the Emancipation Proclamation some French Bishops urged their flocks to pray for American slaves. The *Annales de la propagation de la foi* took the optimistic position that emancipation might lead to a reactive expansion of Catholicism among ex-slaves of Protestant masters. But these were editorial glosses on events rather than attempts to initiate or influence political or religious policy.[31]

In France the two most important attempts at public mobilization related to emancipation came at the end of the war. The first was a campaign for a commemorative medal to be presented to Lincoln's widow. It gathered 40,000 subscribers before the government became alarmed over the domestic political implications. But its sponsors were overwhelmingly radical and secular.[32] The second venture was a fund-raising drive on behalf of the American freedmen. A parallel campaign in Britain yielded up to $800,000 in cash and goods (more, notes Howard Temperley, than all British contributions for anti-slavery since British colonial emancipation).

The French campaign yielded approximately $10,000. This sum certainly also exceeded the total of private French contributions to anti-slavery activity after 1848.[33] Despite wartime musings about the conversion of ex-slaves, potential Catholic contributors in France could hardly have been less wary than their Anglican counterparts about stinting their own modest missions to fund relief and education under the aegis of nonconformist agencies in a Protestant cultural area. French aid to the American freedmen seemed to be the same pale reflection of the larger British effort. The movement, which before emancipation obtained a hundred British signatures for every French one, collected eighty dollars in Britain for every dollar contributed in France for Freedman's Aid.

However, the reaction to the American Civil War was not just one more demonstration of an excitable British evangelical revival pulling along a French satellite movement. The conflict's initially ambiguous implication for slavery was more than matched by divisions in British Protestant opinion on the appropriate position towards the belligerents. It was French ministers who took a collective initiative in favor of the North, a move only subsequently endorsed by sympathetic British clergymen. The Freedman's Aid appeal also reopened opportunities for personal participation in France which had been foreclosed by the aborted abolitionism of the late 1840s. For the first time French women openly assumed roles of organizational leadership.[34]

The British movement, despite its relative generosity, was showing clear signs of a hardening of the anti-slavery arteries. Its successes were calculated more in terms of contributions than individual participation. A few wealthy supporters could determine the relative 'enthusiasm' of a region, whilst those areas of Britain which had suffered from the Northern blockade of their cotton supply could not even be canvassed. The first mass petition campaign triggered in Manchester, in 1787, must have included a majority of signatures from the lower middle and working classes. Eighty years later, the Freedman's Aid campaign could not even be properly organized among a resentful Manchester working class.[35] Popular apathy was for the first time contrasted with Continental initiative. The same document which proposed the termination of the Freedmans Aid movement in 1868 announced that it was still waiting to realize a penny subscription from working men, following the example set by artisans of Paris, by the Swiss peasants and, partially, by Birmingham.[36] The fund-raising campaign failed to evoke a response from even those who had not been embittered by the economic consequences of the conflict. Nonconformity, flourishing and unassailably respectable, was no longer interested in a sustained campaign in favor of ex-slaves. Britain now converged towards the Continental variant of prestigious committees. British anti-slavery, which the old agitator, George Thompson, had hoped to rekindle from the heat of the American conflict, was, in more than one sense, liquidated in a post-war charity subscription.

Here we note a final irony in anti-slavery's potential as a vehicle for mobilization in France. Although the French working class contribution to American freedmen was fragmentary, this may have been due to a more general absence of religious or alternative modes of class mediating organizations. In the France of 1865 anti-slavery had not been converted into a charity appropriated by large subscribers. There were no aging and wealthy veterans of French abolition at hand to capitalize on the past commitment of millions to the glory of their participation. While the unexpected paucity of the workers' response surprised and disappointed the veteran canvassers in Britain, its unexpected extension in France took its inexperienced female organizers by equal surprise. Working class contributions came in without any central planning or canvassing. Only at the end of the campaign did upper class organizers realize, with regret, quite how large a reservoir of sympathy might have been at their disposal. One donation of 1000 francs represented the combined contribution of 10,000 workers. It is unclear whether the female organizers of the French Freedman's Aid drive were aware of the equally unheeded opportunity twenty-one years before, when thousands of workers of Paris and Lyon had launched the first mass petition for emancipation on the Continent. Certainly they were unaware of the contrast between the artisans of Grenoble who had celebrated Grégoire's electoral victory in Isère forty-five years before, and the Liberal notables who had then voted for his exclusion from the Chamber of Deputies. To British abolitionists, the campaign gave pointed notice of diverging class perceptions at the end of a long crusade. To the French it was a glimpse of a cause which might have linked them to at least a portion of the working class.

III

In religious perspective British anti-slavery movements, in their heyday, paid homage to the increasing power of nonconformist values and modes of association. They provided the basis for a cross-class and cross-national appeal to a common standard of human rights. In their independence from state support and subordination they were also more flexible channels for the rapid mobilization of public opinion against a traditional economic institution than the established religious and political organizations of unreformed Britain. Although anti-slavery became increasingly denominational towards 1830, and elicited a counterpoint of class-oriented anti-evangelical criticism, this far from unanimous dissent from below was lacking in the formative period, when the movement claimed the adhesion of Painite deists no less than Clapham saints.[37] Moreover, given both the extraordinary mobilization of Wesleyan Methodists for anti-slavery in 1833 (Table 2), and the occupational structure of Wesleyan and other evangelical nonconformists (Table 3), it is apparent that artisanal England continued to support the movement at its climax. In cross-cultural terms the significant fact remains that an unprecedented and unparalleled proportion of the nation adhered to a common cause for so long,

Table 3

Occupational structure of nonconformity with high participation in anti-slavery petitions (sample 1830–7)

Occupation	English society (%)	Wesleyans (%)	Baptists and Congregationalists (%)
Aristocracy	1.4	0	0
Merchants/			
Merchants/	2.2	1.7	5.4
Manufacturers	6.2	5.8	8.2
Tradesmen	14.0	5.5	7.1
Artisans	23.5	62.7	63.0
Laborers	17.0	9.5	3.9
Miners, etc.	2.5	7.6	2.1
Others	33.2	7.2	10.3

Source: A. D. Gilbert, *Religion and Society in Industrial England: Church, Chapel, and Social Change 1740–1914* (1976), pp. 63, 67.

and shaped a synthesis of political and religious action around the question of slavery which proved difficult to export beyond its zone of origin.

As Halévy long ago noted, the French religious system lacked this burgeoning dissenting and evangelical network. Its religious organizations were economically dependent upon a state generally hostile to associational agitation. Revolutions and threats of revolution caused the surviving elite of both state and church to be wary of mass action for virtually the whole period during which slavery was an unresolved issue in French politics. From the second decade of the nineteenth century, abolitionism in France was also vulnerable to associations with British colonial supremacy, Anglophile Protestantism and secular radicalism. Non-revolutionary British citizens validated their imperial and economic hegemony with a socioreligious crusade, and mythologized their incremental abolition as a testimony to their moral progress. Their French counterparts were left to poke among the shards of their past to make what they could of unsuccessful emancipations, unsuccessful restorations, and imperial humiliations.

Historians cannot overlook the significance of this temporal priority and divergence in the emergence of abolitionism. By 1814 the evangelical William Wilberforce became a national hero precisely because he was an abolitionist saint. It is hardly possible to imagine anyone else who could, with impunity, condemn a treaty which sealed the greatest military triumph in his country's history. At the same moment his closest French abolitionist counterpart, Abbé Grégoire, lived frozen in ostracism, stigmatized as the incendiary of two worlds. His very existence inhibited the organization of another abolitionist society. The belated hero of French emancipation was to be the unbeliever Victor Schoelcher. But in 1814, the difference between the voice of abolition in Britain and France was not *vox Dei*, but *vox populi*. Behind the words of Wilberforce flowed the greatest wave of petitions in his country's history. This was the tide in the affairs of 'men and brothers', that swept the British evangelical to glory in the name of God and humanity.

Notes

1 See, for example, Christine Bolt, *The Anti-slavery Movement and Reconstruction: A Study in Anglo-American Co-operation, 1833–77* (1969); and Betty Fladeland, *Men and Brothers: Anglo-American Anti-slavery Co-operation* (Urbana, 1972). For some explicitly comparative analyses, see E. Genovese, *The World the Slaveholders Made* (New York, 1969), part I; Howard Temperley, 'British and American Abolitionist Compared' in *The Anti-slavery Vanguard*, ed. M. Duberman (Princeton, 1965); David Davis, *The Problem of Slavery in the Age of Revolution, 1770–1823* (Ithaca, 1975). Toward the end of the

eighteenth century, abolitionism emerged as only one of a large number of social reform movements. They aimed at effective political action at the regional, national and, in the case of abolition, at the international level. This rapid thickening of large-scale associational activity outside traditional authority networks was a counterpart to economic development. Abolitionism was thus an aspect of what Karl Deutsch calls 'social mobilization', a process in which major social and economic patterns are broken, and people become more available for new patterns of action. In domestic terms British, although not French, abolitionism served as a very early vehicle both for the formulation of new values and for the transformation of old forms of political pressure into novel contexts. For lack of space, in this essay we are confining the comparison of social mobilization in Britain and France primarily to religious organization.

2 For recent descriptions of the development of British abolitionism in addition to the accounts of Rice, Temperley and Davis, above, see especially Roger Anstey, *The Atlantic Slave Trade and British Abolition, 1760–1810* (1975), part four; Peter F. Dixon, 'The politics of emancipation: the movement for the abolition of slavery in the British West Indies, 1807–1833,' D. Phil. Oxford (1971); Howard Temperley, *British Anti-Slavery, 1833–70* (1972).

3 See Gabriel Debien, *Les Colons de Saint-Domingue et la Revolution: Essai sur le club Massiac* (Paris, 1953); Yves Debbasch, *Couleur et liberté* (Paris, 1967); Valerie Quinney, 'The Committee on Colonies of the French Constituent Assembly, 1789–1971,' Ph.D. dissertation, University of Wisconsin (1967); Ruth F. Necheles, *The Abbé Grégoire 1788–1831: The Odyssey of an Egalitarian* (Westport, Conn., 1971); D. P. Resnick, 'Political economy and French anti-slavery: the case of J-B Say', *Proceedings of the 3rd Annual Meeting of the Western Society for French History* (1976), pp. 179–86; S. Drescher, *Dilemmas of Democracy: Tocqueville and Modernization* (Pittsburgh, 1968), chap. 6.

4 On the abortive antislavery impulse in the slave South, see especially Donald G. Matthews, *Religion in the Old South* (Chicago, 1977), chap. 2.

5 See Stiv Jacobson, *Am I Not A Man and A Brother? British Missionaries and the Abolition of the Slave Trade and Slavery, 1786–1838* (Uppsala, 1972); and G. R. Mellor, *British Imperial Trusteeship 1783–1850* (1951).

6 See *The Encyclopedia of Missions*, ed. H. O. Dwight *et al.* (New York, 1904), Appendices II and VI.

7 A French Protestant newspaper sarcastically asked whether an English 'Evangelical Alliance', which refused to excommunicate orthodox proprietors of slaves and excluded Quakers, could be a model for unity (*Le Lien* (1847), p. 76). On religion as a source of anti-slavery controversy, see Fladeland, *Men and Brothers*, pp. 364–70.

8 Mr S. Delacroix (ed.), *Histoire Universelle des Missions Catholiques*, 4 vols. (Paris, n.d.), III, pp. 14–15, chs. 1–3.

9 Antoine Gisler, *L'Esclavage aux Antilles Françaises (XVIIᵉ–XIXᵉ siècle): Contribution au problème de l'esclavage* (Friburg, 1965), part 3, 'Les Missionnaires'. On the extraordinary degree of clerical creoliza-

tion in the colonies, see the letter of the Prefect Apostolique, Castelli, to Baron Mackau, July 10, 1841 (Archives Nationales (hereafter A. N.)), Archives privées, Fonds Mackau, 156 API.

10 On abolitionist complaints about institutional passivity vis-a-vis colonial pressures or emancipation see *Rhodes House Anti-Slavery Papers* (hereafter *RHASSP*) G/103 (France), letter of Isambert to Scoble, 19 Jan. 1843, *L'Abolitioniste francais*, T. III (1846), pp. 71, 107–122, 270; on defenses of accommodation, see *La Tribune sacrée* vols. 5–6 (February, 1846), pp. 145–151; *L'Ami de la Religion* (1846), p. 413; *Revue Catholique IV* (July, 1839), p. 374 and *V* (July, 1840), pp. 357–63; and above all a letter from Leguay, replying to an attack on the seminary of Saint-Esprit by Ledru-Rollin in the Chamber of Deputies (*L'Ami de la Religion* (April, 1847), p. 287). His reply clearly shows that almost halfway through the century, anti-slavery still evoked Grégoire, unorthodoxy, and fanaticism.

11 Necheles, *Abbé Grégoire*, pp. 205–7, 229, 235–6, 243; John Francis Maxwell, *Slavery in the Catholic Church: The History of the Catholic Teaching Concerning the Moral Legitimacy of the Institution of Slavery* (London, 1975), pp. 98–102; L. Swidler, 'Liberal Catholicism: a lesson from the past', *Cross Currents*, 21 (1971), 25–37.

12 *Ibid.* The Clergy are described as conspicuous by their absence in the late-blossoming Spanish abolitionist movement of the 1860s. (See A. F. Corwin, *Spain and the Abolition of Slavery in Cuba, 1817–86* (Austin and London, 1967), pp. 166–71).

13 Gilbert Osofsky, 'Abolitionists, Irish immigrants and the dilemmas of Romantic Nationalism', *American Historical Review*, 80 (4), (October 1975), 889–912; Joseph M. Hernon, *Celts, Catholics and Copperheads: Ireland Views the American Civil War* (Columbus, Ohio, 1968), chap. 4. For the conspicuous place given to Irish clerical adhesions, see Garrison's newspaper, *The Liberator*, 8 Oct. 1841, 18 March 1842. I have not been able to discover any estimate of the number of Catholics who signed the address. An even greater number of Irish signatures was collected during the campaign to curtail Negro Apprenticeship in 1837–8, but the disproportionately Protestant areas of the country were geographically over-represented. By the late 1840s Irish nationalism was increasingly hostile to the American abolitionists (Hernon, *Celts*, 62). On the appeal to the French hierarchy see the letter of Richard Madden, to Msgr. Affre, Archbishop of Paris, 17 March, 1842, Archevêché de Paris, Archives historiques, Direction des Oeuvres, 4KII, Dossier: 'Pour l'abolition de l'esclavage'.

14 Delacroix, *Histoire Universelle*, III, pp. 66–7.

15 Anita Rasi May, 'The challenge of the French Catholic Press to Episcopal authority, 1842–60: a crisis of modernization', Ph.D. dissertation, University of Pittsburgh (1970), pp. 113ff.

16 See *L'Univers*, 16 Sept. 1847. *L'Univers* clearly encouraged clerical campaigning in favor of abolition and thought anti-slavery activism could be transfered to the education question (*Ibid.*, 25 Apr. 1847).

17 *Ibid.*, 30 October, 1847. On the role of Dupanloup and the attitude of the Archbishop, see *RHASSP* C13/111 Letter of Bissette to Scoble, 27 April 1847. The outspoken defenders of slavery in the Chambers

62   Seymour Drescher

interpreted the signs of clerical defection from 'benevolent neutrality'
as indicating a very dangerous trend in French opinion. See Bibliothè-
que Nationale, N.A. fr 3631, Schoelcher collection, 'compte de M.
Jollivet avec pièces à l'Appui', letters of Jollivet, delegate of Martinique, 29 January, and 29 October 1847, and letter of Jabrun, delegate of
Guadeloupe, 14 September 1847; and A. N. Archives Outre-Mer,
Généralités 173 (1388), letter of Reiset and Jabrun, 29 June 1847. By
the end of 1847 about 30,000 signatures had been gathered for the
1848 petition drive.

18 A. N. C942, Enquête sur les evenements de mai et juin 1848, dr. 4,
'Club des Amis des Noirs'.

19 A. N. Archives Outre-Mer, Généralités; 153 (1284), dr: 'Abolition de
l'esclavage, 1848'.

20 Dwight, *Encyclopedia of Missions*, p. 571, 'Paris Evangelical Mission
Society'; *Le Lien* (1847), p. 86.

21 Serge Daget, 'L'Abolition de la traite des Noirs en France de 1814 à
1831', *Cahiers d'Etudes Africaines*, XI (41), 14–58. By the July Monarchy, *Morale Chrétienne* was restricting itself to merely occasional
reporting on abolitionist activity elsewhere. The more activist *Semeur*
characterized it as moribund in 1833. On the lack of incentive for mass
agitation during a 'golden age' of French Protestantism, see André-
Jean Tudesq, *Les Grands Notables en France (1840–9): Etude historique d'une psychologie sociale*, 2 vols. (Paris, 1964), I, pp. 124, 443–7;
II, pp. 834–8. On the role of the British in the petition campaign of
1846–7, see Temperley, *British Anti-Slavery*, pp. 185–9.

22 *Le Semeur*, 1831–48.

23 See *RHASSP*, C13/110–129, letters from Bissette to Scoble, January
1847 to January 1848.

24 A. N. Archives Outre-Mer, SA 197 (1489), petitions of 1847, in 48
cahiers.

25 Professor Serge Daget kindly furnished me with information on the
percentage of Protestant signatures. The figure on Protestant clerical
signers is in *Le Lien* (17 July 1847) p. 105. At the beginning of 1848 the
petitions which began to reach the Chamber of Peers were again
disproportionately Protestant, as revealed in the presence of Pastors as
the clerical representative. See AN CC 475 (645).

26 A. N. Archives Outre-Mer, Généralitiés, 153 (1276): Dutrône, on
behalf of the French Abolition Society, to V. Schoelcher, of the Provisional Government's Emancipation Committee, 23 March 1848.

27 In 1853 a former leader of the defunct French society informed the
British that there was no hope of reviving the association to promote
abolition in America and Cuba. (*RHASSP*, G/103, Isambert to Scoble,
15 June 1853).

28 *L'Univers*, 7 July, 24 September, 3 November, 8 December, 1858.

29 See Mary Ellison, *Support For Secession: Lancashire and the American
Civil War* (Chicago, 1972); Lynn M. Case, *French Opinion on the
United States and Mexico 1860–7* (1936, 1969) *passim*; Fladeland, *Men
and Brothers*, Chap. 16; Royden Harrison, 'British labor and American
slavery,' *Science and Society*, 25 (1961), 291–319.

30 D. Jordan and E. J. Pratt, *Europe and the American Civil War* (Boston,

1931), especially chaps. 6 and 7, and E. D. Adams *Great Britain and the American Civil War*, 2 vols. (New York, 1924), II, chaps. 14–15.

31 Serge Gavronsky, *The French Liberal Opposition and the American Civil War* (New York, 1968), p. 186.

32 *Ibid.*, pp. 241–2.

33 See Bolt, *The Anti-Slavery Movement*, p. 113, and Temperley, *British Anti-Slavery*, pp. 258–61.

34 *Le Lien*, 16 December 1865 (summary of the Freedmen's Aid campaign). The 10,000 contributors were from the Mulhouse working class. Workers of Paris, and Lyon were also prominently mentioned. 'The fact is', wrote the reporter, 'that we went to them less than they came to us . . . It seemed to us more natural to address ourselves preferably those who possess . . . [but] in certain cases, the sympathy roused is much more important than the gift received. I hasten to compensate for this gap in our publicity, and to herein declare the number of adhesions which came from where we least expected it'. The French Freedmen's Aid campaign received 86,500 francs, held two major public meetings, and included Catholics, Protestants, Jews, and Freemasons, finally achieving that ecumenical image which had been lacking in prior anti-slavery movements although Protestants were again over-represented in the leadership at the first public meeting in the Salle Herz in Paris (See *Le Lien*, 11 November 1865.) During the war, the circular address in favor of the North was signed by almost 800 French pastors, and subsequently by 4000 English clergymen.

35 See Bolt, *Anti-Slavery Movement*, pp. 64–73, and Ellison, *Support For Secession*. The sympathies of a large part of the Manchester business community had also been with the South during the war.

36 *Bolt, Anti-Slavery Movement*, pp. 67, 109–10, on the general apathy among all classes.

37 On the mixture of adhesion and antagonism towards the anti-slavery movement at the time of emancipation, see for example, *The Poor Man's Guardian*, 18 October 1831, 25 February, 9 June, 17 November, 1 December, 1832, 2 March 1833; *The Poor Man's Advocate*, 4 February, 4 August, 1 December, 1832; *The Working Man's Friend*, 26 January, 2 February, 1833; *The Chronicler of the Times*, 12 January 1833. The extent of this class-orientated analysis was pointed out to me by Patricia Hollis of the University of East Anglia.

3

A MODEL OF THE FRENCH ABOLITIONIST MOVEMENT AND ITS VARIATIONS

by Serge Daget

Towards the end of the age of the Enlightenment a group of progressive French intellectuals took a rather close look at the idea of a universal right to happiness and liberty, and launched an attack on the current view that Negroes were practically animals, and on the general acquiescence in their treatment in the West Indies as beasts of burden. They formulated a novel concept of the African as a moral, social, and political being, a concept that struck at the roots of a way of thought engendered by 150 years of slave trading and slave owning.[1] Such a step involved the creation of a new model of humanitarianism whose material objective was the abolition of the slave trade and, in the long run, of slavery.

In their role of progressive intellectuals the abolitionists were closer in spirit to the Revolution their ideas were fostering than to the faltering *ancien régime*, closer to deism than to official Catholicism. Few in number, they made no attempt to gain mass public support. As Henri Brunschwig has aptly expressed it, they belonged to the 'cultivated elite',[2] and this political and social attitude continued to characterize the French abolitionist movement for the seventy-five years of its existence.

Between 1780 and 1848, however, the model of abolitionism was to depart significantly from its ethical foundations. For reasons of space we must confine ourselves to only those problems and manifestations of change that are most relevant to our discussion. When the model came to be implemented, what part was played by non-humanitarian considerations? In other words, how was the move from the ideal to the plane of action effected? Who were the principal actors? When the movement came to life again after the Revolution and the Empire, did it still conform to the original model or had it lost its character? Under whose control was it? When it was finally achieved, did its success conform to the ethical ideas that had inspired its initiators? If the deformation of the model violated the spirit of its earlier ideals, what new aim motivated those responsible? In order to answer these questions, we must briefly trace the development and achievements of the French antislavery societies from the *Amis des Noirs* to the *Institut d'Afrique*.

I

In the final days of the Capetian monarchy France adhered to the old tradition of political alignment between the monarchy and the Catholic church. Two subsequent events had modified this alignment. First, the Protestants, who had suffered persecution and political annihilation, were making their way back into the life of the nation. The years in the wilderness to which they had been banished were coming to an end. Secondly, the intellectuals had deserted Catholicism for belief in a 'Supreme Being'. After 150 years of entrenched Catholicism, they no longer saw morality as the exclusive prerogative of a God enthroned in a church. Within this group of intellectuals, the few abolitionists were careful not to appeal to God or holy writ to back up their wholly secular thinking about the African. However, they began by challenging the theologians who, over the last century, had done a great deal in their writings to reassure the slave traders and slave owners as to the morality of their behaviour and the purity of their consciences, citing scripture to support their ideas.[3] It followed that although the abolitionist started to anathematize the slave trader with 'God sees you', his rationalism changed the verdict to 'the whole world is sitting in judgment on you'.[4] His irreligious morality needed and evolved a secular terminology and dialectic.

At the end of 1788 a small band of moralistic and philanthropic individuals founded the *Société des Amis des Noirs*, modelled on the British and American abolitionist societies; it was active until 1793 and abortively revived in 1798. This was to be the fountainhead and proving ground of French humanitarianism, though its earliest literary manifestations had started twenty years previously.

Its doctrine, for the most part, was pillaged from Thomas Clarkson, whose book denouncing slavery and the slave trade[5] had been translated into French. The slave trade, it was argued, was just a lottery. Far from being profitable, it hindered the development of

French manufacturing industry, since the Africans had few needs and were not interested in bartering for good quality or costly goods. To satisfy the African market, traders had to buy goods from other countries that the French could only produce badly or not at all. The slave trade affected the health of the people of the coastal regions of Africa, and hence that of French sailors: death on those 'unfriendly shores' was one of Clarkson's strongest arguments. The trade involved the state in costly subsidies paid to the slavers: nearly £1,500,000 in 1786 to transport 25,732 Negroes to St Domingo; and £2,815,378 in 1788 on account of higher tonnage rates for the slave ships. The trade cost Africa dear, as well. Indeed the abolitionists' estimates of the wasteful population drain were sometimes startling: '. . . of ten million slaves dragged from the unhappy shores of Africa only 16,000 survive in our colonies' – so, full of good philanthropic intentions, wrote the members of the Lisieux club, 'The Friends of the Constitution', to the National Assembly.[6] But the *Amis des Noirs* had no definite or original solution. In this, too, they drew their inspiration from Thomas Clarkson. However, they preferred the notion of 'consumption' to save the black population, rather than that of 'conversion' to Christianity. The Africans should be allowed to stay in their own land and, before they could realize what was happening, be transformed into eager consumers. The *Amis* thus put forward the theory of the three 'Cs' (Civilization, Commerce, and Consumption) to which the physiocrats among them added a fourth – Cultivation of the land.

What sort of men were they, who created this anti-slavery model, the doctrinal content of which was to remain almost unchanged for three-quarters of a century? The *Amis des Noirs* enlisted four Catholic clerics, including the bishop of Chartres, and one foreigner, an Italian priest living in Paris; their support could serve to contradict the idea of the inability of the official church (which lent its sanction to slave owning) to help the cause of the blacks. But there was a much larger number of Protestants, including Condorcet, who had written a popular lampoon of slavery under the penname of 'Pastor Schwartz', and Clavière, who was to become finance minister during the Revolution. Presiding over the committee, above all the dukes and marquises, was Jacques-Pierre Brissot, former journalist and pamphleteer. One of the most active among members of the revolutionary clubs, he was to become a leader of the Girondins, and was eventually guillotined during the Terror. Lawyers and doctors among the members advised the *Amis* in questions of law and health. Above all, the professions of a quarter of the ninety founder members were symptomatic of the society's interest in political economy and physiocracy, now at its peak period of interest.[7] There were five Tax Farmers-General, two under-secretaries of the finance ministry (one of whom was Mollien), two directors of the Tax Farms, nine high officials of the *Régie Générale*, members of the *Court Des Aides*, together with several merchants, whose presence served to show that the whole of the mercantile world did not live off the slave trade. The participation of the various government finance officers refuted the slave-traders' accusation that the *Amis* were in the pay of the English, or were trying to undermine the French economy – which came to the same thing.

The model of action took shape under the influence of two currents of thought: on the one hand were what we might today call the humane studies, 'anthropological' preoccupations ranging to sociology and universalist philosophy; on the other hand there was economic science, involving rationalizing preoccupations and soon leading to the discovery that it was impossible to achieve the simultaneous abolition of both slavery and the slave trade. The *Amis* found there were two difficulties in the case of slavery: the plantation owners, who could not afford abolition financially, and the blacks themselves – not so much from inability to enjoy freedom but through unreadiness to fulfil any civic obligations. Faced with the necessity of deciding on some priority the abolitionists chose, as the most immediately feasible, the abolition of the trade.

They won some reforms. Then in 1794 a decree of the Convention abolished slavery, without any reference to the slave trade. This was because the Convention was simply recognizing an accomplished fact. In 1790 the slaves in Martinique had rebelled; in the following year those on St Domingo had declared war on their masters.

In all this the Catholic hierarchy remained quite indifferent. Had it suddenly decided to adopt the militant moral stance of the unbelievers and follow the line of the contumacious abbés, such as Raynal, Sibire, Cournand or Grégoire, its members would not have retained the support of the faithful. As to any popular support for these philanthropic ideas, it must be noted that the masses, though not totally illiterate, read very little, and only the simplest matter, so that the possibility of getting their ideas across against the entrenched traditions of the slavers was remote. Abolitionist ideas were not disseminated by word of mouth. On the contrary, it was the slavers who had the ear of the people, constantly reminding them that the slave trade was good for trade generally – not just for the merchant navy, but for peasant textile workers too. In 1802 Bonaparte reinstated slavery *and the slave trade*. He had been advised to do so by colonial 'experts' allegedly acting from the most philanthropic motives, namely to restore tranquillity to the disordered colonies. During the discussions leading up to the Concordat with the Church in 1802 the emissaries from Rome made not the slightest allusion to the question. This was all in line with the *Amis* model: that is to say, it followed from the minority status of the abolitionists, from their vulnerability without popular or Catholic support.

II

With the return of peace and the sanction of the Anglo-French treaty of 1814, the sea was once more open to French shipping. Between 1814 and 1831 the stark facts of French involvement in slavery continued to justify the abolitionist action of the humanitarians. It took them another seventeen years to attain their goal. There was a gradual build-up of preventive measures affecting both land and sea[8]; these were prompted by suspicions that had arisen during this period concerning more than 700 French ships, of which more than half had undoubtedly taken part in the slave trade. But what had been the effect of twenty-five years of Revolution and Empire on the humanitarianism and priorities of our original model?

In the early years of the Restoration 'the world', said Rémusat, 'was full of eye-witnesses of the Revolution'[9]. These had seen the catastrophe of St Domingo, the devastation of the most beautiful island of the West Indies, followed by the restoration of slavery and the slave trade. The ejected planters, seven or eight thousand in number, and the home ship-builders combined to press for the reconquest of the island and the re-instatement of slavery, while repopulating it in the proportion of one third male, two thirds female, so as to ensure a good reproduction rate. The government hesitated to accede to this minority demand; but popular feeling, influenced by a wave of anti-British sentiment caused by the severe peace terms of 1815, was on the side of the private interests. Abolition had been imposed by the British cabinet and hence was insufferable, however honourable its motives, and the French did not think Britain's motives were honourable. British philanthropy was accused of having a well defined ulterior objective. This was to maintain and promote commercial hegemony in the Atlantic under cover of the repression of the slave trade – by the use of warships, in which case, of course, the Royal Navy would be the predominant agency of enforcement.

The revival of the abolitionist cause was faced with two obstacles. In the first place the shipbuilders argued against abolition on the grounds that the slave trade was indispensable for national economic revival: 'it affects the prosperity of our ports, of our colonies, the maintenance of our navy, all of which are closely bound up together'.[10] Another obstacle to the furtherance of the anti-slavery cause was the marginal character of the members of the re-animated movement: for example, Madame de Staël was a Protestant, in a country where Catholicism was newly enthroned as the principal religion of an officially tolerant state and her literary fame as authoress of *Préface à un ouvrage de M. Wilberforce* was based on a panegyrical analysis of German cultural models; while the economist Sismondi, a Swiss Protestant, derived his reasons for supporting British-inspired abolitionist action from the achievements of the French Revolution. Even the few genuine French nationals among the abolitionist minority had questionable political or personal viewpoints. The Comte de Saint-Morys expressed sympathy with the black incendiaries of St Domingo. The Abbé Grégoire, who harshly condemned the sordid interests behind the slave trade, had been one of Napoleon's senators, a member of the Convention and a bishop who had taken the oath of loyalty to the Revolution.[11] After the peace settlement of 1815, to speak of abolition was to get oneself accused of both subversive and anti-national tendencies. In such a political climate the abolitionists could only accede to government policy, and neither influenced nor guided it.

It was in these conditions that the first signs of a distortion of the original model made their appearance: the occasion was the Grégoire affair. During the Revolution he had fought for the social and political rights of half-castes and for the freeing of slaves. His chief characteristic had been a thirst for power which had turned to bitterness when in 1817 his election to the Chamber of Deputies was invalidated and he was unseated. He was to find revenge through his attachment to the abolitionist cause. He had two less distinguished colleagues, the Abbé Giudicelly, a hot-headed Corsican, and Morenas, a Provençal, unstable and impecunious, but cultivated and imaginative. Their opposition to received opinion was political rather than religiously heretical; their principal offence was their assertiveness.

Giudicelly and Morenas had collected information in Senegal about the continued existence of the slave trade. They communicated it to the Ministry of the Navy, but they also published it in the London *Times*, a most provocative act. On a second occasion they exploited the right of petition, so that twice, in 1820 and in 1821, the Chamber of Deputies was jolted by the incapacity of the government to act in the matter of abolition. The ministry and its supporters brushed aside the two representations, but the minister had to deal with the second Morenas petition 'at the political level' on account of its contents, 'which were not of a kind that could be made public'.[12] Can one assert that in all of this there had been any departures from the early model?

If there were, it was not through any lack of appeal to the Catholic hierarchy. In Rome there exist letters of appeal from the Abbé Giudicelly. But the trio could hardly expect much help from the Catholic authorities. Grégoire had notoriously betrayed his vocation. Giudicelly had left the apostolic prefecture of Saint-Louis de Sénégal and at this time was preaching 'patriotic sermons' in the church of St Laurent in the faubourg Saint-Denis. Morenas had been a leading Freemason.[13] Undoubtedly, all three hoped to achieve various personal ambitions by exploiting the publicity aroused by the diffusion of their abolitionist petitions. In retaliation for the scandal of his disqualification in the Chamber of Deputies, Grégoire was masterminding a humanitarian scandal, acting as the *éminence grise* behind Morenas' two petitions. As a result of his activities, Giudicelly was to be approached by the people of Haiti to go there 'as soon as possible so as to become a bishop'.[14] Morenas, having attracted the attention of the leaders of the English movement, especially Clarkson and Macaulay, was reckoning on being offered a colony of his own in one of the British settlements on the African coast, together with a guarantee of neutrality in any conflict with France.[15] A distortion of the model? Perhaps, since hereafter, joining the abolitionist cause could be seen as something that paid off, in personal advancement as well as for the advancement of humanitarianism.

Publicly, at least, the petition gave a fresh boost to the French abolitionist movement. In July 1822 Wilberforce judged that it had made a new start. His optimism had nothing to do with Grégoire and Morenas. Wilberforce was attracted by a new and very different assortment of Frenchmen: by the literary fame of one of the leaders of the new movement, Benjamin Constant, and the political and social standing of another, the Duc de Broglie. This new movement, whose role I have described elsewhere,[16] was the *Société de la Morale Chrétienne*, founded at the end of 1821 and active between 1822 and 1848. The Prefect of Paris summed it up: 'Its principles and its aims are as congenial to every Protestant sect as they must be repugnant to every true Catholic.'[17] It encompassed numerous committees concerned with research into social and international morality. The chief committee, devoted to the abolition of the slave trade, had sixteen members, of whom five were foreign. The Duc de Broglie presided, Rémusat was its secretary. Benjamin Constant was on its editorial committee. Although in the two Chambers of the legislature official tribute was paid to Grégoire and Morenas, they were not, it seems, invited to join the *Société*, or, if they were, they did not accept. Nevertheless, in 1827 Morenas published the first comprehensive work in French on the slave trade, based on English sources along with Grégoire's commentary.[18] The *Société* had the moral support as well as the membership of the Duc d'Orléans, soon to be King Louis Philippe, and the collective and individual repute which resulted from the stature of its French and foreign members. Its central directorate took care not to fall under the influence of the eminence of the English abolitionist movement. All these factors helped the *Société* to survive and function effectively; and its members all shared three characteristics – social distinction, a common religious faith, and a will to act.

Geographically, the dispersion of members corresponded fairly closely to the map of French Protestantism, privileged groups being concentrated in a few big cities, such as Strasbourg, Lyon, Marseilles, and Montauban, with its Protestant theological faculty. The Catholic west was poorly represented, though in Nantes, the chief slaving port, one of the largest shipbuilders in the city, Thomas Dobrée, with his wife, both of the reformed religion, were members. Others came from towns to the north and west of Paris. The total grew slowly from 255 in 1823 to 338 in 1827: French abolitionism remained, as it had started, the concern of a very small group, but it was a group containing some distinguished names, conveying an impression of some class distinction and respectability. Not all members were militant abolitionists.

Fifty-four members belonged to government circles – peers and deputies, heads of the civil service and the armed forces; they were all notables. Capitalist interests with sixty representatives counterbalanced representatives of culture and intellect: the banker rubbed shoulders with the pastor, the business man with the man of letters, manufacturers and property owners with journalists and teachers.

The law was represented by as many as forty-one members. Sixteen doctors and six actors completed the total of distinguishable social categories. There were some eminent names: among the bankers, the André brothers, the Délesserts, the Londoner Hankey, Casimir Périer; among the politicians Duvergier de Hauranne, Vielcastel, Sébastiani de Gérando, Guizot. The journalists included Comte, Dunoyer and Coquerel. Among the twenty-five churchmen were some of high rank – the president of the Protestant Consistory of Paris, the president of the Consistory of the Reformed Church of Paris; and there was the Pastor Oberlin, the fruits of whose social work among the people of the Vosges had amazed all Europe.[19]

This exalted body was active. In May 1825 it raised a petition from 'the people of Paris', renewed the year after, containing the names of 130 of 'the foremost citizens of Paris'. In December 1825, Auguste de Staël, imitating Clarkson, took some soundings in Nantes and brought back proof of ships fitting out for the slave trade; these were immediately passed on to the royal family. The result was the creation of a ministerial committee to take immediate action for abolition. Under pressure from the *Société* 150 merchants from French sea ports signed a petition opposing the slave trade, discounting the trade as a factor in economic growth. There were no signatures from Nantes. After the July Revolution, during a debate on a third and more rigorous abolitionist law moved in 1831 by the Comte d'Argout, Minister of the Navy and a foundation member of the *Société*, homage was formally paid to that body, 'whose protecting arm comes to the aid of all unfortunates . . .'[20] Some months later Sébastiani concluded an agreement with London for the suppression of the trade, based on the right of search. In 1833 de Broglie negotiated an extension of the terms of the treaty.

The *Société de la Morale Chrétienne* thus made an effective contribution to the abolition of the French slave trade. Without underestimating this effectiveness one should also remember that in the 1830s it was rather fashionable to take an interest in social problems; and that after 1826 the combination of diplomatic and economic pressure from Britain and a changed outlook in the French navy made a quick achievement of abolition almost inevitable. A change of government also had a great deal to do with it. With its numerous committees the *Société* provided a training ground for the theorists of the opposition, who came into power in July 1830. They did, in fact, fulfil their promise made eight years earlier to abolish the trade – but it is also significant that a new government, of uncertain legitimacy, badly needed English support.

Is it the fate of the philanthropic spirit to become corrupt or calculating as the philanthropist gets nearer to success? Does philanthropy, like profane love, shut the door on religious morality? It is impossible to generalize. Rather, it may seem fairer to describe the French case as one aspect of 'Gallican' philanthropy, an autonomous variant of universal philanthropy.

The spiritual authorities, acting as Catholics, had never been abolitionist. The re-instatement of Catholicism as the state religion, the revenge of the spiritual over revolutionary materialism, provided no inducement to the Church during the restoration to be any more so. Towards 1826, in fact, Lamennais was promoting the ultramontane doctrine that true political authority could only emanate from the pontifical power. Now the Pope had said nothing about the abolition of slavery or the slave trade at either the Congresses of Vienna or of Verona. Neither in its ultramontane or its Gallican phase, had the French hierarchy ever made a point of preaching to the faithful on the subject of abolition, which it did not favour. A change could only come when the Sovereign Pontiff broke his prolonged silence on the continued existence of the trade and when the faithful followed his example and broke theirs about the situation in the slavers' world. This happened on 3 December 1839, with the publication of the apostolic letter of Gregory XVI.

The issuing of this letter of Gregory XVI owed much to the British cabinet. In July, Palmerston had suggested that the Pope should speak out against the trade. He emphasized that the interests of religion did not clash with the interests of commerce and the 'civilization' of Africa. The question was delicate and involved the etiquette of chancelleries: it was obvious to international opinion that a non-Catholic power had exerted pressure on Rome and deprived the Pope of a chance of taking a splendid initiative. The British envoy at the Holy See disclosed that Gregory XVI was enraged at having been prompted by a Protestant government and felt much closer to the Brazilians, who were keen slave traders, than to the heretical English who were trying to stamp the trade out.[21] A compromise was arranged: the British initiative was not officially published, but the Foreign Office distributed the apostolic letter, especially in Lübeck and Turin, capitals of states that already adhered to the Anglo-French agreements on the right of search. We shall see, later, the consequences of this change of heart by the papacy.

The activities of the *Société de la Morale Chrétienne* coincided chronologically with the period of protestant *Réveil* (awakening) in

France. One is inevitably led to ask oneself if humanitarian concern for slaves had any connection with this awakening. I think not, at least not directly or immediately. The first object of the *Réveil* was spiritual. The fruits of its work were earthly, but of rather local application, like the work of Oberlin in the Vosges, or of Neff in the Alps. According to E. G. Léonard, 'Its propagandists were not, for the most part energetically involved in good works'.[22] The *Société* seems to have been the only body of a predominantly Protestant character in France that took to overseas missionary work, and then not so much for the sake of providing missionaries as for achieving a domestic effect. It is possible that the *Réveil* movement may have lent some support to the renewal of abolitionism after 1822 and up to the petition of the pastor de Félice (dealt with below), but if so it was by remote influence and not by individual involvement – Pastor Oberlin is perhaps the exception, but we know nothing of the extent of his active participation in the *Société*. He was *not* a member of the committee dealing with abolition. The *Réveil*, a religious renaissance, was not closely involved in the renewal of the fight for abolition or in its final victory.

One has to look, therefore, at the secular anti-slavery organizations in order to discover if this victory conformed with the original moral model, or if, on the other hand, it merely displayed a further deviation in the direction of an economic and political ethic already foreshadowed in the case of the *Amis de Noirs*.

There were two feasible methods of operation. The one followed by the *Société Francaise pour l'Abolition de l'Esclavage* (active 1834–48) was long, hard but relatively clear. Founded in 1834 and led by the Duc de Broglie it included the remaining members of the *Société de la Morale Chrétienne*, aided by a few high-powered Protestants, among them Agénor de Gasparin, who had a powerful pen, and his brother, a deputy, worthy successors of their father, president of the *Congrès Scientifique* of France. They were joined on their way by Victor Schoelcher, the atheist journalist.[23] Ever since 1830 he had been paying tribute to the English missions to the West Indies and to the members of the French reformed church. In 1844 he was amazed by the 7000 signatures on the petition raised by the Paris working class, and by the 11,000 on the petition of pastor Guillaume de Félice in 1847.[24] It is not possible to decide exactly what part in all this was played by the Protestant religion, but certainly a fair amount. Such representations cannot compare with those that proliferated in England; nevertheless they indicate a beginning of popular interest in the Negro question and suggest a more or less precise awareness of class solidarity between workers, regardless of race.

Much less is known about the other method, namely the simultaneous achievement of anti-slavery and colonial possessions; one can only theorize about it. From 1817 onwards there were vague ideas, tentative steps towards the rebuilding of a French colonial empire. One was the dream in ministerial circles of turning Guiana into a prosperous colony; another was an appeal for official support, actually discussed in the Conseil d'Etat, for a projected half-colonial, half-philanthropic settlement in Senegambia; another was the investigation of the commercial possibilities of the African coast carried out by Bouët-Willaumez, the future governor of Sénégal and precursor of Faidherbe. But above all other ventures the hazardous conquest of Algeria between 1831 and 1842 stands out. With its government firmly organized by Bugeaud, the colony began to cast an eye on Morocco. In short, this second path was smoothed with undisclosed but ambitious aspirations harboured by the military and quietly encouraged by the government when it suited them politically or for reasons of prestige.

It is against these colonial aspirations that we must see the final incarnation of French abolitionist societies in the period before emancipation in 1848: the *Institut d'Afrique* (active 1842–8). It was a very heterogeneous institution. Created in 1842, it had 213 members of various nationalities within a year. The large number of British members also gave it a Protestant streak as well as a rather '*Entente Cordiale*' political appearance. On the other hand these were balanced in the *Institut* by an equally large number of French legitimists, who assumed an attitude of uncompromising Catholicism and anglophobia. 'Revolutionaries' were present in the persons of Prince Mavrocordato and Isaac Louverture. Wealth, landed property, and the law were likewise represented and, to add the finishing touch, eight bishops and archbishops – now that the Pope had at last committed himself on the slave trade. There was, also, a handful of important experts – Daniel Webster, Macaulay, General Bugeaud and Sir Thomas Fowell Buxton.[25]

In 1843 the *Institut d'Afrique* sent its newly elected members a printed letter. The second paragraph announced that it had been founded 'with the aim of achieving a great work, the colonization of Africa, and the regeneration of the African people by means of the abolition of slavery and the slave trade'.[26] But the three closely printed columns of the Institut's rules and aims went no way towards achieving this three-pronged project. The ideal of emancipation was reduced to an allusion to 'the emancipation of the slaves and their compensation with medals . . .' Beyond that – nothing.

On the other hand the idea of colonization was developed in full. The six committees that devoted themselves to it bear witness, as well they might, to the engrained ignorance of Africa that caused Buxton's failure on the Niger. They sought the advice of Bugeaud, who expressed his appreciation of the honour done him by imparting to the new association 'some ideas that my experience in the self-same places have suggested to me. In the meanwhile . . . I advise the *Institut d'Afrique* to spread the idea that there can be no solid achievement in Africa without European colonization'.[27] The committees, proceeding on 'technocratic' lines, set up model farms, planned to exploit mineral and other rich resources, started up manufactures, hoped expectantly for 'industrial progress', communications between provinces, a customs service, finance, health, education and culture. On the question of religion, the *Institut's* multiplicity of faiths imposed complete silence.

The activities therefore bore little relation to the abolitionist aims set out in the letter to the members. The 'sacred cause of the Blacks' seemed to have been forgotten. The objective was perfectly clear and went far beyond the economic and political means that our original anti-slavery model had expected to employ to end the 'shameful traffic'. But in reducing all the humanitarian idealism contained in the original model to these few words, the *Institut* was almost guilty of moral fraud. In 1845, rather than carry on the fight for abolition it preferred to start a commercial company. This was to have a capital of 2,000,000 gold francs (i.e. $400,000 or £80,000).[28]

Distortion of the model? There is a paradox here, since the slave trade and slavery *were* abolished. But the moral and spiritual forces of the time do not seem to have played much part in this. Once launched, the anti-slavery impulse was not given any special moral or intellectual support. The Protestant *Réveil* gave no noticeable boost to a movement in which the reformed church had always been active. From the Catholics, up to 1839, there was simply a massive silence: indeed, *Le Silence* was the name of a French slave ship in 1820. The masses were fairly lacking in religious feeling, and with moral feelings impaired by grinding poverty they had other things to think about than working for the blacks.[29] They did, however, in small numbers back up the intellectuals.

Religious sentiment played a very feeble part in the French struggle for abolition, and colonization, a goal long unconsciously sought before being actually defined, was the final result of the movement's founding inspiration. The pure humanitarian ethic was desecrated through a deviation in favour of new ideas that re-affirmed the exercise of power over fellow men. The germ of imperialist thought developed in the heart of the abolitionist ethic.

Notes

1   R. Mercier, *L'Afrique noire dans la littérature française. Les premières images, XVII–XVIIIè siècles*, Fac. de Lettres (Dakar, 1962). I. Sachs, *La découverte du Tiers-Monde* (Paris, 1971). M. Duchet, *Anthropologie et Histoire au Siècle des Lumières* (Paris, 1970). L. Poliakov, 'L'Image des hommes du Tiers-Monde: le passé et le présent', *R. Franç. Hist. Outre-Mer*, LX, n° 218 (1973), pp. 86–97.

2   H. Brunschwig, *L'Avènement de l'Afrique Noire* (Paris, 1963).

3   Anonyme (J. B. Bellon de Saint-Quentin), *Dissertation sur la traite et le commerce des nègres, suivie de Trois Lettres d'un Théologien*, s.l. (1764).

4   Collectif, *La Révolution française et l'abolition de l'esclavage. Textes et Documents*, Editions d'Histoire Sociale, 12 vol. (Paris, 1968). See vol. 4, 4, 'L'Homme redevenu homme . . .', by a former infantry captain, s.l. (1790), p. 16.

5   T. Clarkson, *Essai sur les désavantages politiques de la traite des nègres, en deux parties . . . précédé de l'Extrait de L'Essai sur le commerce, de l'espèce humaine, du même auteur, traduit de l'Anglais par M. Gramagnac* (Neufchâtel, 1789).

6   Collectif, *La Révolution française* . . . , vol. 5, pp. 217–31. S. Daget, 'Les mots "esclave", "nègre", "noirs", et les jugements de valeur sur la traite négrière dans la littérature abolitionniste française, de 1770 à 1845', *R. Franç. Hist. Outre-Mer*, LX, no. 221 (1973), pp. 511–48.

7   Collectif, *La Révolution française* . . . , vol. 6, 4, 'Tableau des membres de la Société des Amis des Noirs, année 1789'.

8   S. Daget, 'Le trafic négrier illégal français, de 1814 à 1860: historiographie et sources', *Annales de l'Université d'Abidjan*, série I, Histoire, t. 3 (1975), pp. 23–53.

9   Ch. de Rémusat, *Politique libérale ou fragments pour servir à la défense de la révolution française* (Paris, 1875).

10 Archives nationales (hereafter A. N.) section Outre-Mer, Généralités 154/1288, Begouën-Demeaux, armateurs au Havre, dans une pétition au ministre de la Marine, 3 Oct. 1814, signée par 59 autres armateurs.

11 Mme de Staël, *Mirza ou Lettre d'un voyageur;* Mme de Staël, *Préface pour la traduction d'un ouvrage de M. Wilberforce sur la traite des nègres* (Paris, 1814); Mme de Staël, *Appel aux Souverains réunis à Paris* . . . , dans *Oeuvres Complètes* (Paris, 1828), Tomes 1 and 17, pp. 369ff. Simonde de Sismondi, *De l'intérêt de la France à l'égard de la traite des nègres, 3rd edn. augmentée des Nouvelles réflexions sur la traite* . . . (Genève 1814). H. Grégoire, *De la traite et de l'esclavage des noirs et des blancs par un ami des hommes de toutes les couleurs*, (Paris, 1815), Comte de Saint-Morys, *Aperçu sur la politique de l'Europe et sur l'administration intérieure de la France* (Paris, 1815).

12 A. N., S.O.M., *Généralités* 191/1475, note pour le conseil des ministres du 16 juin 1820. The petition was published by *Corréard*, (Paris, June 1820); *Généralités* 152/1274, for the work of the ministry and the minister's notes, see also *Généralités* 152/1273. For the debates in the Chamber of Deputies, see le *Moniteur Universel*, 26 June, p. 899, and 11 July, the statement of the deputy, Courvoisier. For the second petition, see also A. N., Paris, CC[4 B]431, no. 46, chambre des Pairs.

13 S. Daget, 'J. E. Morenas à Paris: l'action abolitionniste, 1819–21', *Bull. I.F.A.N.*, T. xxxi, série B, no. 3 (1969), pp. 875–85.

14 *Idem; ibidem.*

15 *Id. ibid.*

16 S. Daget, 'La France et l'abolition de la traite des Noirs. Introduction à l'étude de la répression française de la traite au XIXè siècle', Doctorate thesis, Centre de Recherches africaines de la Sorbonne, Paris (1970), not published. For a resumé of this thesis see *Cahiers d'Etudes Africaines*, 41, vol. xi, 1 (1971), 14–58.

17 A. N., Paris, Intérieur, F[7] 6960, Police générale, 12/024, Société de la Morale Chrétienne, Préfet à ministre, 23 août 1823.

18 J. E. Morenas, *Précis historique de la Traite des Noirs et de l'esclavage colonial.* Published by the author and Firmin Didot (Paris, 1828).

19 *Journal de la Société de la Morale Chrétienne*, 1827, *Crapelet* (Paris, 1827). List of members of executive council and various committees, list of members in the years 1826–7, pp. 71–83. See E. G. Léonard, *Le Protestant Français* (Paris, 1955), cf. the chapter on the nineteenth century 'et les oeuvres humanitaires', and p. 206, n. 1. On Oberlin, see p. 205. Also P. and E. Hagg, *La France Protestante* (Paris, 1859).

20 *Moniteur Universel*, Chamber of Deputies, sitting of Tuesday 1 Feb. 1831.

21 *Public Record Office*, Slave Trade, F.O. 84/ 292, F.O. 84/ 328; F.O. 84/ 329 (1839–40), ff. 134–41, 28 June 1839, draft of note to be presented by Mr Aubin to the Papal Government; 25 January 1840, Rome, Aubin to Fox, consul at Florence; f. 137, Note on political viewpoint of Grégory XVI; etc.

22 Léonard, *Protestant Français*, p. 206.

23 A. de Gasparin, *Esclavage et Traite* (Paris, 1838), A. de Gasparin, *De l'affranchissement des esclaves et de ses rapports avec la politique actuelle* (Paris, 1839), V. Schoelcher, *Histoire de l'esclavage pendant les deux dernières années*, s.n. (Paris, 1847).

24 G. de Felice, *Emancipation immédiate et complète des esclaves. Appel aux abolitionnistes* (Paris, 1846). For the petitions, see Schoelcher, *Histoire de l'esclavage*, pp. 131–42 and 414ff.; *idem*, p. 459.

25 *Archives départementales de l'Ille et Vilaine*, Rennes, Commerce, 6[7] M[1], *Institut d'Afrique*, lettre enregistrée et personnelle (Paris, 1843), Rules of the Institut, list of members. See A. J. Tudesq, *Les Grands Notables en France, 1840–9. Etude d'une psychologie sociale* (Paris, 1964).

26 Arch. départ. Ille et Vilaine, cité, *Institut d'Afrique*, Présidence et secrétariat général, lettre personnelle (Paris, 1843), lithographed copy. Signed Prince de Rohan-Rochefort; Hip. de Saint-Anthoine. See p. 1 para. 2.

27 *Idem*, Statuts, col. III, extraits d'adhésions, M. le lieutenant général Bugeaud. Souligné dans le texte.
28 J. C. Nardin, 'Le Libéria et l'opinion publique en France, 1821–47', *Cahiers d'Etudes Africaines*, 17, vol. v, 1 (1965), 96–144, see letter from Edouard Dubuc, correspondent of the Institut d'Afrique. P. Brasseur, 'A la recherche d'un absolu missionnaire: Mgr Truffet, Vicar Apostolic to the Guineas, 1812–47', *C. Et. Africaines*, 58, vol. xv, 2 (1975), 259–85. My thanks are due to Mme P. Brasseur for additional information about the Institut d'Afrique.
29 L. Chevalier, *Classes laborieuses, classes dangereuses à Paris pendant la première moitié du XIXè siècle* (Paris, 1958). J. Vidalenc, *La Société française de 1815 à 1848* (Paris, 1970), 1973, see T. I.

4

ANTI-SLAVERY AND THE DUTCH: ABOLITION WITHOUT REFORM*

by P. C. Emmer

Introduction

'If the world were to come to an end, I would go to Holland, where everything happens fifty years later', the German poet Heinrich Heine is supposed to have said. His apocryphal aphorism certainly applied to the anti-slavery issue in the Netherlands. This country might have been in line with other nations of Western Europe in 1814 as far as the abolition of the slave trade was concerned, but it certainly stood apart by its belated abolition of slavery in 1863.

This paper tries to explain the delay in catching up with the rest of Europe. In the first section the marginal importance of the Dutch slave-holding West Indies to the metropolitan economy will be discussed as well as the rapidly increasing exports of the Dutch East Indies. The second section focuses on Dutch public opinion with regard to the issue of emancipation. In fact, anti-slavery in the Netherlands never gained any popularity as part of a secular movement or as part of a religious one outside a small section of the elite. The mini-abolitionist upsurge during the years 1853–7 may have been partly stimulated by the British and Foreign Anti-Slavery Society's efforts.

As a result of this almost complete absence of economic and moral anti-slavery pressures, abolition was treated as a purely technical matter by both the executive and the legislature. The third and fourth sections show that, after 1844, the ending of slavery was regarded as inevitable by the government and, after 1852, by the slave-owners as well. No doubt the British and French abolitions of 1833 and 1848 respectively might have had a catalytic effect, had their outcome been more positive for their plantation economies. However, because of the post-emancipation decline in exports from both the British and French West Indies, it seemed to take the Dutch government and parliament even longer to work out an emancipation scheme that would not only free the slaves and compensate their owners, but would also increase exports.

In the conclusion, attention will be drawn to the fact that the absence of a sizable abolition movement in the Netherlands might be explained as one of the results of an overall stagnation of the nineteenth-century Dutch economy and society.

Anti-Slavery and the Dutch Economy

The Dutch had been relatively late in acquiring Caribbean colonies. First, they had concentrated on Brazil and it was not until after the final surrender of New-Holland in 1661 that the Dutch conquered most of Guiana during the second Anglo-Dutch War. The previously acquired islands in the Caribbean, with Curaçao as their governmental centre, were suited only for transit trade and for the production of salt, not for the cultivation of sugar and coffee.[1] Not until the second half of the eighteenth century did the Netherlands start to develop Guiana and then only Surinam. Berbice, Essequibo and Demerara remained relatively undeveloped until the British conquest of 1799.

Together, the Dutch Caribbean possessions were not nearly large enough to satisfy the demand for West Indian export crops at home; the Dutch always imported sugar and coffee from Portuguese Brazil and the Spanish, English, and notably French West Indies.[2]

Since the major share of the coffee and sugar imported into the Netherlands was produced on foreign plantations, the Dutch slave-grown products never became a vital ingredient of the Dutch overseas trade. During the third quarter of the eighteenth century an attempt was made at changing this situation. For a period of twenty years the Dutch invested heavily in Surinam, but the high hopes of those investors to turn the only Dutch plantation colony into a second Jamaica or St Domingue did not materialize. The large increase in the capital investment did not result in greater export of cash crops. Surinam had reached the point of diminishing returns and, unlike England, the Netherlands did not resort to protection.[3] The collapse came in 1773, when the Dutch investors suddenly stopped handing out loans to Surinam planters. As a consequence, the Dutch slave trade almost ceased.[4]

Surinam's short-lived supremacy in Dutch colonial affairs made it impossible for it to enjoy the sort of prominent position as 'darling of the empire' occupied by the British Caribbean. In addition, there existed no aggressive and concerted 'West Indian Interest' in the Netherlands, except for some rearguard action by the plantation-owners during the last two decades before emancipation. Among those metropolitan groups interested in the West Indies, there existed no geographical unity. Amsterdam investors had granted the loans to Surinam and Zeeland-based merchants had brought the slaves. After the financial crisis of 1773 only the plantation-owners were interested in a West Indian 'revival'; the slave traders just stopped and switched to other activities. No wonder that the legal abolition of the Dutch slave trade in 1814 did not require any pressure from the government. The records of the two Anglo-Dutch courts, subsequently set up for the suppression of the slave trade, reveal that no Dutch shipping firm could be accused of participating in the illegal slave trade.[5]

Slavery was another matter altogether. The silent abolition of the slave trade had done little or nothing to arouse Dutch public opinion regarding the 'peculiar institution'. The Amsterdam-based plantation owners wanted to see their money back and the Dutch government continued with the old, pre-Napoleonic policy. It left the planters to themselves and assisted the investors in getting as much of the Surinam export crop as possible to Amsterdam by excluding foreign carriers from that colony.

During the first decades of the nineteenth-century Surinam enjoyed an ambiguous economic relationship with the Netherlands. It constituted the economic basis of the Dutch shipping in the Atlantic, but at the same time this shipping and the Surinam exports were of marginal importance to the Dutch economy as a whole. In 1844 the trade between Surinam and the Netherlands amounted to about $1\frac{1}{2}$ per cent of the Dutch GNP.[6] There seemed to be no compelling reason to endanger this economic activity by imposing abolition on the planters, when the Dutch flag was ousted from the non-protected long-distance carrying trade.[7] On the other hand, Surinam remained, as in the eighteenth century, only one of the sugar producers for the Dutch market and it was never the major one. Cuba and Brazil were the main suppliers and after 1834 Java took over. In 1851 Java exported ten times as much sugar to the Netherlands as did Surinam.[8]

The economic marginality of slavery to the Dutch economy had two consequences. No one ever argued that the continued existence of West Indian slavery was vital to the economic growth of the Netherlands. Conversely, there seemed to be no reason to bother the plantation-owners, either in Amsterdam or in Surinam, in their attempts at getting their investments to pay off.

Slavery in Surinam was in fact one of the many backwaters of the stagnant Dutch economy of the nineteenth century. The absence of economic theorizing together with the absence of economic growth stimulated a generally conservative attitude. On the whole, the Dutch economy of that period was strongly oriented towards the past and it was not until the 1890s that the industrial 'take-off' started.[9]

The conservative inclination in Dutch economic thinking and the relatively small number of influential economic liberals worked wonders, however, in the East. In Java, the implementation of the neo-mercantile 'cultivation system' produced large profits, amounting to 20 and 30 per cent of the total income of the metropolitan government during the period 1840–65. These colonial profits enabled the Dutch government to create a modern infrastructure for rail and water transport, to pay off its debts, and to subsidize the administrative deficits of the West Indies and the Gold Coast forts. The financial surplus extracted from Java also helped to pay for the compensation granted to the West Indian slave owners in 1862/3. In 1860, Dutch government expenditure averaged 78.7 million guilders. About 38 per cent of that money was coming from the Dutch East Indies. The amount of money paid as compensation to the slave owners came to about 12 million guilders.[10]

Anti-Slavery and Dutch Public Opinion

The first observation to be made on public opinion in the Netherlands regarding slavery was its relative indifference to the institution. Unlike Britain, Holland never exhibited the pattern of a continuous flow of protests, starting with actions against the slave trade and resulting in a massive popular movement against the economic and moral implications of slavery. In fact, the slave trade never did arouse much protest. The occasional Calvinist vicar, who warned against it, did not seem to carry much weight.[11] In reply, the slave traders could always point to the argument of Jacobus Elisa Capiteyn from Elmina, a black theology student at Leiden

University, who defended the trade in slaves as well as the institution of slavery.[12]

The slave revolt in Berbice in 1763 and the ideas of the French philosophers started a small trickle of Dutch publications in which slavery was attacked.[13] During the early nineteenth century some Ph.D. theses were written on the abolition, all in Latin following traditional academic custom.[14] During the last quarter of the eighteenth century the idea of abolishing the slave trade and slavery had also found a few adherents among the Dutch 'patriots', who supported the principles of the French Enlightenment.

Again, the marginality of abolition within this group itself should be stressed. Around 1800, abolition had become a purely academic issue in the Netherlands because all the Dutch slave-holding colonies had been conquered by the British. The slave revolt on St Domingue had also had an adverse impact on such anti-slavery sentiment as existed, and in the first Dutch constitution of 1798 no mention was made of either the abolition of the slave trade or of slavery.[15] The Dutch translation of Stedman's *Narrative of a Five Years' Expedition* ... did advocate the abolition of slavery in Surinam in an appendix, especially written for the Dutch edition by R. van den Santheuvel.[16] But this suggestion was forgotten long before some of the slave colonies were returned to the newly constituted Kingdom of the Netherlands after 1813.

In Britain, anti-slavery became an issue for both the dissenting Protestants and the secular liberals during the first decades of the nineteenth century. This was not the case in the Netherlands.

The Dutch Reformed Church, the official state church before 1795, did not petition on the issue until 1858. Within this church, however, there existed a small, but influential group of professionals, politicians, and businessmen, who worked towards a new orthodox-Calvinist revival. Initially, this *Réveil* group saw no discrepancy between slavery and the traditional principles of Christianity.[17]

The Roman Catholic Church also remained silent on this issue. The Roman Catholics in the Netherlands had only been fully emancipated after 1795, and the church had no regular episcopal hierarchy. In April 1853, the pope instituted regular bishoprics in the Netherlands, but this led to a storm of protests from the Protestants (the so-called 'April Movement'). Obviously, the Roman Catholics had enough problems of their own and it seemed untimely to agitate on behalf of the anti-slavery cause. The Roman Catholics kept a low profile in politics in general and the small number of Roman

Catholic politicians in parliament were all members of the liberal faction. At that stage, Roman Catholics still embraced the liberal principle of easing the Dutch governmental apparatus into a neutral, secular position, away from the centuries-old link with Protestantism.[18]

Finally, the ideology of political and economic liberalism found few adherent in the Netherlands. The stagnant economic and social situation, as described in the previous section, made 'laissez faire' and 'free labour' or 'free trade' academic concepts, imported from abroad. It was not until 1840 that there even existed a clear-cut group of liberals among the members of Dutch parliament who rejected slavery on secular grounds.[19]

It was also around the year 1840 that the prominent *Réveil* movement within the Dutch Reformed Church changed its attitude towards slavery and started to campaign against it. The *Réveil* adherents had still no objection to slavery in principle, but they became convinced that this institution severely hampered the preaching of God's word among the slaves. They aimed at 'vrijlating' (releasing) the slaves and did not agree with the secular liberal principle of 'vrijmaking' (setting free) the slaves.[20]

This difference between those with a religious affiliation and the secular liberals prevented concerted anti-slavery action in the Netherlands. In 1841 the two groups split on the issue as to whether or not their first common meeting should start with an opening prayer. Stimulated by some visiting members of the British Anti-Slavery Society these two groups petitioned separately in 1842 to the king in order to obtain his support for the abolition of slavery. The minister for the Colonies told the king to abstain. The result was that for another decade the Dutch anti-slavery movement, small as it was, could not even emerge as an institutionalized lobby.[21]

Anti-slavery liberals continued to meet and published monthly the 'Contributions to the Knowledge of the Dutch and Foreign Colonies in Particular of the Manumission of Slaves' between the years 1844 and 1847. This journal contained a number of articles on the British abolition movement and reported the frequent visits by the Anti-Slavery Society's secretary at the time, George William Alexander. Also, one article points to the bleak future of slavery in Surinam even without abolition: around 1900 only 20,000 slaves would remain. Proudly the journal referred to British Guiana, where after abolition sugar exports were rising and to Guadaloupe, where the new machinery of Derosne and Cail produced excellent results on many plantations.[22]

After the setback of 1841, the *Réveil* group did not drop the anti-slavery issue. Its leader, Groen van Prinsterer tried to link abolition with an appeal to all those in favour of the teaching of Christian principles at state schools. However, the two issues remained separate and only later on was the movement towards confessional schools to gain massive support.[23]

In 1853, the Dutch anti-slavery movement finally gathered momentum. The *Réveil* adherents founded a 'Society for the Advancement of the Abolition of Slavery'. Some anti-slavery liberals now also joined, but some remained outside it, because of the strong confessional basis of the Society. Its 'declaration of principles' still rejected 'the so-called philanthropical zeal' stemming from the revolutionary ideas of the French Revolution.[24]

Why this final success in 1853? First, it had become obvious to all 'slave friends' that the government needed an extra push in that year. In addition, there clearly was a second effort from the British Anti-Slavery Society to influence the Dutch scene.

The first stimulus to more abolitionist action had to do with an advisory committee on West Indian slavery appointed by the government in 1853 with a surprisingly low number of anti-slavery members. This seemed to destroy all hopes for a speedy abolition unless the abolitionists took more determined action.

The second motive is less specific for the year 1853, since there had been regular contacts between British and Dutch abolitionists after 1841. The British and Foreign Anti-Slavery Society's conventions in London were regularly attended by some Dutch members, notably Daniel Twiss, a merchant from Rotterdam.[25] At the convention of 1843 he gave a rather good description of the peculiar deadlocked position in which the Dutch abolitionists found themselves. He said: 'The anti-slavery party in Holland can effect but little as our government, although pledged to abolition, is opposed to individuals interfering in the discussion of the question. We must, therefore, recommend the slaves in the Dutch colonies to your protection (Applause)'.[26]

In addition, after 1842 there had been frequent visits by prominent British abolitionists to the Netherlands, among them Alexander Scoble, Elisabeth Fry and her brother Samuel Gurney. Their influence remained limited for three reasons: their contacts in the Netherlands were mainly made among the elitist *Réveil* group, which counted its adherents in tens rather than in hundreds. Secondly, the *Réveil* group had its doubts about the Methodist and Quaker theology of their British visitors. They were no Calvinists.

Thirdly, the Dutch abolitionists were afraid that too much influence from Britain would affect the Dutch character of their own efforts. After the foundation of the Dutch Society for the Advancement of Abolition in 1853, an offer for a public lecture tour by L. A. Chamerovzow was declined for this reason.[27]

During the 1840s the Dutch government was particularly anxious to reserve the abolition issue strictly to itself and in accordance with this policy the king, William II, was advised in 1840 not to accept a petition by the British Anti-Slavery Society addressed to all monarchs of Europe. This refusal was noted by Alexander, who wrote to Groen van Prinsterer, the most important member of the *Réveil* group: 'The king of Holland is the only potentate that has refused to receive the Address of the Convention with the exception of the Sultan of Turkey'.[28] Again, the king did not commit himself, when Elisabeth Fry and her brother talked to him in 1841 about anti-slavery, the teaching of the gospel at state-schools, and prison reform.[29]

According to the *British and Foreign Anti-Slavery Reporter*, however, the Dutch anti-slavery scene looked rather bright:

> In conclusion we may express our cordial satisfaction in finding that the press and people of Holland feel a lively interest in circumstances that affect the character and the honour of the Dutch people . . . There is no part in Europe to which we turn with feelings of more lively hopes and satisfaction in reference to the abolition of slavery than to Holland, short as has been the period in which an anti-slavery Organization has there existed.[30]

Between 1850 and 1858 the contacts between the British Anti-Slavery Society and the Netherlands were intensified and at least eight delegations came to the Netherlands. By now, the British must have lost faith in a large-scale Dutch abolitionist movement: they even subsidized an anti-slavery tour by Mollet from Amsterdam through the country.[31] This concentration of British efforts after 1850 might have helped the Dutch abolitionists to try once more to found a Dutch abolitionist society.

If one can speak of a climax, Dutch anti-slavery reached its peak during the years 1853–7, when the Society for the Advancement of the Abolition of Slavery reached a membership of 670 and when some four smaller, local groups were active in addition, all based in Amsterdam and Utrecht.[32] After the introduction of the first emancipation bill in 1857 by the government, this short outburst of private anti-slavery activities ended. The Society also published a journal, which gives a good insight into the elitist, orthodox-Calvinist character of the society.[33]

The main articles in this journal were centred around the attempts made by the government at introducing a satisfactory emancipation bill. Further, the journal published some reports on the state of the slave economy in Surinam; the Society was particularly interested in the military operations against runaway slaves and the president wrote a letter to the minister of the Colonies asking him to stop these patrols. The journal also contains travel accounts of visitors to British Guiana, paying special attention to the successful production of sugar without slave labour in that former Dutch colony. The published minutes of the annual meetings of the Society show a complete lack of enthusiasm among its members: only seventeen to twenty of them attended.

The liberal, non-religious anti-slavery movement never had the strength to found a nation-wide organisation of its own. The minutes of 1852 of the liberal debating club, 'Felix Meritis', in Amsterdam show the dilemma. The emancipation of the slaves in the West Indies obviously was going to require large-scale government intervention and this was contrary to the liberal theory of 'laissez faire' in economics.[34]

In spite of that short-lived peak between 1853 and 1857 it remains surprising that so few people in the Netherlands took an interest in emancipation. If we look at the number of pamphlets on the issue only 12 were published before 1840; 26 in the period between 1841 and 1853 and 56 between the years 1853 and the abolition of 1863.[35]

J. Wolbers, a well-known anti-slavery publicist, enumerated the causes of this lack of Dutch popular enthusiasm for the 'Great Cause'. He mentioned as probable causes: the general ignorance regarding the West Indies in the Netherlands as well as the internal differences among anti-slavery campaigners themselves. However, Wolbers also points to the clever 'machinations' of the 'reactionary party' in arguing that slavery in Surinam existed only 'in name'.[36] What had actually happened to slavery in the Dutch West Indies?

Anti-Slavery and the Dutch West Indies

The Dutch anti-slavery debate really centered around the abolition of slavery in Surinam. In 1862 there were 30,000 slaves and around 5000 freed slaves in that colony. The slaves in the Dutch Antilles numbered around 6000, and there were around 6500 freed slaves. The position of the Antillean slaves was quite different from that of Surinam slaves.[37] The Dutch Caribbean islands did not produce any cashcrops and consequently the conditions of slavery were generally taken to be far better than in Surinam by contemporary observers as well as by modern historians.[38]

Abolition of slavery on the islands never was much of a problem. Manumission was frequent and in 1848 there were more free blacks than slaves. The sudden abolition of slavery in the French West Indies affected the slaves on the Dutch part of St Maarten; they demanded their freedom and got it.[39] Nearly the same happened on St Eustatius. On the whole there was little fear among the employers on the Dutch Antilles that the supply of labour would collapse after emancipation. It would be fair to suggest that after 1848 slavery on the Dutch Antillean islands could have been abolished without further ado as soon as the Dutch government had made a firm offer to pay compensation to the owners.

Slavery in Surinam, however, was another matter. Abolition in that colony meant a complete social and economic revolution and the planters in Surinam were determined to avoid this. They met with little opposition in their efforts to prolong slavery as long as possible. For the planters, slavery was the only labour supply system that worked and as long as no real alternative presented itself, they were not going to abolish it. Several factors worked in their favour.

The Surinam slaves organized comparatively few uprisings during the period 1816–63. At the very end of the slavery period, around 1862, there were a few slave gangs who refused to go to work or wanted money for their labour. On the whole, however, the slave owners were not confronted with heavy pressure from the slave population.[40] In addition, marronage declined and after 1833 only a relatively small number of slaves escaped to freedom in neighbouring British Guiana in spite of the fact that only one small Dutch naval vessel, positioned in the Corantine river, was assigned to stop them.[41]

Secondly, missionaries with abolitionist leanings were more or less absent in the colony. The Moravian Brethren had a near monopoly in Surinam for the Christian instruction of the slaves. The Dutch Reformed Church was strictly a 'white' church and the Moravian missionaries themselves did not consider emancipation a necessary precondition to Christianization. Some brethren even owned slaves themselves.[42] In the Netherlands, their activities were supported by some private charities, but the Herrnhut Church had almost no adherents in the Netherlands; there existed no institutional link between the slave-church in Surinam and the abolitionist Christians at home.[43]

Thirdly, British abolitionist influence in the colony was small and almost disappeared in 1845, when the last British commissioner at the Anglo-Dutch mixed court for the suppression of slave trade left Paramaribo.[44] The same is true as far as the impact from British Guiana after the emancipation of 1833 is concerned; this colony became increasingly interested in indentured labour after 1845. Before that date the presence of British abolitionists next to Surinam did have some nuisance value, for example government circles in British Guiana offered to buy the freedom of all Surinam marrons. In addition, demands from Surinam government officials to hand over runaway slaves were ignored in Georgetown.[45]

Finally, the Dutch government exerted little pressure on the colonial authorities in Surinam to impose measures which would go against the *communis opinio* of the planters. A governor who wanted to force a set of new working conditions on the planters had to resign. The planters were represented in almost all governmental and judicial institutions of the colony and an appointee from the Hague had to think twice before he acted against their interests.[46]

These four arguments all support the thesis that the Surinam planters were faced with only one pressure to abolish slavery: the declining profitability of their plantation economy. The planters tried to remedy this situation by creating larger plantations, by introducing more machinery and by concentrating on sugar. The Dutch government showed the way by operating a large sugar plantation of its own, using the latest distilling equipment and improving working and housing conditions for the slaves.[47] The colonial government of Surinam also sent two naval officers to various other parts of the Caribbean to report on the results of emancipation elsewhere as well as on new technology in the production of sugar and cotton.[48] In 1851 and 1856 the colonial government finally succeeded in introducing new legislation on the working conditions of the slaves; the planters accepted it this time, since the set rations of food and clothing were more in touch with reality than the former proposals.[49]

After 1848, both the Dutch and Spanish Caribbean retained the system of slavery. However, Cuba and Puerto Rico both had a much better economic future than the declining Dutch Antilles and Surinam. The system was in danger of outliving itself, because the number of slaves was steadily decreasing. The slave owners now

accepted abolition as inevitable but used their willingness to emancipate the slaves in order to get compensation out of the Dutch
government. In the meantime, the Surinam government received
special grants to pay for the experimental immigration of free
contract-labourers from Madeira and China. This was an attempt to
see whether the sudden decline in labour supply after emancipation
could be avoided, as had not been possible in British Guiana after
apprenticeship ended. The results of these experiments with free
contract labour were negative. After 1858, no more free labour was
imported until well after emancipation. From that date onwards the
planters must have realized that the ending of slavery had to have a
dramatic effect on the labour market. For many, the forthcoming
compensation might make it possible to withdraw their assets completely from the colony.[50]

Anti-Slavery and Dutch Politics

Until 1850 anti-slavery was a minor issue within Dutch colonial
politics. There existed no continuity between eighteenth-century
Dutch anti-slavery as part of the Enlightenment and abolition as it
appeared again after 1840.

As mentioned above, some 'patriots' had taken an interest in
anti-slavery, under the impact of the French revolutionary movement. However, the constitution of the Batavian Republic did not
mention abolition. That the radical and moderate 'patriots' could
not agree to such a drastic measure is shown in the minutes of the
debate on this issue in the National Convention of 1797.[51] The
'patriots' decided not to abolish either the slave trade or slavery
itself: the Dutch planters in the West Indies might be induced to
surrender their colonies to the British even before they had been
attacked. But this tactical move by what had by then become the
'patriot establishment' does not imply that the abolition of slavery
remained a mute issue. The 'Committee for the Affairs of the
Colonies and Possessions in America' received a proposal for abolition, in which gradual emancipation was suggested to be paid for by
the slaves themselves.[52]

After 1800, abolition disappeared from the political scene, as did
almost all other colonial problems. Only the Gold Coast forts and
Decima in Japan remained in Dutch hands. All other possessions
had been conquered by the British. In 1814–15 slaveholding
Surinam and the Antilles were returned to the Netherlands in

addition to the Indonesian archipelago. However, the Cape, Ceylon, Berbice, Demerara and Essequibo remained British.

The abolition of the Dutch slave trade had been one of the British conditions to be met for the return of these colonies, and in 1814 the executive issued a special order-in-council to fulfil this demand. In 1818 a bilateral treaty was concluded between Britain and the Netherlands in order to set up instruments of control, mixed naval courts, and naval squadrons. Subsequent changes in Dutch penal law were debated in parliament, but the debate does not reveal any sustained interest in this matter by one or more of its members. Oddly, many of the Belgian members of the House took part in the discussion, which for them must have been purely academic.[53]

After 1818 anti-slavery disappeared again. The administration of the colonies was a province strictly reserved to the executive until a change in the Dutch constitution in 1848. For the Dutch governments of the early nineteenth century slavery was a very minor issue. After the introduction of the highly successful cultivation system in Java in 1832, colonial interests within the government were directed towards the East. It was not until 1844 that the minister of the Colonies reported to the king that the abolition of slavery had become inevitable in Surinam.[54] In 1839, the same minister could still advise the king that slavery in Surinam should remain and that the abolition of slavery in the British West Indies had little impact on the Dutch Caribbean colonies.[55] For what reasons the minister changed his mind is difficult to assess, since it was very much a one-man decision.[56] After 1844 abolition had become a matter of 'how' and 'when' and not any longer one of principle.

Between that decisive year 1844 and 1848 the administration of the colonies and thus abolition remained exclusively in the hands of the government. The minister did not even tell the outside world of his change of heart and as late as 1853 another minister of the colonies had to reassure an M.P. about the government's positive attitude towards abolition. Both the liberal members of parliament and the group of Surinam plantation owners deplored this 'autocratic' system. This second group had been organized in 1844, because the Surinam planters and their advocates at home wanted the newly appointed governor in Surinam removed and also because there were constant rumours that the government might change its mind in favour of abolition.[57]

In 1848 the issue of abolition, together with all other colonial affairs, moved from the control of the executive to the Dutch parliament after a change in the Dutch constitution. As a matter of fact, colonial problems were often used to test the new system of ministerial responsibility. Between 1848 and the year of emancipation, 1863, slavery suddenly became an important issue, but strictly within parliament. Outside parliament the role of both the anti-slavery and pro-planter lobbies were of marginal importance. From their first petition of 1844 until 1852 the planters' lobby was against abolition and after 1852 the lobby concentrated on getting the highest possible amount of compensation for the slaves.[58] The anti-slavery movement, on the other hand, tried to speed up legislative action rather than to argue with the planters' lobby.

After abolition had been accepted by the executive in 1844 more than eighteen years were needed to complete an emancipation scheme which came into effect on 1 July 1863. All the years in between were used to evaluate numerous schemes put forward by the ministers for the Colonies, an advisory committee, and some private individuals.[59]

Another paper on Dutch anti-slavery could easily be filled with the arguments in all these schemes and bills, discussed and introduced by the government and debated in parliament. These arguments were much the same as those used in the debates on abolition in other countries with slave-holding colonies. The only unique debating point was the evaluation of the previous emancipations in the British and French West Indies. Emancipation in British Guiana was closely scrutinized and this explains the special attention given to the importation of contract-labourers in most Dutch proposals for emancipation.[60]

In order to get an impression of the issues at stake in the Dutch debate on emancipation between 1852 (when the government first proposed abolition) and the final law of 1862 (with five abortive government proposals in between) seven main points are selected: the amount of money to be paid as compensation (final law: 12 million guilders); the possible expropriation of the plantations by the state (final law: no); the possible migration of free contract-labourers under government supervision (final law: no); the possible pay-back of the compensation money by the emancipated themselves (final law: no); direct or gradual emancipation (final law: direct); a possible period of apprenticeship (final law: ten years but not for the Dutch Antilles); regular or special civil law for the ex-slaves (final law: regular).

The long debate on technicalities was conducted at leisure without much pressure to quicken the pace of the anti-slavery developments, whether at home or in Surinam.[61] The British ambassador at the time, Lord Napier, might well have been a good judge of Dutch political life: 'The Dutch are little disposed to take a busy and sustained part in politics . . . Some vital questions must be at stake, affecting the conscience, the heart or the purse of the nation to rouse them to exertion. The Pope, or the House of Orange, the finances or the colonies must be in question'.[62]

Conclusion

In looking at the anti-slavery effort in the Netherlands, it is easy to be surprised about the small number of its adherents. However, there should also be surprise about the small number of Dutch Marxist movements, prison reformers, or new, dissenting religious movements during the first decades of the nineteenth century.

However, there was one mass-movement in 1853 among the Protestant Dutch, protesting against the establishment of several Roman Catholic bishoprics in the Netherlands. But this 'April Movement', petitioning to the king against the new organization of the Dutch Roman Catholic Church, tried to keep Dutch society as it was and as it had been since the seventeenth century. The only nineteenth-century Dutch mass-movement which was directed towards change, petitioned for the subsidizing of confessional schools out of the state budget and it was not until the 1870s that it got under way, together with a new Calvinist revivalism among the Dutch Protestants and the founding of the first Dutch Socialist party.

Before the last quarter of the nineteenth century, the Dutch government and parliament were about the only group which at least debated innovative change. Since the right to vote was based on property and sex,[63] they represented about 10 per cent of the highest taxed part of the male population. The small number of voters implies that there was a relatively strong link between the executive/legislative elite and the financial one. Not in a direct way, but indirectly; it would be difficult to speak in the Netherlands of an 'industrial party' or a 'colonial party', where politicians and investors in industrial and colonial firms worked hand in hand.[64] However, this indirect link might explain the governmental and parliamentary concern for the slave-owners and it called for the long and technical debate on emancipation.

Notes

* My sincere thanks go to Ernst van den Boogaart and J. W. Siwpersad, who read an earlier version of this paper. Seymour Drescher's editorial comments greatly improved my English usage.

1 Cornelis Goslinga, *The Dutch in the Caribbean and on the Wild Coast, 1580–1680* (Gainesville/Assen, 1971) surveys the first period of the Dutch presence in the West Indies, but mainly in terms of power politics. More information on the economic impact of the Dutch is found in C. and R. Bridenbaugh's *No Peace beyond the Lines; the English in the Caribbean, 1624–90* (New York, 1972).

2 J. P. van de Voort, *De Westindisch plantages van 1720 tot 1795; financiën en handel* (Eindhoven, 1973), pp. 25–7.

3 P. C. Emmer, 'Surinam and the decline of the Dutch slave trade', *Revue française d'histoire d'outre-mer*, LXII (1975), pp. 245–51.

4 Johannes Postma, 'The Dutch slave trade: a quantitative assessment', *Revue française d'histoire d'outre-mer*, LXII (1975), pp. 232–44.

5 P. C. Emmer, *Engeland, Nederland, Afrika en de slavenhandel in de negentiende eeuw* (Leiden, 1974), pp. 82–126.

6 M. Kuitenbrouwer, 'De vertraagde afschaffing; de besluitvorming over de afschaffing van de slavernij in de Nederlands-Westindische kolonien, 1851–63', *Werkschrift VIII* (Historisch Seminarium, Universiteit van Amsterdam, 1975), p. 42. This contribution has subsequently been published in a modified version as M. Kuitenbrouwer, 'De Nederlandse afschaffing van de slavernij', *Bijdragen en Mededelingen van het Historisch Genootschap*, 93 (1978), pp. 69–98. All citations refer to the previous version. An estimate of the Dutch GNP in 1840 is from J. Teyl, 'Nationaal inkomen van Nederland in de periode 1850–1900', *Economisch- en Sociaal-Historisch Jaarboek*, XXXIV (1971), p. 262.

7 P. C. Emmer, 'Het Atlantische Gebied', in F. J. A. Broeze, J. R. Bruijn and F. S. Gaastra (eds.) *Maritieme Geschiedenis der Nederlanden* (Bussum, 1977), III, pp. 302–7.

8 J. J. Reesse, *De suikerhandel van Amsterdam van 1813 tot 1894, een bijdrage tot de handelsgeschiedenis des vaderlands, hoofdzakelijk uit archieven verzameld en samengesteld* ('s-Gravenhage, 1911), pp. 12/13, XLI, XXXIII and XLII.

9 J. H. van Stuijvenberg, 'Economische groei in Nederland in de negentiende eeuw; een terreinverkenning', in P. W. Klein (ed.) *Van Stapelmarkt tot welvaartsstaat* (Den Haag, 1970), and J. A. de Jonge, *De industrialisatie in Nederland tussen 1850 en 1914* (Amsterdam, 1968).

10 See Teyl, 'Nationaal inkomen', pp. 250, 251 and C. Fasseur. *Kultuurstelsel en koloniale baten; de Nederlandse exploitatie van Java, 1840–60* (Leiden, 1975).

11 W. S. Unger, 'Bijdragen tot de geschiedenis van de slavenhandel II, de slavenhandel der Middelburgsche Commercie Compagnie', *Economisch-Historisch Jaarboek*, XXVIII (1958–60), p. 93.

12 A. van Dantzig, *Het Nederlandse aandeel in de slavenhandel* (Bussum, 1968) pp. 114–16.

13 J. M. van der Linde, *Heren, slaven, broeders; momenten uit de geschiedenis der slavernij* (Nijkerk, 1963), pp. 114–20 and M. Gijswijt,

'Slavenhandel en slavernij als sociaal en politiek probleem. De abolities
door Engeland, Frankrijk en Nederland', *Werkschrift VIII* (Historisch
Seminarium Universiteit van Amsterdam, 1975), p. 8.

14 C. de Jong, 'The Dutch press campaign against the Negro slave trade
and slavery', *Mercurius, Journal of the Department of Economics of the
University of South Africa*, xv (1973), pp. 27–54.

15 G. J. Schutte, *De Nederlandse patriotten en de Kolonien, een onderzoek
naar hun denkbeelden en optreden* (Groningen, 1974), pp. 147–50;
P. C. Emmer, *Engeland, Nederland, Afrika en de slavenhandel*, pp.
180–3.

16 John Gabriel Stedman, *Reize naar Surinamen en door de binnenste
gedeelten van Guiana* (Amsterdam, 1800), IV, pp. 149–85.

17 R. Reinsma, *1863, een merkwaardige episode uit de geschiedenis van de
slavernij, 1963* (Den Haag, 1963).

18 There existed a link between the Roman Catholic bishop on Curaçao
and a Roman Catholic M.P. in the Netherlands: C. Ch. Goslinga,
*Emancipatie en emancipator; de geschiedenis van de slavernij op de
bovenwindse eilanden en het werk der bevrijding* (Assen, 1956).

19 Reinsma, *1863*, pp. 47, 48.

20 *Ibid.*, p. 11.

21 *Ibid.*, pp. 52–67.

22 *Bijdragen tot de kennis der Nederlandsche en vreemde Koloniën, bij-
zonder betrekkelijk de vrijlating der slaven*, 1844–7.

23 Reinsma, *1863*, p. 39.

24 Those among the liberal politicians and theoreticians who were
interested in the colonies started a new publication, the *Koloniale
jaarboeken, maandschrift tot verspreiding van kennis der Nederlandsche
en buitenlandsche overzeesche bezittingen* in 1861, mainly reporting on
the Dutch East Indies.

25 Reinsma, *1863*, p. 6 mentions Twiss as the only Dutch visitor to the
Anti-Slavery conventions in London. *The British and Foreign Anti-
Slavery Reporter* mentions some more Dutch visitors.

26 *The British and Foreign Anti-Slavery Reporter*, 21 June 1843.

27 See Reinsma, *1863*, and Howard Temperley, *British Anti-Slavery,
1833–70* (1972), p. 192.

28 Reinsma, *1863*, p. 13.

29 *Ibid.*, pp. 14, 15 and the *British and Foreign Anti-Slavery Reporter*,
1841.

30 *The British and Foreign Anti-Slavery Reporter*, 23 Feb. 1842.

31 Temperley, *British Anti-Slavery*, p. 190.

32 K. A. Zeefuik, *Herrnhutter zending en Haagsche maatschappij, een
hoofdstuk uit de geschiedenis van zending en emancipatie in Suriname*
(Utrecht, 1973 with English summary), pp. 157–61 and Bert Altena,
'Eene moeijelijke en teedere quaestie; het Nederlandse parlement en
de emancipatie van de slaven in Suriname, 1848–63' (Unpublished
M.A. thesis, Department of History, Vrije Universiteit, Amsterdam,
1976), pp. 29, 30.

33 *Maandblad/Tijdschrift uitgegeven vanwege de Nederlandse Maatschappij ter bevordering van de afschaffing der slavernij* (1855–62).

34 *Overzigt der werkzaamheden van de afdeling koophandel der maat-*

schappij onder de zinspreuk 'Felix Meritis' te Amsterdam, 1 mei 1852/31 april 1853 (Amsterdam, 1853).

35 E. Th. Waaldijk, *Die Rolle der Niederländischen Publizistik bei der Meinungsbildung hinsichtlich der Aufhebung der Sklaverei in den Westindischen Kolonien* ('s-Gravenhage, 1959).

36 J. Wolbers, 'De afschaffing der slavernij, eene volkszaak', *Tijdschrift, uitgegeven vanwege de Nederlandsche Maatschappij tot afschaffing der slavernij*, VII (1861–2), pp. 61–8.

37 Kuitenbrouwer, 'Vertraagde afschaffing', p. 37.

38 Harry Hoetink, 'Race Relations in Curaçao and Surinam', in L. Foner and E. D. Genevose (eds.), *Slavery in the New World; A Reader in Comparative History* (Englewood Cliffs, 1969), pp. 178–89, and *Eerste/Tweede Rapport der Staatscommissie benoemd bij Koninklijk Besluit van 29 November 1853, no. 66 tot het voorstellen van maatregelen ten aanzien van de slaven in de Nederlandsche koloniën*, vol. I, *Suriname* ('s-Gravenhage, 1855), vol. II, *De Nederlandsche West-Indische eilanden en bezittingen ter kuste van Guinea* ('s-Gravenhage, 1856).

39 Goslinga, *Emancipatie en emancipator*, p. 83.

40 A. Th. van Deursen, 'De Surinaamse negerslaaf in de negentiende eeuw', *Tijdschrift voor Geschiedenis*, LXXXVIII (1975), pp. 210–23.

41 E. van den Boogaart and P. C. Emmer, 'Plantation slavery in Surinam in the last decade before emancipation: the case of Catharina Sophia', in Vera Rubin and Arthur Tuden (eds.), *Comparative Perspectives on Slavery in New World Plantation Societies* (New York, 1977), p. 208, n. 9, and J. P. Siwpersad, 'Hoofdlijnen van het slavernij – en emancipatiebelijd van Nederland (1833–63)' (unpublished M.A. thesis, Department of History, University of Groningen, 1975), p. 7.

42 Temperley, *British Anti-Slavery*, p. 191.

43 Zeefuik, *Herrnhutter zending*, pp. 100–19.

44 Emmer, *Engeland, Nederland, Afrika en de slavenhandel*, pp. 103–26 and Siwpersad, pp. 30–44.

45 Siwpersad, 'Hoofdlijnen', pp. 16–29.

46 Kuitenbrouwer, 'Vertraagde afschaffing', pp. 43–5.

47 See van den Boogaart and Emmer, 'Plantation slavery'.

48 J. E. W. F. van Raders and D. L. Wolfson, *Verslag eener reis naar Demerary, Granada en Guadaloupe gedaan op last van zijne excellentie den gouverneur van Suriname in het laatst van het jaar 1845* (Paramaribo, 1846).

49 J. Wolbers, *Geschiedenis van Suriname* (Amsterdam, 1861), pp. 744–7.

50 Kuitenbrouwer, 'Vertraagde afschaffing', p. 65.

51 Schutte, *De Nederlandse Patriotten*, pp. 147–50; Emmer, *Engeland, Nederland, Afrika en de slavenhandel*, pp. 182, 183.

52 Algemeen Rijksarchief, Den Haag, *Collectie Goldberg*, 170, d.d. 29 May 1798.

53 Emmer, *Engeland, Nederland, Afrika en de slavenhandel*, pp. 189–92.

54 Kuitenbrouwer, 'Vertraagde afschaffing', p. 44.

55 Siwpersad, 'Hooflijnen', p. 21.

56 Siwpersad, *ibid.*, p. 22 sees these pressures from British Guiana as crucial!
57 Kuitenbrouwer, 'Vertraagde afschaffing', p. 44; Siwpersad, 'Hooflijnen', pp. 56–60; *Verslag Handelingen van de Tweede Kamer der Staten-Generaal.* 1844/45, appendix xxxiii, pp. 996–1014.
58 Altena, 'Eene moeijelijke en teedere quaestie', pp. 23–27.
59 Reinsma, *1863*, p. 28.
60 See note 38 and *Eerste Rapport*, p. 42.
61 Kuitenbrouwer, 'Vertraagde afschaffing', p. 69.
62 Altena, 'Eene moeijelijke en teedere quaestie', p. 52.
63 Johan de Vries, 'Het censuskiesrecht en de welvaart in Nederland, 1850–1917', *Economisch- en Sociaal-Historisch Jaarboek*, xxxiv (1971), p. 211.
64 There was one M.P. who had direct interests in Surinam during the parliamentary debates on abolition: A. F. Insinger (1849–59), Kuitenbrouwer, 'Vertraagde afschaffing', p. 46.

Part Two
ANTI-SLAVERY, RELIGION, AND REFORM

5

REPEAL, ABOLITION, AND REFORM: A STUDY IN THE INTERACTION OF REFORMING MOVEMENTS IN THE PARLIAMENT OF 1790–6.[1]

by G. M. Ditchfield

I

Among the most important movements for change in late eighteenth-century Britain were those which pointed in the direction of religious liberalism, humanitarianism, and a more representative system of government. Before 1800 they crystallized into the campaigns, respectively, for the repeal of the Test and Corporation Acts, the abolition of the slave trade and the enactment of parliamentary reform. Thanks to the research of Professor Anstey the intellectual connections between these movements, and in particular the theological motivation which helped to inspire each of them, have been illuminated as never before.[2] It is proposed here to examine these connections at the parliamentary level, in the period before any of the causes reached fruition. There are advantages in concentrating for this purpose upon the years 1783–97 and in particular upon the seventeenth parliament of Great Britain, which lasted from August 1790 to May 1796. This parliament witnessed a conjunction of the three issues which did not occur again until the fundamentally different circumstances of 1827–33. In this later period, moreover, comparisons between one parliament and another are complicated not only by the turnover of members at general elections but also by the transition from the unreformed to the reformed House of Commons. For the parliament of 1790–6, on the other hand, there survives a type of evidence which is not available for the years immediately thereafter. It includes partial division lists for two motions for abolition, one for parliamentary reform, and a limited motion for the repeal of the Test Act. With the reinforcement of evidence from the late 1780s it is possible for the parliamentary backing of each to be compared in some detail.

Such a concentration upon parliament might seem to imply neglect of the extra-parliamentary dimension of these causes. The present study recognizes the importance of 'public opinion', but serious qualifications must remain about its effectiveness in the eighteenth century displayed a markedly reactionary tone, with was then responsive, except in the most negative way, to popular external pressure. Even on those few occasions when parliament did apparently bow to the public will, as over Walpole's Excise Scheme, the Jewish Naturalization Act of 1753, or Pitt's Irish trade proposals, the extra-parliamentary forces were resisting change rather than demanding it. Many outbursts of popular feeling in the eighteenth century diplayed a markedly reactionary tone, with strong undercurrents of national and religious prejudice. The Wilkesite agitation and the County movement of the early 1780s both illustrate the difficulties involved in seeking to raise and sustain public opinion in a 'progressive' or 'liberal' direction. Such attempts could either fall flat and allow opponents to claim that the movement was ill-supported, or succeed (albeit briefly) and provoke charges of intimidatory or quasi-revolutionary behaviour.

These difficulties were greatly intensified by the French Revolution. Agitation could prove counter-productive in the political climate of 'reaction' and loyalism during the 1790s. English dissenters campaigning for repeal made this discovery early in 1790; for this reason the leaders of the Scottish attack on the Test Act immediately afterwards resolved not to launch an 'appeal to the people'.[3] By the winter of 1792–3, if not earlier, the same was true of parliamentary reform. Abolitionists did succeed in organising a petitioning campaign in 1791–2 and could claim credit for the passage of the bill for gradual abolition in 1792. For a time anti-slavery enjoyed a wide degree of popular support, while matters seemingly associated with the subversive tendencies of the French Revolution proved bitterly divisive.[4] But by 1793 the anti-Jacobin mood had deterred abolitionists, too, from mass agitation.[5] The few liberal measures which did reach the statute book in the 1790s, such as the Catholic Relief Act (1791), the Scottish Episcopalians Act (1792), and the Libel Act (1792), all succeeded through intelligent promotion by their sponsors within the political establishment. This study, accordingly, is almost entirely a parliamentary one, with its main focus upon the arena where the attention of repealers, abolitionists and reformers, as well as their opponents, was firmly fixed. A recent biographer of Chatham has written 'At no time under the British parliamentary system has public opinion carried weight unless reflected in the division lists of the House of Commons'.[6] Some of these division lists will be examined in this paper.

It is proposed to proceed under three headings: the connection of both abolition and repeal of the Test and Corporation Acts with parliamentary reform; the interaction between repeal and abolition; and the opposition to repeal and the opposition to abolition.

II

The link between the parliamentary voting on abolition and reform has been clearly demonstrated by Professor Anstey.[7] The definition of 'abolitionist M.P.' at its most rigorous would be confined to those members who are named in the only two surviving division lists on abolition bills in this period. The two lists, both incomplete, give the abolitionist minorities for the unsuccessful motions of April 1791 and March 1796.[8] Between them they provide a total of 85 abolitionist M.P.s, of whom 26 appear in both lists.[9] These members were the pinnacle of the abolitionist movement. They also displayed a long-term adherence to parliamentary reform and especially to the four reform motions of 1783, 1785, 1793, and 1797. Table 1 shows that they voted for reform in considerably higher proportions than did the House of Commons as a whole.

Table 1

Abolitionists and parliamentary reform[10]

Date of reform motion	Proportion of whole house voting for parl. reform (%)	Number of abolitionists then in parl.	Number of abolitionists voting for parl. reform	Percentage of reform minority which they formed
7 May 1783	26.70	46	29 (63.04%)	19.46 (29 of 149)
18 Apr 1785	34.05	56	33 (58.92%)	17.37 (33 of 190)
6 May 1793	7.71	77	18 (23.38%)	41.86 (18 of 43)
26 May 1797	16.66	65	25 (38.46%)	26.88 (25 of 93)

A similar correlation can be made between supporters of repeal (of the Test and Corporation Acts) and parliamentary reform. There existed at this time a parliamentary 'dissenting interest' or lobby of some 150 members prepared consistently to uphold the cause of Protestant dissent, even though very few of them were actually dissenters.[11] Their names can be found in the lists of those M.P.s who voted for the repeal of the Test and Corporation Acts in 1787 and 1789.[12] Repeal in this period meant the removal of the sacramental provisions of the Test and Corporation Acts, the purpose of which was to exclude Protestant dissenters from national and local office. The commitment of this group of repealers to parliamentary reform needs to be re-affirmed, since a recent historian has expressed scepticism about the liberal influence which dissenters are often supposed to have exerted upon eighteenth-century politics.[13] He casts doubt upon (although he certainly does not disprove) dissenting support for electoral reform. Such doubts are not justified at the parliamentary level. Well over two-thirds of the 'repealers' of the late 1780s voted, at some stage, for reform.

Table 2

Repealers of 1787–9 and parliamentary reform

Date of reform motion	Proportion of whole House voting for parl. reform (%)	Number of repealers then in parl.	Number of repealers voting for parl. reform	Percentage of reform minority which they formed
7 May 1783	26.70	88	49 (55.68%)	32.89 (49 of 149)
18 Apr. 1785	34.05	119	61 (51.26%)	32.10 (61 of 190)
6 May 1793	7.71	99	20 (20.20%)	46.50 (20 of 43)
26 May 1797	16.66	66	24 (36.36%)	25.81 (24 of 93)

134 M.P.s are known definitely to have voted for repeal in 1787 and/or 1789; 129 of them were in parliament for one or more of the four reform motions of 1783–97. No less than 90 of the 129 (69.77 per cent) voted for parliamentary reform at least once. It by no means follows that the remaining 39 were hostile to reform.[14] This key figure of 69.77 per cent shows the extent to which pro-dissenting M.P.s threw their weight behind reform.[15] Among the handful of M.P.s actually known to have belonged to a dissenting denomination, support for reform was even higher.[16]

The 'dissenting interest' also existed in the parliament of 1790–6. There are two ways of measuring it. First, there were the survivors of the 134 repealers of 1787–90. They numbered 88 in 1790 and 80 in 1796. Not all of them still favoured repeal (or at least immediate repeal) but newly elected M.P.s in 1790 who sympathized with dissent, such as the younger Samuel Whitbread, helped to make up the difference. Secondly, there is the evidence offered by the one occasion on which repeal appeared in this parliament. This was the motion introduced by Sir Gilbert Elliot on 10 May 1791 for the repeal of the Test Act as it applied to Scotland.[17] Elliot's application for repeal was more limited than those of the late 1780s; its aim was to exempt members of the established Church of Scotland from the sacramental provisions of the Test Act, and it did not seek repeal of the Corporation Act. But it drew support from much the same quarters as the earlier motions. In April 1791 Elliot classed M.P.s as 'Pro', 'Con', or 'Doubtful' on the issue of Scottish repeal, finding 167 'Pro', 280 'Con', and 92 'Doubtful'.[18] The figure of 167 'Pro' is similar to the present writer's estimate of 150 as the size of the parliamentary 'dissenting interest' in the 1780s.[19] This motion of 1791 provides more evidence than the other religious issues of this period; it was a direct attack on the Test Act and had it been successful a more general repeal bill would undoubtedly have followed. From it there remains information about parliamentary loyalties which is not available for the debates on Catholic relief or the Unitarian petition of 1792. It is clear that Elliot's 'Pro' M.P.s formed the core of religious liberalism in the parliament of 1790–6.

Table 3

Repealers of 1791 and parliamentary reform

Date of reform motion	Proportion of whole House voting for parl. reform (%)	Number of Elliot's 'Pro' M.P.s then in parl.	Number of 'Pro' M.P.s voting for parl. reform	Percentage of reform minority which they formed
7 May 1783	26.70	93	40 (43.01%)	26.78 (40 of 149)
18 Apr. 1785	34.05	98	34 (34.69%)	17.90 (34 of 190)
6 May 1793	7.71	157	38 (24.20%)	88.37 (38 of 43)
26 May 1797	16.66	95	42 (44.21%)	45.16 (42 of 93)

Like the repealers of 1787–9, the 'Pro' M.P.s in Elliot's canvassing list showed an inclination towards parliamentary reform, as is demonstrated by Table 3. Elliot's 'Pro' M.P.s formed a higher percentage of the reform vote than did the abolitionists on all four occasions and, interestingly enough, although abolitionists voted in

higher proportions for reform in the 1780s than did Elliot's repealers, the position was reversed in the 1790s. Of the 164 favouring
Scottish repeal who were M.P.s at the time of one or more of the
four reform motions, 84 (51.22 per cent) voted for reform at least
once.[20] Of those who did not, 15 were only in parliament for the
ill-supported reform motion of 1793. The particular commitment to
reform in the 1790s is underlined by the fact that 34.81 per cent of
those 'Pro' who were M.P.s at the relevant times voted for reform in
1793 and/or 1797. The comparable figure for those 'Doubtful' was
only 6.98 per cent and for those 'Con' a mere 3.10 per cent. Here
was the real test which proved the reforming sympathies of the
repealers. They were more pro-reform, while the 'Doubtful' members and the opponents of repeal were markedly *less* pro-reform,
than the whole House. During the 'reformers' nightmare' of the
1790s, support for reform declined among all M.P.s but the drop
was far smaller among repealers than among any other group.[21]
They not only made up the backbone of the reform vote but also
formed much of the 'opposition' in the parliament of 1790–6,
appearing prominently in the minorities against the French war, the
transportation of Palmer and Muir (1794), and the suspension of
Habeas Corpus (January 1795). With men like Whitbread and
William Smith in the vanguard, the 'dissenting interest' continued
to exert a reforming influence.

Similarly the majority of parliamentary reformers of the 1790s
favoured repeal of the Test laws. Table 4 sets out the way in which
M.P.s who voted for reform in 1793 and 1797 had tended to support
repeal in earlier years. The motion of 6 May 1793 is of particular
interest. Of the 43 reformers (including two tellers) on that day, no
less than 38 appear as 'Pro' in Elliot's list. Of the remaining 5, 2
were not in parliament in 1791, 2 more were 'Doubtful' in Elliot's
eyes but are known from other evidence to have supported repeal in
the 1780s, and only one was 'Con'.[22] A more conclusive correlation

Table 4

Parliamentary reformers and repeal[23]

Date of reform motion	No. of parl. reformers of 1793 and 1797 who had been in parl. in 1787 and/or 1789 and who had then voted for repeal	No. of parl. reformers of 1793 and 1797 who were in parl. in April 1791 and were classed as 'Pro' by Elliot on Scottish repeal
6 May 1793	21 of 28 (75.00%)	38 or 41 (92.68%)
26 May 1797	24 of 45 (53.33%)	42 of 57 (73.68%)

between reform and repeal could hardly be demonstrated. There was a 'significant reformist component'[24] in the repeal vote, as there was in the abolitionist vote.

III

Parallel to the close interaction between repeal and reform lay that between repeal and abolition. Its existence can be detected both nationally and in parliament.

Most repealers, especially the most active ones, supported abolition. They made at least some contribution to those vital religious and intellectual changes which acted powerfully in the service of abolition.[25] Probably support for abolition was even wider among dissenters than was support for parliamentary reform. Evangelical and 'rational' dissenters were almost completely united in detestation of the slave trade, while many of the former were unenthusiastic about reform or repeal. As one Unitarian wrote in 1792, 'The Methodists are the most violent anti-revolutionists we have, & yet we all join for the abolition of the slave trade.'[26] By 1790, numerous rational dissenters had uttered denunciations of the trade; Priestley, Lindsey, George Walker, and many others were among them.[27] The Cambridge Baptist minister Robert Robinson preached a sermon on 10 February 1788 entitled 'Slavery inconsistent with the Spirit of Christianity', taking as his text the words 'He hath sent me . . . to preach deliverance to the captives.' (Luke, ch. 4, v. 18).[28] This was rapidly becoming the standard tone of dissenting pastors. There is little evidence to suggest that their followers did not agree and much to show that they did.

Such bodies as campaigned for repeal almost always assisted abolition even if the strength of the commitment fluctuated. The Protestant Dissenting Deputies passed a resolution expressing 'Gratitude to Almighty God for the deliverance of our Country from that National Sin' at the moment of triumph in 1807.[29] A similarity of personnel in both causes is evident, of which one of the best examples is that of the Manchester radicals, who spearheaded the petitioning movement for abolition in 1787, the very year of the first repeal motion.[30] Finally Samuel Kenrick, secretary to the delegates of dissenting congregations in Worcester, was an ardent abolitionist; his correspondence with his Scottish friend James Wodrow reveals much of the national partnership between repeal and abolition.[31] Both were incorrigible campaigners. Wodrow, a Scottish Presbyterian minister with a strong interest in repeal, took an active part also in the widespread Scottish campaign against the slave trade in 1792.[32] For his part Kenrick was learning the art of placing discreet pressure on the M.P. for his constituency of Bewdley.[33] As early as the 1770s dissenters had tried, if not with outstanding success, to press parliamentary candidates to endorse repeal and to identify publicly those who did so. This tactic of 'pledging' was employed by abolitionists well into the nineteenth century. The contribution of anti-slave trade activity to repeal and vice-versa should not be underestimated.

In parliament the connection was not quite so clear cut. Some leading abolitionists opposed repeal, among them Pitt, Wilberforce, and Dolben. It was politically impossible for the last-named, as member for Oxford University, to help to dismantle the 'Anglican Constitution', but constituency pressure is only part of the explanation. The 'Jacobinal' reputation of certain sections of dissent in the 1790s, as well as the theological unorthodoxy of the radical Unitarians, undoubtedly deterred some of the more conservative abolitionists from voting for repeal. Wilberforce's suspicion of the repeal case was fully revealed in his speech of 2 March 1790, when he strongly criticised Fox's motion.[34] Similarly there were some repealers, such as Sir Adam Fergusson, Nathaniel Newnham, and Charles Marsham, who opposed abolition – in some cases for constituency reasons, in a few others because of West Indian interests. But most of the relatively small number of repealers who actually turned out for the sparsely attended debates of 1791 and 1796 did vote for abolition. For instance, the surviving M.P.s of the repeal group of 1787–9 divided 23–9 in favour of Wilberforce's bill of 1796. Those 'Pro' repeal in Elliot's list did so by 26–14. This contrasts starkly with those 'Con' who divided 40–23 against abolition in 1796.[35]

Tables 5 and 6 set out the voting on abolition of the 'dissenting interest', using the measurements of 1787–9 and 1791. The 'dissenting interest' seems to have contributed almost as much to

Table 5

Repealers of 1787–9 and abolition

Date of abolition motion	No. of repealers of 1787–9 then in parl.	No. voting for abolition	Percentage of known abolitionist minority which they formed
18–19 Apr. 1791	91	19 (20.87%)	40.42 (19 of 47)
15 March 1796	80	23 (28.75%)	35.94 (23 of 64)
1791 and/or 1796	96	29 (30.21%)	34.12 (29 of 85)

Table 6

Repealers of 1791 and abolition

Date of abolition motion	No. of repealers of 1791 then in parl.	No. voting for abolition	Percentage of known abolitionist minority which they formed
18–19 Apr. 1791	167	22 (13.12%)	46.81 (22 of 47)
15 March 1796	137	26 (18.98%)	40.62 (26 of 64)
1791 and/or 1796.	167	33 (19.76%)	38.83 (33 of 85)

abolition as to parliamentary reform, composing between a third and half of the known abolitionist voting strength of 1791–6. The number of repealers who voted for abolition would certainly be higher if full lists of abolitionist M.P.s (especially for 1791 where forty-one names are missing) were available. Such parliamentary champions of dissent as Fox, Beaufoy, Hoghton, William Smith, and Lord Stanhope were in the forefront of abolitionist ranks.[36] Sir Gilbert Elliot is a particularly fine example of a member who took a leading part in both causes. He voted for repeal in 1787,[37] sponsored the Scottish repeal motion of 1791 and 'voted with Pitt and Fox for the immediate abolition' in April 1792.[38]

A repealer, however, was much more likely to be an abolitionist than vice-versa. It is true that in the 1780s, before the alarming tidings from France, more abolitionists voted for repeal than against it. Of the 63 abolitionists in parliament at the time of one or both of the repeal motions of 1787–9, 29 (46.03 per cent) voted for repeal at least once.[39] They must have outnumbered those who voted against, bearing in mind that the house was far from full on each occasion, and many were absent. But it is questionable whether this level of support was maintained for the motion of 1790, and during and after that year the position changed. Throughout the following decade it becomes harder to detect the extent to which – if at all – abolitionists as a whole were hostile to the Test Act. As Table 7 shows, the abolitionists in the parliament of 1790–6 did not impress Elliot as notably pro-repeal. The preparation of his canvassing list on Scottish repeal coincided with the abolition bill of April 1791 and Table 7 shows how he classified the abolitionist M.P.s.

Two conclusions may legitimately follow. The abolitionist M.P.s overall were almost evenly divided on repeal in the 1790s with perhaps a slight bias in its favour. This was, of course, a more favourable disposition towards religious liberalism than that displayed by the whole house. But the 31 members who made 'known exceptional exertions in the abolitionist cause'[40] were much more

Table 7

Abolitionists and Scottish repeal, 1791

Date of abolition motion	No. of known abolitionist M.P.s of 1791 and 1796 then in parl.	'Pro' repeal in Elliot's list	'Con' in Elliot's list	Doubtful in Elliot's list	Not in parl. Apr. 1791	In parl. Apr. 1791 but not classified by Elliot
18–19 Apr. 1791	47	22	20	4	–	1
15 March 1796	64	26	23	7	6	2
1791 and/or 1796.	85	33	33	10	6	3

inclined in its favour and much more inclined to act as a group. In 1787–9, 29 of them were in parliament and 17 voted for repeal at least once. Of these 31, moreover, Elliot listed 17 as 'Pro', 12 as 'Con' and one as 'Doubtful'.[41] This may be taken as confirmation of the view that most of the parliamentary support which abolitionists gave to repeal was drawn from the 'hard core' or leadership, rather than from the rank and file.[42] Indeed, amongst abolitionist M.P.s outside the 'hard core' there seems to have been a small majority against repeal.[43]

Of all the liberal and reforming causes of the late eighteenth century, abolition was undoubtedly the most persistent. Its advocates were well-informed and well-connected in governmental circles. From the late 1780s until 1807 almost every year saw a parliamentary motion and success was almost achieved on more than one occasion. The 'dissenting interest' played an important part in helping to maintain this momentum. Its members knew that just as the bill for the gradual abolition of the slave trade in 1792 had faded away in the house of Lords, so any repeal measure which passed the Commons would have received similar, if not more summary, treatment in the upper chamber.[44] The fate of the dissenting petitions of 1772–3, not to mention the more recent example of Lord Stanhope's toleration bill in 1789, had taught them that the Lords constituted an obstacle to religious reform. Repealers and abolitionists faced common problems and, in many ways, sought common solutions.

IV

Resistance to the two causes did not spring entirely from the same quarters. After all, the attendances and majorities for repeal debates tended to be higher than those on abolition. Just as repeal, like most other proposals for constitutional change, was more unpopular in the country during the 1790s than was abolition, so the penal code seemed able to rally more M.P.s in its defence than did the slave trade. No less than 294 members voted against the repeal of the Test and Corporation Acts in 1790 while Scottish repeal (1791) and the Unitarian petition (1792) were defeated by the margins of 149–62 and 142–63 respectively. Abolition did not usually encounter adverse numbers on this scale and even managed a limited success in 1792. Nonetheless there existed a demonstrable connection between the opposition to repeal and the opposition to abolition. This is hardly surprising. The 'negative correlation' between votes cast against abolition and hostility to parliamentary reform has been noted by Professor Anstey[45] and would undoubtedly be more obvious if lists of M.P.s opposed to reform were available. Opponents of abolition tended to be equally hostile to repeal.

Apart from impressionistic evidence and the examination of individual cases a study of the opposition to repeal and to abolition is only possible if one compares Elliot's 'Con' list on Scottish repeal with the list of the anti-abolition majority of 1796. These are the only adequate sources for the 'antis' in either case. They present two findings. First, the level of opposition to abolition from supporters of repeal was very low; only 11.25 per cent of the repealers of 1787–9 and only 10.22 per cent of Elliot's 'Pro' M.P.s then in parliament voted against abolition in 1796. Secondly, a much higher proportion of M.P.s who were 'Con' in Elliot's list voted against abolition in 1796 than was the case with 'Pro' M.P.s.

Table 8 sets out the voting against abolition in 1796 of the three groups identified by Elliot. The proportion of the whole house voting against abolition was 76 out of 558 (including tellers), or 13.62 per cent. A comparison between these figures and those in Table 6 reveals that in 1796 whereas Elliot's 'Pro' M.P.s voted *for*

Table 8

The voting against abolition, 15 March 1796[46]

'Pro' on Scottish repeal		'Con'		'Doubtful'	
% voting against abolition	% of anti-abolition vote	% voting against abolition	% of anti-abolition vote	% voting against abolition	% of anti-abolition vote
10.22	18.18	17.86	52.07	10.66	10.39
(14 of 137)	(14 of 77)	(40 of 224)	(40 of 77)	(8 of 75)	(8 of 77)

abolition by 18.98 per cent to 10.22 per cent (26–14) and the 'Doubtful' members were almost evenly divided at 9.33 per cent for and 10.66 per cent against (7–8), those 'Con' voted *against* abolition by 17.86 per cent to 10.27 per cent (40–23). Thus opponents of Scottish repeal in 1791 voted against abolition in 1796 in proportions similar to those by which M.P.s favouring repeal gave abolition their support. The fact that these opponents of repeal formed over half of the anti-abolitionist majority of 1796 tells its own story.

Similarly, a large majority of anti-abolitionists opposed repeal. Only insignificant numbers of anti-abolitionists then in parliament had voted *for* repeal in the late 1780s – 7 out of 40 in 1787 and 5 out of 48 in 1789 – while most of those actually present had almost certainly voted against it. This is confirmed by Elliot's classification of the 77 anti-abolitionist M.P.s of 1796. Sixty-three of them were in parliament in 1791 and Elliot regarded only 14 as 'Pro', with 40 'Con' and 8 as 'Doubtful'.[47] Thus well over half (40 out of 63, or 63.49 per cent) of known anti-abolitionists opposed Scottish repeal in 1791 and, excluding those 'Doubtful', did so in the ratio of almost 3:1.

Some correlation between the opposition to abolition and to repeal can therefore be detected. No doubt it could be explained, at least partly, in terms of hostility to change, a sense of inexpediency in wartime and a common defence of property and the constitution. But there was at least one other common factor and that was the voting of an important group among the M.P.s for Scottish constituencies. Here, thanks to Elliot, more evidence is available than for other members. For not only did he classify his fellow countrymen as 'Pro', 'Con' or 'Doubtful' on Scottish repeal but recorded their actual votes on 10 May 1791.[48] Thus two comparisons among the Scottish M.P.s are possible; between Elliot's canvassing list and the voting on abolition and between the division of 10 May 1791 and the voting on abolition.

These comparisons are simplified by the absence of any Scottish names from the known abolitionist minority of 1791. One is thus comparing Scottish repeal in 1791 and abolition five years later. Although none of the twelve Scottish M.P.s who were 'Pro' in Elliot's canvassing list voted for abolition, only one voted against it. This was Sir Adam Fergusson (Ayrshire), an independent-minded supporter of government and friend of Henry Dundas. Of the ten who actually voted for Scottish repeal, one (N. MacLeod) voted for abolition in 1796 and one (Fergusson) against. The real interest, however, lies in comparing the Scottish anti-repealers with the

Scottish anti-abolitionists. Of the 45 Scottish M.P.s, 12, a much higher proportion than for the whole house, voted against abolition on 15 March 1796. No less than 11 of them belonged to the Dundas interest and could be relied upon to support the 'uncrowned king of Scotland' in parliamentary divisions.[49] Of these 12, 9 had been M.P.s in 1791 and Elliot had considered 6 of them as 'Con', 2 as 'Doubtful' and only one 'Pro' on Scottish repeal. In the event only one (Fergusson) voted for repeal on 10 May 1791 and 4 voted against.

Nineteen of the twenty Scots who voted against Scottish repeal in 1791 were of the 'Dundas interest' and since both Henry Dundas and his nephew Robert, the Lord Advocate for Scotland, spoke against Elliot's motion this was only to be expected. Just as Scottish members had largely voted against repeal in 1787–90,[50] so the 'Dundas interest' operated against both Scottish repeal in 1791 and abolition in 1796. Although Dundas had supported gradual abolition in 1792 his block of votes proved a vital link between the opposition to the two causes. Indeed, bearing in mind the extent of Dundas's influence as government manager of elections and patronage in Scotland, it might seem slightly surprising that more of the thirty members who were attached to him by 1796 did not turn out against abolition. Henry Dundas himself did not vote against abolition in 1796 (although he spoke against it) and it seems clear that his 'interest' worked rather more discreetly against abolition than against repeal.[51] The discretion was necessary because Pitt gave his personal support to abolition while refusing to countenance repeal. In 1791 Dundas was able to marshall his forces and vote against Scottish repeal without difficulty; in 1796 political divergences with his senior colleague had to be kept to a minimum. It was nonetheless largely due to Dundas that only one Scottish member – as far as is known – voted for abolition in 1791 or 1796, or for parliamentary reform in 1793 or 1797. This was Norman MacLeod, member for Inverness-shire.[52] It remains mildly ironic that even he was first elected as an adherent of Dundas, but quickly followed a more independent course.[53]

V

The absence of much formal co-operation between these three reforming causes in the 1790s should not be allowed to conceal their deeper connections. Most Foxite Whigs, for instance, gave active support to all three. But the prospect of a general repeal of the Test laws seemed hopelessly remote after March 1790 and its supporters set their sights upon more limited objectives. For their part abolitionists would have harmed their own cause by a public endorsement of repeal; quite apart from the danger of association with its radical connotations they were not sufficiently united on the subject to advocate it officially. This helps to distinguish them as a body, despite some overlap, from the small cluster of dedicated parliamentary reformers, who were much more likely to back repeal than were abolitionists. Of course all three causes suffered during and after the parliament of 1790–6 from the impact of the French Revolution, but abolition was the least damaged of the three. It was also much less of a 'party' or 'government versus opposition' question than repeal or parliamentary reform – if indeed it was a 'party' matter at all. This was greatly to its advantage. For abolition was a much more broadly-based cause in the 1790s, both in parliament and in the country, than reform or repeal. The opposition to abolition, although powerful and comparable to a considerable degree with that to reform and repeal, could never muster the same numbers as the opposition faced by the latter two. There is therefore no real surprise in the fact that abolition was the first to be achieved; what is perhaps surprising is that repeal was the second and not the third. The link between them undoubtedly existed in the earlier period as well as at the moment of triumph and it is in the parliament of 1790–6 that it can be most precisely measured.

Notes

1   I wish to thank Professor Roger Anstey and Dr Brian Harrison for suggestions and comments during the preparation of this paper. I am grateful to the Trustees of the National Library of Scotland for permission to consult and cite the Minto Papers and to Dr Paul Kelly for advice as to their use. I am also deeply obliged to the Librarian and Trustees of Dr Williams's Library, London, for permission to examine and quote from the Kenrick Papers.

2   Roger Anstey, *The Atlantic Slave Trade and British Abolition 1760–1810* (1975), especially pp. 126–41 and 403–9.

3   Note by Sir Gilbert Elliot, c. 1791; Minto Papers, National Library of Scotland, MS 11203 f. 200.

4   For an interesting example of the consensus achieved in Birmingham by Clarkson's campaign against the slave trade, as distinct from the conflicts over the repeal of the Test laws, see John Money, *Experience and Identity. Birmingham and the West Midlands, 1760–1800* (Manchester, 1977), p. 219.

5 Anstey, *Atlantic Slave Trade*, pp. 277–8 and 410; Seymour Drescher, *Econocide: British Slavery in the Era of Abolition* (Pittsburgh, 1977), p. 140.

6 P. D. Brown, *William Pitt, Earl of Chatham. The Great Commoner* (1978), p. 251.

7 Anstey, *Atlantic Slave Trade*, pp. 283–5.

8 Forty-seven of the 88 M.P.s who voted for abolition at the end of the debate of 18–19 April 1791 are listed in Clarkson, T., *History of the Abolition of the Slave Trade* (re-issue 1968), II, p. 338n. 64 of the 70 M.P.s who voted for abolition on 15 March 1796 are named in Debrett, *Parliamentary Register*, XLIV, pp. 323–4 and in Cobbett, *Parliamentary History*, XXXII, p. 902. The abolition motion of 1791 was defeated by 163 votes to 88, that of 1796 by 74 to 70.

9 Because of the incomplete nature of the lists the figure of 85 abolitionist M.P.s is necessarily an exclusive one. But it is worth noting that they voted for abolition in ill-attended parliamentary debates and that their attendance was in itself a form of commitment to their cause.

10 The reform minority of 1785 includes two tellers and fourteen M.P.s who paired off in favour of reform; the minorities of 1793 and 1797 each include two tellers. The list of the minority on Pitt's motion for reform of 7 May 1783 can be found in C. Wyvill, *Political Papers* (1794–1806), II, pp. 255–7; that on Pitt's reform motion of 18 April 1785 in *ibid.*, pp. 443–5; that on Grey's reform motion of 6 May 1793 in *Parl. Reg.* XXV, p. 508 and that on Grey's reform motion of 26 May 1797 in *ibid.*, XLVII, pp. 656–7. The figures for the abolitionists of 1791 and 1796 which are given here differ very slightly from those of Professor Anstey (*Atlantic Slave Trade*, pp. 283–4). He found 83 abolitionist M.P.s on this reckoning, compared with the present writer's 85 and also estimated slightly different levels of abolitionist support for parliamentary reform.

11 G. M. Ditchfield, 'The parliamentary struggle over the repeal of the Test and Corporation Acts, 1787–90', *English Historical Review*, 89 (1974), p. 564.

12 G. M. Ditchfield, 'Debates on the Test and Corporation Acts, 1787–90: the evidence of the division lists', *Bulletin of the Institute of Historical Research*, 50 (1977) pp. 69–81. There were unsuccessful repeal motions in 1787, 1789, and 1790; lists of the minority exist for the first two.

13 James E. Bradley, 'Whigs and nonconformists. "Slumbering radicalism" in English politics, 1739–89', *Eighteenth Century Studies*, 9 (1975), pp. 1–27.

14 Lists of M.P.s who voted against reform, or abstained, in the motions of 1783–97 have not survived.

15 This figure of 69.77 per cent is the basis of the present writer's claim ('Parliamentary struggle', p. 558) that a repealer was likely to support reform, involving a redistribution of seats and (more speculatively) an extension of the franchise. There is more to this claim than the fact that 55.68 per cent of repealers in parliament in 1783 and 51.26 per cent of those in parliament in 1785 voted for Pitt's reform motions in those years; see Bradley, 'Whigs and nonconformists', p. 4, n. 9. Of course

many of these repealers voted for reform more than once.

16 Six M.P.s were actually dissenters in 1787–9 and 5 of them voted for reform at least once between 1783–97. But the total number of dissenting M.P.s between 1715 and 1790 was at least 47 and not 39 as Bradley ('Whigs and nonconformists' p. 15) states. R. Sedgwick found a minimum of 28 for the period 1715–54 (*The History of Parliament. The House of Commons, 1715–54* (1970), vol. 1, p. 139) while Sir Lewis Namier and J. Brooke identified 19 for the period 1754–90 (*The History of Parliament. The House of Commons 1754–90* (1964), vol. 1, p. 115.)

17 See the present writer's article 'The Scottish campaign against the Test Act 1790–1', *Historical Journal* (forthcoming). Elliot was M.P. for Helston in 1791 and, as Earl of Minto, served as Governor-General of India from 1806–13.

18 Elliot's canvassing list of the House of Commons (April 1791), Minto Papers, MS 11203, ff. 161–76.

19 There was of course much overlap between the repealers of 1787–9 and Elliot's 'Pro' M.P.s on Scottish repeal.

20 By way of comparison, 83 abolitionists were M.P.s for one or more of the reform motions of 1783–97; 51 of them (61.44 per cent) voted for reform at least once.

21 Among Elliot's 'Pro' M.P.s the proportion voting for reform was actually higher in 1797 than for any other of the four reform motions.

22 Elliot's canvassing list; Minto Papers MS 11203 ff. 161–76.

23 In each case the number of parliamentary reformers includes two tellers.

24 Anstey, *Atlantic Slave Trade*, p. 284.

25 *Ibid.*, part 2.

26 Samuel Kenrick to James Wodrow, 10 April 1792. Kenrick Papers, Dr Williams's Library.

27 See R. V. Holt, *The Unitarian Contribution to Social Progress in England*, (2nd edn. 1952), p. 133 ff. There is further evidence of the same sort in H. S. Skeats, and C. S. Miall, *History of the Free Churches of England* (1891), pp. 387ff. and in Clarkson, *Abolition of the Slave Trade*, vol. 1, *passim*.

28 Robert Robinson, *Miscellaneous Works* (1807), vol. IV, pp. 60–113.

29 B. L. Manning, *The Protestant Dissenting Deputies*, (Cambridge, 1952), p. 471.

30 Anstey, *Atlantic Slave Trade*, pp. 265–6; E. M. Hunt, 'The anti-slave trade agitation in Manchester', *Transactions of the Lancashire and Cheshire Antiquarian Society*, 79 (1977), pp. 46–72. For an examination of the role of the Manchester radicals, notably Thomas Walker and Thomas Cooper, in the dissenting cause, see G. M. Ditchfield, 'The campaign in Lancashire and Cheshire for the repeal of the Test and Corporation Acts, 1787–1790', *Trans. Hist. Soc. Lancs. and Cheshire*, 126 (1977), pp. 109–138.

31 The letters between Samuel Kenrick of Bewdley and James Wodrow, Presbyterian minister of Stevenston, Ayrshire, can be found in Dr Williams's Library, MSS. 24. 157. There is a valuable introduction to the correspondence in J. Creasey, 'Some dissenting attitudes towards

the French Revolution', *Trans. Unitarian Historical Society*, 13 (1966), pp. 155–67.

32 There is an interesting description of this campaign in Wodrow's letter to Kenrick of 23 March 1792.

33 Kenrick to Wodrow, 25 September 1790.

34 *Parl. Reg.* xxvii, 189–90; John Pollock, *Wilberforce* (1977), p. 154.

35 See below, Table 8 and surrounding discussion.

36 See, for example, R. W. Davis, *Dissent in Politics, 1780–1830. The Political Life of William Smith* (1971), pp. 64, 89 and 105ff; A. Newman, *The Stanhopes of Chevening. A Family Biography* (1969), pp. 162–3.

37 Sir Gilbert Elliot to Lady Elliot, 29 March 1787; Countess of Minto (ed.), *Life and Letters of Sir Gilbert Elliot* (1874), vol. 1, pp. 142–3.

38 Elliot to Lady Elliot, 3 April 1792, *ibid.*, vol. ii, pp. 4–5. The original is in Minto Papers, MS 11048, ff.82–3 and the letter contains an interesting description of the abolition debate of April 1792. It seems probable that Elliot was one of the 41 M.P.s who voted for abolition in 1791 and were omitted from the list printed in Clarkson. He was no longer an M.P. at the time of the abolition bill of 1796.

39 The figure rises to 29 out of 59 (49.15 per cent) if one counts only those abolitionists who were in parliament for *both* repeal motions of 1787 and 1789. These figures differ marginally from those of Professor Anstey, *Atlantic Slave Trade*, p. 284.

40 Anstey, *Atlantic Slave Trade*, pp. 282–3.

41 One of the 31 (Samuel Whitbread senior, a sympathiser with repeal) was not an M.P. in April 1791 when Elliot's list was compiled. Had he been, the 'Pro' figure would certainly be 18.

42 See Ditchfield, 'Parliamentary struggle', p. 559.

43 This is substantiated by Elliot's canvassing list on Scottish repeal. Of 85 known abolitionists, 21 voted for abolition in 1791 only, 38 in 1796 only and 26 in both years. On Scottish repeal Elliot classed them thus:

	'Pro'	'Con'	'Doubtful'	Not in Parl.	Not listed
1791 only	7	10	3	–	1
1796 only	11	13	6	6	2
1791 and 1796	15	10	1	–	–
Total	33	33	10	6	3

44 James Wodrow predicted the loss of the bill for gradual abolition in the Lords; Wodrow to Kenrick, 30 May 1792.

45 Anstey, *Atlantic Slave Trade*, p. 284, n. 119.

46 The list of the anti-abolitionist majority of 1796 can be found in *Parl. Reg.* xliv, 323–4. The figure of 77 includes the 74 who voted against abolition, plus two tellers, but one 'extra' M.P. seems to have found his way into the list.

47 One of these 63 M.P.s was not listed by Elliot.

48 Minto Papers, MS 11203, f.159. 10 Scottish M.P.s voted for Elliot's motion on 10 May 1791, and 20 against.

49 Anstey, *Atlantic Slave Trade*, pp. 308–9. William Garthshore, private secretary to Dundas and member for Launceston, also voted against abolition in 1796. A detailed survey of the political affiliations of the

Scottish M.P.s can be found in H. Furber, *Henry Dundas, First Viscount Melville, 1742–1811* (1931), part 2 and appendices.

50 Ditchfield, 'Parliamentary struggle', p. 565, n. 1.

51 See Anstey, *Atlantic Slave Trade*, p. 309 and especially n. 80. Here the way in which Henry Dundas's 'conviction of the need to maintain and defend the Empire' and especially the wealth of the Caribbean possessions had by 1796 helped to lead him to an anti-abolitionist stance is fully revealed. It should also be noted that Robert Dundas was a teller for the anti-abolition majority in 1796.

52 MacLeod voted for parliamentary reform in 1793 and for abolition in 1796.

53 Furber, *Melville*, pp. 239–40.

6
A GENEALOGY OF REFORM IN MODERN BRITAIN

by Brian Harrison

The genealogies elaborated in *Debrett*, *Who's Who* and *The Dictionary of National Biography* are only now being complemented by dictionaries of labour and radical biography. Yet even when this valuable work is complete, the importance of inheritance among opponents of the British establishment since 1780 would not be fully grasped without analysis of its structural and intellectual dimensions. Roger Anstey was well aware of these, for at the end of his book on the Atlantic slave trade he found 'a logic in the success of abolition pregnant with future consequences': he argued that anti-slavery techniques could be applied in other spheres and that abolitionism raised the whole question of the limits of authority over the individual; others could take the matter further.[1] I have discussed elsewhere the 'horizontal' linkages between the various types of nineteenth-century reformer at any one time.[2] Here I aim to complement that discussion by analyzing the 'vertical' linkages between reforming movements over time – the genealogy of reform. Three major constituents of this genealogy will be analysed: its internal dynamic; its inspiration, tradition, or myth; and its institutional base within the community at large. Attention will thereby be drawn, in conclusion, to the political party which reformers hoped would become their instrument, but which in reality became their master – the Liberal Party, whose history is as much to be found among its rebels and supposedly non-party dissidents as in its own institutional structure, and whose fertile internal arguments and invigorating rivalries are misunderstood if they are seen as portending ineluctable decay.

I

Nineteenth-century Britain's well-known pattern of government growth has perhaps thrown too deeply into the shade that pattern of voluntarist and philanthropic growth which alone could set it in motion. This reforming dynamic was partly internal to the reforming world itself. A reforming principle or perception once articulated could readily be applied elsewhere. Humane principles, for example, could readily move on to climbing boys, factory children, drunkards, prostitutes, Bulgarians, animals, or murderers. At the foundation meeting of the Society for the Prevention of Cruelty to Animals in 1824, Wilberforce was present and T. F. Buxton took the chair; and the Society for the Diffusion of Information on the Subject of Capital Punishments, formed in 1828, boasted William Allen as its chairman and Buxton and Clarkson among its members. More than half a century later the abolitionist imprint can be seen all over the Bulgarian atrocities agitation, whose National Conference on the Eastern Question was addressed by Sir T. F. Buxton the younger. Likewise, the libertarian principle could advance through Catholic emancipation in 1829 to the emancipation of the Jews in 1858, to the battles fought by Bradlaugh in the 1880s for entry into the House of Commons, to the enfranchisement of women in 1918 and 1928. As for franchise extension, its progressive broadening out was correctly predicted by its Tory opponents in 1831–2.

For reformers as cerebral as Richard Cobden, the full scope of the reforming programme – education, peace, land reform, reduced taxation, and free trade – was perceived at the start. But even Cobden admitted in his famous interview with Palmerston in 1859 that (like so many other reformers) he had been almost unconsciously drawn into public affairs. 'Why did you enter public life?', Palmerston asked. 'I hardly know, it was by mere accident, and for a special purpose', Cobden replied, 'and probably it would have been better for me and my family if I had kept my private station'. Many reformers recognized the full range of the problems they must tackle only incidentally and by chance. The very process of reform often uncovered evils hitherto unsuspected, or exposed loopholes in the remedies already devised. Lord Shaftesbury was led on from factory reform into public health, educational and sabbatarian causes – as well as into further elaborations and extended applications of factory legislation. The Ten Hours movement was for him, as he said in 1845, 'the beginning of all the movements; it had directed general and individual attention to the state of all the classes of the working people; it was, as it were, a representative question – the interests and welfare of all were contended for under the struggle maintained on behalf of this one'.[3]

As for British feminist history, the women who launched *The English Woman's Journal* in 1858 had no idea of the miseries middle-class women endured from unemployment until the lamentations came flooding into the *Journal*'s office. From there the road opened out towards reforms in women's education and thence to women's suffrage. Nor had Josephine Butler ever intended to embrace the prostitute's cause: as a leader in the movements for women's improved educational and occupational opportunity she was drawn into it during 1869 by others. Her attack on state-regulated prostitution led on to a sequence of other causes; it also reinforced the case for women's suffrage which she had always supported – for in the great nineteenth-century tide of reform there were mutually reinforcing eddies as well as strong forward currents. Mrs Butler no doubt wrote from experience when she said that Catharine of Siena had 'like many other reformers . . . at first hoped for a more quick return for her labours; but as the years went on, she learned, as they have learned, that God had greater designs in view'. Her memoirs refer to 'the vitality of our Crusade', which caused it 'to break through the boundaries of its own particular channel, and to create and fructify many movements and reforms of a collateral character'.[4] After 1918 the birth control movement drew its activists ineluctably into wider types of social reform, as well as into the concept of 'planned parenthood', marriage counselling and research on infertility. But perhaps most accidental of all was the reformer's advance into penal reform – including advocates of the free press in the 1830s, Chartists in the 1840s, suffragettes in the 1900s and nuclear disarmers in the 1960s – as a result of the imprisonment their crusading sometimes entailed.

This onward advance of reform was not always uncontested within the reforming movement itself: by the 1860s Joseph Livesey the pioneer teetotaler was vigorously criticizing the prohibitionists who had emerged from the abstinence movement he had helped to create in the 1830s, just as Florence Nightingale and Caroline Norton held back in later life from advances in the feminist cause they had pioneered. Schism was often the vehicle of reforming advance, with exciting disputes *en route* between reformers of the cautious and radical variety. Zealous anti-vivisectionists, for example, split off in the 1870s from the RSPCA, only to fragment further among themselves.

In other cases there was a mutual jostling forward of reforming causes as a result of reciprocal rebuke, retaliation, and reproach. The factory movement launched itself by saying that abolitionists were ignoring greater evils nearer home. Oastler entered the movement with his letters on 'Slavery in Yorkshire' in the *Leeds Mercury*, and the anti-slavery and factory movements each claimed that its own variant of slavery was the worst. From Cobbett to Orator Hunt to Robert Owen to Carlyle, Disraeli, and Engels came complaints that abolitionists neglected the liberties of English working men. And once the factory movement had secured legislation in the textile mills, the textile manufacturers' justified complaint that conditions were even worse elsewhere pointed the way to further regulation. Mutual reproaches between landowners and industrialists lay behind the factory movement, as Sir James Graham acknowledged when opposing the Ten Hours Bill of 1844; if ten hours regulations were introduced, he said, 'it will be necessary to relax others of a countervailing nature'.[5] His prediction was borne out in reverse order: the Corn Laws were repealed in 1846 and the Ten Hours Bill was enacted in the following year. Mutual reproach reappears as an incentive to reform in the 1880s, when the RSPCA generously helped the fledgling National Society for the Prevention of Cruelty to Children at least partly to discredit the accusation that animal lovers were unconcerned about the sufferings of children.

There was even an international dimension to this rivalry in well-doing. The idea that Britain should set a moral lead to the world runs through Wilberforce's anti-slavery, Cobden's free trade, Josephine Butler's moralistic attack on state-regulated prostitution, the RSPCA's humanitarianism, and the Campaign for Nuclear Disarmament's pacifism. Europe could retaliate by enlarging upon British drunkenness and exploitation of the Irish: and Mrs Beecher Stowe could point out, when on her second visit to England in 1856, that 'the view of your great cities flaming nightly with signs of "Rum, brandy, and Gin"; is to the eyes of an American as appalling as the slave-market of our Southern States to an Englishman'.[6]

These reproaches were often unjust, if only because they took so little account of the environmental constituent of social evils – of industry's impact on British drunkenness, for instance, or of agriculture's implications for animal cruelty in France, Italy, and Spain. There is also surely a case for specialization in attacking the evils of the world: when criticized by socialists for their single-mindedness between the wars, pacifists rightly replied that a start has to be made somewhere. Besides, reformers in one cause were by no means always idle elsewhere. Wilberforce complained in 1807 that his opponents 'searched out every recess of misery and vice in their own country, they looked around them every where for evils, and hugged them all to their bosoms', yet he himself supported factory legislation and defended climbing boys. And when Orator Hunt interrupted the anti-slavery meeting of 1830 with accusations of 'a left-eyed humanity', Brougham pointed out that the abolitionists were active in many other good causes – William Allen in educational reform, for instance, and T. F. Buxton in prison reform. Similar objections to women's suffrage were easily refuted in 1911 when suffragists were shown to have contributed between half and four-fifths of the officials in nine reforming movements.[7] Nonetheless, such reproaches, whether just or unjust, helped broaden out the reformer's vision; the crusader's courage was enhanced by his conviction of moral superiority, and the maligned movement or nation could stir itself to shake off the rebuke.

Driving on these reforming efforts was a deeply-held belief in the need for and feasibility of moral progress as an accompaniment to material growth: hence the reformer's rapid movings on from one cause to another. The supply of crusades would never run dry because the smallest kind of abuse served to train the will, if only in preparation for grappling with larger evils. There might be worse sufferings in nineteenth-century society, but the miseries of ill-treated animals were the more attractive as objects of concern because of the animals' very helplessness. 'Benevolence assumes its purest form', William Ewart told the RSPCA's annual meeting in 1845, 'when its author is not only unrequited, but unknown'. Again, if moral progress was the aim, no locality need be too distant for attention. The perception of a moral principle did not depend on actually observing the evil under attack; indeed, attacking an unobserved evil was in a sense more virtuous. Criticized in 1882 for being so ignorant of the districts exposed to state-regulated prostitution, Josephine Butler replied that 'negro slavery was abolished in our British possessions by a body of persons in England who had never seen a negro slave'.[8]

The Victorian pursuit of moral progress helps to explain why vivisection was regarded with such horror: it seemed a betrayal from within the heart of the friendly camp – by the scientific, middle-class professionals from whom most was expected. It was a new vice, the more loathsome because deliberately committed by

the educated and the benevolent. It is hardly surprising that reformers frequently clashed with the practical politician – preoccupied
as he must be primarily with human nature as it is rather than as it
should be, with major rather than minor evils, and with problems
which are pressing rather than remote. Still, the reformers were
girding themselves up for the conflict by creating an inspiring
reforming tradition.

II

Their ideal was the self-educating, rational, and progressive individual whose emancipation would promote moral progress directly
– by encouraging temperance, humane values, sexual purity – and
perhaps also indirectly, by affirming the values and cultivating the
political influence of moralistic social groups. In the 1860s prohibitionists were as hopeful of the working men as was J. S. Mill of
the women: their votes would promote humane values and moral
progress. Each apparent reforming success was incorporated into
the heroic British reforming tradition, and so reinforced it. The
anti-slavery movement's successes in 1807 and 1833 were particularly important here, if only because – by American standards – they
occurred so early. British abolitionism, instead of merely interact-
ing with the host of early nineteenth-century reforming and
humanitarian movements, actually preceded and inspired them,
long before the advent of those anti-humanitarian mid-century
shifts in opinion which limited the influence of American abolitionists after their triumph.[9]

A continuity of personnel gave backbone to the British reforming tradition, from anti-slavery onwards. Anti-slavery men like
James Silk Buckingham, Joseph Sturge and George Thompson
reappear in the temperance movement launched in the late 1820s,
and Josephine Butler's crusade against state-regulated prostitution
half a century later sounded the same note of libertarian moral
self-development; she persuaded an ageing George Thompson to
expound on her platform the values which had inspired his anti-
slavery effort so many years before. The pursuit of moral reform
could even lead Thompson away from libertarianism in its pure
form towards the peculiar form of state intervention which prohibition embodied: at a Leeds meeting of the United Kingdom Alliance
in 1871 he announced that 'he had never gone for half measures',
and that the drink trade was for him 'not an evil to be regulated, but
a gigantic crime to be abolished'.[10] Many reformers feared that

prohibition might infringe that freedom of choice which lay at the heart of moral progress; the line of continuity in reforming personnel is therefore stronger within the libertarian movements for repealing the Test and Corporation Acts and for emancipating the Catholics, the Jews, and women. A daughter of Benjamin Blackwell, active in Bristol's anti-slavery movement, was the pioneer woman doctor Elizabeth Blackwell; and a grand-daughter of William Smith the anti-slavery leader was Barbara Bodichon, central to the campaign for women's employment in the 1860s. There were cheers at the Free Trade Hall woman suffrage demonstration in February 1880 when Mrs McLaren from the platform singled out Elizabeth Pease (now Mrs Nichol) in the audience as still testifying by her presence 'for that political freedom which has, years ago, been granted to the negro whom she helped to make free'.[11]

Libertarian principles were not confined to politics; they nourished British feminism and the Anti-Corn Law League; both challenged an intrusive state machine, and both attacked aristocratic militarism at its root. The League was the first public movement to attract Barbara Bodichon, and the Anti-Corn Law Leaguer Thomas Thomasson was a major figure in financing the crucially important Manchester feminists of the 1870s. Military and imperial interests reinforced the opponents of both movements, whereas feminist links with pacifism were strong enough during the First World War to provoke a major split inside the women's movement. 'Among the women who are "doing their bit" in a multiplicity of ways', *The Anti-Suffrage Review* complained in March 1917, 'Suffragists form only a small proportion, but it is safe to infer that every Pacifist and every No-Conscriptionist is a Suffragist'. Feminists like Mrs Swanwick, Mrs Pethick-Lawrence, and Catherine Marshall operated at the centre of the British peace movement between the wars, and a former suffragette Miss Gertrude Fishwick was still available in the 1950s to play a crucial role in launching the Campaign for Nuclear Disarmament, with its special women's offshoots entitled 'Women against the Bomb' and 'Voice of Women'.

This continuity of reforming personnel is partly explained by temperament; a generalized desire to change the world placed a Cobden, a Lawson, a Francis Newman, or a Pethick-Lawrence in the reforming camp, just as distaste for the reforming temperament ensured hostility from a Cromer, a Salisbury, a Fitzjames Stephen, or a Hensley Henson. But continuity also resulted from the accumulation of reforming expertise; this could be acquired by a single individual in the course of his lifetime's agitation. A man like James

Acland, radical journalist and lecturer for the Anti-Corn Law League, had developed specialized reforming skills which it seemed a pity (both from a personal and a political point of view) to waste; he reappears in 1855 writing pamphlets for the Administrative Reform Association, and by 1867 he was electoral adviser to the Reform League. As for the Reform Leaguer, Liberal M.P. and trade unionist George Howell, his success as an administrator made him 'into something of an organizational entrepreneur'; to each of his reforming movements he 'brought the same combination of self-interest and diligence, discovering in the achievements of pressure group politics the means to his own advancement'.[12]

Continuity in technique, then, reinforced continuity of personnel. The anti-slavery movement elaborated the reforming machine which Wilberforce had inherited from Wyvill, and in the early 1830s took lessons (via George Stephen) from O'Connell's movement form Catholic emancipation. O'Connell's himself a prominent abolitionist, was also consulted by Thomas Attwood when founding his Birmingham Political Union in 1829; speakers at several radical meetings referred to O'Connell's movement about this time. Richard Cobden subscribed to O'Connell's National Rent, and John Morley thought the Catholic Association an important early influence on his Anti-Corn Law League. The sheer pace of nineteenth-century reform is reflected in the fact that reforming impetus was nourished by both reforming success and failure. Francis Place found the successful franchise campaign of 1831–2 'prospective of still greater importance as the first of an inevitable series, which from time to time will increase the power of the people and lessen that of the government'.[13] Yet the Act's failure to enfranchise working men also created the Chartists, who tried to embarrass the Whigs by referring to the arguments and methods they had themselves employed in 1831–2. Condemning the Whig pursuit of popularity at that time, Peel showed some prescience: 'these are vulgar arts of government', he said: 'others will outbid you, not now, but at no remote period – they will offer votes and power to a million of men, will quote your precedent for concession, and will carry your principles to their legitimate and natural consequences'.[14]

With the Anti-Corn Law League, as with other reforming movements, it was important for British history that so many of the activists remained in politics after their signal success. Sir Wilfrid Lawson in 1872 persuaded the United Kingdom Alliance executive to put up prohibitionist candidates in constituencies which lacked them with the aid of a resolution modelled almost verbatim on an

Anti-Corn Law League resolution of 1843; in 1906 he was still describing Cobden as 'the prince of agitators'. And when the *Women's Suffrage Journal* wanted its readers to petition parliament in 1878, it cited a similar League exhortation of 1841 with the comment that 'what was true then is true now'.[15] Cobden had always intended the League to wield an influence of this kind. 'We have been teaching the people of this country something more, I hope, than the repeal of the Corn-laws', he said in June 1845: he also said that the League was teaching the middle classes their moral power and the working classes the effectiveness of non-violent tactics. League methods even influenced the Scottish nationalists in the early 1850s, Cavour's 'National Society' after 1856, and Holland's Anti-School Law League after 1872.[16]

Even where objectives diverged, reforming techniques could readily be appropriated – by socialists of the 1880s repudiating the Liberal tradition, for example, or conversely by Edwardian reformers adapting socialist techniques to libertarian purposes. Mrs Pankhurst found in the Independent Labour Party of the 1890s all the opportunities for public speaking, self-advertisement, and defiance of the law which she later employed so brilliantly as a suffragette. Nor did her eldest daughter Christabel ignore in 1905 the government's quick response to street demonstrations by the unemployed: she later recalled resolving then that 'we must do something like that to get a Woman Suffrage Bill carried'.[17] The London processions of the militant Women's Social and Political Union were modelled on the labour movement's incursions from the East End – though Christabel mistakenly believed that it was the militancy rather than the actual or potential mass support which had moved the government to act in 1905, and she therefore moved forward to the stunt violence of middle-class conspiracy.

In their manipulative approach to the political parties, she and her mother also owed much to the example set by the Irish nationalists, and especially by Parnell. But their movement diverged from Parnell's in lacking the power to coerce the politicians through representatives in parliament, and in the fact that the suffragettes aimed at participating in the Westminster parliament whose role their tactics undermined. They failed to make the tactical and intellectual adjustment which this divergence demanded. Yet counter-productive effort on behalf of a cause which eventually succeeds does not inhibit later reformers from imitating technique. The success of a cause retrospectively justifies all that is done in its name; sufficient it is to have been on the right side. Suffragette tactics in retrospect therefore acquired a certain glamour – though British feminists wisely avoided them after 1914 – and influenced the Campaign for Nuclear Disarmament in the 1950s. The dynamic in reforming technique persists into the present day, many of whose movements for 'community action' originate with the Committee of One Hundred in the 1960s.

More important even than its provision of personnel and technique was the reforming tradition's provision of inspiration. This rested on a reshaping of the past which was inspirationally not less effective for being historically inaccurate. Like many people then and now, Victorian reformers saw history as a storage-cabinet stuffed with precise precedents and justifications for present action. This view gained credibility from the recurrence of similar situations and arguments within the reforming world. In 1917, for example, Earl Russell defended women's suffrage in the House of Lords with the same quotation from Shakespeare that Whitbread had used in defence of the slaves in 1792: 'if you prick us, do we not bleed? If you tickle us, do we not laugh?'[18] Prohibitionists in the 1860s prescribed moral boundaries to the freedom of trade with the same arguments that abolitionists had employed against Cobden and Bright in the 1840s; and in the 1880s their movement encountered all the complexities of the compensation issue which had beset the anti-slavery movement in 1833, though with a different outcome. A different kind of precedent inspired suffragists from the 1890s: here Britain was no longer setting the pace in reform, and British suffragists advertised Australia and New Zealand's revelation that women's suffrage was compatible with national security and social stability.

The precedents were often misleading. Cobden urged Molesworth in 1837 to use the anti-slavery movement's techniques in promoting the ballot, yet the movement failed to take off. In 1853, its organ claimed that the Anti-Corn Law League's success 'shewed how all popular questions were to be won', yet it was not popular pressure which eventually won the ballot in 1872, but considerations of high politics.[19] In its conviction that 'persistent pressure in a righteous cause, is certain to prevail', the United Kingdom Alliance looked back to the anti-slavery and anti-corn law movements, but in 1881 John Morley's biography of Cobden stressed (pertinently for prohibition, as it happened) that the Anti-Corn Law League's success occurred in special circumstances, and that organization could not of itself achieve political success.[20] The numerous failed popular agitations did not feature prominently in the reforming legend: the

Financial Reform Association, the Liberation Society, the Bulgarian atrocities agitation, or even Chartism. Indeed, the class harmony required by the reforming legend involved virtually suppressing the memory of Chartism, which, significantly, was revived only by late-Victorian socialists. The Bulgarian atrocities agitation in 1876, for example, described its forum for discussing the Eastern Question as a 'conference' rather than a 'convention', for fear of stirring up embarrassing recollections of 1839.[21]

Nor did reformers have the time, perspective, and inclination to recognize the limits to their predecessors' legislative impact. Even the apparent successes of the reforming legend – 1832 and 1846, for example – were far more equivocal in their effects than had at first been expected, as Cobden in later life was himself the first to acknowledge. A reform seen by radicals as a mere staging-post on the road to the new society might seem an enticing concession at the time, but too often it turned out to be the terminus. To take a lesser-known instance, the campaigners for abolishing capital punishment achieved, for all their pains, the mere concealment of executions behind prison walls – a concession which helped perpetuate the punishment itself for nearly a century. Furthermore, the reformers were psychologically too distant from the politician's profession to see how counter-productive their efforts often were: to recognize how their principled stance endangered Stanley's compromise measure of 1833 and helped to wreck H. A. Bruce's attempts at comprehensive temperance reform in 1871. Nor is it yet always recognized how damagingly diversionary was militant suffragism between 1911 and 1914. Whereas the political unions and labour leaders in 1831–2 and 1866–7 did their best to restrain mass violence, suffragette leaders chose actually to foment it in the belief that this was the route to success; nor did Christabel Pankhurst perceive that Irish nationalist violence merely complicated Gladstone's Irish course in 1869–70 (planned before the violence began),[22] and actually frustrated his subsequent efforts for Home Rule.

In reality, the history which matters to the reformer is not what actually happens but what he makes up for himself; the engine of reform is fuelled by beliefs about the past, not by the true sequence of events. The succession of apparently victorious crusades was therefore woven into a romantic banner which reformers could hold aloft. 'I believe that Mr Wilberforce and his friends sustained nearly forty defeats in the House of Commons', a suffragist leader declared in 1876, 'and yet they ultimately succeeded'. Josephine Butler's abolitionist family connexions ensured that it was a history of the anti-slavery campaign that was read out to her for inspiration during her depth of depression in 1875. The reformer might be despised and rejected in his own time, but he could reinforce his courage by summoning up allies from the past and envisaging them in the future. 'Do we not owe the Magna Carta to faddists?' asked Mr Saunders, a beleaguered New Zealand feminist in 1891. 'Do we not owe the abolition of slavery to the faddists Clarkson and Wilberforce? Do we not owe the abolition of Catholic disabilities to the faddist O'Connell.'[23]

Liberty was the inspiring rallying-cry of these movements – though it is difficult now fully to grasp its magic for the Victorians, so long it is since it retreated from its central position in the outlook of the left to become the watchword of conservatism. Insofar as the reformers were defending unpopular opinions, their movements promoted liberty directly – whether in press, public meeting, petition or procession. Nothing puckered the nineteenth-century Liberal brow more quickly than instances of individual injustice. 'The contemplation of cruelty in any form was intolerable to him', wrote Josephine Butler of her father, John Grey of Dilston: 'he would speak of the imposition of social disabilities of any kind, by one class of persons on another, with kindling eyes and breath which came quickly'. It is not surprising that his daughter's movement (motivated, like other movements, partly by propagandist considerations) took up cases of individual oppression. Her crusade gave birth to the Vigilance Association for the Defence of Personal Rights and capitalized on Mrs Percy's case after 1875. Anti-Corn Law Leaguers upheld freedom of speech against obscurantist rural mobs in the 1840s; socialist orators upheld it against narrow-minded municipal regulation in the 1880s, and pacifists circumscribed state power during the First World War with a courage which often rivalled that of the trenches. The defence of liberty lies, as Lord Stow Hill recently argued, 'with the protestors against almost everything: the firm-voiced male and female in Trafalgar Square, in the Albert Hall, in Hyde Park . . . it resides in the Nonconformist conscience . . . it resides in the long-haired student, in the lunatic fringe in all Parties, and in all avenues of thought'.[24]

Owing so much to Protestant traditions and rationalist argument, the reformers reared up against the encrusted privilege and superstition associated with aristocracy and Anglicanism all the historical resonances of the liberal ideal. These movements derived continuity from the fact that all were wielding against privilege the courage of the enterprizing, independent-minded citizen, tempered as it had been by a long sequence of contests with an ignorant and over-weening authority. Wat Tyler, Hampden, and Magna Carta often featured in Josephine Butler's oratory, and in October 1908 Christabel Pankhurst at Bow Street magistrates' court announced that 'Magna Charta had been practically torn up by the present government'. Nor was this liberal ideal confined to Great Britain: before the Civil War, American reformers likewise saw the citizen's moral self-development as an effective substitute for discredited and coercive government. On both sides of the Atlantic an energetic voluntarism was the result. Negro slavery had been ended, said J. S. Mill, 'not by any change in the distribution of material interests, but by the spread of moral convictions.' He concluded that 'one person with a belief is a social power equal to ninety-nine who have only interests'; individual willpower could change the course of the world.[25] Marx's British critics in the 1880s believed that there was a direct relationship between individual freedom and British prosperity,[26] and as late as the 1950s the British left was invigorated by a Campaign for Nuclear Disarmament which rejected the idea that men are mere victims of large organizations in favour of the belief that men can both understand the world and change it.[27]

III

The reforming tradition was buttressed by institutions associated with social class, religious grouping, and personal relationship. The genealogy of reform is but one dimension of that making of the English middle class which is the neglected but major theme of nineteenth-century political and economic history; yet the reformers did not see themselves as narrowly representating mere class interest. For them, the middle class was the nucleus, the germ, of the new society. Theirs was a philosophy of the expanding middle, theirs was a battle of the industrious against the idle, of assertive Northern manufacturer against effete Southern aristocrat. Although they often welcomed aristocratic support, reforming leaders aimed to join with working men in a combined assault on aristocratic values. Aristocrats might sometimes preside over these reforming organizations, but it was the middle-class secretary who did the work. 'I have faith in the middle classes', Cobden told parliament in 1843, 'backed by the more intelligent of the working classes, and led by the more honest section of the aristocracy'.[28]

Middle-class status would be enhanced if it provided moral

leadership for society as a whole, and if its anti-slavery and temperance movements successfully distanced 'trade' from a disreputable 'traffick'. Middle-class reformers took pride in the historical role of their class, which they regarded as the source of humane innovation. Humanitarians saw slavery as incompatible with enterprise and invention, and welcomed electricity, the railway, and other inventions as the salvation of the animals.[29] Medieval cruelty and obscurantism were being shaken off, and history was on the side of liberty and humanity. In 1824 one of the animals' earliest champions, Lewis Gompertz, looked forward to the day 'when for almost every vice and every disease there shall be known a remedy; and when almost every evil will find, in some discovery, a cure'.[30] Middle-class self-assertion against aristocratic values was an important strand in Josephine Butler's outlook, and also in a family central to British feminist history, the Garretts; as for Lydia Becker, her espousal of the restricted property franchise for women faithfully reflected her desire to give middle-class women the freedom which she felt aristocratic and working-class women already enjoyed.

The feminist instance illustrates the drawbacks involved in so clear a class identification. The late-Victorian labour movement was moving towards two reforms which directly conflicted with early twentieth-century British feminism: factory regulation specific to women, and adult suffrage. Edwardian England therefore saw British feminists clashing with the more democratic feminist strategies acceptable to the Labour Party and its Liberal allies. Similar class fragmentation among reformers can be seen in the gulf between the political unions and the National Union of the Working Classes in 1831–2; between the teetotaler of the 1830s and the more respectable opponent of spirit-drinking; between the working-class secularist of the 1880s and the more cultivated agnostic; and between the National Sunday League in the same decade, challenging the sabbatarians through the popular excursion, and the Sunday Society's relatively demure espousal of the art gallery and the museum. Chartists interrupted sabbatarian, anti-slavery, and Anti-Corn Law League meetings, and Karl Marx in the 1860s took a delight in exposing the hypocrisy of a Duchess of Sutherland who could espouse abolitionism at the same time as expropriating her own tenants.[31] No doubt many other class-based reforming disputes could be unearthed if more of the reforming movement's private documentation had survived. In 1875, for example, a vigorous dispute went on behind the scenes in Josephine Butler's movement; H. J. Wilson, director of the Sheffield Smelting Company, disliked the idea of any distinct working-class campaign, with paid officials, against state-regulated prostitution.

Yet what was the outcome? Josephine Butler told him that she 'was only too thankful to see the working men thus moving without being *pushed* by people above them'; she delighted in her movement's reliance on those respectable working men, 'men of the most weight and zeal in their towns' who (in her own words) could 'gather round them all the decent men in the place' because they were 'men of character'.[32] Libertarian ideas were widespread among nineteenth-century working men, who conflicted with the anti-slavery movement only when its conduct seemed hypocritical, and never rejected its basic philosophy. The 1906 general election witnessed sandwichmen dressed like Chinese walking about in chained procession very much as Brougham's Yorkshire election of 1830 had seen blackened and chained people being led about 'in order to rouse the feelings of the people'.[33] Here was testimony to the long-standing vitality of a popular libertarianism which even in 1906 could still draw Liberals and labour together, and which was shortly to issue forth in the 'positive' liberalism of the Asquith governments' welfare reforms.

There was often an element of stage-management behind this alleged working-class following; the suffragette leader Annie Kenney referred to the 'poor oppressed, unawakened East-Enders – every reformer using them for his own ends, and we were doing just the same!'[34] If aristocratic government was to be overthrown, it was important for middle-class reformers to demonstrate that their intellect and organization were backed by numbers. Yet the Cobdens and the Pankhursts engineered working-class support less as a political ruse than from the conviction that the forward-looking working man or woman could hardly fail to support their cause; it seemed a pardonable anticipation of the future. Nor do subsequent trends in British history entirely belie the prediction.

The forces of reform were consolidated by a second set of institutions, the nonconformist churches, with frequent assistance from Liberals and evangelicals in the established church. 'Henceforth we will grapple with the religious feelings of the people', Cobden told Villiers in 1841. 'Their veneration for God shall be our leverage to upset their reverence for the aristocracy'.[35] Nonconformists (especially Quakers) who had already forsaken so much for their faith had little to lose by sacrificing more. Evangelicalism yoked them together with Anglicans into May meetings and religious gatherings which were objects of national pride; their direct influence, and the influence of the techniques they developed, affected the whole mood and climate of nineteenth-century reform, even in its more secular dimension. Hence the reformer's preference for the moral over the utilitarian argument; his preoccupation with the impact of his cause on religious allegiance; his claim to be collaborating with the divine plan. 'Vice and immorality never produced prosperity and happiness', said Wilberforce in 1799: 'misery was invariably the attendant on guilt'.[36]

The broadening-out of nineteenth-century citizenship owed much to the evangelical emphasis on the divinity latent in every human being. Wilberforce in 1789 tried to get politicians to imagine themselves into the mind of the transported slave; M. T. Sadler in the 1830s struggled to make M.P.s realize what it felt like to be a factory child; Shaftesbury in the 1840s emphasized the human qualities even of the lunatic; and Josephine Butler in 1871 defended the prostitute with the claim that 'the image of God may be marred, but it never is wholly blotted out'.[37] The enthusiasm behind these reforming crusades owed much to their symbolic character; their aims transcended the immediate improvements under discussion, and to their supporters they seemed but a phase in the moral evolution of mankind, as well as a welcome opportunity to declare one's personal values and distinguish the sheep from the goats. But it owed even more to the supremacy of conscience which evangelicalism encouraged. Here was an engine which could generate in the reformer prodigies of personal effort and a superb indifference to unpopularity, hostility, and even violence. It was conscience which lent the Victorian reforming cause so much of its expansive power, and enabled it to develop a humanitarian entrepreneurship at least as adventurous as anything witnessed in contemporary commerce.

Reform was also reinforced by family connexion. This may at first sight seem surprising, for nineteenth-century reform owed much to the rebellious child: Florence Nightingale, for instance, bitterly complained about 'the petty grinding tyranny of a good English family'.[38] The very commitment to reform often involves ructions within the family, whereas conservatives relish Edmund Burke's reminder of the intimate link between private and public loyalties. Nor would one expect family connexion to be prominent among reformers crusading for an opportunity society in which merit alone should receive rewards. Nonetheless, nineteenth-century reforms owe at least as much to the child's conformity to parental dissidence as to his dissidence from parental conformity. Nor is this surprising in a century when loyalty to parents was reinforced by custom, by religious duty, by economic interest, and the laws of inheritance; or in a century when denominational loyalty and liberal ideals inoculated the non-conforming of all generations against the fear of appearing eccentric. Even today, political scientists emphasize parental influence over the party politics of the child.[39]

Nonconformist separateness encouraged intermarriage. The Quakers epitomize this reinforcement of public agitation with private affection: Croppers, Sturges, Peases, Backhouses, Gurneys, and Brights reappear in movement after movement, and were all related. Indeed, nonconformist M.P.s were almost as firmly consolidated by family connexion as the Anglicans and aristocrats they opposed.[40] The Unitarian Rathbones of Liverpool illustrate the impact reforming loyalties could make on a nineteenth-century family; 'given a knowledge of the conflicts which at various points have agitated Liverpool', writes Mary Stocks, 'one can deduce with accurate precision what the contemporary William Rathbone will be doing: opposing the slave trade, promoting municipal reform, advocating free trade, constructing a health service, abolishing the Poor Law, founding a university'. Nor were twentieth-century Labour M.P.s any less indebted to family traditions of public service. Twenty-six of the thirty-five cabinet ministers in the first four Labour cabinets on whom information is available came from families with such traditions; fifteen of these were drawn from social levels below the upper middle class, where public life opened up through the posts of poor law guardian, parish councillor, Sunday school superintendent, and local preacher.[41]

So unquestioned were family political traditions that the surviving documents shed little light upon them, yet their importance can be illustrated even from within a relatively secular cause like women's suffrage. The centrality of the Garrett family to the early history of non-militant British feminism has already been stressed; the anti-suffragist John Bright was hemmed in at many points by feminist relatives; and Josephine Butler drew inspiration from her father, and support from her husband, her sons, and her five sisters. And however much militant suffragism might tear children apart from their parents, even within the Pankhurst family, it too owed much to family traditions of reform. Mrs Pankhurst's paternal grandfather Robert Goulden had been present at Peterloo in 1819 when the magistrates charged the crowd, and the Gouldens' anti-slavery outlook deeply influenced her childhood. *Uncle Tom's Cabin* was 'so great a favourite with my mother', she recalled, 'that

she used it continually as a source of bedtime stories for our fascinated ears'.[42] Robert Goulden, her father, participated in the
Anti-Corn Law League and supported the North in the American
Civil War. Her husband, Dr Richard Pankhurst, included feminism
among his many reforming loyalties, and profoundly influenced his
youngest daughter Sylvia with his dictum that 'life is nothing without enthusiasm'; his election manifesto of 1895 hung on the wall in
the room in Ethiopia where she died in 1960.[43] Family loyalties also
consolidated the suffragette rank-and-file: 'the truth is that it was
almost the done thing in our family to go to prison', Lady Rhondda
recalled.[44]

Yet these reforming relationships were no match for the British
aristocratic family connexion: as reformers repeatedly complained,
this transcended the political party and was consolidated by a whole
set of social institutions – the country house party, the public school
and university, the county ball, the London season, the Inns of
Court, the hunting connexion, Pall Mall, and Newmarket. The
American observer A. L. Lowell found English 'society' in 1908 'a
national institution . . . not a collection of separate groups in different places, but a single body with ramifications all over the country'.
Unlike other classes 'which are local', he added, 'society is universal'. Only through the most strenuous organization – through May
Meetings, Friends' Yearly Meetings, processions, petitioning
campaigns and electoral crusades – could the reformers even
begin to contest this continuous aristocratic family power. Six
years after 1832, Thomas Arnold acknowledged that family
connexion was the great strength of British aristocracy: 'it acts
through the relations of private life, which are permanent', he
said 'whereas the political excitement, which opposes it, must
always be short-lived'.[45]

Furthermore, conservatives were on the alert, and (at least in
private) uncompromising in their contempt for radical methods.
They knew all about the 'vertical' and 'horizontal' linkages between
radical movements, and depreciated them with the phrase 'stage
army' or (to use more modern equivalents) 'rentacrowd',
'rentamob' or 'do-gooders'. The mounting influences of press and
publicity soon made it impossible for them to brand reforming
crusades as illegal, but they could still pronounce them factitious
and claim that a cause must be very weak indeed if it needs agitation
as extensive as that of the anti-slavery, anti-corn law, or women's
suffrage movements. They could also attribute motive, and make
sarcastic references to paid agitators moving on from one cause to

the next. 'The business of this profession is to discover or invent great questions', Disraeli told parliament in 1848: 'when a great question is settled, it is the ruin of the profession'.[46]

Ruin was indeed often staved off by re-introducing one's organization onto the reforming stage in a new guise – as an African Institution, freehold land movement, National Liberal Federation, or Committee of One Hundred. But the worldly-wise Disraelian analysis ignored the prominence among reformers of voluntary effort, self-sacrifice, and even martyrdom. Undeterred, the conservative then alighted upon the radical's youthful inexperience or psychological instability, for did not C. E. M. Joad's autobiography portray a young man who 'whenever some social disturbance occurred . . . hailed it joyfully as a portent of the coming revolution'? More recently, Bernard Levin has ridiculed the nuclear disarmer Peggy Duff for spending a lifetime 'marching to nowhere' from one impossible movement to another.[47] To their admirers such people seemed selfless idealists, deliberately forsaking power and profit for the benefit of mankind: but to their conservative critics they seemed restless, tiresome, disgruntled and even unstable people, incapable of living with human imperfection and huddling together in recherché sects of the like-minded. 'A party whose mission it is to live entirely upon the discovery of grievances', said Lord Salisbury of radicals in the 1880s, 'are apt to manufacture the element upon which they subsist'.[48]

Yet an attitude of sardonic detachment was hardly feasible for the Conservative Party as a whole when faced by an unmuzzled Gladstone. Lord Randolph Churchill in the 1880s may have been mistaken in thinking that the Conservative Party could become a vehicle for Liberal policies, but he rightly saw that his Party needed to be more energetic in moulding opinion. In this he was assisted by the Liberals recruited to his party after the 1860s, and especially after 1886. Appropriating Liberal propagandist techniques for conservative purposes, the Unionists from 1886 rivalled the Gladstonian Liberals as the party of propaganda. Their new approach owed much to the radical most expert of all in moulding opinion, Joseph Chamberlain. He was temporarily to carry his skills out of the Party again in 1903, when his campaign for tariff reform plundered the strategies of an Anti-Corn Law League whose legend he was subverting. 'At present my work is in the towns', he told Lady St Helier in October 1903, 'as Cobden's was in the first instance – but the agriculturists of all classes must have their turn'. During the 1920s the Conservative Party at last fully reconciled itself to becoming a party of propaganda; in a democratic age, it could hardly afford to act in any other way.[49]

IV

This Conservative manipulation of opinion, yoked to the tenacity of British aristocracy, made it all the more necessary to create a political machine which could resolve the reformers' differences and marshal the electorate behind progressive causes. The Whig/Liberal Party lay to hand for this purpose, but the difficulty lay in wresting it from aristocratic control; until 1886 the aristocracy was never out of power, whichever political party held the reins. Partly for this reason, the reformer's first loyalty lay to his cause, and only precariously was he loyal to the party of the left. Even after 1886, reformers' comments on the Liberal and Labour Party leadership have often been scathing, and their pose frequently non-party. From T. F. Buxton in the 1830s through Richard Cobden and Sir Wilfrid Lawson to the nuclear disarmers of the 1950s, reformers' attacks on the compromising and political outlook of left-wing party leadership were frequent. For Lawson during the 1884 franchise reform debates it was not even important to maintain his party in power: urging woman suffragist M.P.s to ignore Gladstone's threats, he pointed out that a government defeat on the issue would be 'like a resurrection from the dead . . . all of us Radicals would rise once again into life and liberty . . . we should be Liberals once more, instead of poor dummies sitting and voting here as we are bid'.[50]

Nor was the reformer's non-party standpoint a mere pose, for one of his strengths lay in the fact that he could usually draw into political activity important groupings hitherto indifferent or otherwise engaged. As for his support among the politically active, this did not always come exclusively from radicals: the philanthropic or opportunistic Tory was a familiar figure in the nineteenth-century reforming world, and a minority of Conservatives can be found among the prohibitionists of the 1850s, the feminists of the 1860s, or the campaigners against Bulgarian atrocities in 1876. The genealogy of Victorian reform was never a pedigree; in the raggedness of its edges lay one of its major contributions to Liberal growth, for it could thereby bring new recruits to the Party. The Bulgarian atrocities agitation also illustrates the fact that it was not always the evangelical Conservative who could be thus seduced: evangelicals (except for Shaftesbury) were noticeably absent from that agitation whose Conservatives came largely from the ritualist wing of the established church.[51]

Still, an unreconstructed Toryism and a sceptical Whiggery remained the radical's major enemies, and his weapons against them were publicity and popular organization. 'The outdoor men have always scattered the Tories and always will', said Joseph Parkes in 1841;[52] but organizations like the Anti-Corn Law League and the Birmingham Political Union had the additional attraction of throwing the Whigs onto the defensive within the party of progress. The mobilizing of opinion was an instrument whose mood was at first largely defensive, if only because the enemy was so experienced and so well organized. Anti-slavery leaders stirred up public opinion in their efforts at counter-mining Castlereagh's secret diplomacy and the West India interest's machinations. Franchise reformers during the prolonged crisis of 1831–2 had difficulty in keeping their agitation up to the mark, and even the Anti-Corn Law League's apparent triumph in 1846 produced no permanent and co-ordinated middle-class radical machine which could shake Palmerston's supremacy.

There was a further difficulty: the ferment of competing causes simmering on the radical wing of the Liberal Party threatened always to prosper the Tory tactic of divide and rule. The Party was riddled with men like the Sheffield Liberal H. J. Wilson, who felt uncomfortable at religious services because always tempted to move amendments to the sermon. Liberal Party history repeatedly called in question Cobden's belief that 'all good things pull together', and that 'one good, sound, and just principle never can be at war with another of a similar character'.[53] Strategies for improving the human condition cannot easily be placed in rank order and mutually harmonized within a single scale, though the party of progress gains considerable impetus from the reformers' belief that they can.

Liberals found the clash between libertarians and humanitarians particularly embarrassing; only the relative subordination of social and moral reform as a party political issue limited the damage done by the animal cruelty, factory hours, temperance, and public health reformers – eager as they were for state intervention at the local or national level. Humanitarians often clashed with free traders: when the anti-slavery movement relied on the Royal Navy for help in the 1840s, for instance, or when the temperance movement developed a prohibitionist wing after 1853. Bizarre political alliances sometimes resulted from these incidents, with West Indian planters and

anti-slavery M.P.s joining forces in the 1840s, publicans and prohibitionists uniting in the 1860s. Feminists from the 1870s continuously resisted factory legislation specific to women, and major
difficulties were caused to the temperance and feminist movements
by the prominence of disestablishment and Home Rule as political
issues. The mid-Victorian campaign for 'free trade in religion'
threatened to disrupt the temperance movement's alliance between
Liberal Anglicans and dissenters. As for Home Rule, it threw both
temperance and disestablishment into the shade after 1886 and
(together with the Liberal government's alliance with organized
labour) forced the Liberal governments of 1910–15 into a memorable conflict with the advocates of that decidedly liberal cause,
women's suffrage.

With unimaginative party leadership, these reforming disputes
could have been really damaging. Yet the separateness of
nineteenth-century reforming causes should not be exaggerated.
Purely tactical considerations often led reformers to give a misleading impression of sectarian single-mindedness: they wished to consolidate their following and frustrate the familiar conservative
strategy of establishing guilt by association. Anti-slavery had been
damaged, for instance, by its French Revolutionary sympathies;
anti-sabbatarians in the National Sunday League by their secularism; woman suffrage by its links with Josephine Butler. Suffragists
therefore played down their sympathy with the attack on state-
regulated prostitution and Cobden distanced his League from the
movements for teetotalism, peace, and complete suffrage; yet there
were close links between all these causes. Even the promotion of
non-party candidates at elections to advance a reforming cause was
usually only a form of bluff, with the aim of forcing the Liberal
leadership into line. It was in fact one of the strengths of the
nineteenth-century Liberal Party (as of its successor, the Labour
Party) that open discussion was encouraged about ways of improving society. There is an exhilaration about 'the absolute and essential importance of human development in its richest diversity' when
J. S. Mill discusses it in *Liberty*; and his *Representative Government*
sees 'the antagonism of influences' as 'the only real security for
continued progress'. As Gladstone pointed out, 'it is in the nature of
Liberalism to be subject to diversities'.[54]

Furthermore, the Russells, the Gladstones, and the Asquiths
found much common ground among reformers to build upon.
Humanitarianism pervades the movements to promote education,
anti-slavery, temperance, free trade, pacifism, penal reform, and

feminism – with women as beneficiaries of all these causes. 'Our battle is against wife-beating, and other violent crime', said Professor F. W. Newman in a prohibitionist speech of 1865, voicing a theme often recurring in feminist and temperance apologetics. Central to the feminist case was rejection of the idea that political power should rest on physical force: 'war was the result of the dominance of the male half of humanity', said Mrs Pethick-Lawrence in 1915, justifying the holding of a special wartime women's conference at The Hague. Like the Anti-Corn Law League, the feminists attacked a monopoly which seemed to foment war. They were themselves aware of the parallel; for them, as for Richard Cobden in 1842, their own reform and the peace movement were 'one and the same cause'.[55]

The cultivation of human rationality was another common strand. Anti-slavery and peace could clear the territory which temperance, political participation, and education could cultivate. Henry Vincent the former Chartist leader told a Quaker audience in Sheffield in 1846 that 'he always looked on a soldier with horror and pity. He saw, not the living intelligent immortal member of society, but a huge mass of mechanical automata'. Cobden in 1854 saw standing armies as converting men into machines, and Wilfrid Lawson thought it 'almost as difficult for a soldier to be a Liberal as it is for a rich man to enter the Kingdom of Heaven'.[56] Rationality suffered by any situation of enforced supremacy, whether of male over female, manufacturer over consumer, Anglican over nonconformist, landlord over tenant, imperial nation over colonial population, and ultimately state over individual citizen. Moral growth was stifled by denying freedom of choice to the subordinate group and by protecting its superiors from the invigorating influence of criticism and challenge. Education and political participation would cultivate the mind; temperance, the free press, and the ballot would ensure its balanced growth.

Only through liberty could reason be cultivated. Its most urgent claims came from rural English and colonial overseas populations: the Anti-Corn Law League saw itself as promoting freedom in both areas simultaneously, and some Leaguers moved naturally on after 1846 to agitation for land reform. Through peace, religious liberty, political participation, franchise extension, local self-government, free exchange in land and the consequent wider distribution of property and growth in self-reliance, the rural tyranny of squire and parson could be subverted and the arrogant proconsul and meddling diplomat cast down from their seats. Likewise feminists argued that human talent and energies should be free to rise to their own level. Women should have the vote, said Cobden in 1845, because 'they would often make a much better use of it than their husbands';[57] the cause was vigorously championed later by his three daughters.

Women's participation helped co-ordinate all these reforming causes. Opponents of slavery and the Corn Laws had to face complaints that they were encouraging women into public affairs; women's prominence in combating state-regulated prostitution aroused widespread disgust even in the 1870s; and women's prominence in the RSPCA was noted from the earliest days: 470 of the Society's 739 nineteenth-century legacies came from women, and its whole emphasis was switched from prosecution to education by the Ladies' Committee which it formed in 1870. As for vivisection, women were so prominent in opposing it that their efforts should almost be seen as a branch of the feminist movement itself.[58] The Victorian reforming movement was a major forcing-ground for British feminism. Only after the 1860s did a divergence open up within the ranks of reform between anti-suffragists who argued that philanthropy was woman's special role and suffragists who claimed that philanthropy could never be effective unless backed up by direct political influence. Furthermore, women's suffrage, like other forms of franchise extension, often became 'the residual beneficiary of . . . pressure group activity' – the instrument eagerly grasped by reformers anxious to prosper their flagging causes: moral reform, peace, social welfare, temperance. 'Mankind had been running the world for some four thousand years', Sir Wilfrid Lawson declared in 1897, 'and had made an awful mess of it; could women make it worse with hundred-million Budgets, massacres, famine, riots, and frightful war expenditure all over the world? Would they bring in the drink traffic. . . .?'[59]

Given these affinities between Liberal reformers, pressures for co-ordination inevitably arose, even from below. As early as 1847, William Lovett's proposed 'general Association of Progress' aimed at drawing franchise reformers, free traders, religious libertarians, taxation reformers, and temperance enthusiasts together,[60] and more than one scheme for alliances of this type flourished during that dangerous year, 1848. During the 1870s John Bright's dictum that 'you cannot get six or twelve omnibuses abreast through Temple Bar' was often quoted, and in 1873 Joseph Chamberlain publicly advocated an integrated Liberal programme.[61] The 1874 general election saw dissident Liberal temperance and education reformers helping to produce a Tory victory, and Chamberlain moved forward from his narrower preoccupation with the National Education League to creating the National Liberal Federation in 1877. All these developments held out the promise that, as Francis Place had observed in 1833, 'public opinion . . . will continue to grow with increasing rapidity, and will become more and more potent';[62] but they also threatened, and were intended to threaten, the Liberal Party's Whig leadership.

In 1883 Joseph Cowen drew a distinction between the reformer and the statesman: the reformer, he said, 'labours for the future. His ruling passion is duty. He is not perplexed with the corroding calculations of interest or popularity. The statesman is necessarily a trimmer and a temporiser. He labours for the present'.[63] For success in a two-party system it is essential to weld together these two types of personality – for the reformer's energy, enthusiasm, ideas, and idealism are well worth harnessing. Even without encouragement from the Labour leadership, C.N.D. in the 1950s brought new recruits to the Labour Party. 'Protest against the Bomb', writes Parkin, 'was, for many, their first major political experience, and one which thrust them dramatically into the midst of the ideas and personnel of the radical left'.[64] It was because Liberal leaders so successfully carried out this difficult task of integration that the British Liberal Party's reforming achievement was so prolonged and so distinguished.

In this situation, the Liberal leadership had one major asset: the reformers had politically nowhere else to go; Joseph Chamberlain's approach to an alliance with Conservatism after 1886 was always an unlikely outcome. If the reformers could sometimes draw upon Conservative support, so – for their very different purpose – could Liberal leaders. The 1830s were not the only decade when Conservatives enabled the centrist sections of the reforming party to secure reform without revolution. The cards were placed up Gladstone's sleeve not only by the Almighty but also by Conservatives anxious to concede a 'reasonable' settlement which would stave off greater dangers (in 1869 and 1884–5, for instance, though not, to Gladstone's disappointment, in 1885–6). The zealots might bring numbers, ideas and enthusiasm into the transaction, but the Russells, the Gladstones, and the Asquiths could bring a measure of Conservative acquiescence by influencing centrist elements of the Conservative Party and by cajoling nervous or conscience-stricken peers and pliant bishops in the House of Lords. Liberal leaders had three further weapons: a skill in gauging shifts in public opinion; a weather eye, ever open for the pressure group leader with whom business could be done; and an administrative flair, which pushed through legislation incorporating enough of the reformer's demands to undermine his independent standing. Increasingly after 1832, statesmanship on the left – and even to some extent on the right – consisted of 'measuring the force and direction of the popular gale'[65] and in scaling down and imposing a rank-order on its various demands.

To these skills Gladstone added at least one more: the capacity himself to take reforming initiatives – to go out into the country and mould the public opinion to which parliament must respond. However unsuccessful the Bulgarian atrocities agitation might be in its formal objectives, its impact on the integration and drive of the Liberal Party was immense; its historian has noted that while Gladstone was slow to interest himself in the substantive question, he was quick to grasp the political potential of such spontaneous provincial and popular moral indignation. Ten years later, Gladstone applied the lesson by mounting a popular crusade of his own which tamed the Irish nationalist movement by firmly tying it to the Liberal Party machine. In outlining the plight of the Labour Party, Christabel Pankhurst in 1913 likened official Liberalism to a serpent 'which holds reform movements spellbound until it has swallowed them up'. It was 'always quick to notice any new and hopeful movement for reform, and, as it were, to suck from it its strength and add that strength to its own'. But the Liberal Party was by no means the sole beneficiary from this process; her own cause would have escaped deadlock if only she had felt inclined to adapt its programme in such a way as to enable Liberals to digest it.[66]

As political participation widened, then, in the Late Victorian period, and as the press and public meeting forced politicians to operate more publicly, pressure group and political party moved closer together. Christabel Pankhurst complained with some justice from the dock in 1908 (when prosecuted for trying to rush the House of Commons) that Lloyd George and John Burns had committed similar acts at earlier stages in their careers and she pertly added that Lloyd George's 'whole career has been a series of revolt[s]'. The phrase was at least as apposite twenty years later, when an ageing Lloyd George saw his campaign for land reform as but the latest in the long line of Liberal crusades from the Anti-Corn Law League through the Liberation Society to local option.[67]

Yet just as the Victorian pressure group leaders had required a myth or reforming tradition to boost their self-confidence, so the newly-democratized Liberal Party machine generated its own inspiration from the past. The great campaigns for reform culminating in 1829, 1832, 1833, 1846, 1867, 1872, and 1884 were therefore made to seem mere episodes in the Liberal Party's heroic and inevitable progress towards the present – rather than as the unco-ordinated and often embarrassing reproaches to the Whig/Liberal leadership which they had often been at the time. Nor was this the end of myth-making on the left, for the inspirational needs of the Labour Party subsequently discouraged recognition of its profound debt to Liberal ideas, attitudes, and traditions of agitation. Those needs also concealed the fact that only the greatest catastrophe in modern European history could arrest the Liberal Party's gradual digestion of the last in the long line of sympathetic but fractious groupings on its left – the British labour movement. Unlike so many earlier splits among reformers, the schism which resulted was to inflict a lasting impoverishment on the British left.

Notes

1 R. Anstey, *The Atlantic Slave Trade and British Abolition 1760–1810*, Macmillan (1975), p. 412. I gratefully acknowledge here the very helpful comments of Dr Christine Bolt and Professor Donald Read on an earlier draft of this article; they should not be blamed for any misuse I have made of their advice. In the notes which follow, quotations are noted in order of their appearance in the text.

2 See my 'Moral reform and state intervention in nineteenth-century England', in P. Hollis (ed.), *Pressure from Without in Early Victorian England* (1974), pp. 289ff.

3 J. Morley, *The Life of Richard Cobden* (11th edn., 1903), p. 695; E. Hodder, *Life and Work of the Seventh Earl of Shaftesbury* (1886), II, p. 115.

4 Josephine Butler, *Catharine of Siena. A Biography* (1879), p. 237; *Personal Reminiscences of a Great Crusade* (1896), p. 83, cf. Miss Tod in *The Shield*, Nov. 1874, p. 218.

5 Hansard's *Parliamentary Debates, Third Series*, Vol. 73, c. 1215 (18 Mar. 1844), [henceforth cited as *H.C.Deb.* 18 Mar. 1844, c. 1215].

6 Mrs Stowe, quoted in F. J. Klingberg, 'Harriet Beecher Stowe and social reform in England', *American Historical Review*, 43, No. 3 (Apr. 1938), p. 551; see also C. Taylor, 'Some American reformers and their influence on reform movements in Great Britain from 1830 to 1860' (unpublished Ph.D. thesis, Edinburgh, 1960), p. 19.

7 Wilberforce, *H.C.Deb.* 23 Feb. 1807, c. 994; *Anti-Slavery Monthly Reporter*, III, pp. 248, 255; *The Common Cause*, 14 Dec. 1911, p. 625.

8 Ewart in RSPCA *19th Annual Report, 1845*, p. 19, cf. G. S. Evans, in RSPCA *23rd Annual Report, 1849*, p. 18; Josephine Butler in *Parl*[iamentary] *Papers* 1882 (340), IX, Q. 5432.

9 Cf. George M. Fredrickson, *The Inner Civil War: Northern Intellectuals and the Crisis of the Union* (New York, 1965), pp. 192–5. I am most grateful to Professor Eric Foner for generous bibliographical guidance on American abolitionism.

10 *Alliance News*, 14 Oct. 1871, p. 661.

11 *Women's Suffrage Journal*, 14 Feb. 1880, p. 39.

12 F. M. Leventhal, *Respectable Radical. George Howell and Victorian Working Class Politics* (1971), p. 217; for Acland, see Hollis, *Pressure from Without*, pp. 13–14.

13 D. J. Rowe, *London Radicalism. 1830–43. A Selection from the Papers of Francis Place* (1970), p. 95.

14 Norman Gash, *Sir Robert Peel. The Life of Sir Robert Peel after 1830* (1972), p. 12, cf. p. 38.

15 Lawson quoted in J. H. Fowler, (ed.), *The Life and Letters of Edward Lee Hicks (Bishop of Lincoln 1910–19)* (1922), p. 197; for the 1872 incident, see A. E. Dingle, 'The agitation for prohibition in England. A study of the political activity and influence of the United Kingdom Alliance, 1871–95' (unpublished Ph.D. thesis, Monash, 1974), p. 117; *Women's Suffrage Journal*, 1 Jan. 1878, p. 8.

16 Richard Cobden, *Speeches on Questions of Public Policy*, J. Bright, and J. E. T. Rogers (eds.) (1870), I, p. 305. See also William Ferguson, *Scotland 1689 to the Present* (New York, 1968), p. 320; G. M. Trevelyan, *The Life of John Bright* (1925), p. 91.

17 Christabel Pankhurst, *Unshackled. The Story of how we won the Vote* (1959), pp. 48, 66.

18 *H.L.Deb.* 17 Dec. 1917, c. 216; *H.C.Deb.* 2 Apr. 1792, c. 1104.

19 Bruce L. Kinzer, 'The failure of "pressure from without": Richard Cobden, the Ballot Society, and the coming of the Ballot Act in England', *Canadian Journal of History*, XIII, 3 (Dec. 1978), pp. 401, 410.

20 Quoted from United Kingdom Alliance, *23rd Report of the Executive Committee . . . 1874–5*, p. 68; see also Morley, *Cobden*, p. 405.

21 R. T. Shannon, *Gladstone and the Bulgarian Agitation 1876* (1963), pp. 141, 252.

22 J. R. Vincent, 'Gladstone and Ireland', *Proceedings of the British Academy*, 63 (1977), p. 201; cf. Christabel Pankhurst, *The Militant Methods of the NWSPU* (2nd. edn., 1908), p. 15.

23 Quotations from Forsyth, in *Women's Suffrage Journal*, 1 June 1876, p. 85; Saunders, *New Zealand, Parliamentary Debates*, 24 Aug. 1891, p. 522.

24 Josephine Butler, *Memoir of John Grey of Dilston* (Edinburgh 1869), p. 48; Stow Hill, in *H.L.Deb.* 26 Nov. 1970, c. 296.

25 Christabel Pankhurst in *Daily Telegraph*, 26 Oct. 1908; J. S. Mill, *Representative Government* (Everyman edn., 1960), pp. 182–4; see also Fredrickson, *Inner Civil War*, p. 9.

26 K. Willis, 'The introduction and critical reception of Marxist thought in Britain 1850–1900', *Historical Journal*, 20, No. 2 (1977), p. 450, cf. F. Engels, *The Condition of the Working Class in England*, trans. and ed. W. O. Henderson and W. H. Chaloner (Oxford, 1958), p. 89.

27 Frank Parkin, *Middle Class Radicalism. The Social Bases of the British Campaign for Nuclear Disarmament* (Manchester, 1968), pp. 20–1.

28 Cobden, *Speeches*, I, p. 43.
29 See, e.g., Whitmore, in Committee of the Society for the Mitigation and Gradual Abolition of Slavery . . ., *2nd Report* (1825), p. 62; Milbank, *H.C.Deb.* 2 Apr. 1792, c. 1104; W. A. McKinnon, in RSPCA, *28th Annual Report, 1854*, p. 27; Henry Aggs, in SPCA *8th Annual Report, 1834*, pp. 37–8.
30 L. Gompertz, *Moral Inquiries on the Situation of Man and of Brutes* (1824), p. 30.
31 Karl Marx, *Capital* (New York, 1967), I, p. 730.
32 City of London Polytechnic, *Josephine Butler Papers*, Box 1: Josephine Butler to H. J. Wilson, 22 Apr. 1875; Royal Commission on the . . . Contagious Diseases Act, *Parl. Papers* 1871 (C. 408) XIX, Q. 12,921.
33 Quo. from *H.C.Deb.* 15 Apr. 1831, c. 1464 (Mr A. Baring); see also Petrie, Sir Charles, *Walter Long and his Times* (1936), p. 105.
34 Annie Kenney, *Memories of a Militant* (1924), p. 68.
35 British Library, *Add. MSS.* 43662 (Cobden Papers), Vol. 16, f. 27: Cobden to C. P. Villiers, end. 6 June 1841.
36 *H.C.Deb.* 1 Mar. 1799, c. 526; cf. *H.C.Deb.* 6 Apr. 1797, c. 278.
37 Butler quoted from R.C. . . . C.D. Act, *Parl. Papers* 1871 (C. 408) XIX, Q. 12, 943. See also Wilberforce in *H.C.Deb.* 12 May 1789, c. 45; 'Alfred' [Kydd, Samuel], *The History of the Factory Movement* . . . (1857), I, p. 172; Hodder, *Shaftesbury*, II, p. 65.
38 C. Woodham-Smith, *Florence Nightingale, 1820–1910* (1950), p. 93.
39 David Butler, and Donald Stokes, *Political Change in Britain* (1969), p. 47.
40 Elizabeth Isichei, *Victorian Quakers* (Oxford, 1970), pp. 12, 66, 147.
41 Mary Stocks, *Eleanor Rathbone. A Biography* (1949), p. 13, cf. p. 20; see also Jean Bonnor, 'The Four Labour Cabinets', *Sociological Review* (1958), p. 46.
42 Emmeline Pankhurst, *My Own Story* (1914), p. 2.
43 Quoted from Margot Asquith, (ed.), *Myself When Young* (1938), p. 259; see also David Mitchell, *The Fighting Pankhursts* (New York, 1967), p. 322.
44 Viscountess Rhondda, *This Was My World* (1933), p. 161.
45 A. L. Lowell, *The Government of England* (1921), II, p. 509; A. P. Stanley, *The Life . . . of Thomas Arnold* (8th edn. 1858), II, p. 87.
46 *H.C.Deb.* 20 June 1848, cf. 961.
47 C. E. M. Joad, *Under the Fifth Rib. A Belligerent Autobiography* (1932), p. 28; cf. Kingsley Martin, *Harold Laski (1893–1950). A Biographical Memoir* (1953), p. 19. For Levin, see *The Observer*, 5 Sept. 1971, p. 27.
48 Lady Gwendolen Cecil, *Life of Robert, Marquis of Salisbury* (1931), III, p. 65; cf. Paul Smith, (ed.), *Lord Salisbury on Politics*, Cambridge, 1972), pp. 318–19.
49 Lady St Helier, *Memories of Fifty Years* (1909), p. 288; cf. Austen Chamberlain, *Politics from the Inside* (1936), p. 199; see also John Ramsden, *The Age of Balfour and Baldwin 1902–1940* (1978), pp. 231ff.
50 *H.C.Deb.* 12 June 1884, c. 182.
51 Shannon, *Gladstone*, p. 181.

52 Quoted in Geoffrey B. A. M. Finlayson, *England in the 1830s* (1969), p. 102.

53 Cobden quoted in Hollis, *Pressure from Without*, p. 142; Cobden, *Speeches*, I, p. 180, cf. pp. 178, 182; see also Mosa Anderson, *Henry Joseph Wilson. Fighter for Freedom 1833–1914* (1953), p. 30.

54 J. S. Mill, *Liberty* (Everyman edn. 1960), p. 62 (superscription by W. von Humboldt); *Representative Government* (Everyman edn. 1960), p. 201, cf. pp. 247, 267–8; Gladstone quo. in G. M. Young, *Victorian Essays* (ed. W. D. Handcock), (Oxford, 1962), p. 106.

55 F. W. Newman, *The Permissive Bill More Urgent than any Extension of the Franchise. An Address at Ramsgate, February 17th. 1865*, United Kingdom Alliance 1865, p. 4; Mrs Pethick-Lawrence in *Jus Suffragii*, 1 Apr. 1915, p. 302; J. A. Hobson, *Richard Cobden. The International Man* (1919), p. 37; see also *Women's Suffrage Journal*, 1 July 1875, p. 98 (Mrs M'Laren).

56 Quotations from *Sheffield & Rotherham Independent*, 26 Sept. 1846 (Vincent); G. W. E. Russell, *Sir Wilfrid Lawson. A Memoir* (1909), p. 186; see also Sussex County Record Office, Chichester: *Cobden Papers 83*, p. 41: Cobden to Sig. Mauro Macchi, 1 Sept. 1854.

57 Cobden, *Speeches*, I, p. 257.

58 SPCA *6th Annual Report, 1832*, p. 15 (Mackinnon); RSPCA *77th Annual Report, 1901*, pp. 35ff; R. D. French, 'Medical science and Victorian society: the anti-vivisection movement' (unpublished D.Phil. thesis, Oxford, 1972), p. 389.

59 Hollis, *Pressure from Without*, p. 9; Lawson, *H.C.Deb.* 3 Feb. 1897, c. 1213.

60 British Library, *Add. MSS.* 37775, f. 97 (Working Men's Association Minutes, Vol. 3, minutes for 29 Sept. 1847).

61 Bright, *H.C.Deb.* 14 June 1881, c. 559; J. L. Garvin, *The Life of Joseph Chamberlain*, I (1932), pp. 159–61.

62 Quoted in D. J. Rowe, (ed.), *London Radicalism*, p. 114; Place was writing on the extinction of the National Political Union.

63 Evan R. Jones, *The Life and Speeches of Joseph Cowen, M.P.*, (n.d.) p. 225.

64 Parkin, *Middle Class Radicalism*, pp. 162–3.

65 Morley, *Cobden*, p. 152.

66 Pankhurst, Christabel, in *The Suffragette*, 29 Aug. 1913, p. 798; see also Shannon, *Gladstone*, pp. 90, 92, 100, 110–11.

67 Pankhurst in *Votes for Women*, 29 Oct. 1908, p. 81; see also Roy Jenkins, *Asquith*, (1964), p. 513.

7

THE RISE OF BRITISH POPULAR SENTIMENT FOR ABOLITION, 1787–1832

by James Walvin

In 1787, William Wilberforce confided in his diary:

> God Almighty has set before me two great objects, the suppression of the slave trade and the reformation of manners.[1]

This refinement of manners was by its very nature a more diffuse and distant ambition whereas the campaign against the slave trade (and later slavery) was both specific and more immediate. Moreover, it was the ending of the slave trade which was to be realized more swiftly and to be remembered as the most outstanding achievement of those men gathered around Wilberforce and known as the Clapham Sect. Yet the campaign against the slave trade and slavery was not merely the work of a small, influential pressure group. It is the purpose of this paper to suggest that abolition was successful largely because it became unprecedentedly popular – at all levels of society.

Wilberforce and the Clapham Sect were initially drawn together by antipathy to the slave trade. Although drawn from both the established and dissenting churches, this group of evangelicals shared a common inspirational theology which urged them to undertake 'good works'. This theology, fully documented by Roger Anstey, was partly responsible for their abolitionism, but they also drew upon the writers of the European and Scottish Enlightenment.[2] Of course the political influence of the *philosophes* went far beyond the realms of abolition but the campaign on behalf of the slaves, set in train by the evangelicals in 1787, was in itself a major turning point.

The pioneering abolitionists who formed the Abolition Committee in 1787 sought to persuade parliament and ministers of the justice of their case and, equally, to give their efforts as wide a public base as possible. The metropolitan committee sought in effect to create popular abolitionism by careful co-ordination of the efforts of local sympathizers, peripatetic lecturers, tract distribution and newspaper coverage.[3] In fact, the first blows for abolitionism had already been struck by Granville Sharp through his efforts in the 'slave cases' of the 1760s and 1770s. These cases were doubly influential. First, they revealed the political potential of proceedings through the courts and secondly they helped to create a more favourable political and social climate for England's black minority.[4]

At much the same time, new political examples were being offered by the successful extra-parliamentary tactics of the friends of John Wilkes and the British supporters of the American colonists. By 1780, the cumulative result of these tactics had succeeded in creating a remarkably widespread and popular movement intent on parliamentary reform.[5] But it was the problem of slavery, in the form of the infamous Zong case of 1783, which once more attracted growing public attention.[6] Furthermore, political concern about slavery continued to grow in the mid-1780s, largely because of the distinctive problems of London's black minority.

Since the 1760s there had been a sizeable black population in the capital but after 1783 this was augmented by refugee former slaves from the American colonies. Many were utterly destitute and Granville Sharp – an obvious source of relief – found himself trying to assist no fewer than 400 of them. It was clearly beyond the means of one man and in 1786 a committee was founded 'for the Relief of the Black Poor'. Even with Treasury support, this too proved inadequate to the task of relieving black poverty and there emerged, as a political alternative, the Sierra Leone scheme to repatriate London's blacks to West Africa.[7] But the scheme, characterized by corruption and mismanagement, proved little less than disastrous for the first emigrants. Nonetheless, it succeeded in keeping the issue of slavery firmly in the public eye in 1786–7. And when, in 1787, the largely Quaker Abolition Committee was formed, some of its members had already been active on behalf of London's black poor.[8]

The fact that the Abolition Committee was predominantly Quaker was important, for it provided an instant chain of sympathetic friends throughout the country. When, later that same year, the young convert to the cause, Thomas Clarkson, was dispatched on an abolitionist fact-finding and lecture tour of the country, he found abolitionists – many of them Quakers – wherever he travelled.[9] In Manchester, however, his main contacts were Thomas Walker and Thomas Cooper who told him of 'the spirit which was then beginning to show itself, among the people of Manchester and of other places, on the subject of the Slave Trade, and which would unquestionably manifest itself further by breaking out into petitions to parliament for its abolition'.[10] At the promptings of the Manchester men, whose own petition attracted 10,639 names and was reprinted in a number of provincial newspapers, the Abolition Committee urged their supporters to dispatch similar petitions to parliament. By June 1788, more than 100 had arrived. And to accompany and expand this expression of political sentiment, the Abolition Committee published large numbers of abolitionist tracts, books and newspaper articles.[11] New provincial groups were added to the list of supporters of whom perhaps the most significant were the dissenters, notably the Methodists, who were, at the same time, politically organized to press for the repeal of the Test and Corporation Acts. From 1787 until final emancipation in 1838 the role and numerical strength of nonconformity in abolitionist efforts was extraordinary. By the 1820s a substantial proportion of all abolitionist petitions – numbered in their thousands – came from dissenting congregations.[12]

Abolition also needed men within parliament and government, and from 1788, as Roger Anstey has shown, the main abolitionist thrust was to secure a parliamentary majority against the trade. In the process there were some notable political victories. The trade was investigated by a committee of the Privy Council and subsequently regulated by Dolben's Act (1789). But for a variety of tactical and obstructionist reasons, a vote on abolition was not taken until April 1791. Throughout that time, however, abolitionists maintained an effective lobby in parliament and government; nonetheless their parliamentary defeat in April 1791 was overwhelming – if not surprising.[13]

This defeat led once more to a renewed upsurge of extra-parliamentary efforts, the outcome of which was remarkable. By the spring of 1792, 519 abolitionist petitions had reached parliament: that from Manchester contained 20,000 names. Sir Samuel Romilly wrote:

> the cause of the negro slaves is at present taken up with much warmth in almost every part of the kingdom as could be found in any matter in which the people were personally and immediately interested. Innumerable petitions to Parliament and (what proves men's zeal more

strongly than petitions) great numbers have entirely discontinued the use of sugar. All persons, and even the West Indian planters and merchants, seem to agree that it is impossible the trade should last many years longer.[14]

In fact it lasted another 13 years. But when we recall that abolitionism had only begun as an effective political movement five years earlier, Romilly's comment is testimony to the enormous speed and impact made by the abolitionists. Yet, even as he wrote, the very tactics which had created this abolitionist groundswell were being discredited by the impact of the French Revolution.

The plebeian corresponding societies which emerged in 1791–2 to pursue parliamentary reform adopted the well-tried tactics of public meetings, lectures, tracts, networks of correspondents and, of course, the petition. Their Paineite tone and plebeian composition, however, coming at a time of growing alarm about the drift of events in France, created a hardening of attitudes towards their political tactics. When, in the spring of 1793, their reforming petitions arrived in large numbers in parliament, the nation was already at war with revolutionary France (so admired by the radicals).[15] Men began to distrust the politics of popular associations, and ever more doubts were expressed about the efforts of abolitionists, more particularly because of the violence and destruction in the slave society of St Domingue. But it was growing antipathy towards popular radicalism which helped to undermine the public strength of abolitionism. In 1793 the Earl of Abingdon said:

the idea of abolishing the slave trade is connected with the levelling system and the rights of man . . . what does the abolition of the slave trade mean more or less than liberty and equality? What more or less than the rights of man?

A friend of abolition similarly complained that 'People connect democratical principles with the abolition of the Slave Trade and will not hear mention of it.'[16]

There was an undoubted community of interest between the popular radicals and abolitionists. Many evangelicals – notably Wilberforce – favoured parliamentary reform (though Wilberforce was alarmed at what he took to be the threat of revolution in the 1790s) and a sizeable body of abolitionists M.P.s also voted for reform in the 1780s and 1790s.[17] Abolitionism was likewise a distinct theme in the political creed of the artisan radicals in the corresponding societies (as one might expect of men so devoted to the writings of Paine). Thomas Hardy, founder of the London Corresponding Society, affirmed that the rights of man 'are not confined solely to this small island but are extended to the whole human race, black or white, high or low, rich or poor'.[18] Artisan cutlers in Sheffield in 1794 similarly called for the 'total Emancipation of Negro Slaves'[19] (and this at a time when the Abolition Committee was thinking merely of ending the slave trade). Among spokesmen of the radical societies, abolition was a prominent theme. John Thelwall in London, Henry Redhead Yorke in Sheffield, Thomas Walker in Manchester, and Coleridge in Bristol – all addressed their radical audiences about the injustices of slavery and the slave trade.[20] But the fate of the corresponding societies was effectively sealed by the repressive Two Acts of 1795: the societies had been doomed by their own popularity. Moreover, the political consequences of those Acts went far beyond the corresponding societies. By effectively outlawing all public meetings, the Two Acts crippled public abolitionism as much as radicalism.[21] Such a blow was, however, less serious for the abolitionists who had by then secured a sizeable following within parliament. Henceforth, the abolitionists' main task was to exert pressure within parliament and, unlike reform, they had little or no need of the extra-parliamentary pressures which had been so vital in the initial task of lifting abolition from the public to the parliamentary level.

Governmental severity in the 1790s purged the nation of popular politics (with notable though isolated exceptions) for the best part of twenty years. And it is significant that when the public politics of mass meetings and petitioning once more resurfaced – in 1814 – it did so, again, in response to the problem of slavery. The proposal at the Congress of Vienna to renew French slave trading rights produced a massive abolitionist outburst in England, greater by far (and more swiftly aroused) than the initial feeling thirty years before. Within one month some 800 petitions containing 1½ million names were sent to parliament. Samuel Whitbread noted, 'The country never has, and I fear never will, express a feeling so general as they have done about the slave trade.'[22] Abolitionists were also convinced that the petitions were instrumental in changing governmental policy. Clarkson wrote, 'I cannot but think, that we have to thank the Petitions for this Energy. No other satisfactory reason can be given why Administration was so apparently indifferent to the Subject when the Treaty was made, and why so interesting since.'[23] However disappointing the world of Congress diplomacy proved to be to abolitionists, they had shown the speed, strength, and influence of their political reflexes. By 1814 no one doubted that there was a remarkable national antipathy towards slavery and the slave trade. The problem remained, however: how best to direct this feeling against slavery itself?

The abolition of 1807 had done little to help the slaves already in the Caribbean. Moreover, as early as 1810 Wilberforce had become alarmed that the planters seemed able to circumvent abolition by illegally importing slaves.[24] With this in mind, James Stephen devised the notion of slave registration – in effect a census – as a check against illegal importations, and it was introduced into the newly acquired island of Trinidad in 1812. A wider slave registration now became the main abolitionist ambition and they launched a renewed parliamentary campaign to extend registration to all the slave islands. A tactical, plantocratic rearguard action effectively delayed registration from one year to another, and it was not finally enacted until 1810.[25] Once implemented, however, registration yielded dramatic results. The demographic evidence from these slave returns provided the most telling and irrefutable evidence to date of the reality of black slavery. Furthermore it compounded the impression, conveyed by dissenting missionaries active in the Caribbean and by the periodic slave revolts, that slavery was barbaric and the whites unhesitatingly vicious. Abolitionists, now led by younger men, notably by Thomas Fowell Buxton in the Commons, felt that a new public campaign was needed to press for amelioration and, eventually, freedom. And it was felt that the facts about slavery would speak for themselves. James Cropper wrote to Clarkson, 'let us show what the Slavery of the British Colonies is and then our opponents will be speechless.'[26] With this in mind, the remnants of the Clapham Sect and their new, young backers, founded the Anti-Slavery Society in 1823, setting in train a reprise, on an even more startling scale, of the extra-parliamentary tactics which had proved so successful in 1787–92 and in 1814.

James Cropper, for example, felt that 'Public Opinion is necessary to some extent to the successful prosecution of our inquiries'.[27] And, as in 1787, abolitionists turned to Thomas Clarkson for a lead. Now sixty-three, he set out once more, covering 3000 miles in 1823, helping to found 200 local committees, and prompting 100 abolitionist petitions. A year later, a similar tour produced 600 petitions.[28] At the same time, discussions with ministers resulted in Canning's 1823 Resolutions, expressing a formal commitment to eventual emancipation. Not to be deflected by promises, the Anti-Slavery Society remained convinced of the need to maintain public pressure, notably via petitions, both to pin down hesitant ministers and to overcome plantocratic opposition:

will not an uninterrupted Chain of Petitions coming on during the whole of the present Session *show* Ministers that they will not be forsaken . . . will not the voice of the Nation, thus displayed, show the Planters the impossibility of a successful resistance, and will they not therefore be more inclined to submit.[29]

By the mid 1820s abolitionism was more popular than ever before. It was often supported by local government,[30] while ever more parliamentary candidates were, from 1826 onwards, obliged to declare their position on slavery. At the Yorkshire election of that year a candidate declared, 'On the gradual abolition of Colonial Slavery, I am happy to believe there are not two opinions in the country'.[31] And, as testimony to this view, waves of abolitionist petitions continued to descend on parliament. The petition was in fact the annual expression of abolitionist sentiment; between 1826 and 1832 more than 3500 were dispatched to the Lords alone.[32]

These petitions, which were as much a ritual as an expression of opinion, reveal many central features of abolitionism. And they also show how the political arguments had advanced since the movement's early days. By the mid-1820s abolitionists assumed that West Indian slaves possessed those rights which, in the 1790s, the popular radicals had claimed for themselves. The debate about human rights – 'the rights of man' – is a prominent theme in abolitionist literature of the 1820s and 1830s, more especially in the petitions. Slavery, said abolitionists from Norwich, was 'utterly inconsistent with the inalienable rights of man'.[33] Methodists from Yorkshire denounced slavery as 'directly contrary to the natural Rights of Man'.[34] Yet only thirty years before, such sentiments had been denounced by Ministers and judges. Indeed, Englishmen had been transported for asking for these rights for themselves. The abolitionist petitions of the years 1826–32 were steeped in the political vernacular of what had once been artisan radicalism. Moreover, the abolitionists assumed that the slaves' rights were identical to their own English rights. Some spoke of the slaves as 'black Englishmen',[35] others of British-born subjects. Some wanted to see slaves raised 'to the Enjoyment of all the Civil and Religious Rights and Immunities which are the Birthright of every British Subject'.[36] But by the 1820s, abolitionists tended to assume that these rights were divinely ordained rather than secular endowments: 'sacred Rights which belong to all the Family of Man'.[37]

Time and again, abolitionist petitions referred to slavery as a blot on the Christian conscience and an affront to the Almighty. According to dissenters in Derby, slavery was 'a System full of Wickedness, hateful to God, and a Curse and Disgrace to Britain'.[38] Methodists in Barnsley thought it 'repugnant to our Religion'.[39] Women in Hereford denounced it as 'a System alike revolting to the feelings of Mankind as inconsistent with the Counsels of Heaven'.[40] While it seems indisputable that slavery by the 1820s was widely regarded in England as a deeply offensive institution, the strongest objections to it were couched in religious terms. The reasons for this are straightforward. First, a substantial proportion of *all* abolitionist petitions came from religious bodies or congregations. And secondly, the Agency Committee established in 1830 as a ginger group from within the Anti-Slavery Society, issued firm instructions that its lecturers must avoid political controversy and should instead abide by the view that 'the system of Colonial Slavery is a crime in the sight of God, and ought to be immediately and for ever abolished'.[41]

By the mid 1820s, although it is true to say that abolitionists regarded slavery as an immoral and unchristian outrage, it would be wrong to deny the presence of an economic critique of slavery. Early in 1822, James Cropper had privately raised the question of East India sugar, and the artificial protection which kept slave-grown sugar viable and yet costly to the British consumer.[42] By the end of that year, this criticism had broken into print, and by 1826 support for freely-imported East Indian sugar had become a political objection to slave-grown sugar. In the words of one parliamentary candidate, 'The difference in the duty on East and West India sugar operates as a bounty on slavery, and as a tax on the people of England, which they might reasonable require to be removed.'[43] It became clear – and was widely propagated by the abolitionists – that the British consumer was supporting the slave system – a fact increasingly denounced at abolitionist meetings, in their literature and in parliament itself. In some cases this economic critique of slavery became a more general argument for free trade.[44] In April 1827, for instance, 'The Chambers of Commerce of Manchester and Birmingham and the merchants and manufacturers of Leeds and other places' demanded both free trade and an end to the sugar duties.[45] The new industrial nation had come to see that slavery – a product of the age of mercantilism – was inimical to its wider economic interest, a point made half a century before by Adam Smith. Yet, while acknowledging this economic criticism of slavery, it would be wrong to exaggerate it. Whichever evidence we turn to – abolitionists' correspondence, parliamentary debates, tracts, lectures, or local activities – the economics of slavery received very little attention indeed and formed a mere fraction of the literature. If we are to accept the evidence of the abolitionists' own words, they were, overwhelmingly, concerned with slavery as an ethical and religious issue and not as an economic problem. These were not, of course, mutually exclusive viewpoints. But if the ending of slavery was seen by abolitionists as the undoing of an outdated economic system, they rarely said so.

By 1830 the extent and depth of anti-slavery feeling is difficult to overstress, and to a substantial degree this sentiment had been generated by the *Anti-Slavery Reporter* founded in 1825. The *Reporter*, like the Chartists' *Northern Star* at a later date, provided an important organizational framework and a focal point for a diffuse political movement. Established by Macaulay, the *Reporter* provides a mirror into the world of abolitionism in its last and crowning decade. But it is much more than a mere reflection of abolitionism, for its own role was seminal in providing information, guidance and direction to the national cause.[46] It is, for instance, striking that after the publication of the *Reporter*, abolitionist petitions tended to become more uniform and standard, as local groups and congregations copied the examples offered in the *Reporter*'s columns. But, for all the plantocratic claims that the resulting petitions were rigged, copied or merely the result of intemperate excitement, abolitionists themselves never doubted that all the evidence pointed to a massive and genuine support behind the cause.[47]

Perhaps the most striking contribution of the *Reporter* was, however, the prodigous volume of information about slave society which it fed to the public. In one issue after another, the reader learned about the minutiae of slave life; about the slaves' work, housing, family-life, punishments, and religions. Distinguishing between slave islands, offering careful demographic analyses (derived from the registration returns), and comparing Caribbean with North American slavery, the *Reporter* presented an analysis of slave society which was the most sophisticated and comprehensive to date.[48] Plantocratic claims were instantly analysed and answered. So too were government pronouncements, ministerial missives, colonial business and correspondence between Whitehall and the colonies.[49] The reading public came to know more about slave society than ever before; and what they learned they abhorred. But the work of the *Reporter* had even wider implications, for it sought to make public the hitherto private realm of politics: ministers, colonial officials, and official correspondence and publications were exposed to critical public scrutiny. This, inevitably, made life more difficult for the men concerned and in the process the role of the minister began to change: he was now subject to pressure both from without and from within.

What seemed to outrage abolitionists most acutely was the cruelty involved in slavery. To a society not without its own distinctive barbarities, slavery nonetheless seemed to excel in organized and legalized inhumanities. Moreover, it seemed to English onlookers that the slaves' periodic revolts (Barbados 1816, Demerara 1823, Jamaica 1831) and the predictable white repression, provided substance for their feelings that slavery was itself barbaric and only maintained and supported by the most vigorous of white repressions.[50]

By the 1830s the planters' prospects looked bleak indeed: they were beleaguered in parliament and unable to withstand the tide of abolitionism in the country at large. Lectures, sermons, public meetings, tract warfare, newspaper coverage – all helped to spread further the cause of abolition. In the language of an age dazzled by technical potential, parliament was compared to 'the steam engine which required only *the steam of public opinion*, strongly expressed, to enable it to annihilate Colonial Slavery at one majestic stroke'.[51] And this public opinion seems to have reached its peak, or rather a series of peaks, between the establishment of the Agency Committee in 1830 and the calling of the reformed parliament in 1832. It was, furthermore, in these months that news reached England of the slave revolt which had devasted parts of Jamaica at Christmas 1831. It merely confirmed the wisdom of the abolitionists' decision, taken in 1830, to switch the thrust of their attack from gradual to immediate emancipation. Urged on by the Agency Committee and the *Anti-Slavery Reporter*, immediate emancipation swiftly became a popular issue. Joseph Losh, hitherto a gradualist, writing in his diary for November 1830, noted 'An article in the *Anti-Slavery Reporter* in favour of immediate emancipation. This is well and sensibly written . . .'[52] The resulting popular demand for immediate black freedom was carried along by the wider campaign for the reform of parliament and the battle for 'The Bill'. When finally carried, the 1832 Reform Act itself greatly enhanced the prospects of black freedom because reform weakened the old West India lobby, just as the emancipation of the Catholics had augmented the parliamentary strength of the abolitionists. Henceforth, even those publications which had previously taken a pro-planter line, began to beat a tactical retreat and to side with the abolitionists.[53]

Between 1830 and 1832 the public flocked to the abolitionist cause as never before. Indeed the sole restraint on anti-slavery meetings in these years was the physical capacity of the meeting place. In 1830, for example, the General Meeting of the Anti-Slavery Society attracted 2000 people – with 1000 locked outside.[54] Two years later, in May 1832, 3000 people managed to squeeze inside. Nothing like it had been seen since the heyday of the London Corresponding Society in the 1790s. And wherever abolitionists lectured or met between 1830 and 1832, they filled the meeting place – often despite the length of the meeting. The 1832 General Meeting at Exeter Hall lasted from 12 noon till 7 pm. Inconvenient times could, however, affect popular backing. A meeting called in Hexham for 10 am was clearly a mistake, 'The hour being very inconvenient to the shopkeepers and workmen of all kinds, the meeting, though respectable, was by no means numerous.'[55] Abolitionists by this time had no trouble in finding a convenient meeting place – a startling contrast to the fortunes of the more overtly political radical movements. From the corresponding societies of the 1790s through to the Chartists in the 1840s, English radicals had to rely on the tavern or the public place for their venues. But this was not true for abolitionists. Assembly rooms, chapels, courts, town and county halls, guild-halls, taverns – even a Music Hall – were available to the abolitionist cause.[56] And wherever the lecturers from the Agency Committee spoke, they faced packed audiences (of both sexes). Often they had to repeat their lectures to the overspill audience. But perhaps of greatest help were the dissenting churches, though now their facilities were augmented by the premises offered to the cause by the churches of Ireland, Scotland and England.[57]

In addition to these crowded lectures, there was an abundance of cheap or free literature published by the Anti-Slavery Society and the Agency Committee, although a growing amount was issued by the local abolitionist groups which proliferated in their hundreds in the 1820s and 1830s. Even the remotest of spots could boast their own abolition society. Women organized their own anti-slavery societies, often with remarkable political effect.[58] And the abolitionist message was even passed on to the nation's young via children's abolitionist literature.[59] But it was the publishing effort of the Anti-Slavery Society which was most striking. In 1823, for example, it published 201,750 tracts; by 1830 these had risen to half a million.[60] And all this in addition to the pervasive influence of the *Anti-Slavery Reporter*. In the light of such a massive propaganda

160   James Walvin

campaign it may not seem surprising that in 1831–2 some 1½ million names were attached to abolitionist petitions.[61]

It would, of course, be unrealistic to claim that abolitionists alone were responsible for the ending of the slave trade and slavery. Abolition clearly involved a complex process in which government, colonial administration and vested interests sought to reconcile the nation's changing political and imperial values with economic considerations (which were themselves in a state of flux). Yet, since the publication of Eric Williams' *Capitalism and Slavery* the historical debate has concentrated on the economics of slavery at the expense of abolitionism. The purpose of this essay has been to suggest that we need to extend our definition of abolitionism by seeing it as incorporating a genuinely popular movement which spanned not merely the world of formal politics. Abolition in effect created unprecedented public backing for its political ambitions. Moreover, its organization and tactics provided an exemplary model for others keen to persuade parliament and the people of their cause. If the slave trade and slavery could be brought to an end, what else might be changed by similar efforts?

Notes

1 Quoted in E. M. Howse, *Saints in Politics* (1973 edn.), p. 32.
2 Roger Anstey, *The Atlantic Slave Trade and British Abolition, 1760–1810* (1975), chap. 7, 120–125.
3 *Ibid.*, chap. 10.
4 J. Walvin, *Black and White. The Negro and English Society, 1555–1945*, (1973), chaps. 6–8.
5 John Brewer, *Party Ideology and Popular Politics at the Accession of George III*, (1976); E. C. Black, *The Association* (Cambridge, Mass., 1963), I. R. Christie, *Wilkes, Wyvill and Reform* (1962).
6 Walvin, *Black and White*, pp. 92–3.
7 *Ibid.*, chap. 9; Christopher Fyfe, *A History of Sierra Leone* (Oxford, 1962).
8 Anstey, *Atlantic Slave Trade*, p. 249; Walvin, *Black and White*, p. 146.
9 Thomas Clarkson, *The History of the Rise, Progress, and Accomplishment of the Abolition of the African Slave Trade by the British Parliament* (1808), I, pp. 292, 295, 321, 369, 371, 410.
10 *Ibid.*, pp. 415–16.
11 Anstey, *Atlantic Slave Trade*, pp. 256–60; 265–7.
12 *Journal of the House of Lords*, vols. LXII and LXIII.
13 Anstey, *Atlantic Slave Trade*, pp. 267–78.
14 *Memoirs of the Life of Sir Samuel Romilly, Written by Himself* (2nd edn, 1840), II, 2–3.
15 Albert Goodwin, *Friends of the People* (1979).
16 *Annual Register* (1793), 90; *Hansard Debates*, 1792–4, 632–50; R.

and S. Wilberforce, *The Life of William Wilberforce* (1839), II, p. 18.

17 Anstey, *Atlantic Slave Trade*, pp. 179–80, 283–4.

18 Add. MS, 27, 811, f. 4.

19 *Proceedings of the Public Meeting held at Sheffield, April 7th 1794* (Sheffield, 1794), pp. 22–5.

20 J. Walvin, 'The impact of slavery upon British radical politics, 1787–1838', *Annals of the New York Academy of Sciences*, 292 (New York, 1977), pp. 347–8.

21 G. S. Veitch, *The Genesis of Parliamentary Reform* (1965 edn.), p. 326.

22 F. R. Cartwright (ed.), *The Life and Correspondence of Major Cartwright* (1816), II, 84.

23 Letter from Thomas Clarkson, September 1814, Add Ms 41, 267A, f. 60.

24 Howse, *Saints in Politics*, pp. 140–1.

25 *Ibid.*, pp. 140–50.

26 Add MS 41, 267A, f. 113.

27 *Ibid.*

28 Howse, *Saints in Politics*, p. 155; R. Coupland, *The British Anti-Slavery Movement* (1933), pp. 122, 131–2.

29 Add MS 41, 267A, f. 126.

30 Letter, March 1824, (Y 326) and May 1828, *Memorials to the Corporation 1827–33* (K 109), York City Archives.

31 *Speeches and Addresses of the Candidates for the Representation of the County of York in the Year 1826* (Leeds, 1826).

32 *Index to the Journals of the House of Lords, 1820–1833.*

33 *Journal of the House of Lords*, LXIII, 31.

34 *Ibid.*, 101.

35 *Anti-Slavery Reporter*, October 1827, 141.

36 *Journal of the House of Lords*, LXIII, 31.

37 *Ibid.*, 24.

38 *Ibid.*, 32.

39 *Ibid.*, 24.

40 *Ibid.*, 33.

41 Howse, *Saints in Politics*, pp. 162–3; *Report of the Agency Committee of the Anti-Slavery Society*, 1831, pp. 2–3.

42 Add MS 41, 267A, f. 106; 108.

43 *Speeches and Addresses of the Candidates for the Representation of the County of York in the Year of 1826*, 26.

44 *Negro Slavery; or a view of some of the more prominent features of that state of slavery as it exists in the USA and in the colonies of the West Indies* . . . (1823), p. 117.

45 *Anti-Slavery Reporter*, 23, 30 April 1827.

46 *Ibid.*, 1, June 1825.

47 *Ibid.*, 8, January 1826.

48 *Ibid.*, 2, 31 July 1825; 7, 13 December 1825; July 1827.

49 *Ibid.*, October 1827; November 1825.

50 For the slave revolts, see M. Craton, 'Proto-Peasant Revolts', *Past and Present*, Spring 1980.

51 *Anti-Slavery Monthly Reporter*, May 1830.

52 'The Diaries of James Losh', E. Hughes (ed.), *Publications of the*

Surtees Society, CLXXI, II, p. 100; *Report of the Agency Committee . . .* 2–3.

53 *Anti-Slavery Monthly Reporter*, October 1829.

54 *Ibid.*, June 1830; *Report of the Agency Committee . . . 1831.*

55 Hughes, 'Diaries of James Losh', II, pp. 97–8.

56 *Report of the Agency Committee*, 1831, 6–22; *Memorials of the Corporation*, 1827–33, K 109, York Archives, 23 and 26 May 1828; K. K. Macmahon (ed.), 'The Beverley Corporation Minute Book, 1707–1823', *Yorkshire Archaeological Society* (1953), 71, 75, 112.

57 *Anti-Slavery Monthly Reporter*, June 1830.

58 *Accounts of the Receipts and Disboursements of the Anti-Slavery Society*, 1823–31; *First Report of the Suffolk Auxiliary Society . . .* (Suffolk, 1825); *First Report of the Swansea and Neath Auxiliary Anti-Slavery Association* (Swansea, 1826).

59 Opie, *The Black Man's Lament* (1826).

60 *Accounts of the Receipts and Disboursements of the Anti-Slavery Society*, 1823–31.

61 Walvin, 'The impact of slavery', p. 352.

8

'FREE AIR' AND FUGITIVE SLAVES: BRITISH ABOLITIONISTS VERSUS GOVERNMENT OVER AMERICAN FUGITIVES, 1834–61

by David M. Turley

One of the great strengths of Roger Anstey's *The Atlantic Slave Trade and British Abolition* is its subtle treatment of the interaction between abolitionists and the government in 1806–7 which produced the two acts abolishing the slave trade under the British flag. Relations between anti-slavery reformers and politicians were not always conducted so successfully. The present essay focuses on an issue which divided most anti-slavery leaders from the British government in the 1840s and 1850s: were American slaves who had escaped to British territory after the emancipation of 1834 to be safeguarded against return to the southern states? This was a problem which concerned abolitionists frequently only between 1839 and 1843. Its history, however, merits analysis for a number of reasons.

The divergent responses of government and reformers to particular fugitive cases illuminate the losing battle abolitionists were waging to secure the recognition of the natural right of all men to freedom as the basis of government action. It became evident too, that humanitarian objectives could be incompatible with the exercise of British national sovereignty as well as that of foreign powers. Moreover, the precepts of international law, despite the tradition of linking them closely to natural law, were exposed as inadequate supports for the anti-slavery case. That case came to express a tension between the need to employ the terms of

municipal and international law to attract the attention of government and the desire to break through to the moral assertions
of natural law.

The context of anti-slavery efforts on behalf of American fugitives was unpromising. By the time of the establishment of the
British and Foreign Anti-Slavery Society (hereafter BFASS) in
1839 many former active abolitionists no doubt felt that their main
task had been completed. This in part accounts for the sharp decline
both in the number of local anti-slavery societies and in the income
of abolitionist organizations in the following twenty years. British
capacity directly to undermine slavery elsewhere was limited; much
anti-slavery opinion assumed that the government would do whatever was possible. Agitation by reformers, it could be argued, was
therefore less necessary, though it might serve as a useful reminder
to government that its conduct was being carefully judged by a body
of informed opinion.[1]

Abolitionists who continued their work after the end of apprenticeship took no such complacent view of the situation. They were of
a strongly ideological disposition, convinced of the universal validity of moral reform activity. Every significant British anti-slavery
leader would have accepted the American Elizur Wright's assertion
that 'moral force can not be bounded by geographical lines, rivers or
oceans'. Indeed, George Thompson argued that interference in the
affairs of others was no offence since mankind was one great family.[2] Such an expansive vision encouraged large moral ambitions
and a self-conscious consistency to ideological principle.

Activists of the BFASS sometimes expressed dissatisfaction with
government even when it pursued policies which, at any rate arguably, produced results that anti-slavery men wanted. Why was this?
The instance of their opposition to the cruising policy for the suppression of the slave trade in the 1840s suggests that there were
elements in their ideology, pacifist conviction in this case, which
remained untouched by pragmatic considerations.[3] Such a conclusion is confirmed by an examination of the problem of safeguarding
the freedom of fugitive American slaves in the British West Indies
and Canada both before and after the extradition agreement with
the United States in the Treaty of Washington of 1842. A study of
the main incidents seems to confirm the view that the government
could safely be left to handle the problem without interference.
Scholars have realistically concluded that reformers had virtually no
influence on government policy. Yet, with scarcely an exception,
slaves were not returned to their masters in the southern states.

British as well as American abolitionists, however, remained concerned about the problem until 1861.

Since they saw their prime moral duty as securing the natural right of freedom for slaves, reformers found a number of causes for worry. Firstly, a series of ship cases occurred in the West Indies between 1831 and 1842 in which American vessels with slaves on board were shipwrecked, driven into a British port by bad weather or, in the case of the *Creole* in late 1841, suffered mutiny by the slaves who took the ship into Nassau. These incidents provoked discussion of the legal issues and made abolitionists extremely sensitive to the danger that slaves would be returned. Similar, though not identical, problems were raised by fugitives reaching Canada. Together they fed concern over the implications for runaways of the Anglo–American extradition agreement concluded between Ashburton and Webster in 1842.[4]

Secondly, they were anxious because they misread, for a period, the meaning of the Peel government's position and the attitude of authoritative legal opinion on the ship cases. In harmony with abolitionists, some lawyers maintained the authority of municipal law in the West Indies against claims based on international law and, occasionally, even suggested that the natural right to freedom was the basis of refusal of the American claims. Reformers certainly expressed commitment to freedom for the slaves as an absolute and only temporarily and tactically shifted from that position thereafter. Thus when the Treaty of Washington cast doubt on this they were dismayed and suspicious of the consequences. Thirdly, they had a stronger conviction than the politicians that there were grave dangers in relying on local decisions taken in the colonies to achieve anti-slavery objectives. Finally, after failing to get the slaves fully protected against extradition, which their position logically required, the abolitionists remained unconvinced that the difficulties in applying the safeguards on extradition in the 1843 enabling act, linked to the Treaty, had been properly worked out.

The cases of the *Comet* in 1831 and the *Encomium* in 1833 both involved the wrecking of American vessels on the Bahama Banks and the release of the slaves aboard by British officials. In 1835 the *Enterprise* was driven into Hamilton, Bermuda, by bad weather and again the blacks were released by writ of habeas corpus. In October 1840, the *Hermosa* was wrecked on the key of Abaco. Against the captain's request to be landed at an American port, wreckers took all aboard to Nassau where, after proceedings, the slaves were freed.[5]

The probable legal ground upon which the colonial authorities acted, at least in the two earlier instances, was an interpretation of the act of 1824 against the slave trade.[6] The internal and coastal slave trade, however, while morally dubious, remained legal for Americans. This made it difficult to apply the 1824 act in these cases. Moreover, the effect of judgments in earlier ship cases by Sir William Scott (Lord Stowell) was to limit the operation of 'general principles of justice and humanity' in favour of freedom to instances when the municipal laws of the country to which the slave vessel belonged prohibited the slave trade. Such commerce was not illegitimate simply by virtue of the law of nations; states took part in it and their practice had to be respected.[7] Even after the act of 1824 there was clearly no basis for extending the local municipal law of British territories over slave-trading vessels in all circumstances. Nor, while the content of the law of nations could be deemed to draw on the 'general principles of justice and humanity', could the actual practice of states which recognized slavery or the slave trade be brushed aside. The precepts of international law operated most effectively when they became part of the law of a sovereign state, either by statute or treaty. Lacking that basis, their acceptance by a state depended upon courtesy.[8]

The American case for the restitution of slave property, built up over several years by diplomatic notes, speeches from Calhoun in the Senate, and the efforts of Secretary of State Webster struck at this weakness of British municipal law. Paradoxically, it did so by the uncertain argument of the superior force of international law which required aid to a vessel in distress. Calhoun in particular vehemently denied the power of municipal law in such cases to affect in any way either existing rights of property between persons on board ship, or indeed any relations under the law of the country to which the vessel belonged.[9]

The British response was shaped by, but did not originate with, the nature of the American argument.[10] In the cases of the *Comet* and the *Encomium* the law officers accepted the American claim by noting that the incidents had occurred at a time when slavery was still legal in the West Indies, but placed their main emphasis on the fact that the loss of the slaves to their owners was entirely consequent upon their seizure by British officials. As to the *Enterprise* (and the same arguments were later considered to apply to the *Hermosa*), after a temporary reversal of their opinions, the law officers had finally again advised in favour of the American claims. They justified their conclusions by stressing the distinction between voluntary and involuntary entry of a foreign vessel into a British port. The *Enterprise* was in the second category and was entitled under international law to leave port with its cargo intact. Since the holding of persons in slavery did not infringe international law, municipal law failed to alter the situation. But, at the time of the temporary reversal of their initial opinion, the law officers felt that the case turned on a direct conflict between the claims of international law and the sovereignty of the national legislature. The American claim had to be rejected because it rested on the proposition that by the law of nations an independent sovereign state could not enact a law, as Great Britain had done in the Emancipation Act of 1833, stating that slavery should be recognized nowhere within its territory.[11]

Palmerston was important in the controversy because of the way he cut through so many of the legal distinctions offered by his advisers. He vindicated British sovereignty by basing his policy on the state of local municipal law at different times and asserted the conclusive power of the Emancipation Act. He thus concluded that the American claims for compensation on the *Comet* and *Encomium* were justified because slavery had at that time been legal in British dominions. Once the slaves in the West Indies had been emancipated, however, the principle that a slave who touched British territory and breathed its 'free air' became instantly free formed the basis of British policy and had to be strictly maintained. For this reason he rejected the claim on the *Enterprise*.[12]

Abolitionists in England naturally welcomed Palmerston's position on this last case. However, they sharply criticized the grant of compensation to the owners of slaves on the *Comet* and *Encomium*, a decision based upon the same principle of sovereignty as had produced the approved stand on the *Enterprise*. Compensation infringed not the principle of sovereignty but the dictates of natural law because it 'admitted that a man has a right to hold property in man and thereby the eternal principles of justice are violated.'[13] When in late 1841 slaves on board the *Creole* revolted and took the ship into Nassau, the reformers expected a vindication of the mutineers, even from the charge of murder, despite the fact that the incident extended the controversy between the British and American governments at a time when negotiations between the two states were imminent. In the negotiations the United States wanted to include discussion of an agreement for the return of shipwrecked slaves and fugitive criminals; the *Creole* case clinched this concern.

In the Bahamas the authorities released all the *Creole* blacks except the nineteen against whom there seemed some evidence of participation in the revolt and then awaited instructions from London. Abolitionists in England built on both precedent and the argument from eternal justice heard in the earlier protest against compensation. They reminded the new foreign secretary, Aberdeen, of Palmerston's refusal to return slaves who had touched British territory and defined the revolt of the slaves, as did Brougham in the House of Lords, as legitimate resistance to secure their natural right to liberty; the killing of a passenger was a regrettable effect of this vindication of natural right. The blacks could not be given up and must be treated as free British subjects. Brougham was, if anything, even more sweeping in arguing that the Somerset case in England itself[14] and the operation of the Emancipation Act had created 'free air' throughout British territory, the slightest breath of which produced freedom, even against the will of the master and even if it required the use of force. Both Brougham and the London committee concluded by adding to the arguments from natural right, precedent, and statute their conviction that the alleged offences were beyond the competence of British courts, having been committed against American citizens on an American ship.[15]

Aberdeen's reply embraced both the non-competence of British courts in the case and, by implication, the effect of 'free air' in British territory; he concluded that the government had no authority to bring the blacks to trial, still less to detain them in custody or hand them over to a foreign government.[16]

As Tyler's secretary of state, it was Webster's role to argue the case of the *Creole*. He did this essentially by developing the earlier position of Calhoun. Wary of the British argument on the effect of 'free air', the Secretary maintained that the *Creole* blacks had at no time been within British territory until British officials interfered. But, above all, he stressed that the doctrine of the comity of nations took precedence over local law. Comity, or courtesy, led to the expectation that local authorities would help restore the previously existing situation, though this of its nature could not be a mandatory requirement. The officials in the Bahamas, however, had hindered the return of control of the ship to the master and crew and prevented the continuation of the voyage.[17] The American argument was plausible in that, ordinarily, out of comity a state would enforce foreign rights or the precepts of international law in the expectation of reciprocal action by the foreign power in the future. But in the case of the restitution of slaves the power of comity could be considered weakened from two points of view: municipal law was explicitly hostile to the maintenance of slave property and slavery was considered contrary to natural law.

Inevitably the abolitionists waved the argument from comity aside since they defined freedom as a natural right. Lawyers in parliament, equally naturally, supported the supremacy of the national legislature within British territory. The law officers had advised Peel's government that the law of nations did not require the fugitives to be returned and Denman confirmed this in the Lords, bolstering his position with quotations from Coke and Story. The concept of comity, he argued, was relevant only when the laws of all nations could be considered 'reasonable and just'. Only a treaty could provide effective machinery for the return of fugitives, and Denman concluded that the existence of slavery and the slave trade 'formed an insuperable difficulty to our government entering into any such treaty, or persuading the legislature to consent to any such law.' Campbell, Attorney-General at the time of the *Enterprise* case in 1837, declared that with the end of slavery in the West Indies 'a slave was as much free when he arrived in the Bahamas or at Bermuda as if he had reached Portsmouth or Plymouth'. The abolitionists reproduced extensive quotations from these legal–political authorities.[18]

The significant point, however, about some of the legal opinions which repudiated Webster's claims was that they went beyond defence of national sovereignty: Denman alluded to underlying principles of justice, while the pamphleteer-lawyer, Robert Phillimore defended the slaves' 'perfect right of freedom' against 'the imperfect right of courtesy' at the core of the American case. These comments implied that the legislation which had established 'free air' also gained extra force from embodying general principles of right and justice.[19]

Aberdeen's reply to the American minister, Everett, was grounded consistently on national sovereignty but his manner of response reinforced the impression that something more than the enforcement of municipal law was at issue. He stated flatly that the *Creole* blacks were free instantly on arrival at Nassau and 'the undersigned congratulates himself that he possesses no discretionary power in the case'. The general grounds of humanity, the foreign secretary argued, could not overrule the legal position that each country must make its own judgment on domestic matters. In regard to slavery he was rather disposed to appeal 'to the principles of justice than of humanity'. The reply went so far as to confront

Everett with the American tradition of natural rights by quoting at him 'the memorable language' of the preamble to the Declaration of Independence.

> But the undersigned leaves the application of these principles to the deliberate judgment of each independent state; and he feels satisfied in reflecting that the doctrine of Mr Everett will at least establish the supremacy of the law within the jurisdiction of each country respectively, whether its operation shall liberate the slave from his fetters or consign the free man to imprisonment.[20]

This was hardly a less firm rejection of comity than the *British and Foreign Anti-Slavery Reporter*'s view that to ask the British to subscribe to comity in this case was 'as if international courtesies were to have no limit and could require or justify participation in crimes the most atrocious and abhorred.'[21]

With some justification, therefore, anti-slavery men could feel that they were in harmony with legal and political opinion about the position of foreign slaves on British territory as a result of the West Indian ship cases. Agreement on the effect of 'free air' on the status of the slave was complemented by recognition of this effect as a badge of moral superiority for politicians, reformers, lawyers, and public opinion alike. There was even enough in the language of some legal authorities and the foreign secretary to allow the abolitionists to see support for their belief that the emancipation legislation embodied the natural right of all men to liberty and confirmed British attachment to the principle of natural justice. There seemed to be a consensus on the absolute character of the freedom attained by fugitive slaves when they touched British territory.[22]

The opening of negotiations between Webster and Ashburton, however, brought anti-slavery men face-to-face with the inherent tension between their commitment to the 'higher law' of freedom and its embodiment in legislation which derived its force from the sovereignty of Parliament. Through further legislation, or approval of executive action, or failure to prevent action, parliament could qualify any 'absolute' commitment. Abolitionists were aware that only treaty arrangements could deliver fugitives up 'to the vengeance of their [the slave-holders'] laws', so that the very fact of negotiations on an extradition agreement cast a dark doubt over their conclusions drawn from the ship cases.[23]

Both the British and American governments had an interest in an extradition agreement. Apart from concern over the West Indian ship cases, the Americans were dissatisfied with the discretionary powers given to the authorities of Upper Canada under local legislation of 1833 and the vague powers inhering in the governor of Lower Canada. Experience of a number of fugitive slave cases between 1829 and 1842 indicated that American slaveholders could not expect an automatic return of fugitives by the Canadian authorities since, especially after 1838, colonial officials required sufficient evidence of criminality under Canadian law to justify apprehension of a fugitive charged with a crime.[24] The obvious resolution of the problem, from the American point of view, was a specific extradition agreement containing such an enumerated list of offences as would secure the return of the vast majority of fugitives.

The British would have liked an extradition agrement to cover fugitives of other kinds, but were anxious not to concede either a specific agreement on shipwrecked or mutinous slaves or to accept a list of enumerated offences which could easily be invoked to get runaway slaves returned. Both Whig and Tory governments over a number of years had been consistently in favour of restricting the list of offences in any extradition agreement that might be concluded with the United States, and always insisted on the exclusion of 'mutiny and revolt on board ship'. Equally firmly, successive governments stated that no person would be surrendered merely because he had escaped from slavery.[25] Peel's government, however, wanted a general settlement of the outstanding issues between Great Britain and the United States, especially the north-eastern boundary question. As part of a comprehensive treaty, therefore, they accepted an extradition agreement in article ten; Aberdeen's firmness did succeed in excluding 'mutiny and revolt on board ship' from the enumerated offences.

Abolitionists had reason for dissatisfaction. It could be argued that the earlier requirement, which was to be continued, that any fugitive's alleged offence had to be considered criminal under local British law before he could be extradited met Aberdeen's insistence on the 'supremacy of the law within the jurisdiction of each country respectively'. If so, then the rule of action was vulnerable to attack as inadequate since under that rule, and on the eve of Anglo-American negotiations, the fugitive slave Nelson Hackett had been returned to Arkansas from Canada. To steal a horse and saddle might be necessary to gain freedom but to take a watch and coat was excessive self-indulgence.[26] Any agreement, even one in which the conditions for extradition were extremely strict, was seen by reformers as a weakening of the previous position. In the absence of a treaty or local legal provision they believed fugitives were afforded a general protection because the law of nations did not require return and a presumption in favour of freedom might be expected. Above all, the abolitionists reacted with something like shock, especially after the release of the *Creole* captives, to what they took as a sharp blow to their basic conviction that the Emancipation Act had guaranteed absolutely the freedom of the fugitive slave. They were also shaken out of their assumption that the legislation was widely understood as a statutory embodiment of the natural right to liberty. The reformers, therefore, adopted as a logical conclusion the need to exclude slaves completely from the operation of extradition.[27]

This position was entailed by the character of abolitionist ideology and was only departed from briefly in an attempt to get stronger safeguards written into the enabling act when it became clear that the government would not exclude slaves as such from extradition.[28] Nor could anti-slavery men accept the claim that the rule of criminality under municipal law had the beneficial effect for the slave of treating him on equal terms with the free man. Free and slave could not be regarded as equal since if a slave were extradited and then tried and actually found not guilty of his alleged offence, he would still be returned to perpetual bondage.[29] The trouble was that this argument was unlikely to impress the government because, even if true, it did not infringe Aberdeen's principle of the 'supremacy of the law within the jurisdiction of each country respectively'. On the contrary, since slavery was maintained largely by munipal law in the southern states, the principle was properly expressed by such treatment of a slave.[30]

This exposes the fact that as the main basis for British government policy, Aberdeen's rule could modify the effect of 'free air'. More damagingly, it created a principle which, by granting the right of southerners to treat slaves differently from other men, logically prevented any shift of government policy in response to the 'double jeopardy' argument which abolitionists took so seriously. Reformers, therefore, could stand on no other ground in principle than the natural right of man to liberty, above and beyond any legal limitations or, for that matter, guarantees.

In practice, anti-slavery forces had to work for more precise safeguards in the process of extradition by writing them into the enabling act when it was debated in Parliament in the summer of 1843. They were, for example, worried about fraud or perjury by those claiming fugitives. Ministers could only reiterate that the requirement of criminality under local law, the provision in the treaty for unilateral repudiation of the extradition agreement, and the formal requirements for applying through the Federal Government for an extradition would be likely to act as efficient safeguards.

But such reassurances, as the Attorney-General seemed to glimpse at one moment, could not fully meet the anxiety of abolitionists. If the government were to believe Americans capable of perjuring themselves to the extent that special provisions were required against it, he argued, then they should not enter into treaties or even engage in commerce with the United States.[31] Some reformers had concluded precisely that they had sufficient reason to distrust government officials as well as slave-holders and their agents. The columns of the abolitionist paper gave space to John Quincy Adams's role in the *Amistad* case of mutinous slaves who had taken over a Spanish slave vessel and who were released in the United States after an argument by Adams before the Supreme Court. The readers of the paper were therefore aware of the argument of anti-slavery Americans that in this case the Federal government had worked as the agent of the 'slave power'. That applications for extradition had to come through the government in Washington probably gave reformers less comfort than it did Aberdeen.[32]

Indeed, a significant theme of abolitionists in England in the years between 1839 and 1843 was that officials and politicians of various governments were vulnerable to corruption by slave-holders. The conduct of the Spanish minister in Washington, as well as the behaviour of the authorities in Cuba over the *Amistad* and the treaties against the slave trade concluded with Great Britain, were indefensible and influenced by slave-holding interests. The American government's conduct in the same case had been attacked by its own nationals. Even in British colonies where slavery had been ended, the former slave-holders exercising power in the local legislatures 'have but too successfully fettered the liberty they could not withhold and would perpetuate to the greatest possible extent their [the freedmen's] servile and degraded condition'. Not even officials in Canada in the Nelson Hackett case were above suspicion. Fears were reported both privately and publicly amongst abolitionists that local Canadian authorities had conspired with Hackett's American pursuers to mislead the new governor, Bagot, and secure the slave's return to Arkansas.[33]

Slave-holders by their very nature could be expected to continue to commit fraud and corrupt officials. They were 'shamelessly' possessed by 'vindictive passions' and determined to subject to 'punishments the most horrible and revolting' runaways who by their assertion of freedom set an example to their fellow bondsmen. Moreover, they believed 'the clause of the Treaty . . . enables them to do this [recover fugitives] by affording them the best because the easiest, the least expensive and most effectual way of satisfying their cupidity and glutting their vengeance'.[34]

During the passage of the enabling bill which was required to put extradition into effect, the abolitionists and their parliamentary spokesmen maintained their preference for total exclusion of slaves from extradition.[35] Failing that, they insisted that it was necessary in every case that the papers be returned to London for scrutiny to limit the likelihood of fraud in depositions and avoid the danger of corrupt or improper action by local officials.[36] Presumably the reformers calculated that they could reach, and perhaps influence, politicians in Whitehall but not in colonial territories at the local point of danger.

Equally important to their defence of 'free air' was the attempt to clarify the enumerated crimes, and thus help vindicate actions taken by fleeing slaves. The government assured doubters that the taking of property to escape would not be considered a crime; theft was in any case not amongst the enumerated crimes. But ministers would make no additional commitment.[37]

The impact made by the Apprehension of Offenders (America) Act of 1843 can be illuminated by studying two subsequent cases of fugitive slaves. Both cases preserved the freedom of the fugitives and both failed to resolve crucial doubts about the extradition procedure. The first incident, in 1843, involved a group of seven slaves who had stolen a small sloop on the Florida shore and had eventually been taken to Nassau by a British wrecker. There they were claimed by an American provost marshal on a charge of murder allegedly committed during a brief landing at some other point on the Florida coast. The reformers regarded this as a crucial test case because it occurred so soon after the enabling act became law. 'The eyes of the world', Aberdeen was informed, were on the case; the government was expected to be 'discriminating and firm'.[38]

While the slaves were not handed over, the result must have left the reformers with ambivalent feelings; the point which perhaps most concerned them in the operation of the extradition agreement – how a crime alleged against fugitive slaves would be defined by the courts – was left frustratingly without clarification. The judges in the

Bahamas found that the evidence did not enable them to pronounce on whether the slaves' alleged offence was criminal under local law. The claimants failed to provide sufficient information either viva voce or by copies of depositions upon which the original warrant was issued in Florida. The judges hinted that slavery could be relevant in determining criminality by noting that what constituted murder in Florida might not do so in the Bahamas. However, they were unable to clarify this comment and set a precedent. A warrant for apprehending the slaves was refused on the dangerously narrow ground that the claimants had failed to meet the documentary requirements of the 1843 act. If there had been evidence of the kind needed, the judges admitted, 'we should of course have considered ourselves bound to receive it and to issue our warrant for apprehending the offenders'.[39] This may have meant that more evidence in proper form would have made it clear that the alleged offence was murder under local law, or it may have implied the opposite. Until that ambiguity was removed abolitionists could not be satisfied.

The case of John Anderson in Canada in 1860–1 raised similar issues for the last time before the Civil War ended the problem. Anderson had escaped from Missouri in 1853 and had killed a white man, Diggs, who had tried to stop him. When Anderson was eventually discovered in Ontario both a local magistrate and two of three judges in Queen's Bench in Toronto concluded there was sufficient evidence to sustain a charge against the fugitive and issued a warrant of commitment. Anderson's counsel entered an appeal and delay was prolonged by the issue of writs of habeas corpus both from Common Pleas in Toronto and Queen's Bench in England, the latter on the intervention of L. A. Chamerovzow, the secretary of the BFASS. Both metropolitan and provincial reformers pressed action on the Colonial Office, and Newcastle intervened to halt extradition to give time to examine the case in London. Anderson was eventually released.[40]

The near-extradition of Anderson could be argued as sufficient ground for abolitionist anxiety. The crucial point, however, is a different one. The problem remained of whether prima facie evidence of criminality required merely sufficient evidence of the right kind, or involved a definition of the supposed crime. It has been argued that the public silence of British officials was deliberate and allowed them quietly to interpret individual cases in favour of freedom.[41] Equally, silence gave latitude to officials and the judiciary to interpret the 'safeguard' of criminality under local law in ways detrimental to fugitives. The judgments in Anderson's case in the Canadian Court of Queen's Bench illustrated this.

Chief Justice Robinson and Mr Justice Burns both concluded that the committal of Anderson was the correct decision. Robinson understood the phrase 'according to the law of this province' to refer only to the means and amount of proof required and not to touch the definition of the offence. Under local law in Missouri the man whom Anderson had killed had every right to attempt to arrest him. Robinson argued that a man in Canada could not be murdered in pursuit of a slave, because the law did not recognise slaves, but it did not justifiably follow that 'therefore a slave who had fled from a Slave State into this province can not be given up to justice because he murdered a man in that State'. By Canadian law the killing of a man legally authorized to carry out an arrest was considered murder.[42]

Burns was equally explicit in rejecting the plea that no murder had been committed if the killing was intended to secure liberty. 'That argument is a fallacy', he commented, 'for the two Governments in making the Treaty were dealing with each other upon the footing that each had then, at that time, recognized laws applicable to the offence enumerated'. The common-sense conclusion required that the law of the foreign country could not be entirely ignored; if this were not so the treaty lacked a true mutuality.[43]

McLean dissented from the majority opinion precisely because he believed that the phrase 'according to the law of this province' applied to the definition of the crime and not merely to the quantity and character of the evidence. He thought that 'the difficulty of imagining a parallel case suggests the idea that it will be better to take the case of the prisoner as it has been attempted to be established by evidence and apply to such evidence the rules of law by which we must be bound if such a case occurred in this Province'. Thus McLean found for Anderson because he concluded that the slave had committed no crime in escaping to better his own condition 'and the fact of his being a slave can not . . . make that a crime which would not be so if he were a white man.' The fact that Anderson was released did not resolve this difference since he went free on a technicality.[44]

Almost eighteen years after the act of 1843, abolitionists were aware that, although a desirable result had been achieved once again, 'the merits of the case are left untouched'.[45] Indeed, their fears of local decision-making had been intensified; their conviction that uniformity and justice in defence of the effects of 'free air' required intervention in the colonies by Whitehall remained. Only if decisions on fugitives were ultimately taken in London could the reformers themselves hope to have any influence.

The issue of the extradition of American fugitive slaves from British territory was quantitatively insignificant; it involved a handful of cases and a few hundred blacks in the West Indies and Canada. It does, however, throw light both on the intellectual difficulties of the abolitionists and the political constraints within which they worked. At the intellectual core of abolitionists' moral and political intransigence was the natural rights philosophy. They held to this commitment, which was moral as well as intellectual, because it offered an implicit criticism of positive law and political practice, in an era of advance in legal positivism. British courts after the Somerset case had progressively squeezed out the operation of anti-slavery morality based on the 'natural' state of freedom. Legal commentators and judges had also undermined abolitionist claims that there should be a correspondence between natural and international law by giving, in most cases, priority to the actual practice of states.[46] Thus, paradoxically, anti-slavery reformers were swimming against the legal and intellectual tide at the same time as abolitionism was making headway in the western hemisphere from the 1830s.

Politically, it was evident that protection of the fugitives by vindicating British national sovereignty was not the same as the acceptance of a natural right to liberty. The articulation of national sovereignty could contradict claims on behalf of slaves based on natural right. The implications went well beyond the fugitive issue. In their struggle to convert the world to free labour, British abolitionists had no other weapon anything like as strong as an anti-slavery British government; that weapon had been revealed as double-edged.

The element of conflict in the relations between reformers and government manifested over the extradition of American slaves had one more facet. By the beginning of the 1840s anti-slavery reformers often felt remote from the centres of power. The main reason for this was that significant figures amongst them – Joseph Sturge and the journalist Josiah Conder on the committee of the BFASS for example, and George Thompson outside it – defined themselves as Radicals 'not now in favour in High Quarters here'.[47] Provincial activists could confidently assert a continuity between abolition and domestic liberalism and even Chartism.[48]

The orientation of the active part of the BFASS committee

178   David M. Turley

towards political radicalism is evident too in their willingness to rely in parliament, in addition to their usual Whig spokesmen, on M.P.s, whose political complexion was radical or advanced liberal. The minute books note approaches to the militant dissenter, Edward Baines, the radical Sir George Strickland, the philosophical radical, Sir John Bowring and the universal reformer, William Sharman Crawford.[49]

Other noteworthy figures active in anti-slavery affairs both in the country and on the metropolitan committee of the BFASS were dissenting ministers who carried weight in their localities and often in their denominational organizations. Significantly, these men were involved, along with anti-slavery activities, in a complex of dissenting religious organizations such as the Voluntary Church Society, the Liberation Society and missionary agencies. The Rev. J. H. Hinton was prominent on the Broad Street committee of the BFASS, active in the Baptist Union and voluntaryist organizations as well as editor of the *Anti-Slavery Reporter* for a period. In the country, the leading Birmingham Congregationalist, the Rev. John Angell James and the prominent Glasgow minister, Dr Ralph Wardlaw, shared similar interests with Hinton.[50]

Thus, by the 1840s, a significant proportion of the anti-slavery leadership was part of a middle-class – dissenter – radical syndrome markedly different from the evangelical grouping of the earlier years of the century. Such leaders were predisposed to disagree with the outlook of both Whig and Tory governments in some areas of reform activity but, as anti-slavery men, hoped for the co-operation of government to suppress the slave trade, destroy slavery overseas and protect blacks whether free, freed, or fugitive. Inevitably, they were sharply aware of differences of approach which emerged between them and the government on anti-slavery issues. It was necessary to press hard to win over governments to which they were often unsympathetic and which they assumed were frequently unsympathetic to them.[51] The principled intransigence of abolitionists evident on the problem of American fugitives also served as the ideological cutting edge of a group of politically unassimilated reformers.

Notes

1 Howard Temperley, *British Anti-slavery, 1833–70* (1972), pp. 221–47; David M. Turley, 'Relations between British and American abolitionists from British emancipation to the American Civil War', unpubl. Ph.D. diss. (Cambridge, 1969), pp. 301–22.

2 Elizur Wright to Beriah Green, 19 March 1835, Elizur Wright Papers, Library of Congress; George Thompson, appendix VI, pp. 54–6 in Angelina E. Grimké, *Slavery in America. A Reprint of an Appeal to the Christian Women of the Slave States of America* (Edinburgh, 1837).

3 Temperley, *British Anti-Slavery*, pp. 168–83.

4 On Canadian cases see Alexander L. Murray, 'The extradition of fugitive slaves from Canada: a re-evaluation', *Canadian Historical Review*, XLIII (1962), pp. 298–314; Robin W. Winks, *The Blacks in Canada, A History* (Yale, 1971), pp. 168–77. Both of these correct Roman J. Zorn, 'Criminal extradition menaces the Canadian haven for fugitive slaves, 1841–61', *Canadian Historical Review*, XXXVIII (1957), pp. 284–94, who is too sanguine about the influence of the reformers. An account of the *Creole* incident is in Betty Fladeland, *Men and Brothers: Anglo–American Antislavery Co-operation* (Illinois, 1972), pp. 329–32.

5 John Bassett Moore, *A Digest of International Law* (Washington 1906), II, pp. 350–1.

6 5 Geo. IV c. 113 *An Act to amend and consolidate the Laws relating to the Abolition of the Slave Trade* (1824), especially clause XXIII.

7 See especially the cases of the *Diana* (1813), *English Reports*, 165, pp. 1245–8 and of the *Le Louis* (1817), *English Reports*, 165, pp. 1464–82.

8 Robert M. Cover, *Justice Accused: Antislavery and the Judicial Process* (Yale, 1975), Chap. 6.

9 Moore, *International Law*, pp. 350–1; Richard K. Crallé (ed.), *The Works of John C. Calhoun* (New York, 1851–5), III, pp. 9–14. Speech of 14 Feb. 1837.

10 In 1834 Palmerston turned down a Danish proposal for the mutual return of fugitive slaves in the West Indies on the grounds that the recent emancipation measure indicated Parliament would have nothing to do with such a scheme and that the full implementation of the legislation would remove all legal differences between the colonies and the United Kingdom. *Royal Commission on Fugitive Slaves Report . . . 1876* in *Parl. Papers, Reports, Commissioners*, 1876, XXVIII, C. 1516–I, pp. 523–4.

11 Lord McNair, selected and annotated, *International Law Opinions*, (Cambridge, 1956), II, pp. 80–5. Opinions of 19 April 1834; 31 Oct. 1836; 9 September 1837; 20 July 1838.

12 *Parl. Papers, Reports, Commissioners*, 1876, XXVIII, C. 1516–I, pp. 600–1; Moore, *International Law*, p. 351.

13 British and Foreign Anti-Slavery Society (hereafter BFASS), Minute Books, I, 14 August 1839, p. 84, Rhodes House, Oxford; *Emancipator*, 31 Oct. 1839.

14 The Somerset case, decided in 1772, was a test case regarding the status of a Negro in England, in which the subject of the case, James Somerset (an escaped slave threatened with being returned as a slave to Jamaica), was declared a free man. Many contemporaries believed the decision had practically outlawed English slavery, but this was not so, nor was it the final slave case in an English court.

15 *Hansard*, 3rd ser., LX, 1842, 27–30, debate of 3 Feb. 1842; BFASS,

Petitions and Addresses, 12 Feb. 1842, pp. 82–5, Rhodes House.

16 *Hansard*, 3rd ser., LX, 1842, 317–27, debate of 14 Feb. 1842.

17 Daniel Webster to Edward Everett, 29 Jan. 1842 in *The Diplomatic and Official Papers of Daniel Webster while Secretary of State* (New York, 1848); Robert Phillimore, *The Case of the Creole considered in a Second Letter to the Right Hon. Lord Ashburton, & C. & C. & C.* (London, 1842), pp. 49–51; Edward Everett to Aberdeen, 1 March 1842, *Parl. Papers*, 1843, LIX, pp. 464–71. Webster's argument received the sanction of the eminent American lawyer, Henry Wheaton in *Elements of International Law* (Boston, 1855), pp. CXXXIX–CXXXI.

18 McNair, *International Law Opinions*, II, pp. 85–8, opinion of 29 Jan. 1842; *Hansard*, 3rd ser., LX, 1842, 321, debate of 14 Feb. 1842; BFASS, *Third Annual Report* (1842), pp. 144–5; Phillimore, *The Case of the Creole*, pp. 7–10.

19 Phillimore, *The Case of the Creole*, pp. 20–1.

20 Aberdeen to Edward Everett, 18 April 1842, *Parl. Papers*, 1843, LIX, pp. 541–4. The last phrase refers to the habit of officials of southern states of imprisoning free coloured sailors on British ships for the duration of their call at a southern port.

21 Quoted in Henry H. Simms, *Emotion at High Tide* (Baltimore, 1960), p. 217.

22 This conclusion took no account of judicial decisions which had reduced the scope for the operation of natural rights and the effect of the Somerset judgment.

23 BFASS, Memorial to Aberdeen, 12 Feb. 1842, Memorials and Petitions, vol. I, p. 85, Rhodes House.

24 H. Fox Strangeways to Under Secretary at C.O., 28 Feb. 1838, C.O. 42/453, P.R.O.

25 Murray, *ibid.*, pp. 301, 306.

26 *Hansard*, 3rd ser., LXIV, 640–1, debate of 27 June 1842. Hackett had allegedly taken property in addition to that required to assist his escape. Theft was not an enumerated crime for the purposes of extradition under article ten of the Treaty of Washington, though robbery, presumed to include an element of violence, was.

27 BFASS Minute Books, II, pp. 40–1, 6 Feb. 1843; Memorial 'On the Extradition Clause of the Treaty of Washington', BFASS Petitions and Addresses, 1840–3, pp. 188–93; Joshua Leavitt to John Scoble, 27 Dec. 1842, 9 March 1843, S22 G. 84, Rhodes House; Thomas Clarkson to – (1842?), Thomas Clarkson Papers, Howard University, Washington DC.

28 BFASS *Fourth Annual Report* (1843), p. 121.

29 Memorial 'On the Extradition Clause of the Treaty of Washington', BFASS Petitions and Addresses, 1840–3, p. 189; *BFAS Reporter*, 19 Oct. 1842.

30 It worried a Canadian governor in an earlier Canadian case of an American fugitive slave. Sir Francis Bond Head to Glenelg, 8 Oct. 1837, C.O. 42/439, P.R.O.

31 Memorial 'On the Extradition Clause . . .', p. 190; *Hansard* 3rd ser., LXXI, 566–8, 11 Aug. 1843.

32 *BFAS Reporter*, 15 Jan. 1840; 29 July 1840; 24 Feb. 1841; 5 May 1841.

33 BFASS Memorial to Palmerston 9 Nov. 1839, Memorials and Petitions, p. 3; Memorial 'On the State of the Laws and the Administration of Justice in the Colonies' to Russell, 8 July 1840, loc. cit., pp. 18–25; Charles H. Stuart to Lewis Tappan, 9 Aug. 1842, S.18 C22/30, Rhodes House; *BFAS Reporter*, 21 Sept. 1842.

34 Memorial 'On the Extradition Clause . . .', pp. 189, 192, Thomas Clarkson to Aberdeen 11 Oct. 1843, BFASS Memorials and Petitions, pp. 234–6.

35 Aberdeen thought that to do this would vitiate the whole treaty. BFASS Minute Books, II, pp. 46–7, meeting 24 Feb. 1843. On 11 Aug. 1843 Hawes moved an amendment in the Commons but was defeated by 59 to 25.

36 BFASS Minute Books, II, p. 11, 25 Nov. 1842; *Fourth Annual Report* (1843), p. 121; Thomas Clarkson to Aberdeen, 11 Oct. 1843, BFASS Memorials and Petitions, pp. 234–6; Vernon Smith in *Hansard*, 3rd ser., LXXI, 564–6, 11 Aug. 1843.

37 BFASS Minute Books, II, p. 90, 19 July 1843; T. B. Macaulay in *Hansard*, 3rd ser., LXXI, 568–72, 11 Aug. 1843; *Hansard*, 3rd ser., LXX, 472–5, 30 June 1843; *Hansard*, 3rd ser., LXXI, 566–8, 11 Aug. 1843.

38 Thomas Clarkson to BFASS Committee, 5 Dec. 1843 in Annie H. Abel and Frank J. Klingberg (eds.), *A Side-Light on Anglo American Relations, 1839–58 furnished by the Correspondence of Lewis Tappan and Others with the British and Foreign Anti-Slavery Society* (Lancaster, Pa. 1927), p. 153, note 119; J. H. Hinton to Aberdeen, 6 Dec. 1843, BFASS, Petitions and Addresses, II, pp. 13–14.

39 *Parl. Papers, Accounts and Papers* (1844), vol. XXXIX, pp. 297–306.

40 BFASS Minute Books, IV, minute 125, 4 Jan. 1861; Glasgow Emancipation Society, Minute Books, pp. 335–6, 10 Jan. 1861, Smeal Collection, Mitchell Library, Glasgow; Duke of Newcastle to Officer administering the Government of Canada, 9 Jan. 1861, *Parl. Papers Accounts and Papers* 1861, LXIV, pp. 296–7.

41 Murray, 'Extradition of fugitive slaves', p. 313.

42 *Parl. Papers Accounts and Papers* (1861), LXIV, pp. 317–19.

43 *Ibid.*, pp. 327–8.

44 *Ibid.*, pp. 324–6. For a later expert view that the majority decision in Canadian Queen's Bench was correct see Edward Clarke, *A Treatise upon the Law of Extradition* (4th edn., 1903), pp. 250–1.

45 John Scoble to L. A. Chamerovzow, 16 Feb. 1861, S18 C23/88 Rhodes House.

46 F. O., Shyllon, *Black Slaves in Britain* (Oxford, 1974), pp. 125–231; Cover, *Justice Accused*, chap. 6.

47 Joseph Sturge to Amos A. Phelps, 2 Oct. 1841, Phelps Papers, Boston Public Library; Raymond G. Cowherd, *The Politics of English Dissent: The Religious Aspects of Liberal and Humanitarian Reform Movements from 1815 to 1848* (1959), pp. 153–4.

48 Glasgow Emancipation Society, *First Annual Report* (Glasgow, 1835), pp. 8–9. For other reform activities of anti-slavery men George Thompson, Mss Diary for 1846, week beginning 18 May, Raymond

English Deposit, John Rylands Library, Manchester; C. D. Rice 'The anti-slavery interest and the sugar duties, 1841–53' in 'The transatlantic slave trade from West Africa' (Centre for African Studies, University of Edinburgh, n.d.) (cyclostyled).

49 Turley, 'British and American Abolitionists', p. 59.

50 Henry B. Stanton, *Sketches of Reforms and Reformers of Great Britain and Ireland* (New York, 1849), pp. 226, 222–3.

51 In 1847, the parliamentary committee of the Anti-State Church Association selected fifty-three candidates, including Thompson, Sturge and Bowring as worthy of support by dissenters. Crawford and Strickland were pledged to voluntaryism as was Charles Buller who also aided the BFASS, Cowherd, *Politics of English Dissent*, pp. 162–3, 215 n. 65.

9
CONSCIENCE AND CAREER: YOUNG ABOLITIONISTS AND MISSIONARIES

by Bertram Wyatt-Brown

Historians are political creatures, and not always clear-thinking ones at that.[1] In racially conservative times, the 1930s and 1940s, we lambasted the abolitionists as insecure fanatics who started a war nobody wanted. In recent, more liberal days, the 1960s and 1970s, we have called them champions of racial justice and egalitarian fulfilment. Yet foreign missionaries, the abolitionists' contemporaries, are usually overlooked because they had almost nothing to do with home politics. When mentioned at all, they appear as narrow busybodies who imposed a shabby culture on helpless aborigines and opened the doors for imperialists. The contrast is startling. The anti-slavery crusaders were allegedly breaking chains while the foreign missionaries were forging them. Yet both groups stood for many of the same things, especially the end of bondage, whether it was *suttee* or the southern auction block.

Rather than explore the common features of these movements, the tendency is to exaggerate the differences. Both shared many values, hopes, and prejudices. Neither one was very subtle or circumspect about what it wanted; universal moral discipline and restraint on the one hand and personal autonomy and freedom from ancient sins and passion on the other. Foreign missionaries sought to elevate 'heathen' women and other dependents so appallingly maltreated. The abolitionists wished to uplift the 'bleeding' slave. It would be hard to judge which benevolent group deviated the most palpably from the pledge solely to use pacific, Christlike means to right these and other wrongs. Although foreign missionaries were probably more condescending toward the native peoples than abolitionists were in regard to American slaves, both groups had their egalitarian saints and their racially haughty sinners. In any event, the foreign missionaries and emancipationists agreed that literacy should not be used as a means for rulers, priests, and their allies to hold others in the bondage of ignorance. Education, these Christian Yankees insisted, should be available to all, the ordinary people of other continents as well as the blacks at home. Both sets of reformers hoped to create new Yankeedoms in places of darkness, firmly convinced in the exportability of their common culture. Theologically, foreign missionaries and anti-slavery advocates championed the Second Coming and were naïve enough to think the goals achievable in a matter of years. Despite these similarities, political perspectives of the causes and their leaders have muddled our understanding of who the abolitionists and foreign missionaries were.

Instead of recognizing how much alike antebellum reformers and evangelicals were, we have vainly tried for years to single out the abolitionists from the rest for the purpose of condemnation or praise. There was only one distinction that can be substantiated from written remains. Late in their pre-career stage, young adult abolitionists showed a decided fascination with politics as well as repulsion from the alleged corruptions of American party politics. More will appear on the issue later. But aside from this differentiation, no psychological or attitudinal key will ever be found to unlock the mystery of the abolitionists' motives.[2] The obstacle is not just the unprovability of psychoanalytic theory when applied to a group as conventional as abolitionists were. Nor is the problem simply the absence of the necessary historical information, much of which never existed in written form anyhow. Rather the difficulty is the politically biased proposition itself. It assumes an anti-slavery specialness – either toward iniquity or benevolence. Instead, the cause possessed all the shadings of good and ill that evangelicalism, its point of origin, had as well. We can learn much by examining common features that linked the reformers with their fervent brethren in Cherokee villages, Bedouin tents, and jungle clearings. No doubt, other sorts of evangelists or religiously minded laymen could provide reference points. Yet for purposes of drawing comparisons, the careers of foreign missionaries and abolitionists are particularly analogous. Their causes were self-sacrificing, poorly paid, socially problematical, dangerous, and much suspected by those whom they wished to convert.[3]

The most important single factor uniting missionary with abolitionist was that most unwelcome New England export: the evangelical conscience.[4] By examining the moral development of the youngster – the implanting and growth of conscience and character – one can ascertain the progress toward a lifetime's work in benevolence, though not specifically what branch of well-doing might be selected. In fact, many young people raised in pious homes entered science, medicine, parish ministry, or some other occupation with the conviction that the choice fulfilled a self-denying, God-given ambition to serve others. With great intensity and complete sincerity, other individuals did combine, for instance, a legal career with missionary labor (Jeremiah Evarts) or anti-slavery (Ellis Gray Loring).[5] The writer hopes that by focussing on two comparable careers, he can elucidate typical cultural responses within a special setting, the evangelical and chiefly New England environment.[6]

We should start as life does itself – at the beginning. The evangelical style of child-raising was an alternative to an older means that relied on shame, open humiliation, and physical pain to curb presumed child depravity. The latter doctrine had been associated with Calvinism, but actually the idea that children were all but incorrigible and required stern handling should not be identified too narrowly with any sectarian or theological position. In any case, an enlightened approach to childrearing had developed by 1800 and those practicing it belonged to denominations subject to evangelical influences. The new religious sensibility reflected a concern with the atonement of Christ more than the illimitable sovereignty of God, affection as much as obedience in human relations, the inner life more than the outward appearance, the integrity of the person over the demands for conformity. Of course, in the treatment of children, families adopted all sorts of patterns and methods, whether they were Quakers, Methodists, predestinarian Congregationlists, or belonged to some other denomination. On the whole, the children of evangelical parents were subjected to a scheme that, for all its faults, had a specific rationale: a clear expectation of what the results should be, and an attentiveness to the child that contrasted with the indifference that so often had marked the parental ways of the past.

Prescriptive literature, as well as daily practice ascertained from letters and diaries, indicated a growing conviction that calculated, rational, and predictable behavior toward the child shaped character toward self-dependence and appreciation of authority. The contradiction was an inherent aspect of the evangelical spirit. The system was somewhat chary of overt shows of affection – the fear of spoiling the child. But love there was in most cases, and from it a sense of self-confidence developed in the child. Rigorous, a little cheerless, and overly regimented, evangelical childrearing tried to link godliness with consistency, love with conscience, individuality with order, benevolence toward others with sacred duty.[7]

At the heart of the evangelical mode for conscience-building was the mother. Formerly, the authority for disciplining and making decisions about the children was in the father's hands. By the end of the American revolutionary era, the mother had gained the means and the ideology for devoting full attention to childrearing. Formerly she had been preoccupied with such soul-wearying, endless drudgeries as weaving cloth and making soap. But the developing economy provided her not only with such comforts as factory textiles but also the time for making plans about childrearing. Instead of just hastily reacting to the crises of the moment, mothers could concentrate upon becoming devoted child-raisers. It was a calling that every evangelical writer in the new republic assured them was both divinely ordained and patriotic. Through pious clubs called 'maternal associations', Sunday school and church sewing societies, and other newly developed organizations, mothers not only could leave the house to enjoy the exchange of childrearing ideas and gossip but also could display a very active piety which would instruct their own children. Benevolence, all agreed, should be taught by example as well as precept.

The mother's pre-eminence over father was not, of course, peculiar to households from which abolitionists would later emerge. Yet it appeared in most such homes. Thomas Wentworth Higginson, for instance, remembered that he owed his mother his most cherished principles: 'a love of personal liberty, of religious freedom, and of the equality of the sexes . . .' John G. Whittier, anti-slavery poet, also declared, 'I felt secure of my mother's love, and dreamed of losing nothing and gaining much', but his father was to him an elderly, austere presence. In similar fashion Higginson had little positive to say of his father, who had died when Higginson was eleven. 'I was unfortunately too young at that time to feel my loss much'.[8]

The self-conscious, inventive role for mothers encouraged the selection of one child, or perhaps two, for extraordinary attention. Quite early on, the youngsters learned that they must begin plans for the future, although the career was years away. Kenneth Keniston, the Yale psychologist, has called this emphasis upon the moral and career success of the child the creation of 'a sense of specialness'. In traditional fashion, boys heard about especially active roles of benevolent work for men. The future missionary Adoniram Judson was much encouraged, for instance, to play at Gospel preaching when only four. Likewise Wendell Phillips – to parental delight – enjoyed haranguing playmates seated beneath his 'pulpit'-chair. More unexpectedly, evangelical mothers sometimes urged daughters to think of serving Jesus as missionary wives. That career combined domesticity with romantic adventure and service to others. Children's literature included anecdotes from the lives of such heroines as Mrs Harriet Newell and Harriet Winslow. The Rev. Gardiner Spring, biographer of the missionary Samuel J. Mills put the matter this way: 'Many a godly mother can say, – "I have had peculiar solicitudes respecting *this* child. Even before its birth, I dedicated it to the Lord . . ."' Whatever the choice would later be, the child discovered that benevolence and career, when practiced in play, elicited parental blessing. In addition, the youngster became aware that he or she had been selected for a special destiny.[9]

Occasionally the strains of parental intrusion were too great or else the less gifted sibling felt neglected. Sometimes even the most exemplary of families raised ne'er-do-wells. The reasons for failure were bound to be complex, but certainly a sense of inadequacy for matching the high demands of parents – and high accomplishments of siblings – were among them. William Tappan took to drink the way that his younger brothers Arthur and Lewis took to good causes. William L. Garrison's brother was a drunkard. In contrast, the successful child in the experiment acquired the same conviction of future glory that the elders entertained for him. Sally Phillips, mother of Wendell Phillips, told the future abolitionist more than once, 'Be good and do good; this is my whole desire for you. Add other things if you may – these are central'.[10] He took the lesson to heart.

The subtleties involved can scarcely be recaptured from reminiscences, but occasionally one catches glimpses of the sense of specialness arising, particularly among the acutely sensitive and especially when the child had committed some wrong. Isaac Hecker's Methodist mother, for instance, had only to express some mild displeasure to plunge her boy into spasms of abject submission. Everton Judson, missionary to northern Italy, recalled his mother telling him at the age of six or seven, 'My son, I wish I could see you as much engaged in serving Jesus Christ as you are at your play'. He put down his toy and burst into sobs.[11]

In shaping the child's conscience toward benevolence and piety, the evangelical mother well knew the importance of stirring anxiety.

From fear of disapproval and from desire for praise and love, sometimes withheld as penalty, the child learned to listen to his or her inner voice. Sometimes, fear of death, a greater reality for children then than now, was enlisted to serve godly purpose. David Marks, an evangelist to the West, recalled that his Calvinist Baptist mother nightly tucked him into bed with the words, 'Soon my son you will exchange the bed for the grave, and your clothes for a winding sheet'.[12] As adults, many evangelicals expressed resentment for such morbid laments. Yet the remarks met the purpose intended. Anxiety, fear of meaninglessness, abandonment by God and loved ones, became a spur to life. Strangely this kind of anxiety seemed to encourage self-confidence and grittiness, not despair or lassitude.[13] The price, however, was the painful goad to do good, as child and adult; the effort was often taxing and driven.

Non-reformers, non-abolitionists – quite ordinary church-goers – were raised in the same fashion. The difference was that some children took the lessons of conscience and burden of inner doubt with unusual seriousness. They were not necessarily prissy or submissive. Yet, as a rule, the future well-doer was more aware of moral strictures than other youngsters. Theodore Parker offered an insight into his own upbringing. Once at age five, he nearly killed a turtle. But he refrained. Racing home, he breathlessly asked his mother Hannah why he had not struck the turtle. She exclaimed, 'Some men call it conscience, but I prefer to call it the voice of God in the soul of man. If you listen and obey it, then it will speak clearer and clearer . . . but if you turn a deaf ear or disobey, then it will fade out . . . and leave you all in the dark and without a guide'. Parker concluded the recollection with the words, 'no event in my life has made so deep an impression upon me'.[14]

The tale was not as important as the tendency it represented. Likewise in abolitionist biographies and other sources, there were frequent references to parental kindnesses and sympathies toward a local black, fugitive slave, or some other victim of prejudice and ridicule. The anecdotes supposedly had a bearing on the observing child's later entry into philanthropy or reform. In all likelihood, though, similar incidents occurred in many ordinary households, but, lacking predictive meaning, the episodes never received literary notice. One may even doubt the authenticity of the details that abolitionists supplied when illustrating family charity. But there can be no question about the depth of piety, concern for abstract justice, and sensitivity to the needs of others that these incidents came to symbolize. By such pleasing recollections, one often links the past with present interest. For anti-slavery reformers, the memory was especially consoling. These stories inspired the reformers to continue a pattern set before them so early and so well.

Intelligent, strong-willed, and benevolent though many of these evangelical mothers were, they exhibited a certain ambivalence about their children, too. The Calvinist heritage in New England was powerful. Intellectually gentler theologies – Arminianism, Unitarianism, for example – could be adopted as the family religion, but emotionally religious, concerned parents alternated between hope and doubt over human ability to overcome evil. In any case, mothers knew that pampering the young was no way to prepare them for a world of sin and sorrow. Love was offered provisionally, with little spontaneity. Theodore Parker's mother, for instance, had given the boy warmth and warning in equal measure. Moreover, even when a mother was affectionate, her nurturing could be offset by the severity of the father. William McLoughlin, the historian of American religion, argues that evangelical parents produced 'immense amounts of anxiety, self-doubt, and dependence', so that there was a constant and unhealthy desire to please the father, an unrequited effort lasting a lifetime. Certainly, in some instances, that was the result. Take for example John Greenleaf Whittier's childhood. Whittier vividly recalled seventy years afterwards how he had quailed before a weekly trip with his taciturn, unloving father. The Quaker farmer of Massachusetts and his five year-old son had to climb a steep hill at the top of which a screeching gander always waited. As they approached the boy grew terrified lest the goose would peck at him with a fury to match the squawk. The resentments Whittier felt toward his domineering father prevented him from expressing his fear. He never asked his father for help or sympathy on this or any other occasion. Encouragement would not have been forthcoming. The fretful patriarch, then fifty-three, had already been complaining of his son's unmanly sensitivities and later ridiculed his poetry-writing. In Whittier's case, the burden of special holiness and equally intense agony of introspection, reticence, and suppressed rages, as Perry Miller has noted, lasted a full lifetime in reform. Yet, it would be wrong to assume that the abolitionist poet and others under similar psychic pressures did not develop a spirit of independence and deep sense of themselves. Conscience-stricken, even overly anxious, such individuals as Whittier were seldom self-pitying or timidly conforming. Their concern for others, not their disappointments with themselves, was to give meaning to their lives.[15]

Yet all Whittier's examples of familial distresses early in childhood could be replicated a thousand times in the lives of individuals quite outside the anti-slavery orbit. The illustrations, and others like them, are intriguing, and are most suggestive about the effects of family troubles upon the way individuals developed. Perhaps father–child tension was a factor in predisposing the child toward some kind of dream of self-sacrifice – certainly, anxieties of an intense character helped to shape personalities. But, it should be remembered that Wendell Phillips, the Grimkés, the Tappans, William Jay, Elizur Wright and many others had fathers both loving and successful, supportive and yet strict. No single family problem or childhood distress distinguished the anti-slavery reformer from the rest of mankind.

Others – non-abolitionists – registered similar kinds of childhood strain. 'Properly speaking I had no childhood', lamented Orestes Brownson, the transcendentalist and Catholic convert. Isaac Hecker's father, an alcoholic, was a source of perpetual family worry. 'I knew nothing but fear', declared Clara Barton, founder of the American Red Cross. Each of these individuals had peculiarities of character related to their early experiences. There was no common factor, however, to predict their later lives. In Barton's case, the father was a genial, strong-minded figure, but her mother was excessively temperamental. A maiden aunt was even more dangerously violent and was confined in an upstairs room. Forced to sit for hours in an unheated church as a little girl, Clara recalled 'being taken home one bitter Sunday with frozen feet. I had not dared complain and fell in the pew when they set me down.' Like Whittier, she had remained silent for reasons of pride, unexpressed fury, and fear of capricious reprimand. Yet these and other signs of family troubles and childhood reaction affected only personality. They burdened the developing child, but they did not determine future occupation.

Anxiety, so consciously aroused, was a major component of evangelical culture, but it affected no group, abolitionist or otherwise, more than another. Worry about personal righteousness, parental intrusiveness, even severely unhappy childhoods, beckoned some toward benevolence, others to pious ways within business careers, some to indifference, called 'nothingarianism', and a few to outright anti-evangelical 'unrighteousness'. Yet, those who did enter reform came with the instructed conscience, implanted as early as five years of age. The English divine Richard Baxter had told parents: 'It is conscience that must watch them in private, when you see them not; and conscience is God's officer and not yours; and will say nothing to them, till it speak in the name of God'. Almost by definition, missionaries and reformers were untranquil souls. They had learned dissatisfaction with themselves and the world. Yet few ever dared curse the parents who had bound them over to 'God's officer', a drill-master as tough and unyielding as any birch-stick.[16]

As one could anticipate, these children, singled out for specifically moral purposes, were often intellectually gifted. Parents encouraged study and reading for two reasons aside from concern for knowledge. First, reading banked the fires of young exuberance and passions. Secondly, being solitary, reading was one way to shield the child from bad influences. In closely knit communities, the churchgoing children could scarcely avoid the usual hazings, fights, and masculine challenges of one kind or another. Therefore, the child who took to books and study not only pleased master and parent but also separated himself from the unrefined by inclinations for study. The thirst to learn became a form of segregation and as a result, skills accumulated. The anti-slavery leaders Theodore Parker, Theodore Weld, and Elijah Lovejoy were all remarkable for their self-trained memories. Adoniram Judson's mother began her boy's literary training at the age of three. Elizur Wright, Weld (both abolitionists), and David T. Stoddard (a missionary to the Nestorians), stood at the head of their classes. Not only did these and many other reformers and evangelists show intellectual promise, but that promise sped them along the moral, even solitary, paths laid out for them by their parents.[17]

Likewise, women in both causes showed uncommon abilities. Anti-slavery women were bound to be unusually imaginative and alive to moral and political questions. The first women into the foreign mission field, usually as wives of leaders, also proved themselves especially gifted, sometimes even in such unfeminine topics as mathematics and science. Yet, the road for women was a difficult one. Even in evangelical households, too aggressive an approach to scholarly competition was considered unladylike. When Elizabeth Cady Stanton, for instance, won academic honors, her father, grieving lost sons, exclaimed, 'Ah, you should have been a boy'.[18] He did not wish her to deviate from the submissive role assigned to women.

Even for the boys, academic competition was condemned as worldly, but they still struggled fiercely for prizes. After all, the parable of the talents pointed the way. The result was that a tension arose, never to be stilled in the benevolent heart: humility of mind was submission to God. Hope of glory required mental vigor.

Neither parent nor conscience could resolve that contradiction. Though not debilitating in most cases, the dilemma of intellectual hubris and piety proved troublesome for a few adolescents. Charles Torrey's biographer reported that his 'two years [at Exeter Academy] not only fitted him for college but well nigh unfitted him for this world and the next'. Theodore Weld struggled constantly against pride with almost narcissistic zeal. For most, the strain was manageable. Yet, fears of laziness, and of giving in to passion, checked youthful spontaneity. (Ironically, the effervescence thus repressed became in adulthood for some like Weld an elusive object of ambition.[19])

As the school child arrived at adolescence, he or she was thus subjected to contrary goals and drives, but the aim toward a benevolent course of life was already charted. The contradictions were themselves a means to reach the career. Instead of producing a state of permanent confusion or religious rejection, the adolescent physiological turmoil served as a testing time of dedication. The rite of passage toward Christian conversion, observed William James, 'is in its essence a normal adolescent phenomenon, incidental to the passage from the child's small universe to the wider intellectual and spiritual life of maturity'. In addition, it was the time of discovery. Young people were learning who they were and what engaged their fidelity.[20]

The most significant event in the future abolitionist or missionary's life as a teenager was the conversion experience. It was an occasion to be cherished for a lifetime. It marked the beginning not just of manhood but of Christian commitment and a godly career (of some, as yet unspecified kind). Some went through the ordeal in conventional fashion, especially when a revival was underway. Then everybody joined in the excitement. Those with special feelings of fervor and declension did not cross the spiritual divide so smoothly. Sensitive souls by inclination, they suffered acutely. At thirteen, for instance, Henry Lyman, the 'Martyr of Sumatra', happened to swear aloud in front of friends. They teased him with such remarks as 'Oh! Henry Lyman, what will your father say if he heard that?' 'My moral nature' quivered and trembled 'under the shock like an aspen', he recalled. 'I hear even now that oath ringing in my ears . . . that *horrible heavy* mountain that rolled back upon my soul – that withdrawal of the restraints of divine grace.'[21] It was the beginning of Lyman's youthful conversion.

This experience was not idiosyncratic. No doubt, some physicians, businessmen, and politicians also remembered dramatic revival conversions. What matters, however, is that the totality of factors pressed the missionaries and abolitionists toward their destiny. The key point is that very few men and women of the mission and anti-slavery causes failed to experience the converstion rite, or came from religiously indifferent households, or grew up with habits quite out of keeping with the evangelical conscience. Thus, Elijah Lovejoy's wanderings were not peculiar to him, for both inside and outside the anti-slavery circle, others acted similarly, but seldom with such excessive zeal. He walked all the way from Waterville, Maine to New York City, eating almost nothing. He suffered from headaches, a result of the strains of the soul as much as the deficiencies of his diet. His pilgrimage was a penance for not professing faith. The transgressions worried his parents and pious brothers for many years. Selfhood, he appeared to say, could not be forced upon him. Eventually, though, he found relief and regeneration – the delay, if not the depth of agony, was one with which any evangelical could sympathize.[22]

Women abolitionists and reformers also had to suffer at this critical juncture. Raised in an unusually high-minded and pious household in South Carolina, Sarah Grimké at thirteen offered herself as godmother for her baby sister Angelina, but did not feel wholly adequate to the responsibility. As Gerda Lerner, her sensitive biographer, says, 'she was deeply in earnest in her pledge and, years later remembered the profound emotions which caused her to shut herself in her room after the [baptismal] ceremony and pray to make her worthy of the task she had assumed'. Susan B. Anthony, another who fought for slaves and women's rights, mourned over her 'hardened heart' and yearned that she might grow 'more and more refined until nothing shall remain but perfect purity'.[23]

The movement out of declension could take a number of forms, the most untypical being that of Henry C. Wright, later an abolitionist. His conversion seemed to be associated with early childhood experiences in a very direct way – the yearning for an affectionate mother. 'When a boy in my teens, at a Sunday meeting in a country church far in the interior of N.Y. state, a Babe was put into my arms during sermon time, to rest the mother . . . I sat looking into its face – so fair, so beautiful. . . .' The preacher expounded the doctrine of Original Sin and predestination but it *'flashed'* upon Wright that God was not in the preacher's voice. Instead, the true divinity was in the sleeping child. The baby, declared Wright in recollection, was 'the image of God. . . . It was an era – a marked *Event* of my life'. More conventional, however, was the experience of Jonas King, missionary to Greece. Unimaginatively he claimed to have felt a sudden and permanent state of religious commitment after praying in the woods.[24]

The first crisis of spiritual identity, usually begun and resolved in the teens, did not generally lead to a career decision. One reason was that by the 1820s New England's sons (to some extent daughters, too) had a variety of career options, some requiring additional education. To await further maturing, to provide an emotional resting spot, some of those with a sense of special mission became temporary teachers or benevolent society clerks. Charles Torrey, among others, tried schoolkeeping, but the indifference of his performance led him to mourn: 'What shall I do, God knoweth, I do not. . . . Is it my fault that I am not as old as Methuselah? How can I help my youth?'[25] Others delivered inspirational tracts, clerked at national benevolent agency headquarters, edited small reform sheets, and joined summer crusades to free the slave, such as Weld's band of Oberlinites. These offered satisfactions of idealism and commitment, but they were not necessarily permanent.

Ordinarily there was a second crisis of the spirit in the twenties. Though similar to the first in its gyrations of feeling, the second episode concerned career much more than personal identity. The form was the familiar conviction of sin, emptiness, alienation from God, but the question uppermost was: what am I to do in life? Peers, admired elders, perhaps a college professor or more mature student exercised considerable influence in the working out of the problem. Usually the subject put down on paper his innermost feelings, just as he had in the first crisis. The journal made a handy reference for substantiating the unfolding spiritual events, perhaps to please a seminary official. Certainly, memorialists of the missionaries and crusaders found them very useful in writing up the accounts for public edification. In any case, the young collegian, even seminarian felt obliged to undergo the second test of faith, another rebirth, particularly if he was weighing the dangers of foreign work against the conveniences of home.

Just as parents had inculcated conscience, so ministers, church elders, and college faculties guided the young person toward a benevolent career during the intermediate period between parental authority and adult autonomy. Religious societies and presses churned out hundreds of sermons, old works and new, all of which not only demanded belief in a saving Lord but also the witness and sacrifice of spreading the gospel. The policy was no less calculating, intense, and rigorous than the strategy practiced in the home.[26]

Being incorporated into a rather sophisticated religious apparatus, the second crisis was both self-conscious and stylized in a way that the more immature first conversion was not. At Amherst College, for instance, Henry Lyman made a show of spurning a religious revival among classmates. On a spring day in 1827, however, a friend saw him meditating and invited him 'to a grove of pine, beneath whose shade was a sanctuary'. The grove was so designated in conscious imitation of a famous haystack near Andover Seminary where in 1809 Adoniram Judson had led a group of earnest seminarians to pledge their lives to the mission cause abroad. Jauntily, Lyman refused, though he admitted to serious religious doubts, especially about the doctrine of election. A few days passed during which Lyman consulted with President Heman Humphrey, professors, and with both pious and 'gay associates.' Finally, however, he and his solicitous friend repaired to the appropriate site. Lyman's eyes filled with tears as he confessed, '*I am all in the wrong*'.[27] It was the beginning of his second change of heart and purpose. He would become a missionary abroad. The whole incident – the inquiries of the friend, the sacred location, the consultations with believers and (respectable) unbelievers, the meditations, and finally the intimate and emotional admission of sin to the fellow student – seemed novel and exciting to the participants but a considerable tradition and conscious planning lay behind this second ritual of conversion.

The result of the lengthy, hard-won conversion was that young men and women took enormous pride in the grand work of well-doing that opened before them. Yet sometimes well before, sometimes long after the second episode of dedication to God, moments of doubt and declension assailed. Byronic *angst*, particularly over sexual interests, stimulated thoughts of death. John H. Noyes at Dartmouth College, for instance, noted that 'Two patients sorely afflicted with the hypo [that is, hypochondria or depression] have applied to me today for consolation. I advised them never to read Byron, never to think of suicide, and above all repeat every five minutes: 'Faint heart never won fair lady'.[28] Henry C. Wright, a young seminarian and future abolitionist, filled his diary with allusions to the 'mansion' of death that lovingly beckoned. Sarah Grimké remembered a time when 'I craved a hiding-place in the grave. . . . I was tempted to commit some great crime, thinking I could repent and then restore my lost sensibility.' Elijah Lovejoy set his miseries in verse.[29]

These self-indulgent, youthful depressions were a passing phase in the process of working out the role in life. They scarcely should be considered a peculiarity of future abolitionists and idealists. Yet they did have a bearing on later career developments, particularly for those in the foreign mission field and the abolition cause. Both causes were physically dangerous and emotionally taxing. From Andover Seminary, Henry Lyman, for instance, wrote to his sister:

> When these four years have rolled around, I shall probably be in my grave, on a sick bed, or on mission ground. Yes, the pleasures of home, and country, and kindred shall be sacrificed. But what do I say? Rather, the pleasure of leading the benighted heathen to Jesus shall not be sacrificed for home, country, or friends. Would that tomorrow's rising sun might witness my final departure from New England.[30]

The consummation of the romantic feelings that Lyman typified was the contemplation of a glorious martyrdom. In a sense, men like Lyman were engaged in a spiritual wager: if God granted life, the missionary would perform miracles in His service. If God willed death, He was obliged to recognize the sacrifice by conferring salvation. Their pact was not with Mephistopheles, but with the Holy Spirit, and often with the hope of earthly fame as well. The nature of their parent-guided conscience forced them constantly to see this unflattering possibility – the temptation into self-glorification. 'The leading influence of my life', confessed a young abolitionist writing to Theodore Weld in 1850, 'was the love of admiration. . . . Coarse food, hard bed, labor, long walks, fatigues of any kind' were the means to 'get admired'. Steeped as they were in theology, such men well knew how close they flirted with the blasphemy of challenging God to deny them His gratitude. As Pliny Fisk, missionary to Palestine, declared before his final career decision, 'Many unholy motives may induce a man to desire this work. I wish, therefore, to re-examine all my past resolutions and plans, and inquire anew what I ought to do'.[31]

Always self-conscious, forever restless, the products of the evangelical mode of development were well-equipped to meet the clearly marked out goals of New England piety, love of self-reliance, and hatred of sin. They sought to uplift communities allegedly lacking in this cultural trinity. Certainly there was almost a self-absorbed preoccupation involved, but this was quite in keeping with the early channelings of conscience and aggression imparted from childhood. 'By my influence, with God to direct and bless, Africa may be made to arise from her degradation and shake herself from her chains,' mused a seminarian and future abolitionist, Amos

A. Phelps. This was American 'individualism' at a zenith: the single handed conversion of a continent.[32]

Finally, there was the matter of a very significant difference between the abolitionist and the foreign missionary: the attitude toward politics and the moral state of America. For reasons that had little to do with upbringing but much to do with peers and personal experience, future abolitionists had a predilection for changing the minds of those they knew best, not only on religious but also secular topics. Moreover, in contrast to the often squabbling foreign missionaries, they seemed a more gregarious lot, happier in association with each other.[33] One cannot be very definitive about the matter, though, for even abolitionists were well-known for their fractiousness. Yet, it would seem that only future abolitionists vexed themselves over politics. They were provoked by such affairs as Anti-Masonry, Nullification, Sunday mail laws, and the like, in contrast with the apolitical attitude of future missionaries. This orientation was, of course, very logical and self-selective. They put themselves beyond governments, some beyond life itself. Jehudi Ashmun and Samuel Bacon, early missionaries to Liberia, carried matters to extremes hard to match in the abolitionist movement. 'I came to these shores to *die:* and any thing better than death is better than I expect,' declared Samuel Bacon. Ill from consumption and, as always, severely depressed, Ashmun returned to his Liberian post, determined to 'spend' what little remained of life 'dwelling among distant savages'. They both won very quickly the reward they seemed to court so eagerly.[34]

Obviously someone stimulated by events in Washington and the state capitals was not so likely to bury himself, like Ashmun and Bacon, in a fever-ridden country. So too a pietistic turn of mind would scarcely be compatible with a cause so clearly a matter of law, politics, and social control as slavery. For instance, Amos A. Phelps thought of becoming a missionary to Liberia himself. He shortly changed his mind, having already shown considerable fascination with politics – as well as a repulsion from its alleged corruption. By 1830, his worry over Jacksonian 'tyranny,' Fanny Wrightism, Cherokee Indian Removal, and other issues especially worrisome to evangelicals, led him to break with an old schoolmate and friend, William Weeks. In almost a microcosm of Yankee divisiveness over anti-slavery politics later, Weeks denounced Phelps roundly as a *'Politician Minister'*. Once a Congregational ministerial candidate himself, Weeks, a young lawyer, had become a blindly loyal Jacksonian partisan, receiving a postmastership in Canaan, New

Hampshire, as reward. Phelps professed disgust at the news. To complete his new self-image, he renounced Congregationalism and joined the Baptists. The set of decisions had its logic, no less than Phelps' combination of Congregational ministry, Anti-Masonry, Sabbatarianism, and eventual anti-slavery commitment.[35]

On the other hand, the decision to become an abolitionist was almost a secular matter. The conversion cycle of juvenile religious identity and then, in young adulthood, of career choice did reappear in the anti-slavery decision, but only in some instances and seldom with much drama. Weld's Lane Debates ritualized for seminarians the cause of the slave in much the same manner as Judson's efforts at Andover in behalf of foreign missions. But many reformers simply reacted in a variety of ways to the prospect of immediate emancipation. James G. Birney (one of Weld's most prominent converts), Lydia Child, Gerrit Smith, Lewis Tappan, Charles Torrey, Wendell Phillips, Elijah Lovejoy, Henry Wright, Sarah Grimké, and others claimed to have heard an inspiring speech, read a particular pamphlet, reacted indignantly to some slaveholding or Yankee atrocity, all of which signified some sudden heartfelt change. The conversion rite rather demanded such specificity – it made a better story. From what limited records we have, however, it is clear that the process was much lengthier than the reformer cared to admit. Henry Wright, for instance, talked for many months with various friends and critics of the cause – such as James Birney, and Henry Blagdon of Brighton, the conservative revivalist. Birney, then in Boston on anti-slavery business, convinced Wright that bringing the Gospel to the heathen was impossible so long as slavery existed. Blagden, however, took the pietistic side. In his opinion, Wright noted in his journal, such causes as temperance and anti-slavery 'led men to make Religion consist in breaking off from *external sin. Seems to think it wrong to urge men to break off from external sins till their hearts are charged and the fountain is purified*.' Wright believed, though, that the very best way 'to conquer an evil propensity is to cease to indulge in it *outwardly*.' Works, as much as faith, he was implying, were necessary to salvation, a position with secular overtones, though one that evangelicals generally professed. Like almost everybody else in the anti-slavery cause, Wright had had no flashes of revelation. He adopted anti-slavery for intellectual as well as emotional reasons. Over time, however, the anti-slavery commitment developed deep and abiding roots, at least for many of its leaders.[36]

In summary, what the missionary and abolitionist shared often included: a common upbringing under strict, orthodox, evangelical parents; a conversion experience of rich personal meaning; a sense of special destiny, the product of compulsive application to study; a post-parental subjection to pious, admired superiors and elder friends who stirred religious ambitions; and finally a common decision to seek a risk-taking course for the sake of God and personal fulfilment. The sole distinction, aside from the obvious institutional differences between the causes, was a parting of the ways on the matter of politics. One should not, however, overstress the discrepancy. During the 1840s and 1850s, the American Missionary Association, created by abolitionists, served the ambitions of quite politically-minded young evangelicals in the foreign and domestic fields. Some later returned from Jamaica and other lands, as well as from western Indian settlements, to work with freedmen as schoolteachers and chaplains during and after the Civil War.[37] These pious missionaries were keenly aware of domestic moral troubles, a contrast with the views of their missionary predecessors in the 1810s and 1820s.

Quite clearly political interest could well be combined with foreign mission work. The difference between the abolitionist and foreign missionary might really have reflected only a question of timing and opportunity rather than psychological predisposition. In the years following the War of 1812, political matters were momentarily quiescent. Religious revivals and concerns, on the other hand, seized the public imagination. The brightest and most committed idealists of that era naturally turned to the grand adventure of foreign and domestic missions. The 1810s and 1820s were the high mark of the foreign mission field. Gradually, however, foreign work became less a leap into the inspiring unknown. Though outstanding leaders – accomplished linguists, teachers, and physicians – continued to enter the mission field in the decades thereafter, the cause gradually was becoming routine, to some even unpromising. Guilt for *not* joining fellow seminarians in the pledge to Christianize the heathen became easier to bear. At the same time, in the 1830s and 1840s, attention turned to domestic matters, especially anti-slavery. The talented, ambitious evangelical did not follow Adoniram Judson, Mrs Harriet Newell, and Henry Lyman, but instead joined Theodore Weld, William Lloyd Garrison, and the Lane seminarians to brave the clamorous tribes at home. The eventual result was that the abolitionist became increasingly man-centered (since it was the nature of the cause itself), whilst the foreign missionary, on the other hand, remained God-centered.

In any case, the two causes of foreign missions and anti-slavery shared the same sources of inspiration. Their advocates sought to bring order and healing freedom to those they believed mired down in bondage, chaos, and blind ignorance. Yet, in plotting the history of the great nineteenth-century reforms and crucially important movements like the foreign missionary impulse, the historian must consider not merely the character and conscience of those so engaged. Instead one must also acknowledge the remarkable success of their parents, especially the mothers of these persevering Victorians. Discipline and freedom, conscience and career, hope and anxiety were uniquely blended for one generation. The results outweighed the defects. To ask more of these benevolent leaders than they had the sophistication to comprehend would be churlish. Their accomplishments endured. 'No man can begin to mould himself on a faith or an idea without rising to a higher order of experience: a principle of subordination, or self-mastery had been introduced into his nature; he is no longer a mere bundle of impressions, desires, and impulses,' wrote George Eliot, who understood the evangelical mind so well. For all their many failings of credulity, regimentation, and unconquerable seriousness, the missionary and abolitionist, both man and woman, knew there was 'divine work to be done in life,' as Eliot said, and set about doing as best they could.[38]

Notes

1 D. H. Donald, *Lincoln Reconsidered* (New York, 1956), pp. 19–36; M. B. Duberman, (ed.), *The Antislavery Vanguard* (Princeton, 1965), G. Sorin, *The New York Abolitionists* (Westport, Conn., 1971), are among the works arguing for abolitionist particularity.

2 More thoughtful than most anti-slavery scholars is Ronald Walters who reminds us that abolitionists were 'less unique in their anxieties and hopes than in the embodiment they found for those anxieties and hopes'. See R. G. Walters, 'The Erotic South', *American Quarterly*, 25 (1975), p. 200.

3 J. Scudder to S. Worcester, 3 May 1819; S. Worcester to W. Jenks, 25 September 1815; Worcester to J. Prichard *et al.*, 1 October 1815; J. Wood to Worcester, 18 May 1819; J. Wheeler to Worcester, 1 October 1836; J. L. Wilson to R. Anderson, February 12, 1833; Applicant Testimonial Files, American Board of Commissioners for Foreign Missions (hereafter ABCFM), Houghton Library, Harvard University.

4 Common social grounds should also be mentioned, though the topic is beyond the limits of this essay. See D. F. Allmendinger, *Paupers and Scholars* (New York, 1975), esp. pp. 65–94. The ABCFM papers are

also revealing: out of 25 applicants, 1819–35, 6 were orphans or had lost fathers and were in reduced circumstances, yet 25 came from middling social ranks.

5 E. C. Tracy, *Memoir of the Life of Jeremiah Evarts* (Boston, 1845); on Loring, see *Dictionary of American Biography*, xi, pp. 416–17.

6 For a theory of how cultural responses function, see P. Bourdieu, *Outline of a Theory of Practice* (trans. R. Nice), (Cambridge, 1977),

7 A. L. Kuhn, *The Mother's Role in Childhood Education* (Yale, 1947), p. 27; N. F. Cott, 'Notes toward an interpretation of antebellum child-rearing,' *The Psychohistory Review*, 6 (1978), 4, pp. 4–20; C. Strickland, 'A Transcendentalist father: the childrearing practice of Bronson Alcott', *Perspectives in American History*, 3 (1969), pp. 5–76.

8 M. T. Higginson, *Thomas Wentworth Higginson* (Port Washington, N.Y., 1977 ed.), p. 7; S. T. Pickard, *Life and Letters of John Greenleaf Whittier* (Boston, 1894), i, p. 26; D. Hunt, *Parents and Children in History* (New York, 1970), pp. 30–1.

9 K. Keniston, *Young Radicals* (New York, 1968), pp. 44–51, 55–60; E. H. Erikson, (ed.), *Youth: Change and Challenge* (New York, 1963), pp. 1–23; *ibid.*, *Childhood and Society* (New York, 1963), pp. 287–96. See also, B. J. Finkelstein, 'The moral dimensions of pedagogy: teaching behaviour in popular primary schools in nineteenth-century America', *American Studies*, 15 (1974), 3, pp. 79–89; H. S. Sullivan, *Conceptions of Modern Psychiatry*, (Washington, 1952), pp. 18–20; E. L. and R. E. Hartley, *Fundamentals of Social Psychology* (New York, 1952), pp. 485–6.

10 G. Spring, *Memoirs of the Rev. Samuel J. Mills* (New York, 1820), pp. 10–11; C. Martyn, *Wendell Phillips* (New York, 1890), p. 30; *Mother's Magazine*, 1 (1833), no. 2, pp. 68–9, and no. 3, p. 100; see also *The Wife for a Missionary* (Cincinnati, 1835), pp. 93–4, 155.

11 V. F. Holden, *The Early Years of Isaac Thomas Hecker* (Washington, 1939), p. 9; E. P. Barrow, Jr., *Memoir of Everton Judson* (Boston, 1852), pp. 21–2; B. Wyatt-Brown, *Lewis Tappan and the Evangelical War against Slavery* (Cleveland, 1969), pp. 13, 14; J. L. Thomas, *The Liberator. William Lloyd Garrison* (Boston, 1963), pp. 15, 18, 22–5, 282–3.

12 M. Marks, *Memoirs of the Life of David Marks* (Dover, N.H., 1846), p. 14; L. W. Banner, 'Elizabeth Cady Stanton', p. 4, Ms in press kindly lent by the author; E. H. Erikson, 'Reflections on the dissent of contemporary youth', *Daedalus*, 99 (1970), 1, p. 164; *Mother's Magazine*, 2 (1834), 2, pp. 107–9; *ibid.*, 3, pp. 161–3; Henry C. Wright, diary, May 22, 1835 (Harvard).

13 See M. L. Dillon, *Elijah P. Lovejoy* (Urbana, Illinois, 1971), p. 3; R. V. Harlow, *Gerrit Smith* (New York, 1939), pp. 15–16; Holden, *Hecker*, pp. 8–9; R. A. Parker, *A Yankee Saint: John Humphrey Noyes* (New York, 1935); Robert D. Thomas, *The Man Who Would Be Perfect: John Humphrey Noyes* (Philadelphia, 1977), chap. 1.

14 J. Weiss, *The Life and Correspondence of Theodore Parker* (Boston, 1864), i, p. 25.

15 W. G. McLoughlin, 'Evangelical childrearing in the age of Jackson', *Journal of Social History*, 9 (1975), 1, p. 21; Mary Gay to John Quincy

202   Bertram Wyatt-Brown

Adams, 1 January 1841, Gay-Otis MSS, Columbia University Library, kindly brought to my attention by Dr Raimund Goerler; see also Goerler's 'Family, Psychology, and History', *Newsletter Group for the Use of Psychology in History*, 4 (1975), 1, pp. 31–8; J. C. and O. Lovejoy, *Memoir of the Rev. Elijah P. Lovejoy* New York, Anti-Slavery Society, 1838), p. 15; Pickard, *Whittier*, I, p. 26; P. Miller, 'John Greenleaf Whittier: the conscience in poetry,' *Harvard Review*, 2 (1964), 1, pp. 8–24.

16 F. Tiffany, *Life of Dorothea Lynde Dix* (Boston, 1890), p. 11; P. H. Epler, *Life of Clara Barton* (New York, 1919), pp. 6, 12, 14; I. Ross, *Angel of the Battlefield: Life of Clara Barton* (New York, 1956), p. 9; J. B. Stewart, *Joshua R. Giddings and the Tactics of Radical Politics* (Cleveland, 1970), p. 5; H. F. Brownson, *Orestes A. Brownson's Early Life* (Detroit, 1895), p. 4; R. Baxter, *The Christian Directory* (London, 1830), p. 178.

17 B. P. Thomas, *Theodore Weld* (New Brunswick, 1950), pp. 8–9; Wyatt-Brown, *Tappan*, p. 14; Lovejoy and Lovejoy, *Lovejoy*, pp. 17–19; J. P. Thompson, *Memoir of the Rev. David Tappan Stoddard* (New York, 1859), p. 61; Parker, *Yankee Saint*, p. 12; W. A. Hallock, *'Light and Love': A Sketch of the Life and Labors of the Rev. Justin Edwards* (Boston, 1855), p. 17; H. C. Wright, diary, 12 March 1835, Houghton.

18 T. Stanton, and H. S. Blatch, (eds.), *Elizabeth Cady Stanton* (New York, 1922), I, pp. 3, 22–3, 24–5; G. Lerner, *The Grimké Sisters from South Carolina*, (Boston, 1967), pp. 16–25; *The Missionary's Daughter: A Memoir of Lucy Goodale Thurston of the Sandwich Islands* (New York, 1942), pp. 13, 14; *Life and Times of Mrs Lucy G. Thurston* (Ann Arbor, 2nd edn., 1882), pp. 3–6; see also ABCFM records, applicants' files, 1833–5.

19 [Miss Lyman], *The Martyr of Sumatra: A Memoir of Henry Lyman* (New York, 1857), p. 14; H. Schwartz, *Samuel Gridley Howe* (Cambridge, 1956), pp. 4–5, 9; L. E. Richards, (ed.), *Letters and Journals of Samuel Gridley Howe* (Boston, 1906), I, p. 17; Thomas, *Weld*, pp. 156–60; R. R. Gurley, *Life of Jehudi Ashmun* (Washington, 1854), p. 18n; F. Wayland, *Memoir of the Life and Labors of the Rev. Adoniram Judson* (Boston, 1854), I, p. 13; J. C. Lovejoy, *Memoir of Rev. Charles Turner Torrey*, (Boston, 1847), pp. 3–5.

20 E. H. Erikson, *Identity and the Life Cycle: Selected Papers in Psychological Issues*, 1 (1959), No. 1, p. 89; William James, *The Varieties of Religious Experience* (London and Bombay, 1902), pp. 198–200; E. D. Starbuck, *The Psychology of Religion*, (Berkeley, 1899), pp. 224, 262.

21 [Lyman], *Lyman*, pp. 15–16; Gurley, *Ashmun*, pp. 19–20; Wayland, *Judson*, p. 25.

22 Spring, *Mills*, pp. 14–16; James, *Varieties of Religious Experience*, p. 190; F. E. H. Haines, *Jonas King: Missionary to Syria and Greece* (New York, 1879), p. 18; Dillon, *Lovejoy*, pp. 9–10; Thomas, *Weld*, p. 9; D. M. French, 'The conversion of an American radical: Elizur Wright and the abolitionist commitment', dissertation, Case Western Reserve University (1970), pp. 51–5 and D. M. French, 'Puritan conservatism and the Frontier: The Elizur Wright family on the Connecticut

Reserve', *The Old Northwest*, 1, (1975), 1, 85–95; Raimund Goerler, 'Family, self, and anti-slavery: Sydney Howard Gay and the Abolitionist Commitment', dissertation, Case Western Reserve University (1975).

23 Lerner, *Grimké Sisters*, p. 25; I. H. Harper, *The Life and Work of Susan B. Anthony* (Indianapolis, 1889), I, p. 29; M. E. Danforth, *A Quaker Pioneer, Laura Haviland* (New York, 1961), p. 19.

24 Wright, diary, 21 October 1869, Henry C. Wright MSS, Boston Public Library; Haines, *King*, pp. 18–20; 'Memoir of Nathaniel Ripley Cobb', *American Baptist Magazine*, 14 (1834), 3, 316–26.

25 Lovejoy, *Torrey*, p. 29; Samuel G. Howe, diary, April 21, 1829, Houghton Library.

26 On changes in ministry, see D. H. Calhoun, *Professional Lives in America*, (Cambridge, Harvard, 1965); D. M. Scott, *From Office to Profession: The New England Ministry, 1750–1850* (Philadelphia, 1978).

27 [Lyman], *Lyman*, pp. 38, 43–5; L. W. Banner, 'Religion and reform in the early Republic: the role of youth', *American Quarterly*, 22 (1971), 4, pp. 680–2.

28 G. W. Noyes, (ed.), *Religious Experiences of John Humphrey Noyes* (New York, 1923), p. 22; J. Evans, *Memoir of Elder George Evans* (Woburn, N. H., 1857), pp. 7, 10–15.

29 Wright, diary, 1821, pp. 7–11, Wright MSS, Boston Public Library; Lerner, *Grimké Sisters*, p. 53; Lovejoy and Lovejoy, *Lovejoy*, pp. 29–31; M. Fellman, *The Unbounded Frame* (Westport, Greenwood, 1974), Chap. 2.

30 Lyman to his sister, 2 November 1828, in [Lyman], *Lyman*, p. 69.

31 P. Bond, *Memoirs of the Rev. Pliny Fisk* (New York, 1867), p. 71; S. A. Dorrance to Theodore D. Weld, 15 October 1850, Theodore D. Weld MSS, William L. Clements Library, Ann Arbor, Mich.

32 Amos A. Phelps, diary, January 19, 1828, Amos A. Phelps MSS, Boston Public Library; B. B. Edwards, *Memoir of Elias Cornelius* (Boston, 1834), p. 29; E. H. Erikson, *Insight and Responsibility* (New York, 1964), p. 93.

33 Lawrence J. Friedman is preparing a book on anti-slavery, chapters of which will support these remarks.

34 Gurley, *Ashmun*, pp. 1–92, quotations, pp. 27, 28.

35 William B. Weeks to Amos A. Phelps, 15 June 1829, 14 June, 19 August, 1880, Phelps MSS, Boston Public Library; Wright, diary, 8 December 1832, 9 and 11 May and 3 December, 1833, Houghton.

36 Wright, diary, *passim*, January, 1834–10 May 1835, quotation 10 June 1835, Houghton; S. S. Thompkins, 'The psychology of commitment', in Duberman, (ed.), *Antislavery Vanguard*, pp. 270–98; W. H. and J. H. Pease, *Bound with Them in Chains: A Biographical History of the Antislavery Movement* (Boston, 1972).

37 See the American Missionary Association MSS, on microfilm, originals, Dillard University, New Orleans.

38 Quoted by I. C. Bradley, *The Call to Seriousness: The Evangelical Impact on the Victorians* (New York, 1976), p. 202.

Part Three
ANTI-SLAVERY, RACE, AND CLASS

10

RELIGION AND SLAVERY – THE CASE OF THE AMERICAN SOUTH

by Donald G. Mathews

The nineteenth-century abolition movements of the northern United States and Great Britain had in common the great physical and social distances between them and the people they sought to save. They also had in common the moral and religious expansiveness of evangelicalism which joined with political forces to dismantle African slavery in the English-speaking New World. Contrasted to the achievement of anti-slavery evangelicalism, the religion of the American slave South is usually remembered as an aberration, as nothing more than the religious expression of a slaveholding ethos. The failure of southern white evangelicals to sustain an active strategy of undermining slavery is often ignored as a way of evaluating the success of anti-slavery evangelicalism elsewhere; and the even more persistent and remarkable process of Afro-American evangelicalism is also ignored for reasons not altogether clear. This focus on white anti-slavery religion far removed from slavery has sometimes led historians to think of religious 'motivation' as being more divorced from social context than it actually is. Even more detrimental to historical understanding, however, has been the cultural bias to exclude Afro-American religion from analyses even while wrestling with the problem of religion and reform in Atlantic civilization. This essay, therefore, will suggest that religion and slavery can be understood equally well by looking at slaveholders as well as abolitionists, by looking at slaves as well as masters.

I

Evangelicalism – for all its familiarity as a historic movement – was so plastic, so adaptable to different classes and conditions, that to encapsulate it in either simple definition or theological statement is to ignore its essential dynamism. Evangelicalism was not a creed. It was an experience, or to be more specific, it was a conversion experience. Rooted in the reformed traditions of both the continent and Great Britain, evangelicalism brought an intense, personal piety to hundreds of thousands of people in the English speaking world before the end of the eighteenth century. The experience or *New Birth* began as a psychic crisis through which each believer became convinced ('convicted') of utter alienation from the very ground of being, alienation even from the self brought about by ones own sin. The drama of salvation objectified in the Catholic mass became internalized through a Protestant and subjective catharsis. At the moment of self-condemnation the tormented soul cast the self on God's mercy, and, in the depths of despair received forgiveness, healing, and a new beginning so complete as to be 'born again'. Intensity of emotion rather than assent to doctrine characterized this transformation so that correct theology was not so important as a renewed heart.

As if to insist on perpetual tension in the psychic life of believers, evangelicals offered the twice-born a disciplined life. The explosiveness of an individual's conversion was tamed by surveillance within a communion of believers who met regularly 'to set in order the things that are wanting'. Following denominational standards of discipline, each evangelical community carefully scrutinized behavior of its members for 'edification not for destruction': that is to help the weaker brethren and sisters live a holy life; to reinforce through the ritual of inquiry, judgment, and repentance the bonds which held the community together; and to establish clear boundaries between the saved and the damned, to make as clear as possible the concrete uniqueness of evangelical society.

The dialectical tension between experience and order created a persistent sense of personal obligation to do God's work. For some converts, the torment of the interior personal life became a constant warfare, trying to discipline the imperfect self as the believer grew to emotional maturity. For others more able to transcend self-consciousness and project the intensity of inexorable moral warfare into society, evangelical conversion could be the portal into a world of benevolent activities and reform. Whether in the private turmoil of personal discipline or the public drama of reform, evangelicals were characterized by belief in the ability of God's children to do His Will without excuse and to make of their lives a witness to the righteousness, grace, and love of God. Very much in the Christian heretical tradition of 'enthusiasm' (or 'anti-nomianism'), it differed from that mode in the refusal to resolve the tension between ecstasy and order in favor of 'experience'. Springing from both the Puritan and Anglican traditions, evangelicalism differed from them in the refusal to resolve the tension in favor of order. It differed from them also in its diminished reliance on learned men, its suspicion of politics, its tendency to avoid creedal statements, and its preference for the wisdom of the heart over the dispassionate logic of the head. Evangelicalism was also more specifically a mission to the poor, the ignorant, the unloved, and the bound.

A day of vengeful emancipation was not, however, the vision of early evangelicals. Tension between slaveholding and Christian commitment came slowly; but by the end of the eighteenth century, the point in the conversion process at which the tormented believer submitted self to Christ had become a 'model of personal decision and commitment', the psychological and intellectual context within which to fight slavery. Not that all anti-slavery people were evangelicals – they were not; indeed, by the end of the eighteenth century an intelligent and informed man or woman would in Great Britain and many of her former colonies be assumed to be opposed to slavery. But evangelicals' world-view and theology created an especially conducive mental context for anti-slavery action.[1] Many abolitionists believed themselves to be the 'righteous remnant' of the evangelical tradition. The preachers' insistence on immediate repentance of sin became a model for abolitionists' demands for immediate repentance of slaveholding. The strenuous pursuit of a holy life became a metaphor, or perhaps more accurately, a prescription for reform activity. The patterns of thought, the norms of behavior, the earnestness of moral exertion, the legitimating experience of the indwelling of the Holy Spirit – all shaped the mental–moral context within which abolitionists sallied forth to battle with slavery. But it is not at all clear whether abolitionism was evidence of the success of evangelicalism or its failure. More American evangelicals were anti-abolitionist than abolitionist; indeed abolitionists in the United States were by the mid-1830s outcast from the central tradition of evangelicalism. If 'conversion to evangelicalism frequently crystalized vague reformist and humanitarian conviction', it could and did lead ironically to rejection of an evangelicalism unable to transform a 'vague . . . conviction' into an absolute commitment to fight slavery. The result was that abolitionism itself became a 'surrogate religion' to replace an evangelicalism which by the 1830s had declined into 'hollow ritual'.

Popular piety reflected the 'American obsession with the superficial forms of religious life rather than its inner meaning'.[2] The entwining of slavery and religion came to be a moral judgment on both.

II

Evangelicals invaded the South in a variety of ways over a long period of time. In the 1740s New Side Presbyterian itinerants began to preach to isolated groups of dissidents from Anglican formalism; New Light Baptist immigrants from northern colonies became fierce proselytizers in the 1750s and 1760s; a few Anglican evangelicals brought family devotions into the homes of many of the lower classes previously ignored by a tepid and aloof priesthood; and in the 1770s Wesley's itinerants came from England to spread the revival even further. Beyond the obvious differences among these people, there was an essential unity which nourished implications for the evolving social system which could have been revolutionary if they had been allowed to develop to their logical conclusion.

This revolution was conveyed in rhetoric which dramatized the difference between traditional religious mood and the New Birth. The rhetoric was creator as well as the creation of preachers who were personification and symbol of the evangelical community. Chosen in the first place because their fellows had seen within them evidence of 'popular talents' and great piety, the preachers evoked from their audiences either the memory, anticipation or realization of the conversion experience. Whether the stately, carefully worded and highly literate sermons of the New Side Presbyterian, Samuel Davies, or the 'holy whine', harangue, or chant of the Separate Baptists, evangelical sermons were personal and direct encounters between human beings and God. The dry, formal, abstract, and moralistic homilies of traditional preaching which conveyed information and rules from those in authority to those without it contrasted radically with public discourse designed to create a psychological situation in which the community of God's people was recreated for each member who participated in preaching and worship. Authority within this community was not passed on through a self-perpetuating elite but through the persistent quest by evangelicals for men who could prepare them for encounter with the divine. And the talent for creating this encounter did not require formal education or scholarship so much as a perfect resonance between preacher and people which was unlike any traditional view of leadership.[3] The radical character of this interaction of community and elite is underscored by the complaint by a North Carolina Anglican of the New Light Baptists in 1766: 'The most illiterate among them are their teachers; even Negroes speak in their Meetings'.[4]

When black people spoke in evangelical meetings they were in practice rather than principle expressing an essential democracy of experience among people who believed that in worship God revealed His presence as an earnest of what life should really be. If slaves received gifts of the Holy Spirit it was no more than what God had promised – to choose the weak to challenge the strong, to select the ignorant to confound the wise. But ecstasy, possession, or witnessing of and in the Spirit were not the only expression of a revolutionary evangelicalism. The offer of salvation to all meant the essential humanity of all. 'In Jesus Christ', preached George Whitefield, 'there is nether male nor female, bond nor free; even you may be children of God, if you believe in Jesus'. He told them of the 'eunuch belonging to the Queen of Candace. A Negro like yourselves. He believed the Lord was his righteousness. He was baptized. Do you also believe, and you shall be saved . . .'[5]

The meaning of sexual and racial equality before the throne of Grace was not so clear as the proclamation of it, and had to be discovered in the theoretically merciless scrutiny to which evangelicals subjected themselves. But the questions and answers, the certitude and confusion, the elliptical reasoning and the protective emotional defenses of public debate did not all at once make evangelicals decide that owning slaves was a disciplinable offence. There was a long process of moral discovery from the first revivals in the South (1740) until the Revolution (1778); and, convinced as they were that everyone in the community of godly people should think of discipline as self-imposed, discussion had to be resolved not by a majority vote but a more peaceful – and therefore a more Christian – consensus of the community. The achievement of an anti-slavery concensus was difficult in part because the evangelical message was not a call for liberating other people but for freeing the self from whatever enslaved it – sexual fantasy, frivolitry, fear of death, fear of powerful people. The message was essentially apolitical; it did not address the question of power except as it gave believers ability to organize their lives upon principles of self-discovery, self-abnegation, and self-discipline. To link the subjective pilgrimage of the soul to the objective structure of social relationships, the self-condemnation which initiated conversion would have to include slaveholding as an act which imperilled the soul.

Moreoever, whites who had accepted blacks as communicants would have to project themselves into the situation of their fellow Christians, to empathize with them in order to *experience* vicariously the injustice and immorality of slavery.

Whether American evangelicalism could of its own momentum have initiated and maintained an anti-slavery movement is problematic, for the ideology of the American Revolution strengthened and gave impetus to the anti-slavery implications of the New Birth. Early in the conflict with King and Parliament, Americans had in pamphlets, sermons, petitions, and Congressional edicts attacked the slave trade; soon slavery itself came under assault. The concept of slavery which had been so intensely and universally employed to characterize the policies of Great Britain could not fail to become an embarrassment for many Americans, an impossible contradiction with which consistent Revolutionaries found it difficult to live. Revolutionary rhetoric gave evangelical piety some of the concepts with which to enlist believers in the fight with African slavery. Slavery, wrote the founding fathers of the Methodist Episcopal Church, is 'contrary to the golden law of God on which hang all the law and the prophets, and the unalienable rights of mankind, as well as every principle of the revolution . . .' Gradually, evangelicals had begun to debate slavery and emancipation. In 1778 Virginia Baptists prayed to the General Assembly that the 'yoke of slavery may be made more tolerable'. In 1780 a Methodist conference denounced slavery and ordered preachers to free whatever slaves they owned – as one of their number had already done upon his conversion; by 1784 the Wesleyans had gone even further and threatened to expel everyone from the church who remained a slaveholder for more than two years; in 1785 the Baptist General Committee of Virginia declared 'hereditary slavery to be contrary to the word of God'. And the change in attitude came from below – at the local level – as well as from above: in 1786 the Black Creek Baptist Church (Virginia) asked, 'Is it a righteous thing for a christian to hold or Cause any of the Human race to be held in Slavery? Answered, Unrighteous'. So also answered the Presbyterian General Assembly in 1787.[6]

Having once said that holding slaves was 'unrighteous', however, evangelicals had not laid the matter to rest. In fact, the answer could apparently do little more than force members of a local church or class to choose sides in the debate. The Black Creek Church, after its statement of 1786, discussed the matter for seven years. Finally, Brother Noel Vick had had enough, and 'absented himself from the Lord's table on account of Slaves being held by some of the Brethren . . .' After prayer the church won him back as he 'agreed to content himself as much as possible under the case and in the Fellowship of the Church'.[7] Even in a church closely identified with an anti-slavery preacher – David Barrow of Southside Virginia – strict anti-slavery commitment created a profound disturbance, one felt by evangelicals throughout the South. They probed the radical implications of their conversion experience, the rigorous demands of Christian discipline, the remarkable coupling of evangelicalism and republicanism which might yet – they hoped – produce a Christian republic. The debate was not only among statesmen in consituent assembly, as in Kentucky, but also in local evangelical meetings attempting to make theories of conversion and revolution into concrete reality. Much argument emphasized the evil done to Africans when contrasted to their just claims for freedom based on 'the natural equality of man'. 'The same that wounds and pains us', wrote one person, 'wounds and pains them. All our feelings are in them'. The refusal to admit that republican and Christian principles were inconsistent with slavery was the result, radical evangelicals charged, of 'an absurd prejudice' which confused the impact of servitude – the corruption of behavior and the dulling of minds – with innate nature.[8] After years of attempting to provide rules of Christian conduct for believers, evangelicals – or at least the most sensitive of them – were impressed with the traumatic moral dilemmas created by slavery. The resulting degradation of the slave – which all admitted – revealed also the degradation of masters who had so monstrously scarred the image of God. Moreoever, to people who were very fastidious about sexual morality and who wished to keep all families free from 'licentiousness' and conflict, the vulnerability of black families and especially slave women was dramatically degrading. To people who urged fathers to exercise authority over their families with Christian love and care, the helplessness of enslaved fathers and husbands make a mockery of Biblical injunctions of obedience to lawful authority.

Despite emphasis on human equality and justice, however, even the most confrontational and denunciatory anti-slavery preaching could not hide certain mental reservations which favored whites. Angry with slaveholders though they may have been, anti-slavery evangelicals believed that African servitude was a burden shared by white as well as black, a predicament with no easy solution, and one faced by a Georgia farmer writing to his son-in-law in 1790:

'There is one thing that hath long lain on my mind with great weight, and that is concerning slavery . . . I am more & more convinced it is wrong, though I feel a great Struggle in my mind about it. Ease and Self Interest & the grandeur of Life & the thoughts that my Posterity may labour hard for a living, and perhaps not be thought So much of in the world if they had no Slaves to Sett them off in a more grand & easy way. . . . But on the other hand when I consider that these people of their forefathers were born as free as my Self & that they are held in bondage by compulsion only . . . [and] are considered in the Eye of the Law & by the owners no more than dumb beasts It fills my mind with horror & detestation.[9]

Understandable enough, perhaps, but if conscience were to win out over 'worldly honor' and economic success, the conflict had to shift from one's internal life to the community of faithful people in which moral and communal order were supposedly identical. In the process one detects in evangelical anti-slavery activity a divided mind, an ambivalence of outrage and attack on the one hand, and a timid caution on the other. A pamphlet which circulated in Virginia and North Carolina during the 1790s is an example. James O'Kelly was free in his attack on 'bloody overseers – ye devils incarnate!' 'Where', he demanded 'is the true disciple of Christ, poor in spirit, meek in heart, thirsting after holiness, crucified with Christ, dead to the world?' O'Kelly waited for an answer in Christian charity. 'If your present situation is such that you cannot liberate your captives without defrauding your creditors, or reducing your family into deep distress, acknowledge the wrong detention, converse with your dear preachers who feel for you, and emancipate them in a more gradual manner; and we shall rejoice to see your sincerity, and acknowledge you as dear brethren in Christ'.[10] Acknowledgement of the evil of slavery was separated from the act needed to destroy it. But people impressed with gradual emancipation laws of northern states believed that a gradual process begun immediately would allow time to prepare slaves for freedom. Having admitted, however, that slaves needed to be educated for freedom, anti-slavery evangelicals had prepared the way for amelioration of slavery to become a substitute for emancipation.[11]

Besides economic self-interest and a reluctance to be unreasonable about emancipation, there was among southern evangelicals a fundamental distaste for the kind of class conflict necessary to overturn the slave system. For over twenty years Methodist ministers tried to create a set of rules to make anti-slavery sentiment an essential part of the Christian's witness without coming right out and condemning 'Christian' slaveholding. The peace of Christian fellowship and the prestige of converting influential worldlings to

Christ was simply more important than a firm stand against slavery. Moreover, most white evangelicals would have to admit that slaveholders who shared the experience of conversion had as much right to communion as did slaves. The action of Baptists in south-eastern Virginia and northeastern North Carolina during the 1790s reveal the difficulties created by this admission. In 1790 the Baptist General Committee of Virginia announced that slavery was a 'violent deprivation of the rights of nature, and inconsistent with republican government'. Brave words in resolutions, however, are not so informative as the extreme caution of local Baptists who found it difficult to address even the most basic problems confronting black people. The Portsmouth association, for example, could not decide whether to allow a slave to marry after his first wife had been sold, or whether to censure the person who had sold her. The issue was 'so difficult', the majority concluded that 'no answer could be given it'. They pleaded with their members to 'Bear each others weaknesses', and attempted to facilitate such forebearance by not reporting their debate about slavery. By 1796, however, something had happened to make them bolder; the 'times' were *wretched and distressing* because covetousness had led 'Christians, with the people of this country in general, to hold and retain, in *abject slavery* a set of our poor fellow creatures, *contrary to the laws of God and nature* . . . a detested conformity to the wicked *ways* and *customs* of this present evil world'. But this was to have said too much. When the same circular letter to the Baptist churches was sent in 1803, everything but the attack on slavery was reprinted verbatim.[12]

To understand why Portsmouth Baptists finally stopped discussing slaveholding is to understand their experience as metaphor for that of most white southern evangelicals. First of all, debate about slavery was 'delicate' – especially traumatic to a people who wanted to maintain a sense of communal solidarity. Secondly, the most active anti-slavery Baptist preacher in the area, David Barrow, announced that the economic facts of life were driving him from Virginia. He could not support his family, he said, without owning slaves as had other Baptists. This he refused to do as he joined the emigration of other anti-slavery leaders similarly defeated by slaveholders becoming evangelicals and evangelicals becoming slaveholders.[13] But there was also another reason for muffling discussion about the morality of slaveholding. Within three years of Barrow's departure, in Richmond to the northwest (1800) and in contiguous North Carolina to the southeast (1802) there was widespread alarm over conspiracies among rebellious slaves. In the resulting climate of fear, debates about slavery were not calculated to quiet anxious whites. After the turn of the century, throughout the south Atlantic states, evangelicals found anti-slavery debate futile within the churches and dangerous in the world.

As the 'world' changed, so did evangelicals. As the South developed agriculturally and socially, evangelicals were able to become the predominant religious influence because of the weakness of non-evangelical churches and the need for moral order which political parties, laws, courts, and towns only partially provided. Between the Revolution and the War for Southern Independence, the South was characterized as much by the opening up of new tracts of land for exploitation as by the slaveholding which accompanied it. Simultaneous with geographical extension was the intensive development by evangelicals of institutions designed to create society: churches, schools, academies, colleges. The eventual assumption of responsibility for shaping norms, values, and apolitical public discourse by the 1830s contrasted vividly with the self-styled poverty of evangelicals in the 1780s and 1790s. As evangelicals grew in numbers they began to create networks of denominational organizations which became one of the most pervasive subsystems of the antebellum South. Not that evangelicalism in any of its forms – Methodist, Baptist, Presbyterian or even Episcopalian – claimed the loyalties of a majority of Southerners; it most certainly did not. But it was among the most significant formulators of public discourse, codes of behavior, religious feeling, and rhetoric of self-justification.

This social responsibility was made possible because white evangelicals were only partially the same people that they had been in the 1790s. The initial and universal appeal of evangelicalism was that it knew no class, caste, race or sex: in the household of faithful people 'God was no respector of persons'. The appropriate response to this appeal was not social revolution, for that would have entrusted the achievement of society structured on the vision of equality to the self-interested and therefore sinful action of men. The political solution as an appeal to force even in failure would have legitimated the invidious distinctions of class, sex, race, or caste by agreeing that they were just so long as maintained by force. But it was precisely this means of establishing legitimacy which evangelicalism rejected. The definition of personal integrity and dignity could not properly be assigned to the world of politics, for if it were, the logic of social differentiation and stratification would destroy the poor, the bound, the outcast – just the kind of people whose salvation was theoretically the goal of Gospel preaching. It is not surprising that evangelical preaching should have had – as it does to this day – an appeal to people whose reliance upon political solutions which were doomed to failure, would have reinforced the already grave sense of rejection and helplessness.

But women, slaves, free blacks, and poor people were not the only converts to evangelical Christianity. Many were also white men and not poor – some were in fact in quite comfortable circumstances. Moreover, there were converts whose political vision identified them with those who held power on principles defined by the language of revolution and republic. The new political style which elicited and shaped opposition to federalist administrations complemented the expressed egalitarianism of evangelical experience. Indeed, the two modes of evangelicalism and republicanism could be understood as two manifestations of a basic process creating a new public order. Thus a religious mood which offered meaning, comfort, love, and hope to persons regardless of station could be and was embraced by white men who sensed in their political perception that their coming into power was a triumph of the 'common people'. They thought of themselves as persons of middling estate; they spoke of their politics as a revolution, even though in a strict sense it was not; and they professed the piety of modest and humble folk. In the earliest days of evangelicalism their self-description would have been correct, but by the 1830s it was only partially true. Evangelicals were now counted among the powerful as well as the powerless; and the powerful needed order to maintain the racial and class system from which they benefited.[14]

If evangelicalism could, when fused with pristine republicanism, explode into a volatile attack on slaveholding, it could, when separated from that political theory become a repressive discipline. The dichotomy of vision and order which created the internal tension of the evangelical ethos provided resolution not through social so much as personal transformation. The initial evangelical antislavery witness was but one aspect of a general debate about the moral implications of conversion. Acceptance of slaves into Christian fellowship on the basis of their religious experience and willingness to submit themselves to discipline preceded the revolutionary discussion of equality and inalienable rights, and required whites to spell out what they expected of blacks as well as whites in the communion of faithful people. The decision was that both races should assume the same personal discipline, the same rules governing sexual conduct and familial relationships, the same rules of public decorum. With relation to each other, bond and free were to avoid conflict and to assume the responsibilities and obligations appropriate to their social rank. That 'God was no respecter of persons' apparently could mean that the invidious distinctions of the world should be softened by mutual respect, kindness, and acknowledgement of a common humanity. Attempts to create a haven from the world are evident in most surviving evangelical records: the use of the familiar 'brother' and 'sister' in polite address, the inscribing of blacks' names in church books, the acceptance of blacks' testimony against whites, the preaching of black to white.[15] The flaws, however, are also obvious. Despite ritualistic acknowledgement of a common humanity, the logic of slavery reinforced and was in turn reinforced by evangelical emphasis on the holy life as an orderly, disciplined struggle to subdue the unruly self. The gift which white evangelicals decided to give blacks, therefore, was moral order instead of freedom, and slaves were judged Christian and certified as acceptable to whites in so far as they behaved themselves.

Even religious conversion of blacks was thought to be too radical for many non-believing masters. But after abortive servile insurrections in 1822 and 1831, powerful slaveholders began to support missions to 'Christianize' (socialize) the slaves. The missionary ideal was personified in the Reverend Charles Colcock Jones, Sr., of Liberty County, Georgia. He stated the problem of the mission so well and so often that none surpassed his scope, insight, high expectations, or sense of failure. Born into a comfortable slaveholding family, Jones was converted after a serious illness and soon left the South for Phillips Academy (Andover, Massachusetts) and, eventually, Princeton Theological Seminary. In letters to his cousin and fiancée, Mary Jones, Charles confessed his torment over slavery: it crippled and degraded blacks, it gave whites 'fearful' power, it violated 'all the Laws of God and man at once'. Over and over he contemplated the terrible burden of inheriting slaves; should he not free them and escape the South? Mary, who was not especially disconsolate about the 'burden' of slaveholding, suggested that he would do better to return home and assume his proper responsibilities; he did so in November of 1832. The ultimate goal of emancipation he relinquished only with the passage of time. In 1834 both in private and public he could talk about it as the result of missionary activities,

> The Religious Instruction of the negroes is the foundation of all permanent improvements of intelligence and morals in the slave-holding

states. (The *only* entering wedge to the great and appalling subject of Slavery. The only Sun, that appearing through the dark clouds, will shed down pure & holy light, and if the Institution of Slavery is to be abandoned, will cause the nation to relax its hold, and gradually and peacefully lay it off, and then sit down in delightful repose.)

But the statement was in parentheses, and he kept it there for the rest of his life; the focus of his thoughts became the mission itself and what it would do for blacks and whites alike. The mission, he explained to a colleague, 'will convince our northern friends that we are not dead, but alive to duty, and engaged in doing it'.[16]

The mission was but one aspect of a slaveholding ethic that was being formulated in the decades before the Civil War. A few evangelical publicists, ministers, and laymen attempted to sketch out a standard of obligation and duty which called upon white evangelicals to take a hard look at their relations with blacks, and to admit that they had simply not done what they should have in order to honor their Christian responsibility. This effort to apply to society the formula of evangelical conversion – acknowledgement of sin, guilt, need, and salvation – was part of a broader trend among slaveholding apologists to formulate an idea system that could legitimate slavery not only among slaveholders, but also among slaves and non-slaveholders – perhaps most especially among the latter. The success of this effort is still difficult to evaluate, but US historians have recently begun to adopt the view that a paternalistic ethos had come to dominate the South by 1860.[17] This fact meant a political–cultural victory for powerful elites who had persuaded a majority of white southerners to accept secession as a way of perpetuating a system that was to be thought of as 'theirs'. Perhaps; but there were significant differences within the ethos, widely varying views of how and when to exercise power, widely varying styles of racial interaction, widely varying ways of facing the future. One of the most coherent ideologies within the slaveholding ethos was expressed as a specifically Christian social ethic. The general trend seems to have been to transform the moral dialectic of sin and salvation into the tension between assuming and not assuming responsibility for the religious care of black people within the system which victimized them. That the slaveholding ethic accepted an impossible task is clear enough from the vantage point of the present; but it was also clear to many Christian and slaveholding whites. The same mentality that supported the impossibilist demands of immediate emancipation in Boston supported the impossibilist demands of Christian stewardship in Liberty County,

Georgia. Every evangelical knew that unresolved moral struggle was the framework of meaningful life. God demanded impossible things of His people; only if they refused to use impossibility as self-justification could they be saved.

III

The incredible psychic tension which characterized the evangelical dialectic at its core could be either creative or destructive. One of its positive effects was to provide those demeaned by social or physical circumstances with the inner personal resources to transcend their situation by what seemed to be a remarkable act of the will but which seemed to many believers to be an unmistakable gift. Nowhere is this better demonstrated than in the religion of black evangelicals. It is evidence indeed that the power of religious sentiment, conviction, and perception cannot be understood so well by scrutinizing the failure of those who held power as by probing the personal and communal achievements of those who had the gift to be able to affirm the self in the face of everything that denied it – what Paul Tillich once called the 'courage to be'.

The conversion of most African Americans to Christianity came through the institutions, worship, sense of history, and promise of salvation provided by evangelicalism. The process of conversion – whether called socialization, aculturation, or assimilation – still awaits the historian who can trace it over time with appropriate sensitivity to the changing levels of social consciousness and degrees of inter-racial intercourse. We do know that few Afro-Americans became part of the European religious community prior to the 1770s; we also know that despite a relatively low ratio of success among blacks when compared with whites during the early evangelical revivals that African participation in the religious exercises and discipline of the New Birth increased significantly. After 1740 white evangelical preachers, following the example of George Whitefield in South Carolina, began to convert black as well as white; by the 1770s and 1780s, the conversion of blacks and their acceptance into the fellowship of the twice-born was common enough to be assumed characteristic of evangelicals. Explanation of the increasing susceptibility of blacks to this new mode of Christianity must surely begin with what appears to be the universal appeal of evangelicalism – its proclamation that 'God is no respecter of persons' and its acceptance of converts into the inner core of those seeking holiness.[18]

The formula of salvation was of course familiar to English speaking Americans of the Protestant tradition. The innovation of emphasizing direct access to God through His offer of salvation to all, immediately rejected all ecclesiastical routine, made theological nuances irrelevant, and seized access to salvation from the dispassionate and elitist priests of the established churches. Angry rectors or vicars could curse such 'enthusiasm' by those who saw 'visions', received 'revelations from heaven', and 'an instantaneous impulse of the Spirit', but what Anglican priests feared, African converts embraced.[19] The attraction was not the intellectual appeal or egalitarian implications of evangelicalism although it possessed both. More significant was the elemental religious perception of salvation – the cosmological affirmation of self – evoked in preaching which molded congregations into a people bonded to each other through worship. But it was not the worship of awe and adoration so much as the worship of receiving God. It was the interaction between preacher and people, in collective response and individual proclamation as persons of both races played a psychological fugue on themes of salvation, freedom, grace, love, and unity in Christ. That these 'religious exercises' should have made preachers report that 'the Dear Lord attended the word with power',[20] reveals the meaning of such preaching; for in it, the whole community felt the presence of ultimate reality before which everything outside the haven of worship would be insignificant.

If whites saw the power of God in his affecting even 'the poor Africans', blacks must have been drawn to evangelical preaching because it invited them to participate in worship through the evocative similarity of the conversion experience to religious rituals and expression bequeathed them by Mother Africa. The importance of the whites' encouragement of blacks to share worship through singing, praying and preaching cannot be over-emphasized. The attempt by traditionalist churchmen to catechize Africans had been unsuccessful for the most part because it was a process which attempted to induce blacks to become Christian through acceptance of alien ritual, worship, and theology. But evangelical whites invited blacks to participate in worship, to express their own experience of divinity, and the resultant sense of healing and salvation. In a sense, the two peoples were moving towards each other: socially by becoming equal participants in singing, prayer, and preaching; and psychologically by sharing with each other their religious experience. Movement through social as well as psychological space broke down the traditional, mutually reinforced aloofness of class, race, and culture in the experience of conversion. For Africans accustomed to whites who disdained 'impulses of the spirit', the behavior of evangelicals must have been remarkable indeed and acknowledgement of a human bond foreign to the behavior of most whites. The evangelicalism which helped to create the Afro-American Christian churches was different from that of whites who would over a generation later develop the Mission to Slaves (from 1830). This was an evangelicalism still favoring the tension between conversion experience and holiness, grace and law, vision and discipline. It was a religion still open to the anti-slavery witness, still troubled by exploitation and the unjust division of society into the bound and free. Ironically, as time passed, the children and grandchildren of early white evangelicals would begin to make the same approach to blacks as had the priests of the established church; that is, to catechize, instruct, and discipline. The ethos would be distorted by well-meaning missionaries who had lost an inclusive openness, the awed acceptance of African expressiveness, and the profound respect for African piety.

By Emancipation the staying power of black evangelical piety was legendary. Indeed, by 1800 whites knew that black believers would with admirable Christian stoicism endure the vilest indignities and the most painful punishment simply to pray in their own fashion, sense the divine in their own rituals, and witness to Christ in their own way. As one Christian protested in anger and grief after whites had invaded a prayer meeting and beat him until blood rolled down his bruised face: 'This is what I have got for praising of my dear Jesus!'[21] Surely the crucifixion was real to him; but if it were, one could argue, so also was the hope of resurrection which, with its promise of utlimate vindication, must have been consolation for the inability to flee the brutal reality of slavery. In this view, black evangelicalism would be characterized only by a spontaneous ecstasy or possession – experience which for a few fleeting moments would burn away consciousness of oppression to be followed only by traumatic re-entry into a drab and painful life.

Black evangelicalism was more than that. It is unlikely that blacks endured the lash and cudgel 'for praising of my dear Jesus' merely to receive a momentary reassurance that they would one day be raised in glory. The pain would have consummed the ecstasy, thereby destroying in one sensation the message conveyed by the other. Religion that is only compensatory – with its fleeting sense of heaven – provides neither framework nor strategy to endure direct confrontation with the world, and black evangelicalism provided both. It was a way of life structured by blacks into a social and personal discipline which could be expressed in evangelical theology as sanctification and in the lives of evangelical slaves as moral courage and dignity in the face of everything that denied them. But the doctrine associated with sanctification which followed European logic and theology does not explain why blacks should have found it important; and yet, in the minutes of local churches and classes is indisputable proof that Afro-Americans agreed to be bound by principles of order and discipline. This fact, because of the slave system, made whites appear to be dictating to blacks, but the question of black submissiveness is best addressed if one remembers that those who dictate behavior and belief on the basis of common experience, as evangelicals did for each other, are themselves admitting their own accountability to the center of value. Thus when evangelical blacks placed themselves under the moral scrutiny of both black and white, they were in effect forcing whites to admit their common humanity by acknowledging the legitimacy of a common morality.

Evangelical discipline was theoretically the same for both blacks and whites. Although they may have disagreed at different times and places on the morality of premarital sexual intercourse, they agreed on strict fidelity in marriage, and believers of both races attempted to strengthen internal bonds and weaken external threat. Despite ludicrous white sermons on obedience, hard work, self-denial, and sobriety, the ideal of self-discipline was honored in black Christianity. The celebratory worship of shout and dance, ecstasy and release may not always have coincided with the stern morality of stoicism and control; but there is much evidence from both races that Christian slaves could impose upon themselves the strictest moral code. Josiah Henson, for example, assumed the most correct stewardship of his master's money and goods, traveling alone on the white man's behalf even into free territory in which he refused to remain because of his Christian obligation to fulfill all duties assigned him. Only when the master betrayed Henson's trust did the black man flee.[22]

Or consider the letter of a Christian driver to his master: 'I wish to live right, and Serve God faithfully and be prepared, let death come Sooner or later, and I know I can't be unfaithful to my Earthly master, and be faithful to God, but I feel it in me if I am faithful to my heavenly master the best I can, then Every thing Else goes right'.[23] Like many statements made by enslaved Afro-Americans, this one is easy to distort into evidence that evangelicalism was a device to force blacks to internalize white values – to force them into mental slavery. If such had been the case in this instance, however, the man who wrote this particular statement would have ended it with a profession of loyalty to his 'earthly master'. But had he done so, he would have identified the will of God with the will of his earthly master, Charles Colcock Jones Sr., who probably came as close as any white man to the ideal. This, Cato Jones could not do. Even while addressing the master who had honored him with tobacco, clothing, and power – perhaps precisely because he was addressing such a person – Cato had to remind the white man as well as himself that loyalty and authority belonged only to God: if he obeys God, 'Everything Else goes right'. It was not merely that Cato had learned his Christianity from a Presbyterian with a particularly fine sense of divine authority, one who would have insisted on a theologically correct attribution of authority to divine providence. Cato had also learned the power of God under the preaching of Toney Stevens. And it was this proud and powerful black Baptist minister who, in the early career of the white Jones, had led his people out of church in protest against distortion of the Gospel.[24] For the faithful, the God who demanded obedience to Himself alone came between the masters and their slaves just as the former had feared. The fact of Christian discipleship is not to be belittled as 'accommodation' or 'consolation', but valued as the sensitive structuring of patterns of behavior and thought and the committing of self to an ultimate loyalty expressed in masterful self-discipline. It was therefore almost literally an act of Grace to receive within the context of a brutalizing system the strength of pride in self that made the communal bond so strong among black Christians.

Disciplinary processes in biracial churches were supposed to remind both masters and slaves that among God's people the ordinary rules of the world did not apply. This rejection of traditional standards had once helped whites to express the anti-slavery witness; with regard to the slaves, it meant that the churches attempted to provide what the legal system denied – legitimacy of blacks as human beings. The discipline of holiness required formalized marriages, marital fidelity, daily prayers, personal responsibility; but as the anti-slavery witness had been surrendered, so also was the sheltering of slaves against the world. This was especially clear when servants were excommunicated for taking a second spouse after the first had been sold and when those who sold them were honored as good Christians. Church records reveal a persistent determination on the part of both blacks and whites to create a morally stable world; and here and there one finds also disagreement, charge and counter charge between black and white. One senses confrontations about a strict legality that favored whites, a refusal to admit that in some cases blacks were wrong when whites said they were, and a continuous interaction between the two races. If blacks throughout the South met illegally in bush arbors or huts at night to worship the God who promised liberty, they would also continue to worship with the whites. The records reveal blacks being accepted back into communion after having earlier been abandoned to the world. This determination on the part of blacks to be acknowledged part of public Christian life was impressive. After Nat Turner's insurrection in 1831, white Baptists in the area betrayed their Christian bonding with blacks by excommunicating without evidence or stated reason every slave within the area around Southampton county Virginia.[25] But the blacks would not stay away; they came back into the church whose white leaders had so faithlessly abused them; they could not leave the Christian faith to be defined by whites alone.

Conflict between black and white as to how the conversion experience was to be made normative for everyday life revealed the fractured quality of southern evangelicalism. It was, and at the same time was not, the same religion for both races, but the fracture went even deeper than racial divisions for it existed within the blacks' religion as well. There was an 'invisible institution' at the core of Afro-Americans' antebellum experience, a black church removed from whites' scrutiny which met to worship without the inhibitions of white society. Just how much it deviated from Christian orthodoxy in its African or Afro-American uniqueness is difficult to say because its worship and belief system would vary with time and place and also because the religion of Afro-Americans was much less affected by formal creeds and theology than that of whites. The. expressiveness of blacks, limited to shouts of approval, song, and rhythmic body movement when in the presence of whites could, in the presence of the spirit and other blacks explode into holy dance and ecstatic seizures. Just as important – or perhaps even more so – was the discovery and recounting of God's promise to deliver His people from bondage. The invisibility of the black church was not, however, limited to isolation from whites. Even with their masters present, the true meaning of blacks' preaching could be obscured as they received the promises of freedom in 'dark symbols and obscure figures', one black minister recalled, 'to cover our real meaning'.[26] Just at what point 'dark symbols and obscure figures' shaded off into folk religion is hard to judge because the sacred world of slaves, like that of all 'pre-modern' peoples, was so undifferentiated and all-encompassing. Pious Christians could believe in or practice conjuring with no qualms, although others would be just as insistent as whites that belief in commerce with spirits was 'heathen' superstition which had no power to deliver the people of God. Conflict between Christians and those who confessed other faiths such as Islam is evident here and there, and may have been touched off when black evangelicals came too close to exhibiting behavior and beliefs similar to those of the whites.

Black Christianity was not, however, white Christianity warmed over, although they both shared symbols and rituals. White evangelicalism had changed from the social movement of the 1780s and 1790s into the religion of the powerful and well placed. The conversion experience became for 'enlightened and refined' people less an overpowering trauma of self-contempt and transformation, and more an inner maturation betokened by a life of piety and duty. The difference was at first one of degree. With the exception of some in the Cumberland church, Presbyterian evangelicals were never so devoted to revivalism and outward emotional breakdown as were Methodists and Baptists. But the latter, too, were becoming more reserved in their worship, and possibly more 'worldly', too, for they were beginning to put pianos and organs into their churches. These changes were complemented by increased ambivalence among white Christians about the meaning of Afro-American Christianity. Although difficult to document for the entire South, the impression one receives from various ecclesiastical squabbles and the organization of missions is that blacks were pushed ever farther to the periphery of whites' church life. At the same time, however, many whites remained impressed by the slaves' Christian piety, believing it to be a perfect example of the transforming power of Christianity. The increasing distance from blacks could allow this perception to degenerate into sentimentality and self-congratulation for having been the agents of the slaves' conversion. If Afro-American religion sometimes reassured white evangelicals as to the morality of their adaptation to slavery, it also came to represent the primitiveness of the slaves and of the great distance they had yet to travel in order to become more like whites. Blacks could agree that their Christianity was indeed different from that of whites, but it is difficult to believe that they would have had it any other way.

The quality of black evangelicalism which for many persons of both races has distinguished it from much of white religion was its vitality. The expressiveness of congregational singing and the call-

and-response patterns in which singing and preaching merged seemed to make blacks more 'emotional' than 'genteel' whites. Visions of the Divine complemented public worship to provide a bridge of consciousness between individual and community. The result was a social bonding which whites sometimes sensed as an alien force. The religious community of whites was reinforced by the communion service as a special act commemorating the passion of Christ; the revivals, too – which had become institutionalized in the camp meeting – bonded young converts to the church by guiding them from the world into a state of grace. Black evangelicals, however, seemed to recreate the community of godly people in most experiences of public worship. The vitality so vivid in meeting was expressed in other ways as well. The preachers who elicited so much excitement from black congregations, for example, had been chosen for their holy work without certification either by education or license from white churches. Like the earliest evangelical ministers of both races, black preachers were selected because of their 'gift', their ability to call forth from the congregation a sense of the Divine and to assure them of the hope of final salvation. Black leadership, in other words, was a creation of the black community by a consensus of the spirit. The word sometimes used to describe the feelings released in worship was 'liberty'. The connotations are clear – liberation from the fear of death, apprehension about the future, guilt for having done those things one ought not to have done, shame for not having done those things one ought to have done; liberation, too, from the masters. Liberty was an expression of relief, a celebration of escape, and the joy of realizing what one's humanity meant. It was expressed in communal dance, song, and open approval of the preacher's words: 'Yes, oh yes!' 'Amen!' 'That's right – Amen!' In the communal celebration of the Spirit of God was the celebration that the Spirit knew neither rank nor race, and no condition of servitude; it was celebration of human equality – 'God is no respecter of persons'.

   Whites, too, sometimes participated in worship like that of blacks. This was true in both the Old World and the New – the Christian tradition has had a long history of 'enthusiasm'. If class and cultural differences affected religious expressiveness, they are difficult to isolate; indeed, the two peoples sometimes interacted with each other so intensely as to allow them to reach across the boundaries of race and class. Perhaps the difference between black and white enthusiasm was in tendency and nuance. White evangelicalism was becoming less characteristically 'emotional'; responses

in worship among blacks may have been those of the entire congregation rather than of a few individuals; enthusiasm among
whites may have been limited ever more to special rites and times.
Certainly there is evidence to support these possibilities.

One thing, however, is clear. Black evangelicals differed from
whites in the history to which the experience of God fused them. In
the nineteenth century the history of white Americans was becoming more clearly defined as they celebrated the heroes and events
which together had set the foundations of the Republic. The War
for American Independence became a revolution and the American
colonies became a nation destined to transform the ancient Christian expectation of a righteous millennium into concrete actuality.
Past and present for citizens of the Republic sharing in its riches
became equally part of the Providential process through which the
perfect society would one day be realized. Gradually the flight of
Puritans to New England became the flight for freedom of all
Americans; the Revolution became the vortex through which the
new people was tested, purged, and vindicated. The fertile lands in
the West became the New Eden isolated from the contamination of
Europe and – for the most sanguine – also from the Fall.

The history of black evangelicals was much different. Indeed,
any sense of history attributed to blacks and especially to slaves
must take into account that culture, social position, and enforced
ignorance combined to undermine historical consciousness. But
such limitations did not prevent blacks from doing what whites had
been doing for years: making their own history. As the recounting
of a process or telling a narrative of events which explains the
origins of a people, history asks: 'Where did we come from, how did
we become what we are, and how are we different from other
people?' Despite an interest in their African origins and a living
memory of lineage, the slaves did not develop a history of origins. If
they faintly remembered where they had come from they did not do
so in a way that created a collective memory. But history is not
merely memory; it is also an elaboration of previous events and
heroes which signifies what the future will bring. Christianity is
essentially a way of understanding history, placing the salvation of
the individual and community in a chain of events which has not yet
ended. One theme which runs through both Old and New Testa-
ments is messianic expectation and ultimate vindication of the
people of God. Christian preaching from the earliest times to the
present is a proclamation of what God has done for His people and
what He intends to do in the future. In the prophetic tradition of

those who for centuries had renewed the Church by preaching the Word, evangelical preachers told blacks a story with three essential parts: the recounting of God's deliverance of His people from bondage in Egypt: the promise of God's deliverance of His people in the future; the invitation to become God's people now.[27] Thus Moses became one of the leading figures in the Biblical plan of salvation as blacks understood it; but he was almost absent from white evangelicalism. And Christ, the Lord of the Apocalypse as pictured in the Revelation of St John also became a major force in black evangelicalism: 'King Jesus rides on a milk white horse, no man can hinder him!'

The fusion of these two figures in the peculiarly black history of salvation acknowledged the injustice of bondage and promised freedom. Entry into this history through conversion made each experience of God's presence an affirmation of the blacks' human-ity and ultimate vindication. That the ideal of chosen people also characterized white evangelicalism is of course quite true, but the whites' claim to that status relied more on the political destiny of their class and nation than did that of blacks. Relying on their own resources the whites' claim as a New Israel was suspect. Reminder of that fact was reinforced every time they broke gospel discipline in their interaction with blacks. In the history appropriated by slaves, masters came to be identified with Egyptians, oppressors of the poor, rich men careless of their souls, and antichrist. But the expec-tation of final vindication was not merely 'etherealized revenge'[28] because it was not consumed by self-destructive anger or palliated by assurance of reward after death; it was the symbolic projection of the inner tension within evangelicalism between the vision of liberty and the reality of self-discipline. It was a mood which reinforced the Christian slaves' sense of moral integrity and personal dignity sus-pended between Uncle Tom and Nat Turner.

Southern evangelicalism thus sustained slaves as well as slaveholders. Its tension between the experience of God and the repression of sin was resolved by each believer in ways affected by social position, personal sensitivity, individual experience, and cul-ture. The social impact of evangelicalism was subject also to varia-tions of space, time, and collective perception, but without going into all of the convolutions of variant possibilities, it should be clear that evangelicalism was not a force imposed from outside and above upon a subject people so much as an earnest of salvation, a process of enhancing self-discovery and learning self-esteem, a communal and individual expression of the Divine in the face of everything which denied it. A mood which defined decorum and moral responsibility for both master and slave, the religion of masters did not become – as pious masters had hoped – the religion of slaves. This is not to say that slaves did not in many cases internalize much of the ethos which formed the whites' worldview. There is much evidence to suggest that black Christians no less than white adopted the ideal of self-disciplined holiness which could provide the core of a mature and dignified life. But essentially, the evangelicalism of blacks maintained the duality of experience and discipline far better than whites whose religious witness was to 'Christianize' slaveholding rather than to acknowledge it as the context of sin from which Christians should be saved. For blacks, slavery was both the metaphor and actuality of sin; and present salvation was metaphor for the liberty that was to come.

Notes

1 Roger Anstey, *The Atlantic Slave Trade and British Abolition 1760–1810* (1975), especially pp. 157–99; David Brion Davis, 'The emergence of immediatism in British and American anti-slavery thought', *Mississippi Valley Historical Review*, XLIX (September 1962), 209–30; Davis, *The Problem of Slavery in Western Culture* (Ithaca, 1966), pp. 3–18; Anne C. Loveland, 'Evangelicalism and 'immediate emancipation' in American anti-slavery thought', *Journal of Southern History*, XXXII (May 1966), 172–88; Ronald G. Walters, *The Antislavery Appeal: American Abolitionism after 1830* (Baltimore, 1976), pp. 39–44; John L. Thomas, 'Romantic reform in America, 1815–65', in David Brion Davis (ed.), *Ante-Bellum Reform* (New York, 1967).

2 Walters, *The Antislavery Appeal*, p. 44.

3 Donald G. Mathews, *Religion in the Old South* (Chicago, 1977), pp. 1–38; Rhys Isaac, 'Religion and authority: problems of the Anglican establishment in Virginia in the era of the Great Awakening and the Parsons' Cause', *William and Mary Quarterly*, 3rd series, XXX (January 1973), 3–36; Isaac, 'Evangelical revolt: the nature of the Baptists' challenge to the traditional order in Virginia, 1765–75', *ibid.*, XXXI (July 1974), 345–68; Harry S. Stout, 'Religion, communications, and the ideological origins of the American Revolution', *ibid.*, XXXIV (October 1977), 519–41.

4 Quoted in Lawrence Lee, *The Lower Cape Fear in Colonial Days* (Chapel Hill, 1965), p. 226.

5 Quoted in Alfloyd Butler, 'The Blacks' contribution of elements of African religion to Christianity in America: a case study of the Great Awakening in South Carolina', unpublished Ph.D. dissertation, Northwestern University (1975), p. 140.

6 Donald G. Mathews, *Slavery and Methodism: A Chapter in American Morality 1780–1845* (Princeton, 1965), p. 295; Andrew E. Murray, *Presbyterians and the Negro – A History* (Philadelphia, 1966), p. 17;

Walter Posey, *The Baptist Church in the Lower Mississippi Valley 1776–1845* (Lexington, 1957), pp. 89, 90; *Minutes of the Baptist General Committee at their Yearly Meeting, Held in the City of Richmond, May 8, 1790* (Richmond, 1790), p. 7; *Minutes of the Baptist General Committee . . . May 1791* (Richmond, 1791).

7   Black Creek Minute Book 1774–1804, 22 November 1793; 21 February 1794. Virginia Baptist Historical Society, University of Richmond.

8   A Student [Ezekiel Cooper] to Godd and Angell [Maryland Journal], 18 April 1792, Ezekiel Cooper Papers, Garrett Theological Seminary, Northwestern University. David Barrow, *Circular Letter* (Norfolk, 1798); *Maryland Gazette*, 30 December 1790; Jeffrey Brooke Allen, 'Were Southern critics of slavery racists? Kentucky and the Upper South', *Journal of Southern History*, XLIV (May 1978), 169–91; Philanthropos [David Rice], *Slavery Inconsistent with Justice and Good Policy* (Lexington, 1792).

9   Daniel Grant to John Owen, Jr., 3 September 1790, David Campbell Papers, Duke University.

10   James O'Kelly, *Essay on Negro Slavery* (Philadelphia, 1789), pp. 11, 14–15, 31, Duke University Rare Book Room.

11   Duncan J. McLeod, *Slavery, Race, and the American Revolution* (Cambridge, 1974), pp. 45–7; Mathews, *Slavery and Methodism*, pp. 62–87.

12   *Minutes of the Baptist General Committee . . . Richmond May 8th 1790* (Richmond, 1790), p. 7; *Minutes of the Virginia Portsmouth Baptist Association holden at Meherrin Meeting House . . . May 26, 1792* (n.p., n.d.), pp. 2–4; *Minutes of the Virginia Portsmouth Baptist Association May 25 &c 1793* (Norfolk, 1793), p. 4; *Minutes of the Virginia Portsmouth Baptist Association . . . May 1796* (n.p., n.d.), p. 5; *Minutes of the Virginia Portsmouth Baptist Association . . . May, 1803* (n.p., n.d.), pp. 7–8.

13   Barrow, *Circular Letter; Minutes of the Kehukee Baptist Association . . . 1796* (Halifax, 1796), p. 4; also *Minutes of the Kehukee . . . 1798* (Halifax, 1798), p. 3.

14   Mathews, *Religion in the Old South*, pp. 1–38, 71–7, 81–97.

15   The local church records upon which the judgments in this paragraph are based are to be found in the Virginia Baptist Historical Society, the Wake Forest University Library, the Southern Historical Collection of the University of North Carolina, the Methodist Episcopal Church South Collection of Duke University, the South Carolinian Collection on the campus of the University of South Carolina, the state archives of North Carolina and Alabama, the Historical Foundation of the Presbyterian and Reformed Churches at Montreat, North Carolina. See also William Davidson Blanks, 'Ideal and practice: a study of the conception of the Christian life prevailing in the Presbyterian churches of the South during the nineteenth century' (Th.D. dissertation, Union Theological Seminary, Richmond, 1960); Cortland Victor Smith, 'Church organization as an agency of social control: church discipline in North Carolina, 1800–60' (Unpublished Ph.D. dissertation, the University of North Carolina at Chapel Hill, 1966).

16   Charles Colcock Jones to William Swan Plumer, 28 June 1834, William Swan Plumer Papers, The Presbyterian Historical Society, Philadelphia; see also Donald G. Mathews, 'Charles Colcock Jones and the

Southern evangelical crusade to form a biracial community', *Journal of Southern History*, XLI (August 1975), 299–320.

17 Eugene D. Genovese, *The World the Slaveholders Made: Two Essays in Interpretation* (New York, 1969); *Roll, Jordan, Roll: The World the Slaves Made* (New York, 1974).

18 The discussion which follows is my interpretation of material gleaned from the following: Butler, 'The Blacks' contribution to Christianity in America'; Genovese, *Roll, Jordon, Roll*, pp. 168–284; Lawrence W. Levine, *Black Culture and Black Consciousness: Afro-American Folk Thought from Slavery to Freedom* (New York, 1977), pp. 1–80; Mathews, *Religion in the Old South*, pp. 185–250; John S. Mbiti, *New Testament Eschatology in an African Background* (London, 1971); Albert Jordy Raboteau, *Slave Religion: The Invisible Institution in the Antebellum South* (New York, 1978).

19 Lewis Jones to the Secretary of the Society for the Propagation of the Gospel in Foreign Parts, 27 December 1743 as quoted in Butler, 'The Blacks' Contribution to Christianity in America', p. 163.

20 William McKendree, Diary, 6 November 1790, Vanderbilt University Library.

21 'A Journal and Travel of James Meacham, Part II 1789–97', *Historical Papers* (Trinity College Historical Society), x (1914), 92.

22 Robin Winks, 'Josiah Henson and Uncle Tom', in Winks, (ed.), *An Autobiography of the Reverend Josiah Henson* (Reading, Mass., 1969), pp. v–xi.

23 Cato Jones to Charles Colcock Jones, Sr., 3 March 1851, C. C. Jones Papers, Tulane University.

24 The incident is related in Mary Jones, 'Miscellaneous remembrances of Charles Colcock Jones' in the C. C. Jones Papers. Tulane University. Whether or not Stevens was actually the person who led the walk-out is a matter of interpretation. He was the major black preacher among the blacks of Liberty County; his age and his piety would have made him a person Jones was bound to respect.

25 See for example Moore's Swamp Minute Book 1818–38, 24 September 1831: 'In consequence of some present existing circumstances the Conference took into Consideration the impropiety of retaining our colored members in fellowship and on motion, Resolved, to suspend them from the privilege of communion from this time until our next association'. Also Racoon Swamp Baptist church, 30 October 1831, and 12 November 1831, 25 March 1832; Black Creek Minute Book 1816–31, Fourth Lord's Day, September, 1831; Mill Swamp Church Book 1812–40. When black members were once again allowed communion a group of whites left this church, see entry for 6 April 1833.

26 L. S. Burkhead, 'History of the difficulties of the Pastorate of the Front Street Methodist Church, Wilmington, N. C. for the year 1865', *Historical Papers* Trinity College Historical Society), VIII (1908–9), 43.

27 See Levine, *Black Consciousness and Black Culture*, pp. 33ff; Mathews, *Religion in the Old South*, pp. 228ff.

28 Eric Hobsbawm, *Primitive Rebels: Studies in Archaic Forms of Social Movement in the Nineteenth and Twentieth Centuries* (New York, 1965, original copyright 1959), p. 133.

11

THE ANTI-SLAVERY ORIGINS OF CONCERN FOR THE AMERICAN INDIANS*

by Christine Bolt

The distracting as well as inspirational effect of the anti-slavery campaign on ante-bellum reformers in the United States has long been noted by historians; recently, for example, with reference to the embryonic women's movement. But the links and contrasts between those agitating on behalf of blacks and Indians have so far received relatively little attention. It will be the aim of this essay to show that, in the minds of certain American humanitarians, the grievances of American Negroes and Indians were closely linked, being epitomized by their loss of freedom. Such injustice, in each case, demanded from the whites whose greed and cruelty were the primary cause of servitude – virtual and actual – a similar reform programme. Reform, for abolitionists and 'friends of the Indian' alike, involved Christian and secular education, instruction in the work ethic, provision of the means for making a livelihood and eventually of civil rights, with a view to the final integration of non-whites, as free individuals, into the dominant society.

Because of the contrasting legal and general circumstances of the two coloured races, and their divergent reactions to reform proposals, these programmes would be applied at different times and at a different pace. In particular, the fact that some Indian tribes were able to preserve their own viable governments for much of the nineteenth century inhibited the efforts of well-meaning, of often ill-doing, outsiders on their behalf. Nonetheless, it was white exploitation of Indian and Negro slaves which first aroused sympathy for red and black men; which helped to keep concern for the Indians alive when the fate of the far more numerous Negro slaves attracted greater interest; and which finally prompted various abolitionists,

who had supported this order of priorities, to take up the cause of
the native Americans again after the Civil War. For reasons of
space, however, the folly of trying to evolve like policies for unlike
minorities must be detailed elsewhere, as must the invariably hostile
black and red responses to that attempt.[1]

I

Slavery was practised in the New World by many Indian tribes,
especially in the Pacific North West, before the coming of the white
man. Whether or not it was an institution comparable to that which
prevailed in Africa and developed in the Americas, its existence was
capitalized upon by white settlers in what is now the United States in
order to punish their defeated tribal enemies, to share in a profitable
trade, to ease the severe labour shortage in the colonies, and to help
clear native land for immigrant occupation. Early European images
of the Indians as uncorrupted and natural men made it difficult to
justify their enslavement by the newcomers and may have encouraged imports of African slaves, who were less favourably regarded
and easier both to obtain and keep. But black and native servitude
were soon governed by a common body of legislation, while the
resemblances between the justification and reality of each became
more important than the differences between them, just as there
was more in common between Indian and white enslavement of
blacks, or Indian and white enslavement of Indians than many
commentators have recognized, notably in terms of treatment of the
slaves.

Due to the greater numbers of black slaves, whites were more
aware of them than of native bondsmen by the eighteenth century
and no independent movement for Indian emancipation emerged.
Yet the latter's plight had been publicized in London and America
by merchants, missionaries and prominent individuals. And if the
limitations placed by the colonies on Indian slavery were largely
prompted by the need to placate tribal allies, evangelists occupied
themselves with the religious 'needs' of Indians, free and unfree,
before they turned their attention to blacks, albeit the censure of
Indian slave-holders loomed larger than discussion of their slaves
and frequently avoided condemnation of slavery itself. The Quakers were especially anxious to end the native slave traffic, moving
against Indian slavery when Negro servitude was still accepted
among them, though no doubt the pacifist brethren were chiefly
concerned to avert wars, the most likely cause of which was friction

with their red neighbours, resulting from or leading to native enslavement. Unfortunately, sympathy for native bondsmen and belief in the universal gift of grace did not mean that Quakers were able to bridge the gap between the two races: there was no inter-marriage, the Indians remained apart.

As fears of slave insurrections grew with the institution of sla-very, separation of the coloured races was also positively fostered by whites, lest the similar resentments of Indians and blacks under the slave codes should drive them together to seek a collective revenge. Indeed, such occurrences – or threats of them – were not unknown and they were predicted with exaggerated alarm during the Revolutionary conflict. Even abolitionists depicted the two groups as potentially dangerous allies rather than fellow victims, and white Americans were consequently urged to emancipate the black slaves, thereby averting an alliance which, if it materialized, would constitute Divine retribution for the neglect of moral obligations. For their part, in order to avert any red–black fraternization, colo-nial authorities employed friendly Indians as slave catchers, tried to extract treaty promises from them to return Negro fugitives or prisoners, and invaded native territory in search of runaways. This discreditable state of affairs was improved in at least one respect following Independence, when the custom of selling rebel Indians into slavery was abandoned; an 'honorable change of conduct' which, according to one later commentator, 'was a true token of the superior excellence of the government of the United States over others'.[2]

After the necessity for Indian slaves decreased, the obvious differences between Indians and Negroes and the desire to think better of the former as the original Americans shaped by the same environment which had produced a heroic breed of settlers, stimu-lated that counterbalancing of red and black which self-interest had always dictated. If the classic image of the noble savage was being undermined by a changing view of nature and evolutionary concep-tions of man, and it had never provided a key to understanding Indian behaviour, it was a useful excuse for white policies and their disastrous consequences. If the Negro could only prosper in bon-dage, it was alleged, the red man could only endure in freedom: romantic literature abounds with tales of ill-starred or dying Indians. Moreover, it was but a short step to imply that if the native Americans could not easily be slaves, then they had never been enslaved – something which Indians themselves endorsed – and could rightfully be portrayed as the innocent symbols of New World liberties, celebrated while they still survived. As a recent study of the image of red and black men in American art between 1590 and 1900 demonstrates, the Indian was represented as a noble savage and intrinsic, active part of an unspoilt landscape, as a fearsome enemy or hero, and eventually as a tragic victim. By contrast, the Negro, particularly until the end of the eighteenth century, featured mainly as servant or slave, as comic relief rather than object for pity. And to the extent that pity was a necessary fuel for anti-slavery work, it is no accident that abolitionists began to display their most active interest in native Americans just when these conventional pictures were changing, from the 1850s onwards, to show Indians in as much need of assistance as blacks, and both available for salvation through Christianity.[3]

II

Yet during the early nineteenth century, the connection between anti-slavery sentiments and concern for the native Americans, tentatively established in colonial times, was strained by white ignorance of the persistence of Indian bondage and a conviction that, with their removal west of the Mississippi, the tribes were again being detached from white jurisdiction. It was further tested by a growing belief that if the Indians were fast vanishing, then black slaves, who had the great merit of being useful to whites, deserved more attention; and by the embarrassing problem of institutionalized black slavery among the Five Civilized Tribes. Although the Indian habit of enslaving other Indians continued well into the nineteenth century, it was little known about except by travellers who had visited the far western tribes, in areas only slowly brought within American dominion. These tribes were also reached by missionaries when servitude was already declining among them, together with the elaborate, materialistic cultures wherein it had flourished, or when it had been abolished in the United States and, Indian claims to autonomy having been overcome, whites felt at once compelled and entitled to move against the system. But while the consignment to slavery of numerous women and children would have particularly offended an informed public, as usual the first missionaries in the field were at pains to present their constituents in a positive light so as to boost contributions, and to argue the case for gaining the trust of the Indians before attempting substantial alteration of their institutions. This could mean that no such alteration was seriously pursued, as we shall see in the case of the southern tribes and Negro slavery. And evangelists might not even oppose slavery actively: Marcus Whitman knew of its existence among the Indians of the North West but he was not much interested in black bondage in the East and wrote to his brother Samuel from Oregon in 1841 that he was 'no more of an Abolitionist' than he had been when he left home. In the South West, and especially New Mexico, the enslavement of Indians by whites, never officially regarded as involuntary servitude, was tolerated by the local community until its investigation by a Congressional Committee in 1865 caused a national scandal, resulting in termination of the practice three years later.[4]

During the 1830s, however, there was no general unawareness of 'the Indian problem'. According to one opponent, Jeremiah Evarts, the attempt to move the remaining eastern tribes west of the Mississippi 'attracted more attention than any other public measure since the close of the last war'.[5] The Jacksonian legislation to this end stimulated a mass of protest petitions, similar to those later provoked by agitation over black slavery and from the same sections of the populace: New Englanders, religious groups, benevolent societies, and colleges, for whom, at this point, the two causes were equally deserving, equally illustrative of white cruelty, greed and expansionist tendencies, indulged for sectional advantage. Indeed, there were those who argued that the Five Tribes were particularly worthy of aid just because they were civilized and Christianized, not savages or caffres, Hottentots or runaway slaves; and because their rights had been guaranteed in solemn treaties which the federal government now proposed to disregard. It was also necessary to resist the developments of the 1830s because the Indians, unlike the black slaves, had no white allies, that is masters, moved by 'pride and interest' to safeguard their material welfare, so that to allow the extension of state law over their territories would be to reduce them to a condition worse than slavery.[6] To principled observers, particularly abolitionists like Garrison, the Motts, the Grimké sisters, Lovejoy and Mrs Child, it was apparent that both enslavement and removal relied on force not justice, and both would render the United States contemptible in the eyes of the outside world because Americans had proclaimed themselves 'apostles of liberty', declaring it 'was the right of *every man* to enjoy freedom – of every man, whether black, white, or red.' Both implied that moral principles might be disregarded when dealing with non-whites, at the prompting of 'repulsive prejudice'; both would retard rather than advance the civilization of which each race was capable – and in the end both might bring Divine punishment.[7]

Among the prominent figures who at various times opposed Indian removal as well as black slavery we may note Henry Clay, Ralph Waldo Emerson, Theodore Frelinghuysen, Daniel Webster, Edward Everett, John Howard Payne, and Samuel Houston (who hoped to see the Cherokees established independently in the West but was concerned to prevent white injustice in the process).[8] Their hostility was not enough to offset Democratic strength in Congress but the crucial vote on the 1830 Removal Bill was very close, its passage being assisted by some Indian administrators and church-men (notably the Baptist missionary Isaac McCoy), who justified their support for government proposals on humanitarian grounds, believing that the tribes were the losers in their past and existing close contacts with white society, being reduced thereby 'to a servil-ity and degradation more harmful to man than African slavery'. The contest was, as McCoy maintained, to some extent a political and sectional one in which anti-administration feeling was crucial (hence the focus on white abuse of the southern Indians), and one in which there were many considerations besides the natives them-selves. Nonetheless, a number of reformers continued to complain of the warfare and ill-treatment which resulted from Jacksonian policies, Mrs Child and William Lloyd Garrison being especially moved by the treatment of the Seminoles and the fate of Osceola, whom Garrison considered to be the 'boldest, bravest, and most sagacious' chief since King Philip; the Bostonian further noted that the plantation raids of rebellious southern Indians had 'emanci-pated a considerable number of slaves'. It was clear to Garrison and such kindred spirits as abolitionist and Indian reformer, John Beeson, that the same slave-owners in government were oppressing both black and native Americans on the mere surmise 'that these tribes might disturb the plantations of their brother slave-holders, and afford a refuge or retreat for their fugitive slaves'.

Their view was essentially correct. Debates over the future of slavery during the 1840s and 1850s adversely affected decisions on the Indian Department's responsibilities in the territories through-out these years. Men like Houston, with political careers to con-sider, felt obliged to put sectional loyalty before conscience regard-ing Indians and slaves, and such caution notwithstanding, the Texan found himself attacked as a traitor to the South; while Beeson, though a farmer not a politician, claimed that his activities had given great offence to the Democrats, no doubt by having presented black and red men as equally the 'victims of slavery . . . of the slave spirit that has crept into our national councils, and controls all the machinery of our Government'. Once the tribes had emigrated, after being depicted as in dramatic numerical decline, and once a network of anti-slavery societies had been established, it was natural that those who pleaded the Indians' case should concentrate on the Negro. After all, a policy so popular with the majority of white Americans as removal was unlikely to be reversed, and its victims still retained a semblance of autonomy and thus the power to help themselves. Some 'progressive' Indians had even supported removal, whereas there was obviously vociferous opposition to slavery within the Negro community. The few blacks who possessed slaves were ignored, along with Indian ownership of Negroes in the 1830s, by whites who were intent on demonstrating the claims of both to civilization.

Ironically the very religious sects which had sympathized with the Indians, gained by their removal from the East, in that the inconvenience of having to re-establish missions west of the Mississippi was more than offset by the growth of white church membership in the vacated territories.[10] But when missionary work was renewed among the Indians in their new homes, the long-term association of black and red men in religious and secular anti-slavery thought was again undermined, as it had been during the Revolution, though now by the stubborn support for black slavery among the Five Tribes.

Until recently this has been an area of slavery studies comparatively neglected by historians. Slave narratives for the Indian Territory are scarce, apart from those gathered in twentieth-century oral history projects: servitude there was but a small, possibly atypical part of a system which had been longer established in other parts of the country, and its leading slaveholders were not influential in national politics, so that neglect is understandable.[11] Moreover the materials which have been left by the white administrators and missionaries who served in the Territory are equally biased, with both groups minimizing the severity of the slave system to disarm political enemies in the one case and disgruntled financial sponsors in the other. Thus the indefatigable McCoy, when publishing his *Register of Indian Affairs* in the 1830s and his *History of Baptist Missions* in 1840, either ignored the existence of slavery when he referred to the Five Tribes whose civilization he was trying to advertize, or merely indicated in a prosaic fashion the number of slaves held and the extent to which they were church members. Similarly Quaker missionary Thomas Battey could note the possession of Negro slaves by 'the more civilized Indians' without feeling the need for further comment.

McCoy was, however, at pains to refute charges of abolitionism brought against a Methodist missionary, the Rev. D. B. Rollin, by the Creek nation in 1836. There was, in fact, a general association of the representatives of the popular Protestant churches with anti-slavery. In his account of missionary work among the southern slaves, W. P. Harrison referred to the 'rash' attacks on slavery by early Methodist and Congregational missionaries, as a result of which the suspicion of them among owners took a generation to overcome. But McCoy maintained that although 'the missionaries regretted the existence of slavery in the Indian country, they had prudently forborne to meddle with the subject', the Methodist in trouble going so far as to refuse 'to teach the slaves to read in his Sunday school', regardless of their entreaties. Rollin was eventually cleared of the charges against him and assigned a post among the Shawnee. Yet the fact that the Creek chiefs seized their opportunity to try and expel all missionaries, and that the Indian Commissioner was obliged to transfer the accused, indicates the practical and constitutional difficulties which would have faced genuine abolitionists. There also seems to have been considerable opposition among the Creeks to the kind of work required of their children by the missionaries which, records Rister, they asserted 'would reduce them to slavery', as well as to any proselytizing efforts among them which threatened 'the customs of their fathers' and won religious recruits from either the blacks or their own people.[12]

The situation was even more tense among the missionaries sent by the American Board of Commissioners for Foreign Missions to the Cherokees and Choctaws. A very serious rift had developed between, on the one hand, the Board and its eastern, anti-slavery supporters; and, on the other, the field workers who had been welcomed by and needed the support of leaders among the still semi-independent Five Tribes, many of whom (particularly those with white blood) owned slaves. The men on the spot, already likely to be affected by the factional Indian politics which removal had aggravated, argued that the missionary's 'one primary object [was] of securing holiness in the hearts of individuals', and that both masters and slaves were admitted to mission churches on the ground of faith only. They maintained that they were obliged to consume slave produce and employ slave labourers, despite a Board injunction against the practice, because no others were available or because they alone spoke English; and that the evangelists and slaves alike in Indian Territory thought that the institution existed 'in a milder form than that which is generally found in the States', albeit there were 'cases of gross cruelty and oppression'.

This last argument was probably designed as a direct rebuttal of the suggestion among outside censors that slavery imposed by heathen 'savages' must be infinitely worse than the system as it operated in Christian white communities. But as missionary critic of the Board, Charles K. Whipple, pointed out and historians have lately observed, slavery in the South and in the Territory had much the same unfortunate moral and economic effects. Similarly, external condemnation of the institution, together with attempts by whites to recover runaway slaves in the Indian domain, brought schisms within the churches established among the Indians and a progressive stiffening up of the slave codes, in addition to restrictions on the rights of free blacks. No Indian abolitionism ever emerged, not least because the Territory produced no white opponents of slavery to offset the influence of white southerners, although William McLoughlin notes the letter of a Christianized Cherokee, David Brown, to a New England friend in 1825, speculating that 'the Cherokees will, at no distant date, co-operate with the humane efforts of those who are liberating and sending this proscribed race to the land of their fathers'. In the event black slavery was not officially abolished by the tribe until 1863; among the Five Tribes in general it was invalidated by the Washington reconstruction treaties of 1866.

The decision to close the American Board's Indian missions by 1861 was defended on the grounds of the real advance of the tribes and the large returns for an expenditure of many missionaries and of $350,000 on the Cherokee station alone, even if its historian, W. E. Strong, felt obliged to concede that 'the course of the Board was somewhat temporizing'. In Whipple's opinion, by contrast, withdrawal was not a consequence of the Civilized Tribes being 'a Christian people' and the work among them therefore finished, but sprang from the difficulty of reconciling the two different views of the missionary's duty outlined above. Furthermore, such views were strengthened by the fact that considerable numbers of black slaves were involved and by the apprehension of anti-slavery northerners that the Indian Territory might become not only a 'savage' but a pro-slavery barrier to the expansion of freedom loving whites, while the southerners who dominated government posts in the Territory were anxious to show that black slavery 'was profitable and desirable there, affording a practical issue of the right of expansion, for which the . . . [Civil War eventually] began'.

Notwithstanding the denunciations of the Board by moderate abolitionists throughout the 1840s and 1850s, and their partly successful attempts to divert funds to the less conservative American Missionary Association, the outcome satisfied nobody, and was one more example of the recurring conflict between evangelicalism and humanitarianism, demonstrated earlier, for instance, by the history of the Methodist mission to the slaves between 1824 and 1844.[13] In Indian Territory, then, as in the rest of the nation, the debate over slavery involved religious, political, and sectional arguments which often lost sight of the slave himself and certainly did nothing to combat the strengthening of those feelings of superiority which Indian tribes had always entertained towards slaves and outsiders, and which were now – with the spread of black bondage – developing into something akin to white racism, at least among the Cherokees, Chickasaws and Choctaws. And since nineteenth-century commentators firmly believed the condition of Indian women everywhere to be one of bondage to their husbands, and that Indians generally exhibited 'the most slavish cringing before natural phenomena', any adaptation to white civilization which ended these forms of savage 'slavery', even at the expense of acquiring another, was not totally without merit, seen in the context of the times. Indeed, black slaves might be as useful to the Indians as they were to the white missionaries, being able to impart to their masters a knowledge of English, white agriculture and habits.[14]

The Indian educator, General R. H. Pratt, would later actually regret that the natives had not been enslaved and so brought into unavoidable contact with civilized life; 'through forcing Negroes to live among us and become producers', he argued, 'slavery became a more humane and real civilizer and promoter of usefulness to the Negro than was our Indian system'.[15] General Armstrong of the Hampton Institute likewise regarded the reservations as worse for the tribes than slavery was for the black population. Since for the most part only the missionaries were doing anything positive to replace 'heathen' by Christian institutions, it is hardly surprising that in these lonely labours they did not lead the attack on a practice which the southern Indians had copied from white men while it was still widely respectable.[16]

III

Yet whatever its shortcomings, the debate over servitude in Indian Territory helped to keep interest in the native Americans alive, and the attraction of that region to fugitive blacks, however unwelcome they might have been among some of the Indians, encouraged whites, when it was convenient, to see a natural affinity between the two coloured races and to believe that free Negroes could reasonably be urged to move there, whence ex-slaves might follow them if emancipation were ever secured.[17] During the two decades before the Civil War, humanitarians such as Mrs Child, Wendell Phillips, Henry Ward Beecher, and the Motts frequently discussed the fate of Indians and blacks, presenting both as the victims of the white man but regarding Negro slavery as more immediately disruptive to the country and therefore demanding of their attention. Indeed, Helen Hunt Jackson claimed to have converted Phillips to activism in the Indian cause after the War was over. And if they allegedly made an 'abstraction' of the slave, more abolitionists had seen and could identify with black Americans, whose destinies and customs whites had done so much to shape, than had encountered or could begin to understand Indian cultures, which remained surprisingly resilient in the face of centuries of white aggression.

Although prominent reformers often lent their names to a whole range of good causes, it was difficult to be simultaneously effective in more than one, especially if there was a living to be earned into the bargain. Thus Henry Whipple, the first Episcopalian bishop of Minnesota, while he stressed that he and his wife had a lifelong interest in the brown and black races, avoided active abolitionism and took up Indian reform in the West, agitating for the regulation of Indian trade and the removal of the Indian service from politics, before evincing an interest in freedmen's aid and becoming a trustee of the Peabody Fund. John Beeson progressed from helping fugitive slaves to publicizing white injuries against Indians, and though he gained a sympathetic hearing from church groups and New England abolitionists in the 1850s, the support was vocal rather than practical at this stage. He was, in fact, then most unusual in proclaiming that, since oppression of the Indians had preceded and facilitated abuse of the black race, 'their redress is of right and necessity the first step in the order of national reform and of self preservation'.

Nonetheless, just as Mrs Jane Swisshelm was peculiarly hostile to Indians for an opponent of slavery, so among the 'friends of the Indian' Mrs Jackson seems atypical in her youthful lack of sympathy for reform and all notions of black equality, only subsequently finding that native problems were able to spark off an idealism she had not known she possessed. In addition to the abolitionists just named, Frederick Douglass urged Indian reform, with a generosity matched by the black Congressmen who took up the cause. They were joined by such opponents of slavery as Alfred H. Love, Gerrit Smith, Cora Daniels, Harriet Beecher Stowe, Aaron Powell, Samuel Tappan, and Peter Cooper, and Republican politicians James Doolittle, John B. Henderson, George W. Julian and William Windom.[18]

It has been argued by Loring B. Priest that most Americans regarded Negro and Indian problems as being quite distinct and that Indian reform gained nothing as a result of the successful anti-slavery campaign, in part because tribal aspirations were at variance with those of blacks, even as their degree of preparedness for citizenship rights was different.[19] However, although the humanitarians moving from abolitionism to Indian issues might grumble about the enormity of their task, they were encountering the same sort of sectional (now Western) and political (still Democratic) opposition that had impeded their earlier efforts. A similar geographical gulf separated them from the objects of their concern and, though depressed by an initially inadequate response, they drew intellectual inspiration from the past and appealed for support to essentially the same reform 'constituency', with real success by the 1880s. As the popular writer on Indian affairs, J. P. Dunn, expressed it: 'The discussion connected with the emancipation and citizenship of the Negroes . . . educated the people to a just appreciation of the natural rights of all men, and an awakening public conscience pointed to the Indian as a victim of past injustice'.[20]

Their first alliances, the National Indian Aid Association and the United States Indian Commission, admittedly did not inspire organizational activities on a level with those precipitated by the foundation of the American Anti-Slavery Society. For some fifteen years most of the work continued to devolve upon a few dedicated individuals, and the abolitionists who took it up were not the leaders who saw it through to completion. But in the economic dislocation immediately after the Civil War the circumstances were inauspicious for any national reform movement in competition with freedmen's aid; the depression of 1837 had, after all, shown what adverse economic circumstances could do even to abolitionism. Moreover, the fact that Presidents Lincoln and Grant were disposed to see changes in Indian administration, and that the Peace Policy was adopted in 1869 by the government itself, suggested the wisdom of an interval of reflection, before further action should be urged.

Meanwhile, reformers were developing a wide range of arguments on the platform, in pamphlet and petition, arguments which were to influence debate about the Indians until the end of the century. Like the abolitionists, they drew on an evangelical Protestant tradition, pointing to the past neglect of religious duty, in the form of missions to the Indians, but they were less dominated overall by religious considerations and did not produce the old sweeping criticisms of the churches and clergy.[21] Since, outside the government, only evangelists had played a part in the efforts to 'civilize' the native Americans through education, such criticisms would have been out of place. Instead, emphasis was placed on the need to increase expenditure and divert funds from foreign to domestic missionary endeavour. The Women's National Indian Association (founded in 1879) accordingly devoted a good deal of its time and money to the religious and educational labour that 'will be needed long after the political work is done', initiating or helping some thirty-two missionary stations between 1884 and 1893.[22] There were, just the same, manifestations of that anti-sectarianism which had distinguished many of the abolitionists: to be seen, for example, in the sustained opposition of the Lake Mohonk Conferences (begun in 1883) to government aid for sectarian schools.[23]

As abolitionists had done, the 'friends of the Indian' also rejected arguments about the permanent inferiority of non-whites, turning to environmentalism or talk about stages of evolution when taxed to explain Indian wars and ingratitude, apathy or dependence. And although they were prepared to advocate the eventual fusion of red and white, there was something of the familiar uneasiness about miscegenation. A speaker at Mohonk captured the ambivalence nicely when he declared, 'all of us are brethren; and it is not for us to say that even the man of tinted skin is not capable of becoming manly and noble, and able to govern himself'.[24]

Other continuities are striking, notably the proffering of individualistic 'solutions' to race problems and the desire to cultivate in the Indian population, as in the Negro, characteristics admired among white men but always requiring re-affirmation in a changing world: sobriety, thrift, diligence, self-restraint, and self-help. These virtues were to be inculcated by granting educational facilities; the opportunity for individual land ownership; instruction in 'home making', which meant keeping women working within its confines; and civil rights. The free man, of whatever race, might then safely be left to make his own way, spiritually and materially. There was, though, no repetition of the dispute over black suffrage, partly because the slower, piecemeal progress of Indian reformers towards native American citizenship meant that the franchise never became a party political issue. Conversely education, if always seen by abolitionists as one means of giving Negroes acceptability in free society, was accorded a fresh significance after the Civil War by the need to assimilate ever increasing numbers of immigrants as well as non-whites, a need which resulted in a greater emphasis upon the role of the school as the essential institution in the transformation process. Yet no attempt was made to educate Negroes and Indians together, outside Hampton Institute in Virginia, because of the distracting racial tensions thought likely to be involved and the differing responses to such establishments of the intended beneficiaries. From this set of priorities it should be clear that the Indian reformers were no more able to understand the economic forces which were transforming the United States – and dooming the family farmer – than the opponents of slavery had been, although both believed their proposals would aid economic progress, as whites defined it.

While the urgent concern with national destiny and the international struggle for freedom had diminished in the aftermath of Reconstruction, the plight of the tribes was frequently presented as the kind of indictment of a free nation that servitude once was, and British complaints that Indian affairs had 'never been very well managed in the States, not so well as in Canada', were a cause of real annoyance as well as a spur to action.[25] But the greatest source of moral reproach, slavery, had of course been destroyed both in the South in 1865 and among the Five Tribes, whose postwar treaties obliged them not only to emancipate their Negroes but to admit them to citizenship and property rights. The motives behind such legislation, still only partly illuminated, appear to have been mixed: a belated desire to do justice to blacks throughout the nation and to make the Indian Territory yet more attractive as a refuge, combined with a complicating wish to punish those who had aided the Confederacy, though in the end both loyal and disloyal elements within the tribes were made to suffer. Certainly there was no co-ordinated effort to protect the freedmen in their rights after 1866 and the main concern for them seems to have developed when whites saw the potential of an alliance with blacks to open up Indian land to allotment. Hence the Dawes Commission in 1894, with this end in view, made much of the failure by 'the so-called governments of these five tribes' to secure justice for the 'moral, industrious, and frugal, peaceable, orderly' freedmen.[26]

Finally, in organizational terms the old and new movements had much in common, albeit the Indian reformers recognized the need for fresh legislation and the political influence nationally to procure it. The Indian Rights Association (formed in 1882) even maintained a lobbyist in Washington, though delegates to Mohonk shrank from such a course as too worldly.[27] By adopting a practical attitude to politics they avoided one of the most disruptive abolitionist quarrels; and this trait, which co-existed with a strong desire to take politics out of the Indian Service, makes them in one sense the forerunners of the Progressives, notwithstanding the 'anti-institutionalism' (more properly anti-paternalism) of their stance against the Bureau of Indian Affairs.[28]

If the agents and field workers of Indian aid were not in danger from a hostile public and were scarcely circuit riders to the sinful, they utilized the techniques perfected by the abolitionists, namely national societies with state and local auxiliaries, and with 'departments' responsible for various aspects of the work. Close attention was given to propaganda, especially exposure literature, sent to and used by the press nationwide; and to fund raising, though the dues collected from elaborate categories of members were always insufficient. Clever use was also made at meetings of Indian spokesmen, selected, if possible, to be moving but not radical.[29] The crusade appealed, as had anti-slavery, to devout middle-class groups, but lacked abolitionism's acknowledged relevance to working men. There seems to have been little social difference between leaders and rank-and-file, concentrated in the North East, although there was some activity in the West and publicists claimed that 'this Indian question, like the national evil of slavery in the past, . . . [is] a great national question. That it is alike the business and the interest of the people to right a great national wrong'.

A degree of unity prevailed among Indian reformers which set them apart from the opponents of slavery but was as much both their strength and weakness as disunity had been among their predecessors. For if disagreements over politics and reform reduced the abolitionists' practical effectiveness while they gave their debates an ongoing vitality, so the common outlook of the 'friends of the Indian' helped them to secure many of their legislative objectives but made them incredibly unwilling to recognize the unwelcome fact of Indian opposition to their programme, to admit that the native Americans would not be 'civilized' within a generation. Confidence among white reformers that they knew what was best for the Indians exceeded even the confidence shown by the freedmen's aid workers. It also led to positive callousness about the prospective destruction of the tribal unit on the reservation, which allegedly fostered a deadly idleness among those residing there, rather as slavery was once seen to inculcate idleness in the South; but slaves, of course, unlike most tribesmen, were anxious to be cut loose from their bondage.

It would be foolish to pretend that Indian reform was simply an application of anti-slavery principles to a race similarly oppressed but more neglected by white Americans, though some contemporaries felt that after emancipation the approach towards the Indians and freedmen of the South should be the same, namely to make both into useful, educated, Christian citizens. And contacts with the *comparatively* homogeneous black population may have encouraged whites in their fatal tendency to think of and legislate for 'the Indian', ignoring vast tribal differences.[30] Each movement changed with the passage of time and was shaped not only by the normal problems facing voluntary associations but by differing Indian and black attitudes to their efforts. Each was affected by the prejudices prevailing among white contemporaries not active in reform: the contempt for 'primitive' societies in the public at large dangerously augmented such feelings among the 'friends of the Indian'. Each responded to the economic conditions of their own day: the exploitation of the West, which made concentrated settlements of Indians on large tracts of land intolerable to westward-moving whites, dictated the kinds of policies humanitarians could hope to advance with success. The practicality, respectability and consequent influence of Indian reformers gave them far easier access to policy makers than the abolitionists had enjoyed, and they achieved many more attributable victories against far less public hostility, although the results of the assimilation campaign were as disastrous for the native Americans as the failures of abolitionists were for the freedmen. Nonetheless, it is clear that the comparative method may usefully be applied to illuminate the course of American reform endeavours in the area of race, as well as the course of such reform movements in different countries. In the case of the movements surveyed here, it points up what was distinctive about each; but it also reveals important connections. For the movement to help the Indians after the Civil War owed a substantial theoretical and practical debt to that opposition to slavery which had first been aroused in their favour, then deflected with the growth of black servitude, yet finally acknowledged their comparable injuries at the hands of white men and their entitlement to equivalent compensation.

Notes

* I should like to thank Roger Anstey, Stanley Engerman, and Sidney Kaplan of the University of Massachusetts for their helpful comments on an earlier draft of this essay.

1 On the disturbing effect of anti-slavery on feminist efforts to organize, see E. C. DuBois, *Feminism and Suffrage* (Ithaca, 1978), p. 19 and *passim*. For space reasons I have had to cut the first section (and footnotes) of my conference paper comparing red and black slavery and their implications for men of conscience; these themes are elaborated in my forthcoming book, *Red and White in Modern America* (Allen & Unwin).

2 I. McCoy (ed.), *The Annual Register of Indian Affairs*, 2 (Indian Territory, 1837), p. 84.

3 H. Fairchild, *The Noble Savage* (New York, 1955, edn.), pp. 363–4, 461–6; B. W. Dippie, 'The Vanishing Indian: Popular Attitudes and American Indian Policy in the Nineteenth Century' (Ph.D., University of Texas at Austin, 1970), pp. 22–3, 106–7; J. W. DeForest, *History of the Indians of Connecticut* (Hamden, 1964 edn.), p. 151; L. M. Child, *The First Settlers of New England* (Boston, 1829), pp. 29–30, 154, 161, 163–4, 169; R. H. Pratt quoted in L. B. Priest, *Uncle Sam's Stepchildren* (New Brunswick, 1942), p. 176; E. Parry, *The Image of the Indian and the Black Man in American Art, 1590–1900* (New York, 1974), pp. xiii, 35–7, 45–9, 54–5, 58f., 68, 82–3, 100, 172; R. Berkhofer, *The White Man's Indian* (New York, 1978), Pt. 3 and p. 58. But, as R. G. Walters points out in *American Reformers, 1815–60* (New York, 1978), p. 194, both blacks and Indians served some Americans as 'negative reference points', helping them to define what for them was un-American.

4 C. M. Drury (ed.), *Marcus and Narcissa Whitman and the Opening of Old Oregon* (Glendale, 1973), I, pp. 69, 421; II, p. 107; L. R. Bailey, *Indian Slave Trade in the Southwest* (Los Angeles, 1973 edn.), pp. 175–87.

5 W. Penn (pseud. Evarts), *Essays on the Present Crisis in the Condition of the American Indian* (Philadelphia, 1830), p. 101.

6 *Ibid.*, pp. 86–90; the quotation is from C. Colton (ed.), *The Works of Henry Clay* (New York, 1904), 7, pp. 649–51; *Speech of Mr. Frelinghuysen . . . April 6, 1830* (Washington, 1830), pp. 10–17, 22, 25–6, 28; F. P. Prucha, *American Indian Policy in the Formative Years* (Cambridge, 1962), p. 243; G. A. Schultz, *An Indian Canaan* (Norman, 1972), pp. 130–2.

7 For the first two quotations see L. Ruchames (ed.), *The Letters of William Lloyd Garrison* (Cambridge, 1975), IV, pp. 120–1; see also W. P. and F. J. Garrison, *William Lloyd Garrison, 1805–79* (New York, 1885–9) 1, pp. 56, 182–3, 232; G. Lerner, *The Grimké Sisters From South Carolina* (New York, 1973) pp. 92, 270–1; Child, *The First Settlers*, pp. 263–4, 277, 281–2; *ibid.*, *Letters of Lydia Maria Child* (Boston, 1883) p. 220, and *Letters From New York* (London, 1843) pp. 280–2; *Frelinghuysen*, pp. 6–9; and for the last quotation, I. McCoy, *Annual Register*, 3 (J. G. Pratt, 1837) p. 69.

8 These men were not, of course, either committed abolitionists or Indian reformers; but they serve to show that the two causes were publicly linked for a variety of reasons, and their stature made even occasional support by them useful to the more engaged humanitarians.

9 R. A. Trennert, Jr., *Alternative to Extinction* (Philadelphia, 1975) pp. 35, 38–9, 49–50, 113, 184–5; I. McCoy, *Annual Register*, 2, pp. 53, 57, 85, 87; *ibid.*, *History of Baptist Missions* (Washington, 1840) pp. 325, 377–8, 381–4, 499 (source of first quotation), 501, 583, and *Address to Philanthropists in the United States, etc.* (1831) pp. 5–8; Child, *Letters*, p. 219; Ruchames, *Letters of Garrison*, (1971), II, pp. 105 (on Florida Indians and Osceola), 106; IV, pp. 125–6 (for further comments); and *ibid.*, p. 137, for the last Garrison quotation; see also II, pp. 217, 439 and IV, p. 100; J. Beeson, *A Plea for the Indians* (New York, 1858) pp. 83, 100 (for the last quotation); J. Gregory and R. Strickland, *Sam Houston With the Cherokees, 1829–33* (Austin, 1967) pp. 9, 31, 101–2; D. Day and H. Ullom, *The Autobiography of Sam Houston* (Norman, 1954) pp. 155–6, 251–2; T. G. Edelstein, *Strange Enthusiasm* (New Haven, 1968) p. 102; and Berkhofer, *White Man's Indian*, pp. 165–6.

10 W. C. Barclay, *Missionary Motivation and Expansion* (New York, 1949,) 1, pp. 234, 237, 244.

11 See especially R. Halliburton, Jr., *Red Over Black* (Westport, 1977), Chap. 7; D. F. Littlefield, *Africans and Seminoles* (Westport, 1977); W. P. A. slave narratives for Oklahoma and elsewhere; A. Abel, *The American Indian as Slaveholder and Secessionist* (Cleveland, 1915).

12 McCoy, *Baptist Missions*, pp. 325, 417–18, 451, 507, 509–12; *ibid.*, *Annual Register*, 1 (Indian Territory, 1835), pp. 5–9, 11–14; 2, pp. 5–7, 9–10, 12–15; 3, pp. 8–11, 13–19; 4 (Washington, 1838) pp. 36–52; T. C. Battey, *The Life and Adventures of a Quaker Among the Indians* (Boston, 1876), p. 13; C. C. Rister, *Baptist Missions Among the American Indians* (Atlanta, 1944), pp. 66–7 (for the quotations), 68, 81, 83–6; W. P. Harrison, *The Gospel Among the African Slaves of the Southern States* (Nashville, 1893), pp. 149–50.

13 C. K. Whipple, *Relation of the American Board of Commissioners for Foreign Missions to Slavery* (Boston, 1861) from whom all quotations about Board missions are taken, except that attributed to Strong, pp. 3–6, 20–2, 25, 27, 38, 41, 43, 46, 49, 55, 88–95, 136–7, 161, 185, 190, 199, 214–15, 235–41; W. G. McLoughlin, 'Red Indians, Black Slavery and White Racism: America's Slaveholding Indians', *American Quarterly*, XXVI (Oct. 1974), 4, pp. 367–85; W. E. Strong, *The Story of the American Board* (Boston, 1910), pp. 52–3, 186–7; A. Abel, *The American Indian as Participant in the Civil War* (Cleveland, 1919), p. 298, for quotation on southern interest in defending slavery in Indian Territory; D. G. Mathews, *Slavery and Methodism* (Princeton, 1965), Chap. III; R. Berkhofer, *Salvation and the Savage* (New York, 1972), pp. 2, 99, 139, 141–2; B. Wyatt-Brown, *Lewis Tappan and the Evangelical War Against Slavery* (Cleveland, 1969), pp. 313–14; R. T. Lewit, 'Indian missions and antislavery sentiment: a conflict of evangelical and humanitarian ideals', *Mississippi Valley Historical Review*, L (June 1963), pp. 39–55.

14 G. Catlin, *Letters and Notes on . . . North American Indians* (1841), 1, p.
    51, on the condition of Indian women; other quotation from A. F.
    Bandelier, *Final Report of Investigation Among the Indians of the South
    Western United States* (Cambridge, 1890), Part 1, p. 41.

15 R. H. Pratt, *Battlefield and Classroom* (New Haven, 1964, ed. R. M.
    Utley), p. 312.

16 Armstrong quoted in *Proceedings of the Fourth Annual Lake Mohonk
    Conference . . . 1886* (Philadelphia, 1887; hereafter LMC plus date), p.
    27. Greater success among the mass of the Indian population might
    have produced a different missionary response to slavery, as there
    would then have been less need to conciliate the Indian slave holders.

17 See Christine Bolt, 'Red, Black and White in nineteenth-century
    America', in A. C. Hepburn (ed.), *Minorities in History* (1978), chap. 8,
    pp. 121, 124–5; D. F. and M. A. Littlefield, 'The Beams Family: free
    blacks in Indian territory', *Journal of Negro History*, 61 (Jan. 1976),
    pp. 16–35.

18 H. B. Whipple, *Lights and Shadows of a Long Episcopate* (New York,
    1899), pp. 361f., 446 and *passim*; R. W. Mardock, *The Reformers and
    the American Indian* (Columbia, 1971), Chap. 1 and *passim*; R. Odell,
    Helen Hunt Jackson (New York, 1939), pp. 155–7, 277; S. D. Smith,
    The Negro in Congress, 1870–1901 (Port Washington, 1966 ed.), p.
    37; R. Cruden, *The Negro in Reconstruction* (Englewood Cliffs, 1969),
    p. 102; E. A. Gilcreast, *Richard Henry Pratt and American Indian
    Policy, 1877–1906* (Ph.D., Yale University, 1967), p. 158 on Mrs.
    Stowe; on Swisshelm, see P. Walker, *Moral Choices* (Baton Rouge,
    1979), pp. 151–3, 176f. Swisshelm's lack of sympathy for Indians may
    simply have been an extension of her lack of sympathy for blacks
    as 'human individuals' rather than slaves – the means of indicting
    slave masters; her chief political enemy in Minnesota, landowner
    and businessman Sylvanus Lowry, was also a Winnebago and Indian
    agent.

19 Priest, *Uncle Sam's Stepchildren*, pp. 58, 174–6; Gilcreast, *Pratt and
    Indian Policy*, p. 158, agrees.

20 J. P. Dunn, *Massacres of the Mountains* (1886), p. 716; also LMC 1886,
    p. 10 – though one must always bear in mind the problems involved in
    judging the significance of reforms through reformers' eyes. White
    opposition to the proposals of the Indian reformers was clearly not of
    comparable intensity to that which the abolitionists had encountered,
    because whites stood to gain economically from the former.

21 See R. G. Walters, *The Antislavery Appeal* (Baltimore, 1976); Mar-
    dock, *Reformers and the Indian* and Priest, *Pratt and Indian Policy*; F.
    P. Prucha (ed.), *Americanizing the American Indians* (Cambridge,
    1973) and Prucha, *American Indian Policy in Crisis* (Norman, 1976);
    and Christine Bolt in A. T. Barbrook and C. A. Bolt, *Power and Protest
    in American Life* (Martin Robertson, forthcoming in 1980), chap. 3.

22 G. W. Manypenny, *Our Indian Wards* (Cincinnati, 1880), pp. xi, xvi; H.
    E. Fritz, *The Movement for Indian Assimilation, 1860–90* (Philadel-
    phia, 1963), pp. 56f; *Annual Meeting and Report of the Women's
    National Indian Association . . . 1883* (subsequently *WNIA* plus date),
    pp. 10–13; *WNIA, 1884*, pp. 8, 54; *WNIA, 1885*, pp. 13, 32; *Sketches*

of Delightful Work (Philadelphia, 1893); *Report of Missions, 1911* (Philadelphia, 1912).

23 See *A Response to Senator Pettigrew*, Indian Rights Association (hereafter IRA) tract 40 (1897).

24 LMC, 1886, pp. 9–10; *ibid.*, 1906, pp. 75–6.

25 G. Campbell, *White and Black* (New York, 1879), p. 15. On the importance of Indian education, through which 'race distinctions give way to national characteristics', despite its cost and controversial nature, see C. C. Painter, *Extravagance, Waste and Failure of Indian Education*, IRA (1892), pp. 18–19, 21–2; F. E. Leupp, *A Summer Tour Among the Indians of the Southwest*, IRA (1897) pp. 24–6; Prucha, *Americanizing*, p. 221.

26 See M. T. Bailey, *Reconstruction in Indian Territory* (Port Washington, 1972), chaps. 2–3; Bolt, 'Red, Black, and White', pp. 121–3; F. P. Prucha, *Documents of United States Indian Policy* (Lincoln, 1975), pp. 192, 194. The various comissions set up to implement the terms of the postwar treaties, as well as contemporary reports from Indian agents and discontented whites and blacks in Indian Territory, reveal conflicting opinions. In general, whites tended to sympathize with the black desire for land, which did not have to be met from white resources; and those with a degree of Indian blood particularly hoped to gain from the distribution. The Indians resented the terms of the treaties but often felt they had dealt fairly with their freedmen, according to those treaties. And blacks, especially among the Choctaw and Chickasaw, frequently felt themselves to be unjustly treated by racially prejudiced Indians, and looked to whites and blacks outside the Territory for aid. See Bolt, *Red and White*.

27 LMC, 1888, pp. 97–9; *Why the Work of the Indian Rights Association Should be Supported*, IRA (1895). There was no great ideological gulf between the major parties over Indian affairs, with each side using them as a means of embarrassing the other, as when anti-administration papers accused the Radical Republicans of seeking to distract the public from the spectacle of their declining power by encouraging Indian warfare: see R. G. Athearn, 'The Fort Bufort "Massacre"', *Mississippi Valley Historical Review*, XLI (1954–5), pp. 677–8.

28 See Mohonk platforms of 1899, 1901–3, 1916; *Fifth Annual Report of the . . . Indian Rights Association . . . 1887* (Philadelphia, 1888; hereafter IRA plus date), pp. 8–13; IRA, 1888, pp. 32–8; and proceedings of the 1904 Mohonk conference.

29 S. Clark, 'Ponca Publicity', *Mississippi Valley Historical Review*, 29, 1942–3, p. 504; L. E. Burgess, *The Lake Mohonk Conferences on the Indian, 1883–1916* (Ph.D., Claremont Graduate School, 1972), *passim* but especially p. 198; R. Slotkin, *Regeneration Through Violence* (Middletown, 1973), pp. 441–4, has noted the use of 'captivity mythology' by the abolitionists before the Civil War, and in the postwar period the stoical victim continued to play a useful part in reformer propaganda.

30 *Report of Hon. Theodore Roosevelt, etc.*, IRA (1893), p. 14; Burgess, *Lake Mohonk*, pp. 422–7; WNIA, 1884, p. 8; 1885, pp. 39, 42; A. Quinton, *Indians and Their Helpers* (WNIA pamphlet); IRA, 1885, p.

10; 1887, pp. 65–7; *Constitution and By-Laws of the Indian Rights Association* (Philadelphia, 1883); Prucha, *Americanizing*, pp. 36, 46. Working class (like other) whites might, of course, hope to benefit from the sale of 'surplus' Indian land released by allotment. In their rejection of 'gradualism' in favour of 'immediatism', the friends of the Indian differed from many freedmen's aid workers in the 1870s and 1880s, though they were not otherwise immune from the impact of Darwinist ideas, as witness their belief, also prompted by hostile white reactions to giving citizenship to blacks immediately after the Civil War, that Indian education was a crucial preparation for their possession of civil rights.

12

ABOLITIONISM AND THE LABOR MOVEMENT IN ANTEBELLUM AMERICA

by Eric Foner

Among the more ironic conjunctures of antebellum American history is the fact that the expansion of capitalist labor relations evoked severe criticism from two very different quarters: the pro-slavery ideologues of the South and the labor movement of the North. Standing outside the emerging capitalist economy of the free states (although also providing the raw material essential for its early development), the South gave birth to a group of thinkers who developed a striking critique of northern labor relations. The liberty of the northern wage earner, according to George Fitzhugh, John C. Calhoun and the others, amounted to little more than the freedom to sell his labor for a fraction of its true value, or to starve. In contrast to the southern slave, who was ostensibly provided for in sickness and old age and regardless of the vicissitudes of prices and production, the free laborer was the slave of the marketplace, and his condition exceeded in degradation and cruelty that of the chattel slave. The prevailing ethos of northern society – free competition – inevitably resulted in poverty for the many and riches for the few.

The somewhat bizarre spectacle of defenders of slavery justifying the peculiar institution in language redolent of a Marxian class struggle has long fascinated historians, as has the response of anti-slavery spokesmen to the southern charges.[1] Less attention has been paid to the role of a third participant in the complex debate over the relative status of labor in North and South: the northern labor movement. It is well known that relations between abolitionists and the radical labor leaders of the North were by no means cordial during the 1830s and 1840s. But the reasons remain elusive. Nonetheless, the not-too-close encounter between abolitionism and the labor movement not only raises important questions about the constituencies and ideological assumptions underpinning each movement, but also illuminates in a new way that historical perennial, the relationship between capitalism and slavery.

The emergence of the nation's first labor movement in the late 1820s and 1830s was, of course, a response to fundamental changes taking place in the work patterns and authority relationships within traditional artisan production. Labor historians have made the elements of this transformation familiar: the emergence of the factory system, the dilution of craft skill, the imposition of a new labor discipline in traditional craft production, the growing gap between masters and journeymen, and the increasing stratification of the social order, especially in the large eastern cities. Working men responded to these developments within the context of an ideology dating back to the Paineite republicanism of the American Revolution. The central ingredients in this ideology were a passionate attachment to equality (defined not as a levelling of all distinctions, but as the absence of large inequalities of wealth and influence), belief that independence – the ability to resist personal or economic coercion – was an essential attribute of the republican citizenry, and a commitment to the labor theory of value, along with its corollary, that labor should receive the full value of its product. The economic changes of the early nineteenth century posed a direct challenge to these traditional ideals. 'You are the real producers of all the wealth of the community', declared New York's *Workingman's Advocate*, 'Without your labors no class could live. How is it then you are so poor while those who labor not are rich?'[2]

The search for an answer to this question led labor leaders to a wide variety of programs, ranging from Thomas Skidmore's attack on the inheritance of property, to the more typical denunciation of banks, merchants, and 'non-producers' in general, for robbing labor of a portion of its product. Whatever the specific programs advocated, however, labor spokesmen agreed that working men were faced with a loss of their status both within the crafts and in the republican polity. Conditions of labor both in the new factories of New England and in the artisan workshops of New York and Philadelphia symbolized the decline of the 'dignity of labor'. The phrase which entered the language of politics in the 1830s to describe the plight and grievances of the labor movement was 'wage slavery'. A comparison between the status of the northern worker and the southern slave – usually to the detriment of the former – became a standard component of labor rhetoric in these years. In language remarkably similar to the southern critique of northern labor conditions, Seth Luther declared that northern mill workers labored longer each day than southern slaves, and in worse conditions. A New Hampshire labor newspaper asked, 'A great cry is raised in the northern states against southern slavery. The sin of slavery may be abominable there, but is it not equally so here? If they have black slaves, have we not white ones? Or how much better is the condition of some of our laborers here at the North, than the slaves of the South?' The famous Coffin handbill distributed in New York City after striking journeyman tailors were convicted of conspiracy declared, 'The Freemen of the North are now on a level with the slaves of the South'. And the militant female textile workers of Lowell, Massachusetts, referred to themselves during one strike as the 'white slaves' of New England, and their newspaper, the *Voice of Industry*, claimed the women operatives were 'in fact nothing more nor less than slaves in every sense of the world'.[3]

There is no point in further multiplying quotations to demonstrate that the idea of 'wage slavery' played a central role in the rhetoric of the labor movement. Sometimes, 'wage slavery' was used more or less as an equivalent for long working hours or for poverty. But the meaning of the metaphor was far broader than this. The phrase evoked the fears so prevalent in the labor movement of the 1830s and 1840s of the erosion of respect for labor, the loss of independence by the craftsman, and the emergence of 'European' social conditions and class stratification in republican America. Most importantly, working for wages itself was often perceived as a form of 'slavery', an affront to the traditional artisanal ideal of economic and personal independence. As Orestes Brownson explained in his remarkable and influential essay, 'The Laboring Classes', it was not simply low wages, but the wage system itself, which lay at the root of labor's problems. The wage system, said Brownson, enabled employers to 'retain all the advantages of the slave system without the expense, trouble, and odium of being slaveholders. . . . There must be no class of our fellow men doomed to toil through life as mere workmen at wages'. The emergence of a permanent wage-earning class challenged the traditional definition of the social order of republican America.[4]

What was the attitude of those who raised the cry of 'wage slavery' towards actual slavery in the South? It has often been argued that northern workingmen were indifferent or hostile to the anti-slavery crusade, or were even pro-slavery. White laborers, it is argued, feared emancipation would unleash a flood of freedmen to compete for northern jobs and further degrade the dignity of labor.[5] Yet it is important to distinguish the labor movement's response to abolitionism, and, indeed, to black competition, from its attitude to slavery. After all, inherent in the notion of wage slavery, in the comparision of the status of the northern laborer with the southern slave, was a critique of the peculiar institution as an extreme form of oppression (unless one agreed with Fitzhugh that northern labor should be enslaved for its own benefit, a position not likely to find many adherents in the labor movement). The entire ideology of the labor movement was implicitly hostile to slavery: slavery contradicted the central ideas and values of artisan radicalism – liberty, democracy, equality, and independence. The ideological fathers of the movement, Thomas Paine and Robert Owen, were both strongly anti-slavery.

Recent research, moreover, moving away from an earlier definition of abolitionists as representatives of a declining traditional elite, has underscored the central role played by artisans in the urban abolitionist constituency (although not the leadership of the movement). In Lynn, according to Alan Dawley, shoemakers equated slaveowners with the city's factory magnates as 'a set of lordly tyrants'. In Utica and Cincinnati, writes Leonard Richards, artisans were represented far more heavily among the abolitionist constituency than in the mobs which broke up abolitionist meetings. And the careful analysis of New York city anti-slavery petitions between 1829 and 1837 by John Jentz reveals that in most cases, artisans were the largest occupational group among the signers. In New York, the only newspaper publicly to defend Nat Turner's rebellion was not an anti-slavery journal, but the *Daily Sentinel*, edited for the Workingman's Party by the immigrant English radical George Henry Evans. The radical artisans who met each year in New York to celebrate Tom Paine's birthday often included a toast to the liberators of Haiti in their celebrations, and Evans' *Workingman's Advocate* went so far as to claim, rather implausibly, that 'the Government of Haiti approaches nearer to pure Republicanism than any other now in use or on record'. Evans did acknowledge in 1831 that the labor movement sometimes neglected the cause of the slave because of its preoccupation with the grievances of northern workers. But he added that he remained committed to the total eradication of slavery in the South.[6]

1831, of course, was also the year in which William Lloyd Garrison commenced publication of *The Liberator*, the point from which historians usually date the emergence of a new, militant, immediatist abolitionist crusade. As is well known, Garrison addressed the condition of northern labor, and the activities of the labor movement, in his very first issue:

> An attempt has been made – it is still making – we regret to say, with considerable success – to inflame the minds of our working classes against the more opulent, and to persuade men that they are contemned and oppressed by a wealthy aristocracy. . . . It is in the highest degree criminal . . . to exasperate our mechanics to deeds of violence, or to array them under a party banner, for it is not true that, at any time, they have been the objects of reproach. Labour is not dishonourable. The industrious artisan, in a government like ours, will always be held in better estimation than the wealthy idler. . . . We are the friends of reform; but this is not reform, which in curing one evil, threatens to inflict a thousand others.[7]

Of course, Garrison's point about the high regard in which labor was held was precisely what the labor movement contended was no longer true. Four weeks after the editorial appeared, Garrison published a response by the labor reformer William West, arguing that there was, in fact, a 'very intimate connexion' between abolition and the labor movement, since each was striving to secure 'the fruits of their toil' for a class of working men. To which Garrison responded with another denunciation, phrased in the extreme language so characteristic of all his writing:

> In a republican government, . . . where hereditary distinctions are obsolete . . . where the avenues of wealth, distinction and supremacy are open to all; [society] must, in the nature of things, be full of inequalities. But these can exist without an assumption of rights – without even a semblance of oppression. There is a prevalent opinion, that wealth and aristocracy are indissolubly allied; and the poor and vulgar are taught to consider the opulent as their natural enemies. Those who inculcate this pernicious doctrine are the worst enemies of the people, and, in grain, the real nobility. . . . It is a miserable characteristic of human nature to look with an envious eye upon those who are more fortunate in their pursuits, or more exalted in their station.[8]

Thus, from the very outset, a failure of communication marked relations between the two movements. Fifteen years later, the utopian socialist Albert Brisbane called on abolitionists to 'include in their movement, a reform of the present wretched organization of labour, called the wage system. It would add to their power by interesting the producing classes . . . and would prepare a better state for the slaves when emancipated, than the servitude to capital, to which they now seemed destined.'[9] The proposed alliance never did take place, and Garrison's early editorials suggest some of the reasons. It is not precisely that the abolitionists were complacently 'middle-class' in outlook, a characterization found quite frequently in the recent historical literature. Abolitionists – both Garrisonians and their opponents within the movement – threw themselves with enthusiasm into all sorts of other movements to reform American society, from the abolition of capital punishment to women's rights, from temperance to peace. They often criticized the spirit of competition, individualism, and greed so visible in northern life, as the antithesis of Christian brotherhood and love.[10] It will not do to defang the abolitionist crusade: it was indeed a radical impulse, challenging fundamental aspects of American life (and none so deeply embedded as racism). But in its view of economic relations it did speak the language of northern society. Perhaps this is why the movement, so feared at the outset, eventually could become respectable.

In contrast to the labor movement, most abolitionists – as Garrison's early editorials made clear – accepted social inequality as a natural reflection of individual differences in talent, ambition, and diligence, and perceived the interests of capital and labor as existing in harmony rather than conflict. As a result, they were unable to understand, much less sympathize with, the aims of the labor movement or the concept of 'wage slavery'. Their attitude toward labor was graphically revealed in a pamphlet published by the New York abolitionist, William Jay, in the mid-1830s. In the course of a discussion of the benefits of immediate emancipation, Jay sought to answer the perennial question, what would happen to the slave when free:

> He is free, and his own master, and can ask for no more. Yet he is, in fact, for a time, absolutely dependent on his late owner. He can look to no other person for food to eat, clothes to put on, or house to shelter him. . . . [He is required to work], but labor is no longer the badge of his servitude and the consummation of his misery, for it is *voluntary*. For the first time in his life, he is a party to a contract. . . . In the course of time, the value of negro labor, like all other vendible commodities, will be regulated by the supply and demand.[11]

What is particularly noteworthy in this extraordinary argument is, first, Jay's ready acceptance of the condition which caused so much complaint among the labor movement – the treatment of human labor as a 'vendible commodity', and secondly, the rather loose use of the word 'voluntary' to describe the labor of an individual who owns nothing and is 'absolutely dependent' on his employer. To the labor movement, Jay's description of emancipation would qualify as a classic instance of wage slavery; to Jay, it was an economic definition of freedom.

The labor movement, articulating an ideal stretching back to the republican tradition of the American Revolution, equated freedom with ownership of productive property. To the abolitionists, expressing a newer, liberal definition, freedom meant self-ownership – that is, simply not being a slave. It is one of the more tragic ironies of this complex debate that, in the process of attempting to liberate the slave, the abolitionists did so much to promote a new and severely truncated definition of freedom for both blacks and whites. As many historians have observed, the abolitionist conception of both slavery and freedom was profoundly individualistic. Abolitionists understood slavery not as a class relationship, but as a system of arbitrary and illegitimate power exercised by one individual over another. The slaves and, to some extent, northern workers, were not downtrodden classes but suffering individuals, and it was this liberal, individualist definition of personal freedom which not only cut abolitionists off from the labor movement, but, as Gilbert Osofsky argued, prevented them from making a meaningful response to the economic condition of the Irish-Americans, despite a principled effort to overcome nativism and reach out for Irish-American support in the 1840s.[12]

The intense individualism of the abolitionists, historians are agreed, derived from the great revivals of the Second Great Awakening, which identified moral progress with each individual's capacity to act as an instrument of God, and opened the possibility of conversion for all as the prelude to eliminating sin from society and paving the way for the Second Coming. Religious benevolence was, it seems clear, the primary root of antebellum reform.[13] But it was not the only root, and historians' single-minded emphasis on revivalist Protestantism as the origin of immediate abolitionism has tended to obscure the equally sincere anti-slavery convictions of the radical artisans, so many of whom were influenced by Enlightenment deism. Indeed, the tensions between the labor movement and evangelical abolitionism were part of a larger confrontation during the 1830s between evangelicism and the powerful opposition it generated within northern society. As Jentz has shown, the New York Workingmen's leaders were intensely hostile to the evangelical campaign, viewing it as an attempt to unite church and state in a campaign for special privileges incompatible with the principles of republicanism. The campaign against the Sunday mails, led by Lewis and Arthur Tappan shortly before their involvement in abolitionism, aroused considerable opposition among free-thinking artisans and these same radical artisans were estranged from the anti-slavery movement because of the presence of evangelicals like the Tappans in leadership positions. Nonetheless, when New York's anti-abolitionist riot occurred in 1834, George Henry Evans defended the right of the Tappan brothers to freedom of speech. Later, he again praised abolition as a 'just and good cause', while not resisting the opportunity to add, 'many of the Abolitionists are actuated by a species of fanaticism, and are desirous of freeing the slaves, more for the purpose of adding them to a religious sect, than for a love of liberty and justice'.[14]

In the eyes of Evans and the radical workingmen for whom he spoke, moveover, Tappan the intolerant Sabbatarian was not unrelated to Tappan the wealthy merchant who was one of the very men helping to transform labor relations at the expense of the laborer. Certainly, the Tappan brothers were not averse to using their economic power to coerce artisans into supporting their various causes. In January 1830, a tailor complained that Lewis Tappan approached him with a petition against the Sunday mails and, when refused, threatened that the tailor would get no more of the trade of his brother Arthur's mercantile firm. To the tailor, Tappan was a 'redoubtable champion of Calvinism, illiberalism, etc'. To the Tappans, the 'infidelity' of men like Robert Owen and George Henry Evans was as offensive as their economic views. Indeed, before leaders of the benevolent empire like the Tappans took control of New York City's abolition movement, anti-slavery had a reputation for being 'largely composed of irreligious men, some of infidel sentiments'.[15] The great revival of the 1830s changed that, identifying abolitionism with evangelicism and, one presumes, alienating anti-slavery men like Evans from organized abolitionism. But, given the large number of artisans who signed abolitionist petitions, we should not let the evangelicism of the abolitionist leaders obscure that portion of the anti-slavery constituency whose roots lay in the rationalism of the Enlightenment and in republican notions of equality and liberty, rather than in Christian benevolence.

For most of the 1830s and 1840s, relations between the abolition and labor movements remained strained. Open attacks on labor organizations, such as that in the first issue of *The Liberator*, were not, however, typical of abolitionist liberature. By the end of the 1830s, abolitionists were making an attempt to appeal to workingmen for support. Yet, whereas labor leaders tended to see abolition as a diversion from the grievances of northern labor and slavery as simply one example of more pervasive problems in American life, abolitionists considered the labor issue as artificial or secondary.

Whatever problems northern labor might face, whatever legitimate grievances it might articulate, were all rooted in the peculiar institution. Slavery, said abolitionist literature, made all labor disreputable and was the cause of the degradation of labor in the North. 'American slavery', as one abolitionist resolution put it, 'is an evil of such gigantic magnitude, that it must be uprooted and overthrown, before the elevation sought by the laboring classes can be effected'. Both abolitionists and labor leaders spoke of the alliance between the Lords of the Loom and Lords of the Lash – the textile manufacturers of New England and slave-owners of the South – but each drew from it a different conclusion. To the labor movement, factory owner and slave-owner were both non-producers who fattened on the fruits of the labor of others; to the abolitionists, what was objectionable in the factory owners was precisely their pro-slavery political stance, not their treatment of their employees.[16]

During the 1840s, a handful of abolitionist spokesmen did attempt to forge an alliance with the labor leaders, moving toward a critique of labor relations in the North. John A. Collins became convinced on an abolitionist trip to England that the condition of the working classes deserved attention from opponents of slavery. Slavery, he concluded, was but a symptom of a deeper problem. 'The cause of all causes', the deep underlying root of poverty, war, intemperance, and slavery was private property, 'the admitted right of individual ownership in the soil and its products'. In 1843, Collins joined the communistic society at Skeneateles in western New York State and the next year began publishing *The Communist*. Still later, this peripatetic reformer returned to the Whig party, convinced that only governmental power could effect social reform. His mercurial career did not exactly generate enthusiasm among his erstwhile abolitionist colleagues. Garrison condemned the Owenite environmentalism which lay behind Collins' utopian experiment, interpreting it to mean that men were not individually responsible for their sins. And Frederick Douglass accused Collins, not without plausibility, of 'imposing an additional burden of unpopularity on our cause' when Collins attempted to introduce socialist ideas at abolitionist meetings.[17]

Probably the most prominent abolitionist who attempted to rethink the relation between northern and southern labor conditions was Nathaniel P. Rogers, editor of the *Herald of Freedom*, published in Concord, New Hampshire. (I leave aside here John Brown who was, in this as in everything else, *sui generis* among abolitionists. Brown's career of business failures in the 1830s and

1840s, usually taken by historians as evidence of maladjustment, may have made him rather more skeptical of the virtues of the northern economic order than other abolitionists. Interestingly, the Provisional Constitution Brown drafted to apply to territory he planned to 'liberate' in the South included a provision that all property captured from the enemy or produced by the labor of his associates would be held 'as the property of the whole' and used 'for the common benefit'.[18]) Rogers proposed a grand alliance of the producing classes North and South, free and slave, against all exploiters of labor. Living amidst the burgeoning factory system of New Hampshire, Rogers concluded that the abolitionist movement had not only been blind to social conditions in the North, but had directed its appeals to the wrong constituency. 'We have got to look to the working people of the North, to sustain and carry on the Anti-Slavery Movement', he announced in 1843. 'The people who work and are disrespected here, and who disrespect labor themselves, and disrespect themselves because they labor – have got to abolish slavery. And in order to do this, they must be emancipated themselves first'. Rogers soon took to organizing anti-slavery meetings at which the condition of northern workingmen received more attention than the plight of the slave. 'Very little time was wasted in talk about floggings and starvings, etc.', he said of one such meeting, 'tyranny here at the North; northern servitude and lack of liberty were our main topics. The working people were admonished of their own bondage and degradation'. It is easy to understand why veteran abolitionists might find such meetings disquieting. At one New Hampshire gathering, the *Herald of Freedom* was denounced as an 'infidel paper' and members of 'the Priesthood', as Rogers called the local clergy, attempted to break up the meeting.

Rogers was unique among abolitionist leaders in his complete rejection of the ethos of technological progress and his acceptance of the idea of conflict between capital and labor. Many abolitionists condemned an excessive spirit of greed in northern society, but most were fascinated by technological change, viewing it, indeed, as yet another evidence of the superiority of the northern social system to that of the slave South. Rogers, however, could write: 'The money-built Railroad, like all other labor-saving machinery, makes the rich, richer, and the poor, poorer. . . . Monopoly and capital seize on the labor-saving machine, and wield it to the poor man's destruction'. Northern labor, 'the slave of Capital', was bought and sold 'at auction' as in the South, and the abolitionist movement,

Rogers insisted, should demand 'Liberty for the New Hampshire day-labourers' as well as for the southern bondsman.[19]

Rogers' position was, to say the least, atypical of the abolition leadership. This was made abundantly clear in a lengthy series of letters and editorials which appeared in *The Liberator* in 1846 and 1847. The issue of 4 September 1846 contained a letter Wendell Phillips had addressed to George Henry Evans, whose quest for a solution to the problems of poverty and inequality had come to focus on land policy. Along with the emigrant Irish radical Thomas Devyr, Horace Greeley, and a few others, Evans now identified land monopoly as the root cause of poverty and demanded the free distribution of homesteads to settlers on the public lands, and a limitation on the amount of land any individual could own. Land monopoly, which caused low wages and poverty in the eastern cities, was the underlying reason for the 'wages slavery' which, Evans still believed, was 'even more destructive of the life, health and happiness than chattel slavery as it exists in our Southern States'. Moreover, insisted the land reformers in a striking anticipation of the debates of the Reconstruction years, the emancipated slave would simply 'be subject to the slavery of wages, to be ground down by the competition in the labor market' – a view of the post-emancipation situation quite different from that of William Jay quoted above. Phillips, while admitting the validity of some of Evans' criticisms of the concentration of land ownership, was forced to take exception to the equation of 'wages slavery' with slavery in the South, proposing once again the abolitionist definition of freedom as self-ownership. Whereupon Evans responded, 'the men robbed of their land *are* robbed of themselves most effectually'.[20]

This exchange touched off a series of editorials and letters lasting well into the following year. William West rushed to Evans' defense, insisting land reformers did not ignore the plight of the slave. 'They do not hate chattel slavery less, but they hate wages slavery more. Their rallying cry is, "Down with all slavery, both chattel and wages"'. Some months later, Garrison accused land reformers of 'magnifying mole-hills into mountains, and reducing mountains to the size of mole-hills' in comparing labor conditions in the North with slavery. 'To say that it is worse for a man to be free, than to be a slave, worse to work for whom he pleases, when he pleases, and where he pleases', was simply ridiculous, Garrison insisted. Moreover, it was 'an abuse of language to talk of the slavery of wages . . . The evil in society is not that labor receives wages, but that the wages given are not generally in proportion to the value of the labor performed. We cannot see that it is wrong to give or receive wages'. Nothing could have made more clear the gap which separated the social outlook of the abolitionists from that of the labor movement. Garrison, defending capitalist labor relations, viewed the ability to contract for wages as a mark of liberty, and he was wholly unable to appreciate the coercions implicit in the market-place for labor and the wage relation itself. As the indefatigable William West responded, it seemed 'surpassing strange' that Garrison had 'lived forty years' and still could believe that the northern laborer possessed complete freedom to work when and for whom he desired.[21]

The debate continued in the pages of The Liberator until October, 1847, when Edmund Quincy closed it with yet another abolitionist defence of northern labor relations. But, apart from a slight diversion in which one correspondent explained that the rule of Christ on earth required a shift to communal ownership of property, the most revealing contribution came from the pen of Wendell Phillips. Once again denying the applicability of the concept of 'wage slavery' to northern conditions, Phillips perceptively observed that 'many of the errors on this point seem to me to proceed from looking at American questions through European spectacles, and transplanting the eloquent complaints against capital and monopoly, which are well-grounded and well-applied there, to a state of society here, where they have little meaning or application'. Phillips was certainly correct in asserting that many labor leaders viewed American conditions 'through European spectacles'. The ferocious attack on the evangelical movement in the 1830s, for example, was seemingly more relevant to the situation in the Old World, where the established churches were bulwarks of the status quo, than the very different religious environment of the United States. But Phillips perhaps failed to appreciate fully the central importance of fear of 'Europeanization' as an ideological inspiration of the labor movement. Later in his career, of course, Phillips would himself emerge as an eloquent defender of the rights of labor. But in 1847, his prescription for the grievances of the workingman left little room for social reform or institutional change: 'to economy, self-denial, temperance, education and moral and religious character, the laboring class, and every other class in this country, must owe its elevation and improvement'.[22]

Perhaps the differences in perception which characterized relations between abolitionists and labor leaders down to the late 1840s are symbolized by the fact that when The Liberator in 1847 reprinted an article identifying the condition of northern workers as 'white slavery', it did so in its column, 'Refuge of Oppression' – a portion of the newspaper reserved for items from the pro-slavery press.[23] Garrison could not free himself from the conviction that, by diverting attention from slavery in the South, the labor movement was, in effect, playing into the hands of the defenders of slavery. Yet at this very moment, changes were taking place within both movements which would transform the relations between labor leaders and anti-slavery. One set of changes involved the emergence of opposition to the expansion of slavery as the central political question of the late 1840s, and the vehicle by which anti-slavery became, for the first time, a truly mass movement in the North. Increasingly, the abolitionists were pushed to the side, while free-soilism took the center of the stage as the most available mode of anti-slavery and anti-southern protest. Evangelical abolitionism, it may be suggested, had done its main work in the 1830s. It had succeeded in shattering the conspiracy of silence surrounding the question of slavery. But because it also generated a powerful opposition within northern society – not only from pro-slavery forces, but from those who could not accept the impulse toward 'moral stewardship' which was so integral a part of benevolent reform – evangelicism could not make of abolition a majority sentiment. The more secular, rational, and moderate free-soil position could succeed in a way abolitionism could not.

At the same time, the labor movement, devastated by the depression of 1837–42, was turning toward more individualist and self-help-oriented solutions to the problems of northern workingmen.[24] Evans' own emphasis on the land question, which linked social justice so closely to individual ownership of private property, while seemingly abandoning the co-operative thrust of the labor movement of the 1830s, reflected the change. Evans, as we have seen, still insisted that true freedom required economic independence, but he appeared to be abandoning his critique of the wage system itself. Land reform, not a change in the system of production and labor relations, would solve the problem of urban poverty and offer every workingman the opportunity to achieve economic independence, in the form of a homestead.[25]

Free soilism was not only the means by which anti-slavery rose to political dominance in the 1850s, but also the meeting ground for the two strands of anti-slavery thought which had remained estranged in the 1830s and 1840s. The ideological debate between labor and abolition was solved, in a sense, by the early Republican party, for whom the difference between the condition of labor North and South became a potent political rallying cry. The Republican ideology has been analyzed in detail elsewhere;[26] here I want only to suggest that while the Republicans absorbed much of the moral fervor of the abolitionists – while at the same time making that fervor politically respectable and abandoning the abolitionist demand for equal rights for free blacks – their conception of labor and their definition of freedom had much in common with the themes articulated by the labor movement. In the hands of Abraham Lincoln, the workingman's right to the fruits of his own labor became a devastating critique of the peculiar institution. The Republicans accepted the labor leaders' definition of freedom as resting on economic independence rather than, as the abolitionists had insisted, on self-ownership. To Lincoln, the man who worked for wages all his life was indeed almost as unfree as the southern slave. The anti-slavery of a man like Lincoln (who was personally something of a deist) seemed to connect more directly with the artisan anti-slavery tradition than with evangelical abolition. But like the abolitionists, Lincoln and the Republicans located the threat to the independence of the northern working man outside northern society. It was not the wage system but the expansion of slavery, which threatened to destroy the independence of the northern worker, his opportunity to escape from the wage-earning class and own a small farm or shop. For if slavery were allowed to expand into the western territories, the safety-valve of free land for the northern worker and farmer would be eliminated, and northern social conditions would soon come to resemble those of Europe. The Republicans therefore identified themselves with the aspirations of northern labor in a way abolitionists never did, but at the same time, helped turn those aspirations into a critique of the South, not an attack on the northern social order.[27]

It has recently been argued, in quite brilliant fashion, that the abolitionist movement in England helped to crystallize middle-class values and identify them with the interests of society at large. By isolating slavery as an unacceptable form of labor exploitation, abolition implicitly (though usually unintentionally) diverted attention from the exploitation of labour taking place within the emergent factory system. 'The anti-slavery movement,' in other words, 'reflected the needs and values of the emerging capitalist order'.[28]

Professor David B. Davis, who is, of course, responsible for this interpretation, does note, almost in passing, that in the 1790s anti-slavery maintained strong links to the radical artisan societies, who were anything but defenders of 'the emerging capitalist order'. Yet he gives the impression, perhaps inadvertently, that labor anti-slavery either died out, or was subsumed within an evangelical abolitionism which represented the hegemony of middle-class values in nineteenth-century England. A somewhat similar point has recently been made by Alan Dawley regarding the United States. In his study of the transformation of work in Lynn, Massachusetts, Dawley argues that the crusade against slavery diverted attention from the evils of the factory system, stunted the growth of ideas critical of the regime of the factory owners, and, in general, crowded labor radicalism 'off the center stage' of political debate. Had it not been for the dominance of the slavery issue in the 1850s and 1860s, Dawley suggests – rather implausibly, I might add – an independent labor party might have emerged in the North. As it was, the Lynn shoemakers joined hands with their employers in a crusade against the South, instead of directing their assault against targets at home. 'It is difficult to avoid the conclusion that an entire generation was side-tracked in the 1860s because of the Civil War'.[29]

Did the crusade against slavery foreclose the possibility of radical criticism within northern society? Toward the end of the nineteenth century, the great reformer Edward Bellamy made a similar point about Horace Greeley. Greeley, who had been attracted to communitarianism in the 1840s and had authored stinging condemnations of nothern labor conditions, by the next decade, as spokesman for the Republican party, was glorifying northern labor relations in contrast to those of the South. 'Horace Greeley,' wrote Bellamy, 'would very possibly have devoted himself to some kind of socialistic agitation had not the slavery agitation come on'. Bellamy considered Greeley's change of heart inevitable and necessary: 'slavery had to be done away with' before social reform could commence in the North. But others were not so certain. Even during the 1830s and 1840s some labor leaders had accused the abolitionists of being the stalking horses for northern capitalists, seeking to divert attention from the labor issue in the North. One anti-abolitionist pamphlet charged that abolitionists themselves were employers who 'bask in the sunshine of wealth obtained by pilfering the mechanic's labor'. More typical was the perception of an alliance of abolitionists and capitalists, expressed, for instance, in a poem originally published in England and reprinted in an American labor journal, describing the death of a factory girl from starvation:

That night a chariot passed her
While on the ground she lay,
The daughters of her master
An evening visit pay.
Their tender hearts are sighing
As Negroes' woes are told
While the white slave was dying,
Who earned her father's gold.[30]

Unfortunately, this is not only bad poetry, but bad history. The Lords of the Loom were not interested in hearing about 'Negroes' woes'. Far from being in some kind of tacit alliance with abolitionists, they were among the most pro-slavery and anti-abolitionist groups in the North. This fact, it seems to me, casts a certain doubt on the Davis thesis – at least if one wanted to apply it to America – and the arguments of Dawley. Or, perhaps, it simply points up again the ambiguity of the abolitionist heritage. In the hands of a Garrison, anti-slavery did, indeed, promote the acceptance of the free labor market and the capitalist order of the North. So too did the glorification of the northern social order by the Republicans in the 1850s. But that fact should not lead us to forget the other anti-slavery tradition, that of the early labor movement. Eclipsed by the rise of evangelical reform, sidetracked, perhaps, by the free-labor ethos of the Republican party, the labor-oriented critique which linked slavery to labor conditions in the North rose like a pheonix from the ashes of the Civil War, to inspire the great crusades of the National Labor Union, the Knights of Labor, and even the Irish-American Land League.[31] If anti-slavery promoted the hegemony of middle-class values, it also provided a language of politics, a training in organization, for critics of the emerging order. The anti-slavery crusade was a central terminus, from which tracks ran leading to every significant attempt to reform American society after the Civil War. And the notion of 'wage slavery', and the traditional republican definition of freedom it embodied, lived on to help frame the social conflicts of late nineteenth-century America.[32]

Notes

1 See Harvey Wish, *George Fitzhugh, Propagandist of the Old South* (Baton Rouge, 1943); Richard Hofstadter, *The American Political Tradition* (New York, 1948), chap. 4; Eugene D. Genovese, *The World The Slaveholders Made* (New York, 1969), pt. 2.

2 *Workingman's Advocate* (New York City), 13 March 1830. On artisan radicalism, see Eric Foner, *Tom Paine and Revolutionary America* (New York, 1976).

3 Seth Luther, *Address to the Workingmen of New England* (Boston, 1832), p. 25; Philip S. Foner, *History of the Labor Movement in the United States* (New York, 1947), I, p. 272; John R. Commons, *et al.* (eds.), *A Documentary History of American Industrial Society* (Washington, 1910–11), V, p. 317; Bernard Mandel, *Labor: Free and Slave* (New York, 1955), p. 77; Thomas Dublin, 'Women, work and protest in the early Lowell Mills', *Labor History*, XVI (Winter 1975), pp. 109–10; Lise Vogel, 'Their own work: two documents from the nineteenth-century labor movement', *Signs*, I (Spring, 1976), pp. 794–800.

4 Walter Hugins, (ed.) *The Reform Impulse* (New York, 1972), pp. 99–101.

5 Leon Litwack, *North of Slavery* (Chicago, 1961), p. 160; Joseph G. Rayback, 'The American workingman and the anti-slavery crusade', *Journal of Economic History*, III (1943), pp. 152–63; Lorman Ratner, *Powder Keg* (New York, 1968), pp. 62–7.

6 Alan Dawley, *Class and Community: The Industrial Revolution in Lynn* (Cambridge, Mass., 1976), p. 65; Leonard Richards, *Gentlemen of Property and Standing* (New York, 1970), pp. 140–1; John B. Jentz, 'Artisans, evangelicals, and the city: a social history of the labor and abolitionist movements in Jacksonian New York' (unpublished Ph.D. dissertation, Graduate Centre, City University of New York, 1977), pp. 54–6, 125–35; New York *Daily Sentinel*, 17 September 1831; *Workingman's Advocate*, 17 October 1835; 1 October 1831.

7 *The Liberator*, 1 January 1831.

8 *The Liberator*, 29 January 1831.

9 *The Liberator*, 5 September 1846.

10 Ronald G. Walters, *The Antislavery Appeal* (Baltimore, 1976), 121.

11 Hugins, *The Reform Impulse*, p. 168. See also the essay by Jonathan A. Glickstein, '"Poverty is Not Slavery": American Abolitionists and the Competitive Labor Market', Lewis Perry and Michael Fellman (eds.), *Antislavery Reconsidered* (1978), pp. 195–218. The italics in the Jay quotation are in the original.

12 George Fredrickson, *The Black Image in the White Mind* (New York, 1971), pp. 32–4; Aileen Kraditor, *Means and Ends in American Abolitionism* (New York, 1969), p. 244; Gilbert Osofsky, 'Abolitionists, Irish immigrants, and the dilemmas of romantic nationalism', *American Historical Review*, LXXX (October, 1975), pp. 908–10.

13 See Gilbert Barnes, *The Anti-Slavery Impulse* (New York, 1933); Anne C. Loveland, 'Evangelicism and immediate emancipation in American anti-slavery thought', *Journal of Southern History*, XXXII (1966).

14 Jentz, 'Artisans, evangelicals, and the City', pp. 97, 192–3; *Workingman's Advocate*, 19 September, 21 November 1835.

15 *Workingman's Advocate*, 30 January 1830; Lewis Tappan, *Life of Arthur Tappan* (New York, 1870), p. 329; Bertram Wyatt-Brown, *Lewis Tappan and the Evangelical War Against Slavery* (Cleveland, 1969), pp. 46–7.

16 Williston H. Lofton, 'Abolition and labor', *Journal of Negro History*, XXXIII (July 1948), pp. 249–83; Mandel, *Labor: Free and Slave*, p. 93.

17 John L. Thomas, 'Antislavery and Utopia', in *The Antislavery Vanguard*, ed. Martin B. Duberman (Princeton, 1965), pp. 255–6; *The Liberator*, 28 August 1846; *Life and Times of Frederick Douglass* (New York, 1962), p. 228.

18 Stephen Oates, *To Purge This Land With Blood: A Biography of John Brown* (New York, 1970), pp. 245–6.

19 Mandel, *Labor: Free and Slave*, p. 77; *Herald of Freedom* (Concord), 2 June, 6 October 1846; 11 April, 2 May 1845.

20 *The Liberator*, 4 September 1846; Salem *Ohio Homestead Journal*, cited in *The Liberator*, 21 April 1848.

21 *The Liberator*, 25 September 1846, 19, 26 March, 2 April 1847.

22 *The Liberator*, 26 March, 9 July, 1 October 1847. On this debate, see also Kraditor, *Means and Ends*, pp. 248–50.

23 *The Liberator*, 9 July 1847.

24 David Montgomery, 'The shuttle and the cross: weavers and artisans in the Kensington Riots of 1844', *Journal of Social History*, v (Summer 1972), pp. 411–46.

25 *Working Man's Advocate*, 6 July 1844.

26 Eric Foner, *Free Soil, Free Labor, Free Men: The Ideology of the Republican Party Before the Civil War*, (New York, 1970).

27 See Eric Foner, 'The causes of the Civil War: recent interpretations and new directions', *Civil War History*, xx (September 1974), pp. 197–214.

28 David Brion Davis, *The Problem of Slavery in the Age of Revolution* (Ithaca, 1975), pp. 347–61.

29 Davis, *Problem of Slavery*, pp. 364, 373; Dawley, *Class and Community*, pp. 196, 238–9.

30 Michael Fellman, *The Unbounded Frame* (Westport, 1973), p. 105; Foner, 'Causes of the Civil War', p. 206; Mandel, *Labor: Free and Slave*, p. 66; Rayback, 'American Workingman', p. 154; Foner, *History of the Labor Movement*, I, p. 272.

31 See Eric Foner, 'Class, ethnicity, and radicalism in the gilded age: the Land League and Irish-America', *Marxist Perspectives*, I, 2 (1978), pp. 6–55.

32 Barry Goldberg, 'Beyond Free Labor' (unpublished doctoral dissertation, Columbia University, 1978), provides compelling evidence of the persistence of the idea of 'wage slavery' among labor leaders after the Civil War, as a rhetorical device for criticizing the emerging industrial society. Paradoxically, he observes, labor reformers played down the differences between chattel slavery and wage slavery, but they identified strongly with abolitionism, ignoring that movement's response to the labor movement of its own time. As late as 1895, the British writer John K. Ingram felt compelled to include an appendix on the 'lax' use of the term 'wage slavery', in his *A History of Slavery and Serfdom* (Condon, 1895), pp. 263–4.

13
ECONOMIC ASPECTS OF THE ABOLITION DEBATE

by Stanley L. Engerman and David Eltis*

Given the recent outpouring of writings on the economics of slavery
and on economic and other aspects of the abolition movement in the
United States and Great Britain, it might be useful to take stock of
some broad contours of these writings, both to see how the views of
the anti-slavery movement have been altered and to indicate those
areas of fact and interpretation where more work will be helpful.
The debate on the relationship between economic trends and interests on the one hand, and the abolition of the slave trade and slavery
on the other, has taken its place as one of those perennials which
will, no doubt, remain of central interest and never be satisfactorily
resolved. While new information will influence and shape the
debate, and the range of possible answers has been narrowed down,
the issue has taken an importance which means that its analysis
often tells us as much about the scholar and his political views in the
present-day world as about the historical issue. While Eric Williams
did not initiate the discussion, in retrospect it appears that it was the
publication of *Capitalism and Slavery* (1944) which defined the
context of the current debates, and even now most writings on
British anti-slavery seem to both start and end by comparing their
conclusions with those of Williams.[1]

Put most simply, Williams shifted the context of the debate about
British slavery and anti-slavery in several ways. One, which will not
be discussed in detail here, was to make slavery and the slave trade a
central part of the study of the British Industrial Revolution, by
emphasizing those arguments (used at the time by the pro-slavery
and slave trade defense) pointing to their economic importance to
the British economy. A second shift was his direct confrontation
with the then-prevailing view of anti-slavery and its success, a view
which now seems to have overemphasized the role of a disinterested

moral crusade in ending the slave trade and slavery. Williams, by contrast, argued for the crucial role of economic factors in explaining the rise and success of the anti-slavery movement. Earlier writers, such as Coupland, did not deny that the 'value and therefore the weight' of the West India interests 'had been undermined by insuperable economic forces', nor that the American Revolution 'had swung the commercial balance of the Empire over from West to East'. Nevertheless, as Fage points out, Coupland's primary focus was on 'the *campaign* of a group of Britons' for abolition, a concern with the abolitionists which led him to emphasize the moral dimension.[2] Williams, however, made central the economic factors he saw as influencing abolition, as well as the political influence of the specific economic interest groups which he thought would benefit from the ending of slavery. The specific economic factors, and their relationship to political success, may no longer seem as simple as they were in Williams' view, but no-one since 1944 has been able to avoid extensive discussion of the economic context within which the anti-slavery movement occurred. Yet, by focusing on the presumed issue of morality versus economics, too much of the subsequent debate has been concerned simply with whether Williams was right or wrong, an approach which can do more to obstruct than to help understand these questions.

To a large extent the customary counterposing of economics and morality is an unnecessary distinction, and it would appear that, for several reasons, the implied contrast of motives is overdrawn. While such a position may seem to ignore the reasons the debate has attracted such attention and emotion, it may help place a number of recent arguments in sharper focus. One important aspect of the relationship between economics and morality was presented in 1776 by Adam Smith:

> The late resolution of the Quakers in Pennsylvania to set at liberty all their negro slaves, may satisfy us that their number cannot be very great. Had they made any considerable part of their property, such a resolution could never have been agreed to.[3]

One might paraphrase Smith in more technical jargon as saying that the demand curve for morality (as most demand curves) was downward sloping: the cheaper the thing to be obtained, the more will be 'purchased'. More directly, it suggests that the success of anti-slavery was influenced by the social and economic importance of slavery, a proposition which may seem both trivial and of some explanatory power in explaining the pattern of developments in the

Americas. A corollary to Smith's point is suggested by Seymour Drescher's comment on the closing phase of the British anti-slavery campaign: 'The hair-splitting utilitarian calculus of demographic and economic stress might presage colonial stagnation but not cataclysmic ruin. That was enough to seal the fate of the slave trade.'[4] Thus a reform which seemed relatively limited in the costs imposed was more easily accepted than one which would have been expensive to the politically interested parties.

A second reason why the attempt to separate economics and morality is difficult is that the mix of motives which led one group to make anti-slavery a major political issue need not have been the same as those which explain the ultimate success of the movement. While even Williams does not seriously attack the motives of the 'Saints', many remain skeptical that such humanitarian impulses can account for the diffusion of the movement and its political appeal. That there might be differing explanations for these two issues is not surprising, as indeed is suggested by Anstey's central contention about 'altruism ... concealed beneath the cloak of interest'.[5] To some the thrust will be on the 'altruism' of motives, to others the 'interest' which presumably affected the voting. Behind this attempt to distinguish origins from factors in success is, perhaps, the fundamental question at issue between Coupland and Williams, an issue to which recent writings provide uncertain guides. Worded most briefly, the question is: 'Did the abolitionists matter?'[6] To Coupland, the answer is clearly yes; to Williams, probably no, despite his description of the abolitionists as the 'spearhead' of the onslaught, since the trend of economic interests alone might perhaps have generated the same outcome. It is when the same question is posed of other writers that the answer may seem less clear, and the depiction of the changes in belief and practice more difficult to examine.

There is a third reason why the distinction between economics and morality is weakened. The role of the ideology of specific interest groups within a nation at a given time is one which does not permit this easy separation. With this broad conception of ideology, there seems little basis with which to distinguish economic from humanitarian, and other political and social, influences. It is precisely the purpose of an ideology to merge divergent strands into one world-view, by a process which not only integrates seemingly different aspects, but which also places certain elements outside the central core of beliefs.[7] One striking aspect of the anti-slavery creed was the belief that economics, religion, and humanitarianism, indeed all aspects of the anti-slavery argument, came together to point to the same outcome.[8] There was no reason for the motivations to be separated, and it would be difficult to believe that any individual could convincingly make the sharp categorization implied by either Coupland or Williams. Thus, it could be argued that, even if the success of anti-slavery was linked to the emerging bourgeois ideology, and that in turn to the shifting economic base, this would represent a markedly different role for economic factors than presented by Williams, and one which would permit agreement between ostensibly pro- and anti-Williams groups.

With these perspectives on the economic approach in mind, we wish to pursue two related themes. The first concerns the use made of various economic contentions in the arguments for British and American abolition, and the manner in which their interpretation has been affected by recent work on the economics of slavery. The second relates more directly to the crucial economic aspects of early nineteenth-century ideology as they influenced the slavery debate, and to the post-slavery developments in the British West Indies, to see what questions they posed for the abolitionists and how they were resolved.

II

It remains quite difficult to sort out the various economic arguments about the slave system which existed among contemporaries and persist today among historians. There are several different arguments, not all of them consistent, which, however, have often been linked. It will be useful to try to separate these arguments and to see what they imply about slavery and the post-slave world. In doing so we can better understand the dynamics of the earlier debates as well as subsequent interpretations both of slavery and of the anti-slavery movement.

If an economic system were inefficient (in either the short or the long-run) there would be measures which would raise its output and thus provide increased benefits to producers and/or consumers. Yet the issue of who would benefit is not obvious, and the group (or groups) in society which lost income due to slavery would be different depending on how these costs were presumed to arise.[9] Moreover there is a subtle difference between arguing that economic difficulties exist at a point in time, and the expectation of problems in the future if current forces were to continue. This is a distinction too often ignored, and theoretically-based tendencies to be realized in the future have too often been read, rather, as current, or very-soon-to-be-established, conditions. Some of the economic writings on slavery, particularly in the US, have been based on this confusion, which, however valid were the projected tendencies, can lead to some misunderstanding of the actual political and social conditions. A related position is one which confuses declining, or falling, profits with actual prolonged unprofitability. While an earlier 'golden age' might have yielded higher returns, and the response of planters was very much to complain, plead distress, and try to reverse these forces, this does not mean that actual profits were negative. The paradox of planters' pleas of distress at a time when prices paid for slaves were rising may suggest that things were not as dire as often maintained.

Similarly arguments which suggest that another form of labor organization might have been more profitable than a slave labor system need not imply that the latter was, in the customary sense of the term, unprofitable in yielding returns to plantation owners. Thus to argue, as was frequently done, that free labor would have yielded even higher profits than slave labor, need not imply that the ongoing slave economy was unable to provide economic benefits to the planters. Larger profits might have been earned, but, as the accumulations of wealth would indicate, the slave system was not without its financial compensations. This does not, of course, mean that slavery was always profitable, but it suggests that too frequently imprecise and inaccurate uses of the concept of profitability have figured in the debates. Another distinction to be noted is that between the profitability of slave production and the relative importance of the slave-based economy to the nation or to its metropolitan area. To argue for little or declining importance might help explain why, in some cases, abolition was more easily achieved; it does not indicate that slavery was unprofitable. Zilversmit's discussion of abolition in the northern United States clearly makes this distinction, while some aspects of the discussion of British abolition have, at times, not been as precise on this difference.[10]

The classic argument of the unprofitability of slavery to the planter was made by Adam Smith, although the same basic argument had been made by several Physiocrats, and by Hume and Millar in England, among others. Smith argued primarily on the basis of labor incentives ('A person who can acquire no property, can have no other interest but to eat as much, and to labour as little as possible'), which affected work input as well as limited the development and introduction of new technology.[11] He also pointed to the limitations to the proper management of individual subsistence by 'a negligent master or careless overseer', a special example of the more general drawbacks of hired and absentee management.[12] With only the briefest mention of the impact of slavery in other parts of the world, Smith argued that despite the large profits, slave labor in the Americas was inefficient, and that it was only the very large returns possible from sugar and tobacco production which explained the persistence of slavery. The high profits permitted the masters to indulge their 'love to domineer', even though still greater financial returns could presumably have been made with free labor, a point in seeming contrast to the basic emphasis on rational self-interest in Smith's work.[13] This basic argument, with its emphasis on the economic inefficiency of slave labor and of costs to slave-owners due to the presumed absence of incentives to slave labor, remains the essential starting point for the economic aspects of anti-slavery thought. We should note, however, that whereas in the past, historians accepted the assertion of the inefficiency of slave labor as an empirical statement, more recently they have seen it as an indication of a basically ideological position.[14]

While much of the earlier anti-slavery argument had used the lack of incentives, and related propositions, to argue for the unprofitability of slavery to the planters, and although Williams does quote Smith, this is not essential to the central part of Williams' argument. He criticizes Smith for not distinguishing between the earlier and later stages of colonial development, so that although 'other things being equal, free men would be preferred', 'in the early stages of colonial development, other things are not equal'.[15] More specifically, Williams argues that the great demand for plantation labor could not have been met by free labor, thus making slave labor necessary. For the years after the American Revolution, to which Williams applies the Ragatz thesis (including declining profitability), the argument of inefficiency is not essential to his main point. It might be noted that Williams conceived overproduction of sugar, not underproduction, as a factor contributing to the success of anti-slavery both in 1807 and 1833. Wilberforce in 1789, and later Stanley also, argued that, based on what could be described as inelastic demand, reductions in sugar output, for whatever reason, would ultimately benefit the planters.[16]

Williams locates the cause of slavery's demise and the costs of its unprofitability elsewhere. Whatever the costs to planters, the major burden of the existence of slavery was felt by British producers and consumers who were forced to purchase in a protected market.

And, not only were they forced to purchase in a protected market, British taxpayers paid a heavy part of the burden of West Indian defense. Thus the argument implies a loss of potential income to residents of Britain, with a corresponding gain, via this redistribution, to West Indian planters.[17] The losses to Britain emphasized by Williams were those suffered by the capitalists, forced to pay higher wages for labor and to suffer reduction in their export markets from restrictions on imports of foreign sugar and other colonial commodities.[18]

Thus Williams effectively counterposed the interests of industrial-capitalists with those of planter-capitalists. Relative to the costs of colonial commodities available from Brazil, Cuba, and elsewhere, there was presumably an unnecessary outlay by the British. An important issue was thus the relationship between slavery and protection. The same protective system, however, remained in operation after the ending of the slave trade and slavery, until almost the middle of the nineteenth century, creating the dilemma for the British that the elimination of colonial protection would lead to widening markets with benefits for the remaining slave economies in the New World. Thus the extent to which 'unprofitability', as discussed by Williams, reflected slavery or protection remains unclear.[19] In essence Williams seems to be arguing that the islands were profitable for the British through most of the eighteenth century, while, whatever the returns to planters, they had become an economic burden prior to abolition.[20]

Williams does raise the possibility of increases in income to other groups in British society with the weakening of West Indian slavery, albeit without any necessary implication for the profitability or unprofitability of the islands. There is, of course, the contention of an East Indian interest among the abolitionists, which was ready to fill in holes in the market after the excess protection of the West Indies was eliminated, and a potentially widened trade with Africa has also been pointed to as a possible benefit of the elimination of the slave trade.[21] Nevertheless Williams' contention that 'this connection between East Indians and certain abolitionists has not been fully appreciated', has not fared well in the subsequent research on this topic, and indeed the search for any cluster of economic interests which might expect to directly derive higher incomes from abolition (as opposed to the removal of protection) seems unlikely to be a rewarding line of investigation.[22]

There remains another set of arguments about the profitability of slavery and its impacts upon long-term development worth noting, given its great emphasis in the debates about US slavery. It has been argued that, whatever the profitability to the individual planter, slavery in the South had a long-term impact of lowering national income by leading to an inappropriate economic structure. Presumably in the absence of slavery there would have been a more extensive development of an urban–industrial base, and the slave South would more closely resemble the northeastern states. Numerous arguments have been proposed to support these points (and numerous objections raised as to their validity). Here it might be useful to note three points. First, the implied counterfactual adjustment to the absence of slavery would presumably have been different on the mainland than in the West Indies. For the mainland, many argue that the major adjustment to the elimination of slavery and/or the power of the planter class would have been a shift from agriculture to industry, raising economic productivity. While there was also some discussion that higher output within the agricultural sector would follow a shift to free labor in the South, in the case of the West Indies it is only within the agricultural sector that adjustment was expected to take place. The debate had little to say about any West Indian shift to other economic sectors; rather the implication was that the shift from slave to free labor would not have reduced the heavy dependence upon agriculture. Although aware of the problem, in general the anti-slavery critique did not discuss in any detail the measures which might have ensured that freedom would have led to higher measured output, rather than a shift of freed labor to nonmarket production.[23]

Secondly, even if the shift to industry posited for the South were to have occurred and yielded a higher national income, it need not imply that slavery was backward, stagnant, or inefficient, or that it would have become so within a short time-span. Clearly the thrust of most recent work on slave economies has been to indicate that the earlier Marxian–Weberian view of slavery as a backward economic system is of doubtful plausibility, whatever the answer to the question of whether or not the South should have industrialized. And, thirdly, while much debate has centred on the relationship between slavery and capitalism, and on whether slavery was capitalistic, this discussion need not be entered here.[24] It seems fairly clear that planters were generally commercially-oriented, responded to price and output signals, and worked at developing labor incentives and efficient productive techniques. While to some this smacks of capitalism, to others there are enough differentiating characteristics from developed industrial capitalism to argue against the latter word being applied to slavery. Nevertheless few now would argue that slavery was not a dynamic aspect of capitalistic development in the modern world, or that, within slavery, economic expansion was not possible.

The marked expansion of the US South in the eighteenth and nineteenth centuries, the continued growth in the use of slave labor and of plantation output in the West Indies, and the ability of slavery to persist in Brazil until 1888 by adjusting to changing market conditions, have all made the previously easy connection of anti-slavery and progress seem more dubious, and serve to raise issues with those parts of the anti-slavery arguments which implied that slavery was a fetter upon economic growth. As we shall discuss, the studies of the post-emancipation response have further indicated that the abolition of slavery, however great the benefits in welfare to the formerly enslaved, did not often raise measured output, and that, to some extent and for whatever reason, the pro-slavery defense seemed to have predicted the economic future better than did the anti-slavery attack.[25] And, on the specifics of the economic conditions in the West Indies, Drescher has ably argued for a vibrant and expanding economy until at least the 1820s, with profitable new areas of settlement available at the time the international slave trade closed. Nor was the growing importance of the West Indies in British trade in the early nineteenth century suggestive of a collapsing economic system.

All these contentions do not, of course, answer all the questions about the economics of slavery, nor do they necessarily imply that Williams' economic arguments (such as those based on the costs of purchasing in protected markets) were incorrect. Yet, in historiographic context, they have certainly meant a shift in the approach to his questions, and a broadening of the interpretation of economic aspects of anti-slavery thought and practice. As the search for beneficiaries of abolition (besides the slave) yields less certainty, the motivations involved seem to become less straightforward and direct, even if, to some, no less ultimately economically based.

III

In this section we present two arguments relating to indirect economic benefits from the ending of the slave trade and slavery, one briefly, the other in greater detail since it has become the focus of much recent work.

In his discussion of the success of the anti-slave trade movement

Anstey placed great stress on the abolitionists' ability to project the 1806 bill closing the trade to Britain's 'enemies and competitors' as being in the national interest.[26] Three points might be noted here. One is that the parliamentary abolitionists frequently used various forms of the national interest argument before 1806, including bills which prohibited the slave trade to foreign colonies, but that generally they deliberately attempted to lift the debate to grounds rather more elevated than that of profit and loss, in the belief that that was where their best chance of long-run success was to be found.[27] Thus against the 1806 ploy described by Anstey, one can discern a strong, but not as successful earlier countertendency in the campaign to present, if not the wolf of economic interest in sheep's clothing, at least a sheep in sheep's clothing. Secondly, though it seems implicit that closing most of the slave trade made closing the remainder less expensive, it seems as plausible to argue that the new British monopoly control made the final closing more, not less, expensive to the colonial interests. Thirdly, while national interest may have been reflected, in part, in direct economic gains to the British within the short-term, it also included a strong element of the avoidance of 'a great augmentation of the enemy's colonial resources'. Thus one can view the argument as either a case for direct economic gains (presumably going mainly to sugar planters) or else as a measure for inflicting economic damage upon British enemies with little (if any) direct profit to the British. In neither case is there an obvious relationship between this view of the determinants of abolition and earlier arguments about the profitability or unprofitability of slavery in the long-run. While still under discussion, it seems of importance to note that the major anti-slavery success of 1806 is seen by some as based upon an appeal to national interest.

The most prominent strand in recent writings on anti-slavery has, however, been the emphasis on the role of ideology as a determining influence. In many ways, these are difficult arguments to describe. To the immediate post-Williams scholar, heavily influenced by economic determinism, the very fact of abolition seemed sufficient proof of the slave system's unprofitability: why else was it terminated? The ideological arguments, in contrast, have no necessary implications for the actualities of the economics of slavery, and, indeed, almost any view of profitability would be consistent with the interaction between ideology and anti-slavery.

There are, of course, different attitudes taken towards the nature and role of ideology. One recent view, that of David Brion Davis, stresses the importance of the attack upon slavery as part of the ideology of the emerging class of bourgeois industrialists, playing an important hegemonic role in their emergence in British culture and society.[28] While the anti-slavery argument may have 'reflected the needs and values of the emerging capitalist order', there is, at times, an implication some draw from Davis that there was something like a deliberately manipulative element in the way anti-slavery was used as part of the control of other groups and classes within society, and some have questioned the sincerity of belief by the industrialists in the humanitarian basis of anti-slavery thought.[29] That contemporaries may not have clearly distinguished economic from humanitarian grounds is suggested by, among other things, the strong appeals to individual responsibility which is found in many of the sermons of the Society for the Propagation of the Gospel in Foreign Parts.[30]

Moreover, in several senses, Davis's presentation of a 'free labor' ideology as espoused by the industrialists in England stresses points different from those in the 'free labor' ideology examined by Eric Foner in his study of the northern United States in the mid-nineteenth century.[31] To Foner the anti-slavery inference of the ideology was dominant in the working class, or at least among those artisans who believed that upward mobility, self-employment, and the ability to avoid a lifetime of wage labor were possible. Foner indicates that in the US the 'free labor' ideology became the basis for an anti-industrialist argument, being, in many ways, a continuation of the earlier attitudes of a society of small farmers and artisans. While the perceived differences in economic opportunities between Britain in the early nineteenth century and the US in the middle years of that century may account for some of the variations in the rise of and use of the 'free labor' ideology, there remain important unresolved issues in regard to the locus of this 'free labor' ideology and the role it played in class relations.

There are further questions about the determinants and consequences of these ideological elements. The manner in which various scholars approach this issue, with emphasis placed on different factors, may seem to isolate strands of belief which are really indissoluble. Although Anstey, Davis, and Drescher may seem to agree on the central role of ideology as a factor in anti-slavery, they do draw quite differing implications. Anstey comes closest to the previous humanitarian argument by stressing the religious background of anti-slavery belief; Davis is more suggestive of Williams in pointing to the compatibility of the anti-slavery creed with the needs of the new industrialists; while Drescher points to abolitionism as 'more a vehicle adopted by under-represented and dynamic social, regional, and religious groups than a channel whereby entrenched interests in Parliament sought to legitimize their old authority', and he emphasizes the impact of 'mass-interest petitioning'.[32] It might, perhaps, be suggested that the disagreements relate less to ideological impact than to questions relating to individual motivation, and the seriousness of belief of the holders of the ideology. Thus without deeper psychological probing (if at all), it seems difficult to see a useful way to disentangle these views. At the least it is difficult to see how acceptance of any of these positions implies rejection of the other.

Perhaps it is worth reiterating that much of the debate on abolition has always attempted to separate the economic from the humanitarian motive in a way which would have puzzled the abolitionists themselves. Smith's explanation of why planters used slaves when they were obviously the most expensive form of labour (see above) had profound moral and humanitarian as well as economic implications, however weak the initial premise. These were explored by Claphamite, Foxite Whig, and classical economist alike in the 1790s and 1800s, with arguments that were not only mutually consistent but were usually used interchangeably by all segments of the anti-slavery movement. Thus when Wilberforce, Smith, Stephen, and the others presented the policy part of their 'humanity, justice and policy' trilogy around which the abolitionist speech was frequently constructed, we can surely say that they were doing more than just tactically pandering to the free market or even national interest prejudices of the British ruling class: they were laying bare part of their own deepest convictions.[33]

Perhaps the best personification of the intermixing of the economic and humanitarian strands of abolition (it would be hard indeed to isolate an evangelical or even religious strain here) was Palmerston. Anti-slavery was much closer to the heart of Palmerston's world-view than the usual 'benevolent crotchet' treatment assigned to him would seem to indicate. Roger Anstey has recently made a strong case for seeing the preventive policy of the British government against the nineteenth-century slave trade as institutionalized, and part of what Robinson and Gallagher called the 'official mind' of the Foreign Office.[34] Anstey's Robinson and Gallagher analogy is valuable but perhaps does not go far enough, for in the mid-century the official mind believed above all that progress, morality, and the growth of markets for British goods would be facilitated by the development of British principles of government and a free market system in the rest of the world, both of which British policy should encourage. Free trade and free labor were obviously foundations of this system, which was expected to benefit *all* countries. Those countries which persisted in the slave trade were subjected to the same infuriatingly patronizing treatment that the West Indian planters had received before 1807. 'There is a want of a thorough appreciation of the real interests of Portugal here', wrote the British minister in Lisbon to Palmerston and the sentiment also reappears frequently in the Brazilian correspondence.[35] Palmerston, of course, was one of the main architects of this policy and to treat his anti-slavery stance as an eccentricity or even as merely a search for markets in Africa (as Gavin has come close to doing) is to miss its inseparable interconnection with the more widely recognized parts of his philosophy.[36]

In any event neither the Davis, Anstey, and Drescher approaches nor these cursory comments on Palmerston do much to connect the need and use of ideology with the actual conditions of slaves and the profitability of slavery in the West Indies. These arguments, therefore, do not so much as really deal with the Williams questions, but rather step around them at critical junctures (as, indeed, did Williams). They do provide a better context for the observed temporal relationship between anti-slavery and industrial capitalism in England, yet still leave unanswered many questions about the specifics of this relationship.

IV

Central to the discussion of the ideological component has been the distinction between free and slave labor. As noted, earlier interpretations accepted as correct the arguments about the relative inefficiency of slave labor, and it is only when questions about this 'fact' have been raised that its ideological role has been made more prominent. It is striking how relatively complete was the unanimity on this point in the anti-slavery argument, and how strong were the beliefs that the slave system provided no incentives, except fear, to the workers and also how effective would be self-interest as a motive in eliciting output. This last point was so taken for granted, that it had achieved the status of a 'truth' without people noting the slender empirical evidence on which it was based. The sensitivity on this point might account for the attention given to the experiments of Joshua Steele on his Barbados estate in the late eighteenth century (which in effect made serfs out of the slaves), and the interest in the free German producers of cotton in Texas described by Olmsted, as well as in the frequent North–South comparisons within the United States.[37] When confronted with more direct comparisons within the South, however, it was argued by the anti-slavery camp that slavery led to the degradation of free labor, and thus created the group of poor and relatively unproductive whites.[38] Given this, the theoretical propositions as to relative incentives under various labor systems and the benefits of free labor were easily supported.

There were two related strands of the 'free labor' ideology, coming to the same conclusion, but with somewhat differing implications. The strand given most attention was that of the benefits to the worker of freedom, self-interest, and opportunities for social mobility, leading also to a higher productivity and thus some advantages to the hirers of labor. There was, however, a variant of this argument suggesting a rather negative aspect of free-labor incentives. Hume, Smith, and Marx, among others, pointed to the advantage of free labor to hirers, since hunger was presumably a better incentive than fear, and the amount of labor forced from a free worker was thus presumably in excess of the labor expected from a slave.[39] The implication, undrawn, would seem that 'wage slavery' was more desirable to the entrepreneur (and less so for the worker?) than 'chattel slavery', and freedom was not an unmixed blessing in material terms.

Clearly the ending of slavery in the West Indies posed certain important issues for believers in 'free labor' efficiency. While three basic patterns did develop, in none of them did free labor show a markedly superior performance to the slave economy in the production of export commodities, particularly sugar. In several of the smaller islands, immediate post-emancipation sugar output exceeded that prior to 1834, there being a particularly sharp rise only in Barbados.[40] This was accomplished without a major coercive return to the plantation system, although high population densities meant little alternative land was available to the freedmen. A second pattern was illustrated by British Guiana and Trinidad, areas in which sugar output initially fell, but, with the introduction of indentured labor from the other islands, as well as India and China, the plantation system again became dominant and total sugar output two to three decades after emancipation markedly exceeded that at the end of the slave period.[41] The third, and most frequently discussed, was the case of Jamaica, which had a marked decline in the output of sugar and other export products, persisting for a rather prolonged period.[42] Wherever possible, the freedmen tried to acquire land for themselves, which they used basically for self-sufficient production, and to become, in Mintz's term, a 'reconstituted peasantry'.[43]

As pointed out by Temperley, the 'failure' to produce higher levels of output by freedmen in the West Indies was regarded as an embarrassment by anti-slavery forces, and they worked hard at providing explanations for this failure of their predictions. In an excellent example of this genre, Charles Buxton pointed to the drawbacks of competing with slave labor in Brazil and Cuba, where imports from Africa were still occurring and slaves could presumably be treated more harshly than were free workers.[44] Yet Buxton noted other factors which might help place the slave versus free labor debate in better context. He attributed some of the difficulties to the failures of plantation management, with the carry-over of undesirable patterns from the slave period, in addition to numerous other financial and economic strains. In particular, he blamed the planters for the failure of ex-slaves to return to the plantation, charging they were unable (or unwilling) to pay adequate wages to induce them to leave their own small farms, because of the planters' refusal to innovate and the debt-burden carried over from slavery. This failure to regain plantation labor had, of course, been anticipated by the planters who had argued that in the absence of the coercion possible under slavery they would be unable to attract a plantation labor force, though they would deny that even without past debt they could possibly pay the higher wages argued for by Buxton and still make profits. (This logic underlay the earlier arguments that slave labor cheapened the commodities purchased by European consumers, as well as the related contention that emancipation would result in a loss in land values to the planters, and thus cost them more than the prices of the freed slaves.)

It might perhaps appear that the planters and the abolitionists were arguing from different premises, and that the emphasis by the former on the proposition that the outcome in terms of measured output might differ from that expected by the latter was correct, but the abolitionists could respond that this outcome was to be attributed to the planter unwillingness to permit a 'true' free-labor market. The basic issue was earlier posed quite directly by cynical planter interests, who suggested that the abolitionists buy up plantations and thus at one stroke prove their point and relieve hard-pressed planters.[45] As most planters noted, and as was pointed out by Mill and McCulloch among the classical economists, slave and free labor would often be involved in different activities because of the drive of free labor to avoid certain types of work wherever possible. (A similar point had been made by Stephen in 1802, in his discussion of policies to settle Trinidad, although his position seems to have shifted over time).[46] While it seemed obvious to most abolitionists and economists that free labor would be more efficient than slave labor doing similar work, to the planters it seemed clear that, with emancipation, the nature of the work done by ex-slaves would change, and lead to lower measured output (and perhaps even lower material income for the previously enslaved).

Related to this is the more general failure to consider the meaning of free labor in the West Indian, as opposed to the British, context (perhaps surprising given the earlier Haitian experience). In the customary depiction of the British case, particularly after the extension of enclosures and the reduction of the yeomanry, little land apparently remained available to those wishing to avoid movement to urban areas and wage work. Thus the 'peasant option' was limited, and free labor with appropriate wage incentives could generally be expected to have led to a higher measured output. In the West Indies, however, many islands still had reserves of 'free' land which were available for settlement. Thus the ending of slavery did not mean that workers would be compelled into working for wages for others. Nor did it imply they would necessarily choose to work on their own land in order to maximize income from market output. Rather a third alternative, self-sufficient production, remained possible, and this seemed to be the preferred alternative for ex-slaves. Thus ending slavery led to a withdrawal of labor from the production of marketed output where possible, and the benefits of freedom did not lead to a higher market production.

Planters were, of course, concerned with these alternatives, and, with varying degrees of success tried to restrict land availability and to force labor input by various vagrancy laws and by regressive tax policies.[47] This 'peasant option' and its full implications were not satisfactorily explored, and, Wilberforce, for one, seemed to suggest mainly that the availability of land to freedmen would preclude their working at too low wages, without accepting that it might mean a fuller withdrawal from the wage labor force.[48] The prediction of the 'free labor' ideology was not accurate for the West Indies, since it ignored one of the most important benefits of freedom which the ex-slaves were enabled to pursue. A reduction in work input and change in the type of work and size of plantation worked on after emancipation have been characteristic of most societies after the abolition of slavery, indicating that, whatever else its benefits, a conflict between free choice in the labor market (even with sharp constraints) and increased market output was to be anticipated, and that the presumed advantages of 'free labor' of ex-slaves to consumers were not so obviously to be realized. Perhaps we might learn something about abolitionist motivation if we distinguish between those individuals who found this disturbing and to be explained away and those who were quite willing to accept this outcome in the interest of humanity.

Notes

* For useful comments on an earlier draft we wish to thank Daniel Field and Herbert Klein, in addition to the participants at the Bellagio conference, particularly David Brion Davis and Seymour Drescher.
1 (Chapel Hill, 1944).
2 In Reginald Coupland, *The British Anti-Slavery Movement* (1964), p. xxi. See also pp. 62, 123.
3 Adam Smith, *The Wealth of Nations* (New York, 1937), p. 366.
4 Seymour Drescher, *Econocide: British Slavery in the Era of Abolition* (Pittsburgh, 1977), p. 140.
5 Roger Anstey, *The Atlantic Slave Trade and British Abolition, 1760–1810* (1975), p. 408.
6 And, if so, why? Even if some might argue that their contribution to the abolition of the slave trade, either by direct political activity or heightened moral concern, was not crucial, this would leave open the debt of subsequent reform movements to the moral feelings and arguments generated by the abolitionists. Dale H. Porter, in *The Abolition of the Slave Trade in England, 1784–1807* (Hamden, 1970), pp. 141–2, raises the question of whether Wilberforce's personality and tactics may have delayed, not accelerated, the ultimate success of the anti-slavery movement.
7 This world-view itself might, in its broad terms, also be accepted by groups in conflict about any set of specific policy issues: e.g., the ideology of the anti-slavery movement could be compatible with that reflected in the planter beliefs, yet because of disagreements on the predicted results of ending slavery (and other reasons) there would remain differences of opinion as to the desirability of abolition.
8 While the typicality of the argument may be debated, James Cropper posited that 'He who has made it the interest of man to do right, has fixed a period to the gains of those who dare presume to debase his creatures', and thus 'is it not reasonable to suppose that these are the means appointed by the Supreme Governor of the universe, for the extinction of slavery ... ?' James Cropper, *A Letter Addressed to the Liverpool Society for Promoting the Abolition of Slavery* (1823), pp. 6, 23. On this see David Brion Davis, 'James Cropper and the

British anti-slavery movement, 1821–3', *Journal of Negro History*, XLV (October 1960), pp. 241–58.

9 In this discussion we shall omit the obvious costs to the enslaved. While these costs did shape the environment of the debate and the discussion of the costs of prolonging slavery, and while the slaves' patterns of behavior were not without influence on these debates, they were politically relevant in a quite different sense than were the costs to British producers and consumers.

10 Arthur Zilversmit, *The First Emancipation* (Chicago, 1967). On the Dutch case, where unimportance to the metropolis did not mean an early end to slavery, see the essay by Emmer in this volume.

11 Smith, *Wealth of Nations*, p. 365. For an earlier (1624) variant of some of the economic arguments, see Mary S. Locke, *Anti-Slavery in America* (Boston 1901), pp. 9–10. It should be remembered that Smith reflected the changing attitude to labor which emphasized the productivity and incentive aspects of high wages, in contrast to earlier writings stressing the 'benefits' of low wages in inducing higher labor force participation. On this changing attitude to labor see, in particular, A. W. Coats, 'Changing attitudes to labour in the mid-eighteenth century', *Economic History Review*, XI (August 1958), pp. 35–51.

12 Smith, *Wealth of Nations*, pp. 80–1.

13 Smith, *Wealth of Nations*, pp. 365–6. In his *Lectures on Justice, Police, Revenue and Arms* (New York, 1956), pp. 94–104 and 222–36, there is a related discussion of the economic aspects of slavery.

14 See, for example, the writings of David Brion Davis, and Howard Temperley, 'Capitalism, slavery and ideology', *Past and Present*, 75 (May 1977), pp. 94–118.

15 Williams, *Capitalism and Slavery*, p. 6.

16 See William Cobbett (ed.), *The Parliamentary History of England*, XXVIII (12 May 1789), 54, and *Hansard's Parliamentary Debates*, 3rd series, XVII (14 May 1833), 1210.

17 For one estimate of this redistribution, see James Stephen, *The Slavery of the British West India Colonies Delineated* (1824), I, p. xxxii. There is, in the contemporary literature, a frequent running together of arguments against colonies and against slavery. See, e.g., J. B. Say, *A Treatise on Political Economy* (Philadelphia, 1836), pp. 203–13. Say is of interest in that he argues both for the profitability of slavery to the planter and the long-term costs due to the opposition to 'the introduction of a better plan of industry'. In response to the first contention, see the discussion of Adam Hodgson, *Remarks During a Journey Through North America* (New York, 1823), pp. 291–335 (to whom Say later wrote a brief letter of modification).

18 It should be noted, further, that those arguing for a popular upsurge against slavery do not point to any direct self-interest reflecting a response to the higher prices presumably paid for imports. Clearly such a basis for an attack on slavery would seem possible, and recent work by James Walvin, 'The public campaign in England against slavery, 1787–1834' (forthcoming in David Eltis and James Walvin (eds.), *The Slave Trade and Abolition*), would suggest some concern with the price of sugar.

19 Drescher resolves (or perhaps sidesteps) this issue by arguing that until at least the 1820s both official British policy and the real interest of British manufacturers lay in protection not free trade. Thus there would have been no ex-ante beneficiaries even if the protectionist system, the prime target of Williams' industrial capitalists, had been destroyed with the slave trade. Drescher also points to the slave trade as the purest example of free trade in the British commercial system. See *Econocide*, pp. 55–63, and 'Capitalism and abolition' in Roger Anstey and P. E. H. Hair (eds.), *Liverpool, the African Slave Trade, and Abolition* (Liverpool, 1976), pp. 167–95.

20 While Williams does not point this out, protection could have conceivably benefited the slave. This was tacitly admitted by some anti-slavery supporters arguing for sugar duties in the 1840s. Ending protection might benefit the manufacturer, but it would also result in a reduction of the slaves' standard of living. It is a measure of the commitment to the free-market ideology that the abolitionists did not even hint at the issue until after slavery was abolished, and even then only a part of the movement was in favor of continued protection. It was left to a West Indian supporter to point this out in the 1820s – see R. Wilmot Horton, *The West India Question Practically Considered* (1826).

21 There is, of course, a major difficulty in these and similar arguments since, for any conceivable action there would, no doubt, be some group that would benefit economically. Thus the issue is not, as is often done, to point to a group which could benefit or, *ex post facto*, did benefit, but, rather to indicate the political power balance between gainers and losers and the actual dynamics of the political process. It is the examination of this latter point that makes the political analysis of Roger Anstey and Seymour Drescher of such central importance.

22 Williams, *Capitalism and Slavery*, p. 188. It should be noted that an equalization of the sugar duties would have, in the opinion of some of the East Indian interests, forced the West Indian planters to use free labor, thereby increasing substantially the West Indian returns (to the presumed detriment of the East Indies?)

23 See David Eltis, 'Abolitionist Perceptions of Post-Emancipation Society' (forthcoming in James Walvin (ed.), *Slavery and British Society*).

24 It might be worth noting, however, that some of the apparent differences between Drescher and Davis stem from their concern with different aspects of capitalism. Drescher regards slavery as the 'preeminently capitalist institution' and equates it with profit-making and the market system. Davis is more concerned with industrial capitalism.

25 See, for a summary presentation of some recent work, an article by Stanley Engerman, 'Notes on the patterns of economic growth in the British North American colonies in the seventeenth, eighteenth and nineteenth centuries', (forthcoming in Paul Bairoch and Maurice Lévy-Leboyer (eds.), *Disparities in Economic Development Since the Industrial Revolution*).

26 Anstey, *Atlantic Slave Trade*, pp. 364–90.

27 See, for example, W. Pitt, *Parliamentary History*, xxix (23 April 1792), 1262, and the comments of Fox and Stephen noted in Drescher, *Econocide*, p. 140.

28 David Brion Davis, *The Problem of Slavery in the Age of Revolution, 1770–1823* (Ithaca, 1975), pp. 343–468, especially pp. 350, 384–5, and 466–8. The similarity of the arguments concerning labor inefficiency under serfdom on the continent to those in the anti-slavery debate are suggested by the discussions in Jerome Blum, *The End of the Old Order in Rural Europe* (Princeton, 1978), especially pp. 315–23 and in Daniel Field, *The End of Serfdom* (Cambridge, Mass., 1976), especially pp. 8–50. Such comparisons often featured in the late-eighteenth and early-nineteenth century attack on slavery, an aspect of the ideological discussion worth more attention.

29 For a discussion of some of these questions, see the review article by J. R. Pole, 'Slavery and revolution: the conscience of the rich', *Historical Journal*, xx (June 1977), pp. 503–13. Put baldly, one might discern two separable 'economic' arguments in Davis. One is that slavery came to be seen as morally indefensible in the light of, amongst other things, new relations between capitalists and workers. The causation here is indirect, related to the responses of capitalists to the social changes of the time, which were seen as both justification and as causes for guilt in their attitudes towards free labor. It might be argued that the capitalist would have been prepared to tolerate substantial losses in income from the destruction of slavery, because he fully accepted the liberal ideology. The second argument suggests that abolition was successful because it fitted the economic needs of capitalists: any losses from abolition would be outweighed by the broader economic gains which the capitalists derived from their new relationship with workers. If there had been nothing in it for the capitalist measured in terms either of income or prestige, abolition would presumably not have occurred. Yet, while dwelling on the gains of the propertied, Davis tends to treat them as effects rather than causes of abolition, and it might seem inappropriate (as well as futile) to attempt to reduce the complexities of the examination of the origins of abolition to a cost-benefit analysis for a particular class. It seems, therefore, that the more plausible interpretation of 'economic' causation is the first of these arguments.

30 See Michael Greenberg, 'Slavery and the Protestant ethic', *Louisiana Studies*, xv (Fall, 1976), 209–39.

31 Eric Foner, *Free Soil, Free Labor, Free Men* (New York, 1970).

32 See Seymour Drescher, 'Capitalism and the decline of slavery: the British case in comparative perspective', in Vera Rubin and Arthur Tuden (eds.), *Comparative Perspectives on Slavery in New World Plantation Societies* (New York, 1977), pp. 132–42.

33 The phrase is from the 1806 Resolution condemning the slave trade, *Hansard*, 1st series, vii, 802. But see Wilberforce's remarks in *Parliamentary History*, xxviii (12 May 1789), 49, and George Stephen's in *Anti-Slavery Recollections* (1854), pp. 253–8. Temperley, 'Capitalism, slavery and ideology' has suggested the compatibility of the post-Smithian capitalist ideology with anti-slavery, without, however, committing himself on the extent to which the abolitionists themselves shared that ideology.

34 Roger T. Anstey, 'The pattern of British abolitionism in the eighteenth and nineteenth centuries', in this volume.

35 Jerningham to Palmerston, British Public Record Office, London, Foreign Office, Slave Trade Series (henceforth FO/84) (2 July 1838), FO 84/250.

36 See R. L. Gavin, 'Palmerston's Policy Towards East and West Africa, 1830–65' (unpublished Ph.D. thesis, Cambridge University, 1958). Similar comments could also be made of Castlereagh and Canning. The latter, e.g., wrote in a secret dispatch that His Majesty's Government was 'strongly . . . impressed' that the slave trade was 'the point upon which must turn the whole question of our future relations with Brazil'. Canning to Amherst (28 February 1823), FO 84/24.

37 On Steele, see William Dickson, *Mitigation of Slavery* (1814). Pitt and Francis, amongst others, picked up references in West Indian literature to slaves who worked twice as hard on their own garden plots as they did on the plantations and the occasional planter like Sir Phillip Gibbs and Sir James Johnstone was prepared to link better treatment with increased output, but one can only describe the empirical evidence as thin. On the Texas Germans, see Frederick Law Olmsted, *The Cotton Kingdom* (New York, 1953), pp. 306–7, 373–4, 502–3 (but see also pp. 505–6). For a brief discussion of the context, se⸱ the introduction by Arthur Meier Schlesinger, pp. xl–xlii. The North–South comparisons are, of course, quite numerous. The diffic⸱ ⸱ies of African 'free labor' in Sierra Leone were, of course, a major source of concern to the abolitionists.

38 For similar arguments made about Brazil, see Joaquim Nabuco, *Abolitionism* (Urbana 1977), pp. 104–38. See also Jill Sheppard, *The 'Redlegs' of Barbados* (Millwood, N.Y., 1977). Given recent writings on the work ethic, it does seem that the existence of slavery is not a necessary factor in 'giving work a bad name'. The general point about the impact of slavery upon white labor (of both slave-owners and non-slaveowners) was, of course, an early feature of the attack on slavery, presented by (among others) Franklin, Smith, Steuart, and Millar.

39 Perhaps these were tactical arguments, but it is striking that many of these comparisons suggested that it was cheaper to provide subsistence to free workers than to slaves. Many abolitionists pointed to the advantage of free labor to hirers, but were unwilling to draw out the full implications of the lowered standard of living. See, for example, Charles Stuart's remark: 'The happiness of the free labourer is not that he always has abundance, for he is often in want, but that he is dependent mainly upon God, and his own exertions'. *The West India Question* (1832), p. 15.

40 For data on sugar output, based on Deerr, see William A. Green, *British Slave Emancipation* (Oxford, 1976), p. 246. See also pp. 163–293, for a discussion of these patterns. It was frequently noted at the time (see, e.g., John Davy's *The West Indies, Before and Since Slave Emancipation*, 1854) that Barbados was the most 'overpopulated' of the West Indian islands and that this was instrumental in its 'successful' retention of a plantation-based sugar economy (as well as a cause of outmigration to other islands). See also Douglas Hall, *Five of the Leewards* (Barbados, 1971), and Woodville K. Marshall, 'The ex-slaves as wage labourers on the sugar estates in the British Windward

Islands, 1838–46' (forthcoming). A similar tripartite distinction among the West Indies had been discussed by Herman Merivale, in his *Lectures on Colonization and Colonies* (1861), pp. 300–48.

41 In Trinidad there was only a small decline with emancipation, but a major spurt in sugar output did not occur until after 1846. On these areas see, in particular, Donald Wood, *Trinidad in Transition* (1968), and Alan Adamson, *Sugar Without Slaves* (New Haven, 1972).

42 See, in particular, Douglas Hall, *Free Jamaica* (New Haven, 1959), Philip D. Curtin, *Two Jamaicas* (Cambridge, Mass., 1955), and Gisela Eisner, *Jamaica 1830–1930* (Manchester, 1961).

43 Sidney Mintz, *Caribbean Transformations* (Chicago, 1974), pp. 146–56.

44 Charles Buxton, *Slavery and Freedom in the British West Indies* (1860). See also [W. E. Forster], 'British philanthropy and Jamaican distress', *Westminster Review*. LIX (April 1853), 171–89, and Douglas A. Lorimer, *Colour, Class and the Victorians* (New York, 1978), pp. 123–30. For a similar discussion of French emancipation, see Augustin Cochin, *The Results of Emancipation* (Boston, 1862).

45 Benjamin Vaughn, *Parliamentary History*, XXIX (2 April 1792), 1086.

46 The position Stephen took in *The Crisis of the Sugar Colonies* (1802), p. 191, and in a letter to Lord Liverpool in 1814 (both noted by Drescher, *Econocide*, p. 156), is explained with more detail but less certainty in *The Slavery of the British West India Colonies Delineated* (1824–30), II, pp. 381–3. Stephen was quite sensitive to the impact of the availability of new areas on the continued profitability of slavery (I, pp. 80–1, 470–1).

47 See the discussions in Curtin, *Two Jamaicas*, pp. 101–57, and Green, *British Emancipation*, pp. 191–260.

48 Before abolition the anti-slavery group talked loosely, both in Parliament and amongst themselves of a 'free peasantry'. See R. I. and S. Wilberforce, *The Life of William Wilberforce* (1838), 5, pp. 158–9, and Charles Buxton (ed.), *Memoirs of Sir Thomas Fowell Buxton* (3rd edn., 1849), p. 103. But the fullest exposition of Wilberforce's views (in the course of which he appears to show himself oblivious even of the enclosure movement in England) appears in Wilberforce to the King of Hayti, 18 October 1818, in R. I. and S. Wilberforce (eds.), *The Correspondence of William Wilberforce* (1840), 1, pp. 385–6. The meaning of 'free peasantry' may, of course, have varied, and tactically any pointing to a withdrawal from the production of market output would conflict with the arguments of the benefits of free labor to consumers in Britain from the larger output of free labor.

14
ANTI-SLAVERY AND BRITISH WORKING-CLASS RADICALISM IN THE YEARS OF REFORM

by Patricia Hollis

In July 1832, the London-based National Political Union, a radical middle-class pressure group organized by Francis Place to ensure the passing of the Reform Act, circulated its list of seven pledges to be extracted from candidates for the new parliament. The pledges were: parliamentary reform, law reform, tax reform, trade reform, church reform, the freedom of the press, and the abolition of slavery. Some three months before, members of the working-class National Union of the Working Classes (NUWC) had published their programme of reform to be discussed at a National Convention. They too urged parliamentary reform, law reform, tax reform, trade reform, church reform, and the freedom of the press. They added other proposals: currency reform, an end to flogging, hanging and the standing army, and self-rule for Ireland. Significantly, they did not seek the abolition of slavery.[1]

Most nineteenth-century reforming pressure groups sought or possessed an authentic working class constituency. Movements to improve public health, free the press, welcome foreign refugees, obtain further parliamentary reform, seek secular education, reform land tenure, disestablish the state church, repeal monopolies, abolish the Contagious Diseases acts, and build international peace, all recruited working men with more or less grace, goodwill, and conviction.[2] The temperance movement and the Anti-Corn Law League acquired former Chartists as lecturers. Anti-slavery, in its techniques, its use of paid lecturers, its extraction of pledges, its mobilizing of the provinces and of dissent, was one of the most innovative and radical pressure groups of the period. Despite much jeering, it was the first to organize its female friends into Ladies'

Auxiliaries (and the later suffragette movement was to look back on anti-slavery, temperance, and the Anti-Corn-Law League as the organizations in which women acquired their political education and 'came out' in public);[3] but it failed to forge a working-class constituency. In the 1790s, some of the most ardent abolitionists had been the London Corresponding Society and its provincial members, until Wilberforce, embarrassed by their sympathies with France, had moved from pressure-from-without to pressure-from-within, a parliamentary campaign free of working-class radical contamination.[4] In the 1840s, George Thompson was to make anti-slavery once more a central radical concern, and his Anti-slavery League of 1846 recruited former Chartists William Lovett and Henry Vincent.[5] From 1823 until the Garrisonian 1840s, however, the abolitionist cause attracted little working-class support, much working-class indifference, and considerable working-class hostility. Given the distrust with which reforming pressure groups were viewed, it is perhaps understandable that for their part anti-slavery leaders preferred to acquire a more respectable constituency than that of working men,[6] to pre-empt any criticism that they were seeking to intimidate parliament with an unruly mob out-of-doors. Given also that the anti-slavery platform was placed on 'the high ground of Christian duty'[7] rather than, as with the Anti-Corn Law League, urged in the name of the national interest, it was more appropriate to receive testimony from ladies and ministers to the religious imperative than from artisans demonstrating the classless, 'interest'-free nature of the cause. Anti-slavery leaders in any case were no radicals, and had little sympathy with a more democratic impulse. They were working for the slaves, never with them. Buxton, for one, showed his anger, impatience and contempt for working-class Chartists at the Norwich meeting they invaded.[8]

Anti-slavery may not have sought working-class support, but it might nonetheless have acquired it, despite itself. There was a strong moral impulse within artisan, Owenite and Chartist thought, which valued the dignity of the individual, the pride of independent labour, the autonomy of adulthood, and which was so often noncon-formist, anti-deferential, upright and Gladstonian. Joseph Sturge, founder-member of the Agency Committee, understood and respected it, the parliamentary radicals and the Manchester reformers organized it into Suffrage Unions, Leagues, and Associations. But the anti-slavery crusade instead aroused active working-class opposition, the antagonism of Henry Hunt and William Cobbett, scathing editorials from Hetherington and O'Brien in their

Unstamped radical papers, and hostile resolutions from working-class political unions. The banners of Northern trade unionists appropriated abolitionist slogans for their own white slaves. In Birmingham in April 1833, and in Norwich in November 1840, anti-slavery meetings were broken up by working men.[9]

William Cobbett, that master of English polemic whose critique of 'Old Corruption' generated the demand for parliamentary reform; Richard Oastler, 'King Richard' of the Northern factory movement, who linked the Tory paternalist impulse to protect factory children with the trade unionist demand for a ten hour day; and Bronterre O'Brien, 'the school master of Chartism', whose journalism in the Unstamped *Poor Man's Guardian* and then in the *Northern Star* taught a generation of working men to 'read' capitalism as the systematic theft of their labour: these three men were the most powerful radical voices of their time. They led the attack on the anti-slavery campaign. Cobbett contrasted the lot of the Negro field labourer with that of the English field labourer, Oastler contrasted the lot of the adult black slave with that of the white infant factory 'slave', O'Brien contrasted colonial chattel slavery with European proletarian wage slavery. All three were quite clear that the Negro slave was the better off. All three labelled the abolitionists as hypocrites, indifferent to poverty and suffering at home. And all three suggested that the abolitionists financed their philanthropy abroad by increasing the exploitation of their white 'slaves' at home.

Cobbett had long loathed the 'cant' of the 'humanity people'. His magnificent *Rural Rides* of 1825 had insisted that agricultural labourers were worse treated than felons, worse treated than Negro slaves. By late 1830, as the Government viciously suppressed the Swing Rising, Cobbett's invective sharpened. English agricultural labourers 'have been harnessed like horses and asses, and made to draw carts and waggons . . . [with] drivers set over them, just as if they had been galley slaves; they have been sold *by auction* . . . [and] kept separated from their wives by force to prevent them from breeding'. And in his lectures to working men at the Rotunda he described the sale of English labourers. 'In Norfolk last winter . . . it was the practise to bring the poor men every month into the church porch . . . and sold by hammer to the highest bidder'. White men '*can be sold*', and white men *are sold*, by the week and the month all over England. Do you call such men free, on account of the colour of their skin?'[10] 'Fat and greasy negroes' were bought and sold, not 'for their blood and bones, but for the labour they bring'. So too were Englishmen. They were slaves in everything but name. What

Cobbett had damned, few working men would care to defend. His phrases were to echo across working-class journalism over the next decade.

Whereas Cobbett, by virtue of his hatred for Wilberforce, his nose for humbug, and his racialist prejudices, was instinctively opposed to emancipation, Richard Oastler, and his co-worker, the former missionary Rev. George Bull, were abolitionists. Oastler, an Anglican Tory protectionist estate steward, claimed to have shared platforms with Wilberforce and received stones and blows intended for him. Prodded by John Wood, a Tory worsted manufacturer, he 'saw' the lot of factory children around him. His famous letter on Yorkshire slavery to the *Leeds Mercury* on 16 October 1830 signalled the start of the Northern Short Time Movement. While Yorkshire itself was represented in parliament 'by the giant of anti-slavery principles', while its inhabitants were famous for their 'religious zeal', for their temperance and reforming principles, and for their missionary exertions, thousands of young children were labouring from 6 a.m. to 7 p.m. with only thirty minutes break in 'those magazines of British infantile slavery – the worsted mills in the town and neighbourhood of Bradford'.

Oastler mobilized the support of sympathetic Tory manufacturers in the worsted industry, of medical men and Anglican clergy, behind Hobhouse's parliamentary bills to give factory children some protection. But the bills were emasculated in Parliament by the capitalist-liberal-dissenting interest. The growth from 1829 of the Lancashire cotton spinners' unions organized by John Doherty which linked up with the nascent Yorkshire trade union movement, gave Oastler's agitation a new direction. From the autumn of 1831, Tory paternalism and trade union radicalism together created a network of Short Time Committees across Lancashire and Yorkshire, to demand a bill that would limit children's labour, enhance the value of men's labour, and be observed by mill-owners.[11]

Pamphlets, petitions, poems and speeches insisted that England's white infant slaves were worse off than adult colonial black slaves. One popular banner carried frequently in procession showed a deformed man with the inscription, 'Am I not a man and a brother?' and underneath it, 'No White Slavery'. Robert Blinco and William Dodd provided autobiographies of themselves as factory slaves. Dozens of verses were published on the same theme; popular novels, such as Francis Trollope's, *The Life and Adventures of Michael Armstrong, the Factory Boy*, employed the images of infant slavery. Oastler and his factory reformers deplored the wrongs of

Negro slavery, but they insisted that charity should begin at home.[12]

Their first criticism of 'spurious' philanthropy was that the conditions of English factory children were far worse than those of Negro
slaves. Their hours were longer (up to eighteen hours a day), their
food, clothing and health poorer.[13] John Cleave, the London radical, was struck as Shaftesbury was, by the deformities of factory
children. Coming out of the factory gates they reminded him of a
box of crooked alphabet letters. Their punishments were worse:
they were beaten with thongs more cruel than any West Indian
whip, battered with bully rollers, sometimes locked into dark wells,
even hung upside down. English children, said Oastler, 'might be
said, not to live, but to linger in a dying state'. John Wade in his
famous *Black Book* claimed that 'the horrors of the middle passage' did 'not transcend those of the INFERNAL FACTORY
SYSTEM'.[14] The children's physical health was being destroyed, and
their moral health was also in danger. The Tory high Anglican, Sir
Robert Inglis, insisted that Lancashire children were not brought by
God into the world merely to be little cotton machines. Their
immortal souls were in peril, for such children were 'without God'
and as much slaves in mind as in body.[15]

Not only were children worse treated than adult slaves; in so far
as they could not consent to their lot they were true slaves. Even
tough political economists like Brougham and Poulett Thompson,
who argued that child labour was essential to the family economy
and the wealth of nations, had to admit that children were not
morally competent to give their consent to any labour contract.
They could not be a free party, they were entitled to protection.
And if they did not get that protection from parents, due to parental
ignorance, destitution, or greed, then they were entitled to it from
the State. Leonard Horner, senior factory inspector, complained in
1840 of 'the inhumanity, injustice and impolicy of extorting labour
from children unsuitable to their age and strength – of subjecting
them, in truth, to the hardships of slavery (for they are not free
agents) . . .' The Short Time campaign's pamphlets quoted approvingly the *Derbyshire Courier*: 'We make laws to provide protection
to the Negro: let us not be less just to the children of England'.[16]

'The great emancipators of negro slaves were the great drivers of
white slaves', a Mr Oates explained at a public meeting. 'The reason
was obvious. The labour of the black slaves was the property of
others, the labour of the white slaves they considered their own'.[17]
The exploitation of factory children financed the very philanthropy
of their masters, their subscriptions to Bible Societies, to anti-

slavery societies and to chapel building.[18] Oastler, as his contacts with working men expanded, developed his critique to encompass working men, as well as their children.

> Slavery I would assist in destroying everywhere; I would not *confine* my sympathies to slaves in the West Indies, believing as I do that we have a still more horrid system of slavery at home. Our workmen, their wives, and their children are slaves. Tell me not of the 'free labour' of a poor famishing artisan, covered with rags and broken in spirit; standing in the presence of an unfeeling, unprincipled Task-Master, possessed of thousands of pounds, bargaining for the price of his labour, his wife and children pining at home . . . If he applies to the Overseer, he is disdain-fully sent back to his Task masters, and told to be *thankful* for half wages. If he stand out, in the hope of getting a better price for his labour, and meanwhile should be seen begging for a piece of bread, the law declares *he becomes vagrant*, and without a crime, he finds the prison is his *legal* home. Yes, this is the 'freedom' that the unprotected British labourer enjoys in this boasted land of liberty. And those Crucibles for extracting in the shortest time, the health and strength of human beings, Factories, I would regulate and controul by law.[19]

Oastler was always careful to insist that he was an emancipationist, but English children had first claim on his compassion. Bronterre O'Brien, Hetherington, Cleave and the London radicals of the NUWC grouped around the Rotunda opposed emancipation itself. They deplored slavery; but to emancipate the Negro in a capitalist society was to pass him from chattel slavery to the 'more servile and more profitable' state of wage slavery, where he would be worse off. Better the Negro remain 'unfree'. O'Brien had none of Oastler's confidence that the factory system, the outward and visible sign of capitalist economics, could be ameliorated by law without a trans-formation of the existing political and social system.

O'Brien, editor of the leading working class Unstamped paper, the *Poor Man's Guardian*, more than any other man, structured working-class perceptions of their new society. His editorials denouncing property, profit and privilege, were discussed in clubs, pubs, and classes of the NUWC from Plymouth to Perth.[20] He shared Cobbett's and Oastler's contempt for cant, for the Buxtons who preferred their objects of benevolence at a distance and posses-sing 'a black hide, thick lips and a woolly head'. Tell Buxton of British children 'pining' in factories, of English adults 'yoked' to gravel carts, of Irish families struggling to survive on sea-weed and raw porpoises, and Buxton was 'cold as marble'. But tell him that 'a sleek and stupid negro' was getting a dozen lashes for not doing what he was well fed for doing, and 'Buxton's eyes are bathed in sensibility'.[21] A correspondent complained to the *Guardian* that the entire anti-slavery campaign was merely 'a gull' to make English working people believe that their own wrongs and miseries were trivial when contrasted with those of other nations. Foreign matters, like foreign wars, Paine had taught working men, were calculated to distract attention away from home affairs.[22]

In any case, London-working class radicals were quite willing to believe the West Indian planters when they asserted that the conditions of the slaves had been much exaggerated. Several debates of the NUWC, the forum of London radicals, argued how much better off were the black slaves than the white ones. Cruikshank, who engraved woodcuts for the Unstamped press, illustrated a pamphlet showing that the black slaves were 'totally free from the cares, the troubles, the poverty and even the labour and anxieties of the British poor'. Negroes enjoyed comfortably furnished dwellings, without rent or taxes to pay; they were never separated from their families, unlike the English workhouse poor, and could even choose their own masters – 'the removal of them is never attempted but with their own *free* consent and approbation'. They enjoyed medical care – 'their health is preserved from interest as well as from humanity'; they were provided with appropriate clothing 'suitable to the climate'; their labour was 'very moderate and well proportioned to their powers', working only from sunrise to sunset, having Sunday off, and time to cultivate their own land. They all had ground attached to their houses, could keep livestock, and acquire money for luxuries such as mahogany furniture. Their punishments were no more severe than Englishmen received for petty offences. And Cruikshank finished the pamphlet with a drawing of an elegant Negro ball, alongside the straw-strewn hovel of an English 'slave'.[23]

White men were told that at least they were blessed with freedom. But everyone agreed that slavery was labour without reward. As black and white were bought and sold for the labour in them, a sale of labour took place in each case. 'Traders in human labour' could hire white slaves or buy black ones. John Smithson went on to argue, 'He that can purchase the labour of a starving community, can dole out their pittance to suit his own purpose, almost the same as if he had purchased their flesh and blood, and very often with much less risk to himself'.[24] Once purchased, the Negro became part of his master's property and enjoyed the protection accorded to property. The white 'slave' was no man's legal property 'not because he is free . . . but because he is not worth possessing'. A stout black slave might be worth £40 or more to his master. A white 'slave' was worth '£30 less than nothing', for that was what the upper classes were willing to pay to see him emigrate. The birth of a black child was welcomed by master and slave alike; the birth of a white child with a curse. Indeed a poor white man or white child was worth far more dead than alive – to anatomy students.[25]

So-called free working men were wage slaves. 'What are called the working classes', wrote O'Brien, 'are the slave populations of civilized countries'. They were mortgaged from the cradle to the owners of land and capital, unable therefore to own their own labour, and forced into a wage slavery none the less real because it was impersonal and systematic, where the chattel slavery of the West Indies was personal and individual. The conditions of wage labour were worse than those of chattel labour, because property owners extracted greater profit from their wage slaves than from their chattel slaves. The greater the profit, the greater the theft. 'We pronounce there to be more slavery in England than in the West Indies . . . because there is more unrequited labour in England'.[26] Blacks hitherto had been free from the 'deadly effects of competing with themselves as labourers'. Once emancipated, black slaves would become wage slaves, undercutting each other's wages. Their new masters would be capitalists who no longer had any financial interest in promoting their health, but would seek to extract the last ounce of labour from them. Emancipation would allow the master to get more work done and to pay less for it. The sole object of 'the ranters of Exeter Hall', wrote O'Brien, was 'to proletarianize' the Negroes for the benefit of employers and usurers. The planters themselves had always admitted they would have preferred free labourers to slaves, if only they had had a reliable source of it for hire. But guarantee him 'a surplus population of starving proletarians to be ever ready at his hand', and the planter will become an instant abolitionist. The slave, said the *Voice of the West Riding*, 'had better remain in his present condition'.[27] Stanley's proposals, thundered the *Destructive*, were 'a humbug from beginning to end. The slave will not be one jot freer should it become law than he is now . . . The power of taking away the fruits of his labour is that in which the slavery consists.'[28] Working men would only be free if they possessed the means of production and political power. Until labour and capital are 'united in the same hands', O'Brien wrote, the people will continue slaves, 'and the slavery will only increase in rigour with the opulence and duration of the system'.[29]

When Stanley proposed to emancipate the West Indian slaves by a grant of £20 million, many abolitionists and most radicals were outraged, abolitionists because the grant rewarded sin, radicals because it increased taxes. O'Brien's wrath could not contain itself. He joined with Cobbett to insist that the money would come from taxes 'wrung out of the productive classes in the shape of rents [and] profits . . . Every additional tax brings additional slavery upon the people'. White slaves were liberating the black slaves at their own expense. West Indians, 'a set of idle luxurious thieves', would now live off white slave labour instead of black.[30] If slave labour was so unprofitable and free labour so preferable, as economists argued, then the West Indians could be entitled to no compensation at all. But if money had to be found, why not take the £20 million from church revenues? It was churchmen, after all, who were most anxious for the repeal of slavery. Yet it was the Church which enslaved men's minds so that they could neither perceive the nature of their wage slavery nor rebel against it. Christianity had been responsible in Western Europe for the overthrow of chattel slavery and the substitution of wage slavery: 'chattell slavery . . . in consequence of the workings of the Gospel, gradually assumed the form of *wages*-slavery, and generated modern proletarianism . . .'[31]

Working-class radicals believed that emancipation was both a species of moral humbug and an extension of economic exploitation for both black and white. The Blackburn working men's Political Union spoke for many when it resolved to condemn the activity of the anti-slavery men, which only 'mislead the people, while it aggravates the oppression of the slave'.[32] They understood that the moral and the economic arguments advanced by abolitionists (the Christian conviction that slavery was sin and the political economists' insistence that slavery was inefficient) were mutually supportive. For few Victorians would have distinguished between the two. In a society when philanthropists comfortably referred to God as the Great Banker, the Heavenly Accountant, and their lives a moral balance sheet; as Figaro said, taking literally the maxim that 'He that *giveth* to the poor *lendeth* to the Lord' and looking for an adequate rate of return in the life hereafter; at a time when Andrew Ure could advise millowners to organize their 'moral machinery on equally sound principles with their mechanical', and so improve their product and increase their profit, for 'Godliness is great gain'; or when Cobden could argue without embarrassment that free trade was living Christianity, because it meant buying in the cheapest market, selling in the dearest, and in so doing 'carrying out to the fullest extent the Christian doctrine of "Doing to all men as ye would they should do unto you"'; in such a society humanitarian and commercial vocabularies reinforced each other.[33] Common to them all was a concern that social discipline should stem from a shared and internalized moral order; common also was a belief that the law (rather than the older Tory preference for personal patronage on the one hand or the newer Chartist demand for the vote on the other) could and should protect all men equally.

The good society, according to this account, was a voluntary association of economically active and morally strenuous adults. The pauper was both morally infirm and an economic parasite. His idleness meant less capital for investment, employment and wages. Lacking the will to work, he was also likely to be vagrant, intemperate, dissolute. One remedy was to make the poor law less 'soft' on paupers; the other response was to recreate in the pauper the will to be independent, to restore him to moral fibre and productive labour by philanthropic reclamation and religious redemption. Scientific philanthropy therefore tried to remove the cause of destitution – moral infirmity – rather than merely alleviate its social consequences – distress. Casual almsgiving was deplored since it 'rewarded' that dependency which was itself the problem; statutory relief was disliked since its very impersonality meant it could not discriminate between the deserving (the widow, the orphan, and the blind) and the undeserving (most of the rest), between God's poor – poor devils – and the devil's poor. The tools of scientific philanthropy were the unexpected home visit, the tract and the leaflet, the chapel and the schoolroom, and the occasional judicious gift of a mangle.[34]

Moralizing the poor therefore, was a form of economic aid. It was not by accident that some of the keenest proponents of a scientific philanthropy, rooted in political economy, should be among the keenest abolitionists; and that some of the most ardent abolitionists were those who were most anxious to extend social and moral discipline among the English poor. And it was therefore not surprising that they should arouse first the suspicion and then the hostility of working-class radicals. For the ethic behind anti-slavery was that slaves were denied moral responsibility, to the detriment of their eternal souls. To be fully human was to have an immortal soul for which one was personally responsible and everlastingly accountable. But the precondition of moral adulthood was economic self-reliance and self-dependence, the capacity to contract, freely to offer one's labour for sale and to negotiate its terms, to be accountable under the law and to the law. Wages rather than the whip would make each man his *own* slave driver, his own moral policeman; and the result, whether among British workmen or West Indian slaves, would be a more disciplined and hence more profitable labour force, and a more disciplined and hence more stable society. Moral maturity, economic efficiency and social order were truly synonyms: and working class radicals when they attacked anti-slavery were also attacking the constellation of religious, economic, social, and philanthropic thought behind it.

Wilberforce himself, of course, while a reformer of the criminal law, earned the undying hatred of Cobbett by founding the Society for the Suppression of Vice, with its relentless sabbatarianism. His friend, the lawyer Sir Thomas Bernard, active in the African Institute, founded in 1797 the Society for Bettering the Condition of the Poor, as an attempt to decasualize late-eighteenth century almsgiving. The young Robert Owen was an ardent abolitionist, and his early communitarian schemes were treated with much suspicion by the radical *Black Dwarf* as 'pauper-barracks' designed to 're-moralize' and discipline the poor. Thomas Chalmers, the Malthusian Glasgow clergyman who was a welcome guest in the Gurney household, was only one of the more outspoken proponents of making the poor utterly responsible for their lot by abolishing statutory poor relief. As he told the Select Committee on the Irish poor in 1830, 'I think there is a great deal of sound political economy in the New Testament . . .'[35]

The convergence of these strands of thought is embodied in William Allen, a Quaker Spitalfields chemist, a Benthamite, an early sponsor of Robert Owen, and an energetic abolitionist. He opposed statutory poor relief and was disarmingly explicit about the social utility of philanthropy: it ensured that the poor man must always ask himself, 'Is my conduct such as to procure me friends in the hours of need? . . . He must be anxious to produce his conduct in the light. He must not withdraw into obscure and wretched corners, where he may indulge his vices unobserved . . . He must endeavour to live under the eye of others, and study to make his conduct the object of their regard'.[36] Stung by Oastler's accusation of spurious philanthropy, Allen founded in 1832 with Samuel Hoare (Buxton's brother-in-law), and William Crawford, the short-lived Society for the Improvement of the Condition of Factory Children. But with total consistency he was disturbed as much by the moral as by the physical evils suffered by children. Their moral and religious education was so neglected that the factory system 'as now conducted' was 'a dreadful and extensive source of juvenile depravity'.[37]

Lord Brougham, the Whig lawyer, and staunch political economist, who since 1824 had been one of the most effective publicists of abolition, was along with William Allen an enthusiastic promoter of popular education. His Society for the Diffusion of Useful Knowledge (SDUK) commissioned Harriet Martineau, the Norwich Unitarian journalist and a life-long abolitionist, to write stories, palatable to working-class taste, illustrating the truths of political economy. Three of her best known reflect the same convergence of vocabularies. *The Manchester Strike* explained that wages were solely dependent on the ratio of population to capital. Trades unions were futile at best, violent and tyrannical at worst. *Cousin Marshall* demonstrated that charity was unproductive; it was a 'false' humanity, since it absorbed portions of the wage fund which alone could create the employment and wages which the poor needed. The *Tale of Demerara* showed Alfred, heir to a plantation, returning home after years in England, convinced that free labour is both cheaper and more humane than slavery. He aptly points out, 'Scarcely any free blacks receive parish relief in comparison with whites'. And at the end of the *Tale*, Martineau lists her main points:

> Where the labourer is not held as capital, the capitalist pays for labour only. Where the labourer is held as capital, the capitalist not only pays a much higher price for an equal quantity of labour, but also for waste, negligence, and theft on the part of the labourer. Capital is thus sunk, which ought to be reproduced. As the supply of slave labour does not rise and fall with the wants of the capitalist, like that of free labour, he employs his occasional surplus on works which could be better done by brute labour or machinery.[38]

Her summary was approvingly included by Josiah Conder in his pamphlet, *Wages or the Whip*, which was to be quoted again and again in the parliamentary debates on emancipation. Working-class radicals were not slow to dismiss the SDUK publications as 'water-closet' literature; and to argue that the knowledge which their Unstamped press would circulate would be *truly* useful knowledge, designed to make the poor *discontented* with their lot.[39] John Joseph Gurney, a much-respected Norwich philanthropist, and the father-in-law of Buxton, in 1831 still tied abolition to sabbatarianism and social order just as Wilberforce had done forty years before. 'What a shameful rebellion against the law of God, is the denial of a *sabbath* to our colonial slaves: and how deep the guilt of that nation which permits the continuance of so impious a cruelty'. For the neglect of the sabbath led to 'vice, misery and confusion'. 'Ungodliness is the worst of all foes to moral virtue and civil order – to the decency, harmony and happiness of society; ungodliness and sabbath breaking act and react'.[40]

The parliamentarians were no less explicit. The radical M.P., J. S. Buckingham, a leading temperance reformer, put it neatly: 'Slavery was sinful, cruel, impolitic and unprofitable'. Sinful, because it offended the spirit of the Gospel, cruel because it flouted the rights of man to the protection of the law as enshrined in the British Constitution, impolitic because it was unsafe, and unprofitable because coerced labour was inefficient labour. The Negro was no different from other men, said Buxton. If he was offered wages, he would work for wages: he was not asking that Negroes should be exempt from labour, only that they should have the right of human beings to work for a wage. And the evangelical Lord Suffield told the House of Lords: 'The negroes were men – they had souls – they were responsible to their Creator. But how could they be responsible if they were not free agents?'[41] To be free, to be responsible, to be fully human, was to possess the capacity to contract, to be free to sell one's labour, to live under the law. Where Negroes had been freed, they had proved highly efficient. In Trinidad, said O'Connell, 774 Negroes, the property of the Crown, had been emancipated, and had not only increased in population (thus permitting the laws of supply and demand of labour to operate), but they had become 'industrious', and with it, naturally, 'fulfilled every moral duty, and had become extremely religious'. The dictates of Christianity, humanity and political economy went hand in hand. J. J. Gurney likewise testified to the Christianity, industry, sobriety, and order of the freed and resettled slaves of Sierra Leone; and Conder's pamphlet, *Wages or the Whip*, while recognizing that freed Negroes might at first work simply for money and finery, insisted they would soon experience higher motives 'to steady industry, sobriety and fidelity to their employers, which are supplied by the principles of Christianity, when brought to bear upon the character'.[42]

Peel, and Colonel Torrens, M.P. for Bolton, were unpersuaded. They did not doubt that free labour was more productive than coerced labour, nor that wage labour was desirable for the moral discipline it imposed. But, unfortunately for the abolitionist argument, the soil in parts of the West Indies was too rich to make daily toil necessary, and there social order would be at risk. Torrens, one of the most interesting and complex of post-Malthusian economists, and in temporary alliance with Fielden to urge protective legislation for factory children, explained that in Barbados and the old colonies, the land was all occupied and densely populated, wages would be low, and so the Negro would be forced to offer himself for hire. Thus these colonies could be granted immediate emancipation 'because there the Negro population would become free labourers compelled to earn subsistence by working for wages, and would be concentrated within the limits of civilization and moral and religious instruction'. But in Trinidad, Berbice and Demerara, where there was still fertile and unoccupied land, he favoured a period of apprenticeship, because if the Negroes were 'let loose', they would not work for wages,

> but would become dispersed throughout the fertile forest, withdrawn from communication, common cooperation, and from all means of intellectual improvement and religious instruction. Why did an enlightened and religious people demand the abolition of slavery in the colonies? . . . It was that in those colonies the negro race might be formed into civilized and Christian communities, and not into tribes of squatters and bushmen relapsing into their original heathen barbarism.[43]

Christian faith, and moral and social discipline, in other words, could only be inculcated where the laws of political economy were at work, where population pressed upon the means of subsistence, and where therefore the labouring poor remained labouring. Since Malthusian laws would clearly not operate in many West Indian islands, then the Negro 'must be educated to habits of industry by increasing their wants', must be trained, in Peel's words, 'into a taste for the comforts and even the luxuries of existence' to keep him hard at work and within moral discipline.[44] The alternative, repugnant to those demanding immediate emancipation, was a long period of apprenticeship.

To Peel, Stanley, and Althorp, under pressure from both abolitionists and planters, apprenticeship offered an additional layer of moral and social discipline beyond that of wage labour, as well as an additional compensation to the West Indian interest. The Negroes, Stanley told the House, were unlikely to engage in 'laborious industry' until 'population presses upon food', and that would not happen while the 'depopulating influence of slavery prevails'. So he recommended apprenticeship, less for the planters' sake than for the Negroes themselves, to train them to be 'fit for freedom'. Brougham's SDUK paper, *The Companion to the Newspaper*, loyally defended apprenticeship as a means of improving the slave's 'moral and intellectual nature'.[45]

Working-class radicals had a sensitive ear for such rhetoric. Cobbett, Oastler, and O'Brien attacked the hypocrisy of the humanity-mongers in freeing the black slaves to the neglect and at the cost of white slaves. But they also understood that behind the Christian and economists' arguments for abolition lay a concept of moral adulthood, of being accountable for one's actions, both here and in the life to come. Abolitionists, whether Tory or Liberal, evangelical or dissenter, accordingly attacked the childish unruly recreations of the poor, and their unmanly and harmful dependence on poor relief. Left to themselves, the white poor, like the black slaves, were children in a giant's frame, uncertain, irresponsible, unstable, pagan, indolent. Sabbatarianism, temperance, religious tracts, more stringent poor relief, a limited, religiously motivated, popular education, the promotion of the self-evident truths of political economy, were simultaneously methods of social discipline, aids to moral growth, and contributions to national wealth. Working-class radicals read such endeavours as a systematic concerted attack on the traditional rights of the poor.

Cobbett was quick to point out in 1825 that Buxton, who sought to free the black slaves, was trying to restrict the white 'slaves' beer houses; and eight years later Cobbett conducted his parliamentary campaigns against anti-slavery and sabbatarianism concurrently. The day after he opposed the 'humbug' of emancipation, he was pointedly complaining that Sir Andrew Agnew's Bill for the Better Observance of the Sabbath was being supported by petitions organized 'in the same manner as the Anti-slavery committee was accustomed to recommend the people'.[46] Oastler complained that those who were most ardent for abolition were the harshest masters of factory children and the most generous of philanthropists, subscribing to bibles 'to keep the poor people from sin' and building chapels 'for the poor children to sleep in' wherein they might be told of the great sufferings of the heathen. And while the labour of the poor was left unprotected, Oastler argued, their traditional rights were being invaded by the anatomy bill (which violated the body of the poor man in death), by coercive sabbatarianism (which denied the poor man his traditional pastimes), and above all by the new poor law (which denied him his legal right to poor relief). In J. R. Stephens' words of 1838, 'If the poor have no right to the rates, then the rich man has no right to his rents'.[47] Bronterre O'Brien with his customary clarity explained that political economy was a *post hoc* justification for the systematic theft of labour, that Christianity was a political doctrine inculcating passive obedience to that theft, and that sabbatarianism, temperance, scientific philanthropy, and the new poor law were styles of social discipline and species of class legislation.

The abolitionists had worked to reform the criminal law at home, just as they were anxious to bring the black slave within the protection of the law abroad. It was the dubious trial of John Smith, following the Demerara revolt, that mobilized Brougham's anger behind abolitionism. Slaves should not be placed 'as a body without the pale of the law, whenever a white man may be pleased to wrong them'. Just as men worked harder for wages than for the whip, so they were more law-abiding not where they most feared capital punishment but where they most fully accepted the mores by which society was ordered and understood the laws they were called upon to obey. Being a citizen, whether black or white, had little to do with political power; it meant being free to sell one's labour and to enjoy the protection of the law. That, said Gurney, was why the British peasant was better off than the Negro slave, whatever his physical conditions.[48]

Correspondingly, one of O'Brien's most bitter attacks on the law was embedded in an editorial on Negro slavery. 'Talk not to us here of the law "applying equally to all parties . . ." The question is not whether the rich are liable to the same punishments as the poor for the same offence, but *what description of offences are made punishable by law*?' The rich did not need to burgle property, for example, since they already burgled the poor through their rents, tithes, taxes and profits. It was poverty that led to crime. The laws of England, both old and new, were class legislation, designed to protect property, punish poverty, and legalize the theft of labour. 'The repeal of unjust laws . . . is all that is needed to terminate poverty and slavery for ever.'[49]

Anti-slavery, then, aroused working-class hostility: black slaves were already better off than white slaves; freedom for the blacks would be bought by further oppressing the white slaves; and once freed, black slaves would become as badly off as white slaves. They would work harder for less; and in experiencing capitalist labour they would also experience the full array of capitalist social discipline. They would become slaves in mind as well as in body. The depth to which this working-class analysis had penetrated beyond the pages of pamphlets and the press into the provinces and into the speech of ordinary working men, may perhaps be best illustrated by an extended example.

In November 1840, the county freeholders of Norfolk called a public meeting in St Andrew's Hall in Norwich to form an auxiliary of the British and Foreign Anti-slavery Society. The local Chartists sat in the front. The Bishop of Norwich opened the proceedings, analysed the signatures of the lords and knights petitioning for it, and told the meeting in fine style that slavery could no longer be tolerated. At which there were shouts of 'Poor Laws' and some noise. When the Bishop mentioned Wilberforce, he was interrupted with cries of 'Put down slavery at home'. The Bishop proposed to speak his sentiments manfully, at which there was much groaning. John Weyland, the local M.P., was the next speaker but had some difficulty in getting himself heard. Then Dover, the Chartist leader, stood up to speak. Weavers such as himself, he said, were free – free to earn 8s a week for their labour. The Bishop got £12,000 a year. In any case, he rather doubted the integrity of the Bishop. Only recently he had presided at a temperance meeting one day, and was to be found at wine parties the next. Dover went on:

> What is slavery? . . . For a man to be the individual property of man is to be a slave. If a man is called upon to produce and don't receive an equivalent, he is a slave. Do then the men who produce everything receive a fair equivalent? (Cries of No, No) . . . Our answer is, that there is a great gap between the producer and receiver, which must be filled up . . . Those men who have the management of affairs ought to fill it up, so that there shall not be so many people starving whilst others are rolling in luxury.

This was greeted with cheers from the Chartists. Labourers, said Dover, produce wealth for gentlemen to enjoy. They were important members of society. 'Why should not those who have an interest in the affairs of the country have a voice?' After all, with a dig at the platform, if they were paid up members of Bible Societies or assurance societies, they would expect to play a full part in the proceedings. 'If a man is put down without having a fair voice, that man is a slave, and he ought to be if he is content to remain so'. Men who were unrepresented were political slaves. And, he continued, 'There is another kind of slavery – mental slavery: the system is to pay thousands a year to enslave the minds of the people, teaching passive obedience and preaching doctrines they have never acted upon . . .' And he moved: 'That this meeting views with deep regret the many proofs of despotic slavery now increasing at home, and it therefore pledges itself to use all its exertions to put a final stop to slavery wherever it is found to exist'.

Dover was seconded by Thomas Hewitt. At a previous meeting Gurney had started his speech by talking about North America. Hewitt would not go so far. 'I will begin at the workhouse door', and he described weavers left to live on $1\frac{1}{2}$d a day, children with straw for their beds. Mr Gurney should have explained to the Negroes that they were better off than Englishmen, they did not have a Queen to pay for at £385,000 a year, nor 14,000 parsons. 'They call us firebrands, but we are determined not to go on with the useless stuff you would persuade us to, but sweep you all off the earth unless you work for your own living'. And with much enthusiasm, three groans were moved for the Bishop of Norwich, for the Whigs, and for the New Poor Law.

At this point, the platform attempted to regain control of the meeting. After several speakers failed to get a hearing, Gurney called to Dover, 'Get me a hearing, friend Dover. Any man who has not a fair hearing is a slave, you know: if so, I am a slave then'. Dover retorted, 'What! Mr Gurney, are you got so unpopular here in Norwich as to be obliged to call upon a common weaver to get you a hearing?' He turned to the Chartists, and to the orchestra, but the noise continued, and Dover added, 'I can't gag them you know; we have no gagging bills'. So Gurney moved his resolutions amid noise that made him inaudible. Buxton, who was on the platform with him, had by now lost his temper and told the Chartists, 'You have succeeded in disturbing the meeting . . . You, for the purpose of gratifying your own passions, have interrupted the cause of human-ity and Christian charity'. He was jeered and the meeting broke up. Reporting the event, the *Northern Star* congratulated the Chartists on 'asserting the dignity of man, the universal right of nature, and their own consciousness of wrongs inflicted on them, in the face of the collected elite of a whole country'.[50] Breaking up an anti-slavery meeting had become a statement of class consciousness by working-class radicals.

Notes

1   D. J. Rowe (ed.), *London Radicalism 1830–43: A selection from the Papers of Francis Place* (1970), pp. 103–5; *The Cosmopolite*, 7 April 1832.

2   See P. Hollis (ed.), *Pressure from Without* (1974).

3   'The emancipation of women', *Westminster Review*, 128 (1887).

4   Roger Anstey, *The Atlantic Slave Trade and British Abolition, 1760–1810* (1975), pp. 277–8.

5   Lovett had in 1837 written an Address on behalf of the London Working Men's association which had criticised American working men for not overthrowing slavery. See W. Lovett, *Life and Struggles* (1967 edn.), p. 107f.

6   M.P.s presenting petitions to the House were very aware of this, as just one day's petitions, those of 15 April 1833, demonstrate. Buxton presented a petition from the clergy, bankers, manufacturers and resi-dents of Glasgow; another from the secession church of Scotland; and a

third from the Sunday School teachers of Newcastle. Lord Howick presented one from the burgesses of Northumbria; Mr Hardy, petitions from several dissenting congregations in Yorkshire; and Mr Blamire presenting petitions from Cumberland 'bore testimony to the high respectability of the subscribing parties to these several petitions . . .' *Hansard*, House of Commons, 15 April 1833.

Compare Oastler's comment to a Halifax meeting: 'Had the present been a black slavery meeting, there would have been the parsons, the dissenters and the ladies; and it would have been a "very respectable meeting". But when the crime came home to themselves . . . they were *skulking* today, they will be at the missionary meeting tomorrow'. (*Report of a Public Meeting on Lord Ashley's Factory Bill, 8 April 1833*)

7 *Report of the Agency Committee*, June 1831, p. 3.

8 *Norfolk Chronicle*, 21 November 1840. Joseph Sturge was an honourable exception. For Buxton, see account of Norwich meeting below, · attributed in Note 50.

9 *Birmingham Journal*, 20 April 1833; for Norwich, see below, Note 50 and appropriate text.

10 *Rural Rides* (Penguin edn., 1967, pp. 261–2); *Political Register*, 4 Dec. 1830; *Cobbett's Lectures on the French Revolution and English Boroughmongering*, nos. 1, 3, delivered at the Rotunda 1830. Cobbett's deep hostility to emancipation was temporarily to waver in 1832 when he belatedly realized that the West Indian planters occupied the rotten boroughs by which English slavery was maintained. 'The fruit of the labour of these slaves abroad has long been converted into the means of making us slaves at home'. *Political Register*, 4 Aug. 1832.

11 For the background to the factory movement, see C. Driver, *Richard Oastler* (1946); J. Ward, *The Factory Movement 1830–55* (1962).

12 For example, *The Destructive*, 13 April 1833; Sadler's speech at Fixby, *Leeds Intelligencer*, 30 Aug. 1832.

13 See W. Dodd, *Experience and Sufferings*, reprinted in W. Dodd, *The Factory System Illustrated* (1969 edn.), p. 318; cf. Charles Wing, *Evils of the Factory System* (1837).

14 *Poor Man's Guardian*, 31 March 1832; *Gauntlet*, 20 Oct. 1833; R. Oastler, *Report of a Speech delivered at Preston*, 22 March 1833, p. 7; J. Wade, *The Black Book* (1832 edn.), p. 382.

15 *Hansard*, House of Commons, 9 May 1836, col. 761; (Ashley in his speech compared the hours worked by Negroes with those of factory children, *loc. cit.*, col. 747); see also R. Oastler, *Leeds Intelligencer*, 20 Oct. 1831, *British Labourer's Protector and Factory Child's Friend*, 5, 19 Oct. 1832.

16 L. Horner, *On the Employment of Children in Factories and Other Works* (1840); *Derbyshire Courier*, 28 April 1832.

17 *Speech of Mr Oates, at a Meeting at Ashton under Lyme*, 27 March 1832.

18 *The British Labourer's Protector and Factory Child's Friend*, 5, 19 Oct. 1832.

19 R. Oastler, *Facts and Plain Words* (1833), p. 16.

20 See NUWC debates, reported *Poor Man's Guardian*, 31 March 1832,

22 June 1833, 10 Aug. 1833, 17 Aug. 1833. See resolution from Blackburn, *Poor Man's Guardian*, 15 June 1833. For the background to the Unstamped press, see P. Hollis, *The Pauper Press* (1970). At its peak, the *Guardian* was selling some 16,000 copies an issue, far out-selling the Stamped orthodox press. *The Times* for example sold around 1000 copies an issue.

The NUWC had at its height some 86 London classes, and some 50 affiliated provincial unions. See I. Prothero, *Artisans and Politics in Nineteenth-Century London* (1979). *The Guardian* was its medium of communication.

21 *Poor Man's Guardian* 17 Nov. 1832. Compare O'Connell's comment, himself an ardent abolitionist, on an Irish issue: 'Oh! I wish we were blacks! If the Irish people were but black, we should have the honour-able member for Weymouth coming down as large as life, supported by all the "friends of humanity" in the back rows, to advocate their cause'. Quoted C. Buxton, *Memoirs of Sir Thomas Fowell Buxton* (1898), pp. 167–8.

22 *Poor Man's Guardian*, 2 March 1833.

23 R. Cruikshank illustrated, *The Condition of the West India Slave con-trasted with that of the Infant Slave in our English Factories* (1833).

24 *The Substance of a speech delivered at Leeds 23 Sept. 1830 by John Smithson, published at the request of a number of the Working Classes*.

25 *Poor Man's Guardian*, 17 Nov. 1832, 1 Dec. 1832.

26 B. O'Brien, *The Rise and Progress of Human Slavery; Poor Man's Guardian*, 1 Dec. 1832; *Destructive*, 8 June 1833.

27 *Poor Man's Guardian* 9 Aug. 1834; B. O'Brien, *The Rise and Progress of Human Slavery*, p. 94; *Voice of the West Riding*, 29 June 1833. See also *Gauntlet*, 9 June 1833. Many of O'Brien's points were later made by former Chartists, Dunning, Reynolds, J. R. Stephens, and the *Bee-hive* on the American Civil War. R. Harrison, *Before the Socialists* (1965), revises too simplistic an identification of English working men with the American North. Older working-class leaders and journalists who regarded the industrial capitalist rather than the aristocrat as the main enemy were more likely to favour the Confederacy. And these were mainly former Chartists, Owenites, and Tory democrats like Stephens, who could not forgive the Manchester school for the New Poor Law, their opposition to factory reform and to Chartism. (Harri-son, *Before the Socialists*, pp. 55–6.) Compare M. Ellison, *Support for Secession, Lancashire and the American Civil War* (1972).

28 *Destructive*, 18 May 1833.

29 *Poor Man's Guardian*, 8 Dec. 1832.

30 *Poor Man's Guardian*, 15 June 1833, 9 Aug. 1834, 22 June 1833; *Gauntlet*, 20 Oct. 1833; see also *Crisis*, 10 Aug. 1833.

31 *Poor Man's Guardian*, 15 June 1833; O'Brien, *Rise and Progress of Human Slavery*, p. 96. Compare Richard Carlile's remarks on the clergy: 'The Priests are as much a political body as a standing army, the former are kept up to keep your mind in awe, the latter your body . . .' *Republican*, 22 Feb. 1822.

32 *Poor Man's Guardian*, 15 June 1833.

33 *Figaro in London*, 8 Sept. 1832; A. Ure, *Philosophy of Manufacturers* (1835), pp. 417–18; R. Cobden, *Hansard*, House of Commons, 27 February 1846.

34 For a general account of the development of philanthropy in the period, see D. Owen, *English Philanthropy* (1965).

35 *Black Dwarf*, 20 August 1817; T. Chalmers, *Evidence to the Select Committee on the State of the Poor in Ireland* (1830), qu. 3584; and more generally, Rev. W. Hanna, *Memoirs of the Life and Writings of Thomas Chalmers* (1850).

36 W. Allen, 'A review of Highmore's Pietas Londonensis', *Philanthropist*, III (1812), p. 4.

37 W. Allen, *The Society for the Improvement of the Condition of Factory Children, 1832*.

38 H. Martineau, *Tale of Demerara, Illustrations of Political Economy* (1832), p. 101. Harriet Martineau noted in her *History of the Thirty Years Peace* (1877), 3, p. 15 'The British peasant thought affectionately of the black brethren whom he, as a freeman and a tax-payer, had helped to release from bondage'.
   More generally on the activity of the SDUK, see R. K. Webb, *The British Working Class Reader* (1965).

39 J. Conder, *Wages or the Whip*, 1833; *Poor Man's Guardian*, 7 April 1832; *Destructive*, 7 June 1834.

40 J. J. Gurney, *Brief Remarks on the Sabbath* (1831), p. 89, 101.

41 Buckingham, *Hansard*, House of Commons, 7 June 1833, col. 473; Buxton, 30 May 1833, col. 162; Suffield, House of Lords, 4 June 1833, col. 356.

42 O'Connell, *Hansard*, House of Commons, 30 May 1833, col. 315; J. J. Gurney, *Substance of a Speech Delivered at a public meeting on the Subject of British Colonial Slavery* (1824), p. 21; Conder, *Wages or the Whip*, p. 90.

43 Torrens, *Hansard*, House of Commons, 25 July 1833, col. 1263–6.

44 Slaney, *Hansard*, House of Commons, 10 June 1833, col. 533; Peel, House of Commons, 30 May 1833, col. 341f. O'Brien devoted an outraged editorial to Peel's speech in *Destructive*, 8 June 1833.

45 Stanley, *Hansard*, House of Commons, 14 May 1833, col. 1216; Althorp, 10 June 1833, col. 543; *Companion to the Newspaper*, 5, June 1833.

46 *Hansard*, House of Commons, 25 March 1833, col. 998.

47 Oastler, *Speech at Preston*, p. 6; J. R. Stephens, reported *Northern Star*, 10 Nov. 1838.

48 'Abolition of the slave trade and slavery', *Edinburgh Review*, Oct. 1824; J. J. Gurney, *Substance of a Speech* (1824). The Anti-Slavery Society of 1823 virtually developed out of the campaign to reform prison discipline; Lord Suffield, Dr Lushington and Buxton himself were among its leading members.

49 *Poor Man's Guardian*, 8 June 1833; O'Brien, *Rise and Progress of Human Slavery*, p. 100.

50 *Norfolk Chronicle*, 21 Nov. 1840; *Northern Star*, 28 Nov. 1840. For Norwich Chartism more generally, see J. K. Edwards, 'Chartism in Norwich', *Yorkshire Bulletin of Economics and Social Research*,

November 1967. The previous year, Norwich Chartists had packed the city churches and insisted on sermons preached on the text: 'Go to now, ye rich men, weep and howl for your miseries that shall come upon you . . .' *James*, 5, i.

Part Four
CULTURAL IMPLICATIONS

15
LITERARY SOURCES AND THE REVOLUTION IN BRITISH ATTITUDES TO SLAVERY

by C. Duncan Rice

During the century between the Seven Years' War and the American Civil War, a complete revolution in Western attitudes opened the way to the downfall of slavery. Moses Finley has observed that 'throughout most of human history, labour for others has been performed in large part under conditions of bondage.'[1] Adam Smith would have agreed. When he discussed it with his 1762–3 jurisprudence class, most Europeans still took slavery for granted. He concluded that it was 'almost impossible that it should ever be totally or generally abolished. In a republican government, it will scarcely ever happen that it should be abolished.'[2] Yet at the beginning of the American war between the states, the Confederate diarist Mary Boykin Chesnut, who was habitually acid about modernity, wrote casually that 'we are human beings of the nineteenth century and slavery has to go, of course.'[3] In the trivial space of a hundred years – perhaps sixty in the British case – slavery had passed from being a given factor on the social landscape, to being incompatible with the beliefs of thinking men and women in the Atlantic community. Disapproval of slavery ultimately became the kind of cultural assumption which requires no evidential support, with something of the reflexive force of the taboo against incest. In this paper I suggest that systematic use of literary sources would help chart the process by which assumptions on slavery were inverted.

We would be closer to understanding this sudden change if Roger Anstey had completed his work. He did not allow the contemporary fascination with social change, with the dynamic, to narrow his focus to the abolitionists who went to the barricades over slavery, or to the sources they left behind them. He was able to think in the wider context of shifting cultural attitudes precisely because his ideal was to draw on the entire written record of the period.[4] Yet so much remains to be done. Anstey himself had just begun to consider the crisis of ideological authority precipitated by the Bible's failure to solve the problem of slavery, to assess the significance of changing views on redemption and the atonement, and to explore the theological matrix of anti-slavery thought.[5] Several other approaches are still untried. Even British magazine sources remain unexplored, and we have no full study of incidental newspaper references to slavery and abolition. Except where sermon titles actually mention slavery, the literature of the pulpit, arguably the richest resource of all, is wholly unexploited. No-one has collated direct and indirect references in works in the curricula of British universities; nor has this been done for surviving files of lecture notes on moral philosophy, classics, and law, except in special cases like Smith's. There must also be references to slavery in materials used in primary and secondary schools, and indeed in children's fiction and periodicals, where Americanists have made a useful beginning.[6] Such sources speak more plausibly about what the culture took for granted concerning slavery at any given time, than reform writing deliberately aimed at the future.

The same is true of literary material. I do not mean by this that we need a more exhaustive analysis of poetry and fiction produced for specifically anti-slavery purposes. Anti-slavery literature in itself reveals nothing more than the standpoint of the pressure group that produced it. It must be clearly distinguished from references to slavery in works written for other purposes. This distinction is ignored in the two works which have examined the British literary response to slavery, and both are flawed in other respects. Eva Beatrice Dykes' *The Negro in English Romantic Thought* is at worst a compilation, at best an attempt to use the African to illuminate the romantic imagination. Wylie Sypher's *Guinea's Captive Kings* is concerned less with views on slavery than with the way in which sensibility changed British attitudes to the Negro, to primitivism, and to savagery.[7] It is worth remembering Wilberforce's dismissal of Sterne's 'delicate sensibility' as 'distinct from plain practical benevolence', and Coleridge's savage contrast between 'a false and bastard sensibility' and the benevolence which 'impels to action, and is accompanied by self-denial'.[8] However, compassion for the slave would certainly have been articulated more slowly without the cult of humane sensibility, which so dominated polite eighteenth-century letters. No scholar thought this theme more important than Roger Anstey.[9] The difficulty in assessing its influence accurately is that the texts which speak most expressively to the new frame of mind do not mention slavery. It is a more modest enterprise, though still a daunting one, to set about gathering and identifying the casual references to slavery, brief and less brief, which are scattered through the body of eighteenth and nineteenth century literature – in the novel, in poetry, and in the polite essay.

This material can be most illuminating. Nonetheless, there are serious problems about using it, and indeed about using imaginative literature to explore any historical problem. David Davis' experimental *Homicide in American Fiction* is in some respects a model of the way in which the assumptions and associations of the novelist enrich our understanding of a changing matrix of values[10] – but Davis has the advantage that violence and/or death have intimate imaginative possibilities which have made them central to practically all Western literature. References to slavery are sparser, and usually tangential to the texts in which they are embedded. I have already mentioned the problem of isolating propaganda from references representing assumptions held commonly by the writer and his public. In the eighteenth century, there are also passages on slavery which are really inserted as intellectual set pieces, for instance in Hector McNeill's obscure novel on Guadeloupe, or in Henry Mackenzie's *Julia de Roubigné*, where the hero describes his scheme of slave management by humane incentive.[11] However, Edinburgh intellectuals were busily discussing such plans in the abstract at this time, and Mackenzie actually wrote *Julia* when he was actively co-operating with government attempts to block abolition of the slave trade.[12] The Negro must be the only victim of oppression who does not plead explicitly for sentimental tears in his earlier *Man of Feeling*. Yet it is usually easy to tell when an author's comment on slavery is nothing more than an intellectual's debating exercise. Twenty year's later, when Mackenzie's friend Sir Walter Scott used forced dancing on slave ships as a metaphor to demonstrate that oppression increases enthusiasm for liberty, there is no mistaking his assumption that readers of goodwill would share his views.[13]

Some of the problems are more apparent than real. It is not always easy to detect the use of anachronistic examples[14] – but this hazard is not confined to fiction, and in any case the material is not intended to yield hard factual evidence. Finally, there is the temptation to assume that even famous texts were more influential than they were. For instance, it has often been said that Turner's superb 'Slavers Throwing Overboard the Dead and Dying – Typhoon Coming On' was inspired by line 980 (and following) of 'Summer' in Thomson's *Seasons*.[15] There is really no evidence for this view. It is as likely that the painting was a response to the atrocity stories based on the *Zong* case – more anachronisms – which were circulating in London before and during the World's Anti-Slavery Convention of 1840.

Casual literary references are valuable in spite of their difficulties, and in spite of their incapacity to yield substantive conclusions. Every author, consciously or subconsciously, writes for many audiences. No one has yet developed a satisfactory conceptual apparatus for distinguishing between them. What I am interested in here is the evidence which can be drawn from the writer's relationship with what Peter Rabinowitz has called the 'authorial audience'. As he puts it, 'the author of a novel designs his work rhetorically for a specific hypothetical audience. Like a philosopher, historian, a journalist, he cannot write without making certain assumptions about his readers' beliefs, knowledge, and familiarity with conventions'.[16] I believe that comment on slavery and abolition presented incidentally and without expectation of a hostile response, should help us plot the stages by which the assumptions of the reading public changed. What follows are some examples of the insights such allusions can provide. I must stress that I present them as methodological illustration rather than as a research contribution, for I have come upon them serendipitously in other reading, mostly in the novel. All the examples are British, most are fairly well known, and none is written about slavery and abolition for its own sake. They vary widely in the class and range of readership they must have reached. Although the period was one of unprecedented advance in literacy, none of my illustrations could have had a mass readership in the modern sense. The first are drawn from Defoe, for whom abolition would have been a piece of windmill-tilting; the last comes from Dickens, upon whom abolitionists had begun to pall. Collectively they suggest that a more systematic survey of such material would make a useful contribution to our understanding of the shift in attitudes to slavery.

Defoe's fiction suggests a reading public which, while it could feel occasional sympathy for the slave, even accept his anxiety to become free, still had no doubts about the morality of slavery itself. It is entirely consistent with his polemical work. The much quoted passage from *The Reformation of Manners* (1702) is not 'truly humanitarian', but exactly what its subtitle says – 'a Satyr', a nonconformist's satire which construes the total behaviour of its objects as religious declension. Throughout his economic writings, Defoe takes slavery for granted. *An Essay on the Trade to Africa* (1711) makes a contribution to the African Company controversy without once mentioning blacks or the slave trade. *A Plan of English Commerce* (1728) argues for the colonization of West Africa to produce tropical staples, by using slaves locally rather than carrying them across the Atlantic.[17] The assumption of the novels is also that there is no question about the morality of slavery as such. However, it can only be moral and therefore profitable if it is used, and if its victims are managed, on the same principles which providentially govern all human economic behaviour.[18] Even in *Captain Singleton* (1720), the mutineers control the slaves they have taken in war through a system of incentives administered by their Prince. Once they complete the crossing of the African continent, they set him free and reward him with a pound and a half of gold dust drawn from the common stock.[19]

Defoe's preconceptions are clearer in the earlier *Robinson Crusoe* (1719). The whole book is a hymn of praise for the principle of ordered individual accumulation. Every one of Crusoe's misfortunes, including his shipwreck and exile, stems from going beyond conscientious profit-making into speculation. While attempting a second foolish voyage trading in West Africa for gold and slaves, he is captured by Moroccan rovers out of Sallee. He escapes from slavery by sea, with the help of Xury, a Moorish boy, and tries to reach the English settlements on the Senegal. When they go ashore for water, Xury offers to be eaten by the 'Wild mans' if this should be necessary for his master's escape. After they are rescued by a Brazilian Guineaman, Crusoe recognises Xury's loyalty by refusing to sell him to the Master as a slave. Instead he binds him over for ten years for sixty pieces of eight.[20]

When Crusoe is landed in Brazil, Xury's price becomes part of the capital with which he sets up an Ingenio or sugar plantation. He begins to prosper and simultaneously to feel deep discontent. He is 'coming into the very Middle Station, or upper degree of low life', the prosaic condition he originally left his home in Yorkshire to escape. Things go even better once he begins to buy slaves, but he cannot resist the gambler's madness which is eventually going to plunge him 'into the deepest Gulph of human misery that ever Man fell into.'[21] Hearing of his Guinea experience, his merchant friends persuade him to go off to gather slaves for smuggling into Brazil. He is tempted by being offered a cut of the profits without having to contribute capital. The result is his shipwreck on an island off the coast of Trinidad, where he remains for a period which significantly coincides with the years from the Restoration of 1660 to the Glorious Revolution of 1688. When he is rescued and returns to Britain, he finds that his trustees have kept his plantation ticking over steadily. It has expanded according to the benign principles of economic growth, and he can retire as a very rich man in the new community created by the Revolution. The general message is clear: slavery is normative, an acceptable weapon in the process of capitalist accumulation. On the other hand, its relationships may be slightly modified by human bonds, and it is not in any way exempted from the normal dangers of irrational economic behaviour.[22]

Defoe makes the same points, though in a modified form, in *Colonel Jack* (1722). It is the story of a poor outcast from the London slums, and his lifelong search for gentility. It projects Defoe's own desperate anxiety over economic and social insecurity in much the same way as *Crusoe*. Jack is in turn pickpocket, highwayman, and soldier, but his first successful venture only begins when he is kidnapped and shipped illegally to Virginia as an indentured servant, or, as he and Defoe's readers would have seen it, as a slave. He becomes his owner's overseer, and revolutionizes the management of his plantation by treating the slaves kindly. The owner is sufficiently impressed to free Jack and set him up in a plantation of his own, which also prospers greatly. His story includes a lengthy digression on the incentives needed to use slave labour most profitably.[23] This is not in any sense a criticism of slavery. Defoe's plantations, like Crusoe's kingdom, are 'islands of ideal social order.'[24] Though it has peculiar economic advantages, slave labour must be managed according to normative economic principles.

Like Crusoe, and indeed the real-life Defoe, Jack's fatal weakness is that he cannot resist accelerating the normal course of economic events. He cannot escape the gnawing awareness that he has not become a gentleman – though his failing is not that he is a slaveholder, but that he is a provincial:

> I looked upon myself as buried alive in a remote part of the world . . . and, in a word, the old reproach often came in my way, that even this was not yet the life of a gentleman.
>
> It is true that this was much nearer to it than that of a pickpocket, and still nearer than that of a sold slave; but, in short, this would not do, and I could receive no satisfaction in it.[25]

Jack leaves when things are going well, is taken by a French privateer, and ransomed to London. He gets married, flees from his wife and her relations, enters an Irish regiment in France, and ultimately joins the Old Pretender's abortive expedition of 1708. He escapes to Virginia, to find in spite of everything that his plantation has continued to expand and prosper under a faithful overseer. After various other reverses, he makes a second fortune in the contraband trade to Spanish Florida. In the end he returns to London to retire on the steady income to which his earlier self-discipline has entitled him.

Defoe and his readers still took the place of slavery in the process of accumulation completely for granted. Jack's and Crusoe's plantations are the one stable force in their mature lives. But the beneficiaries of slavery are not in any sense safe from the dangers of their own irresponsibilities. Moreover, Defoe takes great pains to stress that labour relationships with black slaves should be governed by the same humane principles as those with free and half-free whites. What this amounts to is an attempt to bring slavery into consistency with eighteenth-century assumptions about social justice and the work ethic.

This consistency was too contrived to survive. In the following decades it gradually broke down as sentimental concern for the Negro heightened, as intensified religious anxieties produced a more acute understanding of the plight of the slave, and as growing concern over moral self-control made the passionate world of the slaveholder seem more and more threatening. More fundamentally, the assumptions made by Defoe's generation became less tenable as the humanity of the Negro – which Defoe himself had not denied – came to be accepted all but universally. No passage is so revealing in this respect as the description of the Negro girl in Book IX of *Tristram Shandy* (1767), sitting in the window of a sausage shop: 'a poor negro girl, with a bunch of white feathers slightly tied to the end of a long cane, flapping away flies – not killing them – 'Tis a pretty picture! said my uncle *Toby* – she had suffered persecution, *Trim*, and had learnt mercy –'.[26] They conclude that 'it would be putting one sadly over the head of another' for God to give a soul to them and not to the Negro. Even in the infatuated world of Uncle Toby and Corporal Trim, there is no cavil about black humanity, no question about extending the balm of Shandean sentiment to black people. *Tristram Shandy* is the most important and widely read novel of the century, the most representative of contemporary hopes and anxieties which it both articulated and reinforced. The haunting image of the girl in the window speaks tellingly for polite society's changed image of the Negro. The sentimental revolution against slavery was complete by the 1760s, as indeed was the theoretical argument against it.

These victories raised the problem of what to do about an institution which was generally discountenanced, but which appeared to be immovable. A common response was to take refuge in the assumption that slavery, though undesirable, was an irremediable human affliction analagous to plague, war, disease, and famine. Clearly this was not a response the early abolitionists found acceptable, and we have paid too little attention to it, but is one common at certain stages of most reform movements. It is well expressed in *Jonathan Corncob*, an extraordinary anonymous novel published in 1788. Although Sypher discusses it briefly, he does not mention that it is a clever parody of *Candide*, in spite of some conventions drawn from Sterne's *Sentimental Journey*.[27]

Jonathan Corncob is an American *picaro*, whose adventures are set in the revolutionary period. Like Candide, he and all those for whom he cares become the victims of an incomprehensible world which offers nothing constant but its hostility. Jonathan is imprisoned by the revolutionaries, flogged by the British Navy, and put in irons by a US privateer. Even the cartel ship which is to release him is shipwrecked. His legs are scalded in a classically pointless tavern brawl, and he catches syphilis from his landlady's daughter. His Puritan father is practically beaten to death as a loyalist. His Cunégonde, who rejoices in the name of Desire Slawbuck, begins adult life by losing her teeth due to a pathological love of molasses. She is seduced, kidnapped, made a beast of burden by a Hessian, ravished, and imprisoned. She loses her breast to the teeth of a revolutionary's dog. Jonathan and his friends live in a demented and sadistic world, where the only road to sanity is a nihilistic apathy towards evil. The book closes with his resolution that the only worthwhile human activity is the reading of novels. Even Voltaire's 'We must go and work in the garden' has become optimistic.

This uncontrollable world reduces slavery to one among the host of agencies which arbitrarily promote human suffering. Jonathan is exposed to it when his adventures carry him to Barbados. An old woman dying in a ditch takes the place of the maimed Negro in *Candide*. Although Jonathan profits from his host's provision of a mulatto woman for him, he gradually moves from a sadness that so hospitable a society should be subject to hurricanes, to a conviction that its corruption calls for them as a providential judgement. The Barbados sequence closes hilariously and bitterly when the hurricane does strike, but the hurricane itself takes on the same quality of arbitrary destructiveness as the Lisbon earthquake which is its counterpart in *Candide*. Jonathan records its casualties from local reports as a grim comment on slavery:[28]

Men, women, and children, buried beneath the ruins of buildings		527
Drowned		134
	Total	661
Loss of black cattle:		
Oxen lost by different casualties		745
Which, with 4273 head of negroes		4273
	Makes the amount	5018

The slaves become victims of the same holocaust as their oppressors.

The revulsion against slavery gathered force too quickly for this kind of nihilism to become intellectually entrenched. By 1816, Jane Austen could assume enough of a consensus against the slave trade to use it to attract attention to the plight of governesses.[29] Faulty views on slavery were soon being used as a literary shorthand for being ethically behind the times. In *The Last of the Lairds* (1826), one of Galt's signals of Malachi Mailings of Auldbiggings' moral opacity is his failure to see that being a slave was worse than being a schoolboy – 'a whip has but ae scourge, our schoolmaister's tawse had seven', which Dominie Skelp applied not to the insensitive back but to a more tender part 'that for manners shall be nameless'.[30] The same happens in *St Ronan's Well* (1832), where Scott presents the gulf between barbarism and modernity at its crudest. Captain MacTurk, his down-at-heel highland ruffian, is unable to comprehend that African and American Negroes do not have his own archaic attitude to the code of the duel. Faced with this moral paradox, he fumes at being compared to 'a parcel of black heathen bodies . . . that were never in the inner side of a kirk while they lived, but go about worshipping stocks and stones, and swinging themselves upon bamboos, like beasts as they are.'[31]

Another sign of the change was the deteriorating stereotype of the planter. At the end of the eighteenth century, he was appearing on the provincial stage as a comedy villain. In Archibald McLaren's *The Negro Slaves* and *A Wife to be Sold*, for instance, Captain

Raccoon is the embodiment of spite, ignorance, and cowardice.
Even his lovemaking is doltish:

> Raccoon   I wou'd die to please you.
> Lucy   That's the very favour we were going to ask you. Here's a
>   pistol: kill yourself – You cannot conceive how much it would
>   oblige my mistress.[32]

It is difficult to imagine McLaren's stereotype worsening, but it did
become more subtle. One of the rare lapses in Scott's brilliant *Bride
of Lammermoor* came when he cast around for a metaphor to
express old Lady Ashton's firmness in refusing the Master of
Revensweed's suit for Lucy Ashton. He came up most infelicitously
with a boarding school mistress spurning 'a half-pay Irish officer,
beseeching permission to wait upon the heiress of a West Indian
planter.'[33] In the 1840s, Tucker's *Ralph Rashleigh* (not published
until eighty years after it was written) describes Australian convict
life, often uses trade propaganda imagery to attack the penal system, and has one of the hero's underworld associates pass himself
off as a planter. The transition from successful fence to wealthy
West Indian would not be a socially difficult one.[34] Even as late as
Thackeray's *Vanity Fair*, when old assumptions might have been
weakening, Becky Sharp's most pampered schoolfellow is a West
Indian heiress.[35] To be a planter, or even to have planting wealth,
was to be vulgar and flashy, on the fringes of polite society.

When Scott published *The Heart of Midlothian*, thirty years after
Jonathan Corncob, it was no longer pointless to kick against the
pricks of slavery. The Haitian revolution had come and gone, and
the British slave trade had been abolished. Scott's villain was
George Stanton, the seducer of his heroine Effie Deans. He was a
West Indian, by then a useful shorthand for depravity. Scott needed
no elaborate description to demonstrate that he had been corrupted
by his upbringing in slave society. He had grown up 'in the society of
Negro slaves, whose study it was to glorify his every wish . . . and as
the young men of his own rank would not endure the purse proud
insolence of the Creole, he fell into that taste for low society' which
led to his ruin.[36] Apart from debauching Effie Deans, it transpires
that he was the murderer of Captain Porteous in the great Edinburgh riot of 1736.

Even more revealingly, the book closes with a complex salvation/
enslavement metaphor which is lost on modern readers, but which
Scott clearly assumed his public would pick up at once. Stanton is
himself enslaved to sin by his upbringing, and Effie's child is the

corrupt fruit of their sinful union. When the baby disappears, she only escapes hanging for infanticide after her sister Jeanie goes to London to intercede with the Duke of Argyll and the Queen. Eventually Effie marries Stanton. Their son reappears in Argyll at the end of the novel. It transpires that he has been sold as a boy to one Dunacha dhu na Dunaigh, whose name incidentally translates as Black Duncan the Naughty, and who is an operator in the trade in white slaves from the Highlands to Virginia. The boy has become a young outlaw nicknamed 'the Whistler'. The intricacies of the plot allow him to kill his father George Stanton, at which point he is captured by the authorities. He is released by his aunt, Effie's sister Jeanie Deans, who has throughout been the redemptive figure determined to save her sister from enslavement to sin and its consequences. She does save the Whistler from prison, but he is subsequently kidnapped and sent to the colonies as a slave anyway. We are told that he escapes to live among the Indians, 'with whom his previous habits had well suited him to associate.'[37]

The paradigm is that the original father is enslaved to sin by his contact with chattel slavery, and subsequently reduces those close to him to his own condition of moral bondage. His son rejects Jeanie Dean's guidance towards salvation and liberty, and is reduced to the same physical slavery which began the cycle. Jeanie Deans fails to redeem either father or son, and her success with her sister is problematic. However, her virtuous, ordered life, and the progressive society she represents, are contrapuntal to the aberrations both of slavery and sinfulness.

After West India emancipation, the British public soon reached the stage where it was no longer necessary to think out or justify an anti-slavery standpoint. Abolition had become the one harmless reform cause, an anodyne commitment which carried no ideological risk. In Disraeli's *Sybil*, when things are going badly for the prime minister, his agent Tadpole ruminates that he should 'make some kind of a religious move . . . if we could get him to speak at Exeter Hall, were it only a slavery meeting, that would do.[38] Anti-slavery views seldom had to be articulated, except when writing for American audiences, or to raise support for American abolitionists. However, the slave could still be a useful weapon in argument. For instance, W. E. Aytoun, the compiler of the nostalgic *Lays of the Cavaliers*, had a substantial American sale, especially in the South. When he found that authors like Dickens and himself could not collect American royalties, he was quick to denounce slaveholders, in the certain knowledge that this would strike a sympathetic chord among his British public. His 'Apostrophe to Boz' trotted out the usual catalogue of anti-Americanisms, including the threat that half an hour's conversation with Judge Lynch would make you

> . . . understand more clearly that you ever did before
> Why an independent patriot freely spits upon the floor,
> Why he sneers at the old country with republican disdain,
> And, unheedful of the negro's cry, still tighter draws the chain.[39]

Slavery had become another means of defining what Britons were proud not to be.

By the fifties, every British writer could assume an anti-slavery consensus. When Mrs Craik wanted to dramatize the death of her hero and heroine in *John Halifax, Gentleman* (1856), an influential work on social mobility, she used one simple expedient. John died after thirty-three years of marriage, followed immediately by his wife Ursula.[40] This was not an arbitrary number of years. For Mrs Craik's readers, thirty-three had a triple symbolic force. It was the age at which Christ died, as well as the date of the West India Emancipation Act, and thus a number which triggered the three charges of atonement, redemption, and liberation. For mid-Victorians, the anti-slavery position had become a reflexive part of their belief system.

On the other hand, the case of Dickens demonstrates that disapproval of slavery did not necessarily mean enthusiasm for continued abolitionist efforts. We know too little about romantic racism in Britain, and particularly about its relationship to romantic nationalism. However, it is clear that the 1850s saw the image of the Negro become cheapened, and the active abolitionist impulse weaken, in part as a factor of the emotive forms of anti-slavery enthusiasm stirred up by Harriet Beecher Stowe's visits.[41] At the same time, though the consensus of opposition to slavery was left largely undisturbed, Carlyle's *Nigger Question* (1849) signalized the emergence of a new and particularly ugly form of racism. It is not helpful to dismiss Carlyle and others like him as 'pigmies, enmeshed helplessly in the prejudiced sloughs of their own bias.'[42] His thought was the logical product of his Calvinist attitude to work, combined with a particular romantic perception of ethnicity, and a genuine sense of the urgency of domestic social issues. Dickens' famous passage in *Bleak House* is also symptomatic of a sharp change in British attitudes to helping the Negro, but it is significant that it does not imply the slightest approval of slavery. It is entirely consistent with his lifelong distrust of Exeter Hall philanthropy, and his anxiety that foreign good causes would divert attention from pressing domestic problems. Even in 1853, it did not go without bitter abolitionist criticism.[43] However, the significance of the Mrs Jellyby episode is not that it was new for Dickens, but that the changed atmosphere of the decade made it acceptable for a respectable middle-class novelist to deride abolitionists in a way which would have been unthinkable in the 1830s or even the early 1840s.

Dickens had always had mixed feelings about the moral vision of the abolitionists. Even in *Pickwick* (1836), where his social views are still in flux, there is a well-known comment on the inconsistency between the interest of the Muggletonians in the slave trade and their staunch opposition to all factory reform.[44] Incidentally, this was precisely the opposite of Coleridge's contempt of forty years before, for reformers who felt able to ignore the slave trade 'provided the dunghill be not before their parlour window.'[45] It often seems that reformers cannot win. Dickens also anticipated the Mrs Jellyby passage in 1848, in a review of William Allen's account of the disastrous Niger expedition. It was a persuasive exposure of philanthropic incomprehension of West African realities, and a denunciation of Buxton's fantasy of civilizing Africa while so much remained to be done at home. 'Such schemes are useless, futile, and we will venture to add – in despite of hats broad-brimmed or shovel-shaped, and coats of drab or black, with collars or without – wicked.'[46] The animus behind his attack was anti-abolitionist rather than pro-slavery.

The same is true of the 'Telescopic Philanthropy' chapter in *Bleak House*. Mrs Jellyby is obsessed with schemes for the improvement of the natives in Borrioboola-Gha, on the left bank of the Niger. Her squalid household, a pandemonium of unkempt children, slatternly servants, and smoking fires, is a paradigm of the withering evils which have escaped her attention at home. Though Mrs Jellyby believed that the domestic poor could be colonized on the Niger, where it was hoped they would teach the natives to turn pianoforte legs, her fine eyes had 'a curious habit of seeming to look a long way off. As if . . . they could see nothing nearer than Africa!'[47] The chapter is devastating, but it is remarkable less for its content than for what it reveals about Dickens and his British public. Neither had the slightest doubt about the iniquity of slavery. Even Susan Nipper, in *Dombey and Son*, thought that to be 'a black slave and a mulotter' was the lowest and hardest of all lots.[48] But both were coming to the conclusion that the time had come to call it a day on anti-slavery until more immediate problems were solved.

332   C. Duncan Rice

Literary references of the sort I have mentioned give a wider perspective on attitudes to slavery, a sharper sense of what was changing outside the circle of active commitment. My examples are not much more than throwaway lines. But it is precisely because of their casual quality that they and others like them give a sense of when it was and was not acceptable to write certain things about slavery, and where and when certain standpoints could be taken for granted. What amounts to a cultural revolution cannot be understood without using the evidence, however indirect, which is embedded in that culture's literature.

Notes

1 'Slavery', *International Encyclopedia of Social Science*, D. L. Sills (ed.), (New York, 1968), XIV, p. 308; 'A peculiar institution?', *Times Literary Supplement*, 2 July 1976, pp. 819–21.
2 Adam Smith, *Lectures on Jurisprudence* (ed.) R. L. Meek, D. D. Raphael, and P. G. Stein (Oxford, 1978), p. 181.
3 M. B. Chesnut, *A Diary from Dixie* (ed.) B. A. Williams (Boston, 1949), p. 164.
4 Roger Anstey, *The Atlantic Slave Trade and British Abolition, 1760–1810* (1975), pp. 91–153.
5 Anstey, *Atlantic Slave Trade*, pp. 126–41, 184–99; Anstey, 'Reflections on the Lordship of Christ in history', *Christian*, III (1975), 69–80.
6 J. C. Crandall, 'Patriotism and humanitarian reform in children's literature', *American Quarterly*, XXI (1969), 3–22.
7 E. B. Dykes, *The Negro in English Romantic Thought* (Washington, 1942); W. Sypher, *Guinea's Captive Kings, British Anti-Slavery Literature of the Eighteenth Century* (Chapel Hill, 1942).
8 W. Wilberforce, *A Practical View of the Prevailing Religious System of Professed Christians in the Higher and Middle Classes of Society, Contrasted with Real Christianity* (1797; reprinted New York, 1856), p. 272n.; S. T. Coleridge, *The Watchman* (ed. L. Patton), *Collected Works*, II (Princeton, 1970), p. 139.
9 Anstey, *Atlantic Slave Trade*, pp. 145–8.
10 D. B. Davis, *Homicide in American Fiction, 1798–1860* (Ithaca, 1957).
11 H. McNeill, *Memoirs . . . of the Late Charles Macpherson* (Edinburgh, 1800), pp. 124ff.; H. Mackenzie, *Julia de Roubigné. A Tale* (1797), reprinted in *The British Novelists*, XXIX, 208–14.
12 H. W. Thompson, *A Scottish Man of Feeling* (1931), pp. 150–1, 262.
13 *Old Mortality* (ed.) Angus Calder (1816; Penguin edn., 1975), pp. 70–1.
14 H. House, *The Dickens World* (1941), pp. 29–30.
15 C. B. Tinker, *Painter and Poet. Studies in the Literary Relations of English Painting* (Cambridge, Mass., 1938), pp. 149–52; A. D. McKillop, *The Background of Thomson's Seasons* (Minneapolis, 1942), p. 165; D. B. Davis, *Problem of Slavery in Western Culture*, p. 353.

16 P. J. Rabinowitz, 'Truth in fiction: a re-examination of audiences', *Critical Inquiry*, IV (1977), 126.

17 Cf. Sypher, *Guinea's Captive Kings*, pp. 158–9; [D. Defoe], *An Essay upon the Trade to Africa, in Order to Set the Merits of that Cause in a True Light and Bring the Dispute between the African Company and the Separate Traders into a Narrower Compass* (1711); D. Defoe, *A Plan of English Commerce, being a Compleat Prospect of the Trade of this Nation, as well the Home Trade as the Foreign* (2nd edn., 1730), pp. 333–4.

18 On the economic views expressed in the novels, see M. E. Novak, *Economics and the Fiction of Daniel Defoe* (1962: reprinted New York, 1976).

19 *The Life, Adventures and Piracies of the Famous Captain Singleton* (1720; Everyman edn., 1963), p. 167.

20 *Robinson Crusoe* (1719; Norton Critical editions, ed. M. Shinagel, New York, 1975), pp. 17, 29.

21 *Ibid.*, pp. 30–2.

22 On Defoe and the problem of respectable mores, see M. Shinagel, *Daniel Defoe and Middle Class Gentility* (Cambridge, Mass., 1968).

23 Daniel Defoe, *The History and Remarkable Life of the Truly Honourable Colonel Jack* (1722; Folio Society edn., 1967), pp. 140–61.

24 M. Price, *To the Palace of Wisdom, Studies in Order and Energy from Dryden to Blake* (Carbondale, Ill., 1964), p. 274.

25 Defoe, *Colonel Jack*, p. 182.

26 L. Sterne, *The Life and Opinions of Tristram Shandy, Gentleman* (1759–67; Riverside edition, Boston, 1965), p. 466.

27 *Adventures of Jonathan Corncob, Loyal American Refugee* (1787), pp. 146–7; Sypher, *Guinea's Captive Kings*, pp. 278–80.

28 *Jonathan Corncob*, pp. 146–7.

29 *Emma* (1816; New English Library edn., 1964), p. 238.

30 J. Galt, *The Last of the Lairds* (1826, Blackwood's edn., 1896), p. 271.

31 W. Scott, *St Ronan's Well* (1832; A. & C. Black edn., Edinburgh, 1879), II, p. 277.

32 A. McLaren, *The Negro Slaves . . . being the Original of the Blackman and the Blackbird* (1799); *A Wife to be Sold, or, Who Bids Most? A Musical Farce. To which is Added the Slaves, A Dramatic Piece* (1807), p. 23.

33 (1819; Macmillan edn., 1908), p. 342.

34 J. Tucker, *Ralph Rashleigh*, ed. C. Roderick (1929; Folio Society edn., 1977), p. 60.

35 (1847–8; Nelson edn., 1901), p. 5.

36 (1816; Collins Classics edn., Glasgow, 1952), pp. 313–14.

37 *Ibid.*, pp. 458–9.

38 Quoted in I. Bradley, *The Call to Seriousness: The Evangelical Impact on the Victorians* (1976), p. 176.

39 W. E. Aytoun, *Stories and Verse*, (ed.) W. L. Renwick (Edinburgh, 1964), pp. 313–14.

40 D. M. Muloch [Mrs Craik], *John Halifax, Gentleman* (1856; Panther edn., 1972), pp. 461–2.

41 I have looked at this problem in some detail in my forthcoming *The*

Scots Abolitionists, 1833–61. For a brilliant analysis of the corresponding phenomenon in America, see G. Fredrickson, *The Black Image in the White Mind* (New York, 1971), pp. 97–130.

42 I. G. Jones, 'Trollope, Carlyle and Mill on the Negro: an episode in the history of ideas', *J.N.H.*, LII (1967), 185–99. Cf. I. Campbell, 'Carlyle and the Negro question again', *Criticism*, VIII (1971), 279–90; I. Campbell, *Thomas Carlyle* (1974), pp. 115–18.

43 Thomas, Lord Denman, *Uncle Tom's Cabin, Bleak House, Slavery and the Slave Trade* (1853), p. 5.

44 *The Posthumous Papers of the Pickwick Club* (1836; Penguin edn., 1972), p. 131.

45 Coleridge, *The Watchman*, p. 139.

46 F. G. Kitton (ed.), *To be Read at Dusk and other Stories, Sketches and Essays by Charles Dickens* (1898), p. 70. See also House, *The Dickens World*, pp. 86–91.

47 *Bleak House* (1852–3; Everyman edn., 1972), p. 34.

48 *Dombey and Son* (1848; Chapman & Hall edn. with Phiz illustrations, n.d.), p. 48.

16
ANTI-SLAVERY AS A FORM OF CULTURAL IMPERIALISM

by Howard Temperley

It is often noted that cultures tend to overrate their own ways of life and to underrate those of their neighbours. This is not, of course, a universal rule and there are many exceptions. Nevertheless, it is an observable fact that people tend to be not only attached to their own manner of doing things, a harmless example of the power of habit, but also to regard them as natural and better, and in extreme cases as standing proof of their own superior character and virtue. 'The morals of our people', wrote John Adams in 1774, comparing Bostonians and Philadelphians, 'are much better; their manners are more polite and agreeable; they are purer English; our language is better; our taste is better; our persons are handsomer; our spirit is greater, our laws are wiser, our religion is superior, and our education is better.'[1] Adams was being unusually forthright but such beliefs are of long standing in the Western tradition, and no doubt in other traditions too, and are, among other things, the source of much popular humour.

What is of concern in the present context, however, is not these feelings as such, but the fact that from them can arise moral imperatives requiring action. Needless to say, the two do not necessarily go together. For the most part the sort of judgements which members of one society make about the members of another require no sort of action at all. They are simply part of that largely unconscious process of cultural triangulation whereby individuals and societies locate themselves in relation to history and to the world about them. This is one, and indeed perhaps the principal, way in which cultures achieve a sense of their identity and purpose. It is, after all, often easier to define something in negative terms – as *not* being like something else – than in positive terms, particularly where the entity being defined is something as intangible as a culture. No doubt partly for this reason, many of the commonest responses associated with perceptions of cultural difference are defensive in character, and involve building barriers against outside influences. Only in certain exceptional circumstances, it would seem, do men feel called on to go out and actively proselytize on behalf of their own cultural beliefs.

Until relatively recent times, such examples of this phenomenon as Western history offered were mainly associated with the practice of the Christian religion and, in particular, with the assumption that Christian principles constituted a universal standard which it was incumbent upon all men to adopt. In support of this contention could be cited Christ's own injunction to his disciples to go out and preach the gospel among the heathen. To this extent, Europeans, as Christians, were under a specific obligation to proselytize on behalf of at least certain aspects of their culture; and since in practice it was by no means easy to distinguish those aspects from others – deriving, for example, from social organization or technological change – there was often a good deal of confusion about what exactly was being preached. Moreover, there was usually room too, particularly after the Reformation, for differences of opinion about whom it should be conveyed to, since ideas about Christian principles and practices differed widely as between one set of professing Christians and another. And since it was the universal practice for Europe's rulers to claim that they ruled their societies according to Christian principles, and indeed derived their authority from that very fact, there was a persistent tendency for Christian evangelism to become mixed up with the ordinary processes of politics.

A notable example of the way in which this operated was the habit of European explorers in the Age of Discovery, and for some time after, of defining Christianity in broadly cultural terms, referring to themselves as Christians and to the alien peoples they encountered as savages. Yet what enabled these explorers to feel superior to and, in practice, to dominate, these non-European societies had at least as much to do with technology and social organization as with theology. Of course, missionary activity played an important part in Western expansion; and in an ultimate sense no doubt Christianity had at least something to do with those developments which made the Age of Discovery possible. But few today would regard the settlement of the Americas or the conquest of Asia and Africa as specifically *Christian* achievements.

Although much has been made of such feelings of superiority in explaining the rise of modern slavery – the almost universal belief that hereditary servitude should be limited to persons of non-European stock, for instance, and the frequently stated view that bondage was an effective means of bringing about their conversion – they have less frequently been referred to in relation to its demise. Nevertheless, it is worth pointing out that there was at least some superficial resemblance between the anti-slavery struggle and religious conflicts of earlier times. To begin with, the anti-slavery cause is often referred to as a 'crusade'. This is a term which has been much debased, but as applied to the abolitionists it is not altogether inapposite. Abolitionists believed in active proselytizing, although it must be confessed that this proved more effective as a means of whipping up enthusiasm among potential supporters than among those whose actual behaviour they were intent on reforming. This too, however, was a characteristic not unknown in the struggles from which the metaphor was taken. Nor, for that matter, was the eagerness with which, when preaching failed, they used the arm of the state as their instrument. And, in the event, it usually was state intervention, backed up by the threat of force, and not infrequently by its actual use, that carried the day. Whatever else the anti-slavery struggles may or may not have been, they were an attempt by the advocates of one set of beliefs to impose their values – which embraced much more than simply the way labour was organised and remunerated – on the exponents of another.

This, of course, was not quite how the abolitionists themselves would have described the conflict. To them it was a matter of moral duty. Slavery, quite simply, was wrong. It was wrong because it violated specific biblical injunctions, because it brought suffering to its victims, and because its baneful presence perverted the normal workings of whatever social system contained it. On the other hand, the idea that what they were engaged in was essentially a religious struggle, was one with which they were entirely familiar. Indeed, as men brought up in the Christian tradition, who saw in what they took to be Christian principles the ultimate source of guidance in human affairs, it would have puzzled most of them to learn that it could be interpreted in any other way.

This attitude is well exemplified in Thomas Clarkson's *History of the Rise, Progress and Accomplishment of the Abolition of the African Slave Trade by the British Parliament* (1808) which is notable both as the first attempt to provide a comprehensive account of the origins of the movement and as an example of the way in which these developments could be interpreted in religious terms. According to Clarkson, what set the movement going had nothing to do with economics, politics, or events in the material world, or, for that matter, with a sudden change of heart among Christians generally, but was specifically traceable to the teachings of a handful of figures who, as it happened, were mostly also recognised as among the leading ministers of the day by the various sects to which they belonged. From this, he noted, could be inferred the 'great truth' that 'the abolition of the Slave-trade took its rise, not from persons who set up a cry for liberty . . . nor from persons who were led to it by ambition . . . but where it was most desirable, namely from the teachers of Christianity in those times'. And in an accompanying fold-out map he shows how, beginning as tiny springs and rivulets, each marked with the name of some prominent 'forerunner or coadjutor', the waters converged to become streams and rivers and, ultimately, 'the torrent which swept away the Slave-trade'. Most striking of all, perhaps, is his description of how, by a process of intellectual diffusion, this transformation was brought about:

> An individual, for example, begins; he communicates his sentiments to others. Thus, while alive, he enlightens; when dead, he leaves his works behind him. Thus, though departed, he yet speaks, and his influence is not lost. Of those enlightened by him, some become authors, and others actors in their turn. While living, they instruct, like their predecessors; when dead they speak also. Thus a number of dead persons are encouraging us in libraries, and a number of living are conversing and diffusing zeal among us at the same time.[2]

Thus baldly stated, Clarkson's account may strike the modern reader as singularly naïve. It is also, frankly elitist. It sees the impulse to abolish the trade, which, by implication, included within it a rejection of the institution of slavery itself, as being voiced first by leading thinkers whose ideas in due course percolated down and informed the body politic. Essentially, Clarkson's account was a model of the kind of historical explanation which attributes change to events occurring first in the realm of ideas, rather than in the march of events, and in his case in the ideas of identifiable individuals who, as often as not, were among the leading philosophers and theologians of their time.

At the other extreme, it may be pertinent here to note the work of Eric Williams whose *Capitalism and Slavery* (1944) presents the issue largely in terms of the interplay of economic interests. He does not, it is true, entirely discount the influence of ideas. The abolitionists were adept propagandists who raised anti-slavery sentiments 'almost to the status of a religion in England',[3] and thereby helped to win over the masses to their cause. Some, although by no means all, were genuine idealists. And, of course, the struggle may be charted in terms of arguments employed, often with extreme cunning, by the two sides. In this sense the conflict was far from mindless. But, at bottom, it was essentially a matter of imports and exports, of a declining plantocracy and a rising bourgeoisie, of one set of economic interests struggling against another – in short, of forces which, although not entirely impersonal, were beyond the power of any group, however clever or idealistic, to control.

It is perhaps also relevant to note that the tendency of more recent accounts of the movement has been to steer a middle course between these two views, although in David Brion Davis's two volumes, *The Problem of Slavery in Western Culture* (1966) and *The Problem of Slavery in the Age of Revolution 1770–1823* (1975) we have by far the most ambitious attempt of recent times, or, indeed, of any time, to place the movement within the context of the culture, or perhaps one should say cultures, which sponsored it. Particularly noteworthy is Davis's analysis of the attitudes of leading thinkers upon whose beliefs the question impinged. This, and his relating of the problem of slavery to issues of freedom and social discipline generally, has significantly altered the boundaries within which future discussions of the topic will be conducted. Plainly any extended account of recent developments in the field would need to deal with the many conflicting tendencies which he sees as operating within Western society and, in particular, with his use of the Gramscian concept of ideological hegemony as a means of drawing these together. But for the moment, all we can do is to note that from his account as it has been developed so far – at least one further volume is projected – no very clear overall picture emerges.

Since these efforts to arrive at a solution by means of intellectual and social analysis have proved so inconclusive it might be supposed that historians using an economic history approach might be able to throw light on the issue. And so, in a sense, they have, although not in such a way as to advance the argument significantly.

Following up the lines of investigation suggested by Eric Williams, they have found not only that Williams's own evidence fails to support his conclusions, but that when further evidence is collected it shows that the dominant economic interests in Britain, far from being impelled to weaken or destroy slavery, would have profited from strengthening and extending it. This has been the work of many hands, but most notably Seymour Drescher in *Econocide: British Slavery in the Era of Abolition* (1977) has turned Williams upside down (and offered a devastating critique of other major theories too) by showing that Britain's sugar colonies were in a healthy condition up to the time of the abolition of the slave trade in 1807, and that their subsequent decline was largely the *result* of humanitarian intervention.[4] Meanwhile, the application of econometric techniques to the study of ante-bellum slavery in the United States has provided additional evidence of the continuing vigour and economic viability of that institution.[5] The overall effect of taking economic measurements, therefore, has been to suggest that economics had little to do with the matter. Paradoxically, we seem further away from a solution now than we were a generation ago when it was generally assumed that slavery was economically regressive and that anyone with no better reason for disapproving of it would have been apt to oppose it on those grounds.

In sum, the negative findings of the economic analysts, combined with the enormous increase in knowledge concerning the scope, flexibility, long duration, and continuing viability of slavery, have emphasised the difficulties involved in explaining why it was that at a certain point of history men turned against it. Why was it not attacked earlier – or later? Why, indeed, was it attacked at all? To say that it was contrary to the precepts of much late-eighteenth and early-nineteenth century thinking is no real answer, for it begs the question as to why eighteenth and nineteenth century thinking was different from that of other periods. This is not to deny that ideas acquire a momentum of their own and that much can be learned by following the logic of their development. For this reason it is under-standable that Clarkson and Davis should concentrate on the beliefs of those normally regarded as among the leading thinkers of their day, since much of what they said anticipated and, to a degree, moulded popular thinking on the subject. In this respect, however, it is worth noting that Clarkson's own assumptions differed from those of Davis and other more recent investigators to the extent that he did not see humanitarian beliefs as *originating* with the figures whose ideas he described. In an ultimate sense, it was Providence, the Divine Spirit, or the Divine Influence, which spoke *through* them. This is something he emphasises in the first chapter of his book and to which he continually alludes in the two volumes that follow. Whatever else may be said of Clarkson's explanation it is eminently logical, given his assumptions, and always allowing that the ways of Providence are mysterious. This, however, is a device which Clarkson's modern successors, obliged to account for the same developments in strictly secular terms, are unable to adopt, although many of them have felt the need of it, as shown by their fondness for such notions as Adam Smith's 'invisible hand', Antonio Gramsci's 'ideological hegemony', and vaguely defined notions of 'capitalism'.

Much of the modern speculation about the origins of the movement can, in fact, be seen as reflecting an awareness that explanations based on thought and ideas alone are unsatisfactory, not least because they invoke the fallacy of endless regression. It is the old problem of the Ghost and the Machine. At some point ideas have to be related to the cultures which nurtured them, not just by showing how some beliefs led on to others but how those beliefs in general reflected the manner in which those cultures organised their material affairs. For, unless we accept some version of Clarkson's idea of Providence or, alternatively, assume that ideas lead a disembodied life of their own, we must suppose that one of the principal agencies in shaping them has been the everyday experience of men and women in the individual societies within which these ideas have arisen.

Thus, if we are seeking to explain why men and women in the late-eighteenth and early-nineteenth century found slavery no longer acceptable, it may be useful to begin by asking ourselves simply, what were the prevalent tendencies of that time and what influence might they have had on attitudes towards slavery? And here we may start by noting the enormous increase in wealth which occurred during those years. 'The characteristic which distinguishes the modern period in world history from all past periods', Volume 6 *The Cambridge Economic History of Europe* (1965) observes, 'is the fact of economic growth. It began in [eighteenth-century] Europe and spread first to the overseas countries settled from Europe. For the first time in human history it was possible to envisage a sustained increase in the volume of goods and services produced per unit of human effort or per unit of accessible resources.'[6] Carlo Cipolla begins his introduction to Volume 3 of the *Fontana Economic History of Europe* (1976) by emphasizing much the same point, ending his observation with the declaration that 'From then on, the world was no longer the same.' What these statements refer to, however, as the succeeding chapters make plain, is not simply the new elements of machine production and factory discipline – the images normally conjured up, along with belching steam and drab urban landscapes, by the Industrial Revolution – but a process of sustained economic growth the effects of which first became apparent in Britain and which manifested itself, initially at least, in the form of an increase in international trade, and, from the 1740s on, a steady increase in population. Only at a later stage did there occur the technical innovations which revolutionized cotton and iron manufacturing, preparing the way for the further expansion of trade overseas and more economic production at home. Such developments have a special significance in the case of Britain, since she became the world's first industrial power, but similar processes may be observed at work elsewhere. In France, too, from the beginning of the eighteenth century onwards, economic growth followed a continuously rising curve.[7] And perhaps nowhere in the world was the relative increase in population and wealth more remarkable than in North America, a process which, it has often been noted, lay behind Britain's desire to establish tighter control over her colonies there and so became an important factor in bringing about American independence.

All these developments are familiar to the point of triteness and it would be tedious to labour them were it not that they go far towards explaining the growing influence of the idea of Progress which, as has often been noted, was one of the principal distinguishing features of so much eighteenth- and nineteenth-century thought. It was not, to be sure, an entirely new idea. But it is plausible to suppose that its eighteenth- and nineteenth-century ascendancy reflected in part at least the everyday experiences of people of that period, just as its partial eclipse in more recent times owes much to the horrors of the present century.

This is not, of course, the only view which can be taken of the developments of these years, and many historians have chosen to emphasize instead the suffering, impoverishment and exploitation which accompanied the transition from agrarian to industrial modes of production. So far as the slavery debate is concerned, this has manifested itself in suggestions that attempts to enlist sympathy for far away slaves were designed, either consciously or unconsciously, to divert attention from other evils nearer home. That this may sometimes have been the case cannot be disproved, although evidence for it is hard to find, and, if what is being suggested is behaviour based on unconscious motives, possibly unfindable. However, it is hard to see a movement as formidable as the assault on slavery, with all its implications for radical change, simply, or even largely, as a form of negative response. Altogether, it is more plausible to suppose that anti-slavery marched in step with, and not in opposition to, the major trends of the period.

And here it is worth noting two aspects of the growth in wealth which could not but have a powerful influence on how men responded to it. First, it was of no small significance that the most dramatic increases in wealth were to be found in free-labour societies. This was pre-eminently the case with Britain, which had long prided herself on the freedom of her institutions and was widely admired abroad on that account. But the same, broadly speaking, held true of north-west Europe as a whole, whose rulers, although still some way from accepting the idea of a free market in labour, were less restrictive in this respect than they had formerly been. Probably the societies with the strongest ideological commitment to free-labour were the northern states of the American Union, where slavery had never played a significant economic role, and where it was, in any case, by the first decade of the nineteenth century, well on the way to disappearing. To be sure, all these societies profited in one way or another from the employment of slaves elsewhere. Nevertheless, the fact remains that they participated in the general increase in wealth without themselves employing slaves, at least to any signficant degree.

Secondly, it is worth noting that the increases in wealth which were occurring were generally associated with a loosening of traditional social controls. This goes against what we have often been told about the 'new industrial discipline' and it is certainly true that in factories, mines and other places of employment, workers were often regimented to a greater extent than ever before. But this in part merely reflected the fact that in other respects they experienced fewer constraints. In the towns and cities in which an increasing proportion of the new wealth was created, and into which the surplus population from the countryside drifted, workers no longer lived under the eye of the authorities to the same extent as in the communities they had left. The act of moving was itself testimony to the greater flexibility required by the new methods of production. Whether this meant that workers were 'freer' than before is a question that can be debated, but plainly some of the old rigidities were disappearing as new market forces asserted themselves.

It is always dangerous to introduce the name of Adam Smith into any discussion of eighteenth-century attitudes because of his association with the free trade movement and the fact that free trade principles were not generally accepted until much later. However, if we think of Smith simply as the advocate of a free market economy, it is plain that much of what he said reflected trends already discernable in his own day. As with so many other notable economists, and indeed intellectual innovators generally, his achievement is to be judged less as a triumph of abstract thought than as a shrewd assessment of an ongoing process and his willingness, above all, to accept unconventional conclusions – most notably the view that the freest system would, at least in the long run, prove the most productive. As an abstract proposition, this belief has very little to commend it. Much human history goes to prove precisely the opposite: namely that a relaxation of controls leads to chaos. Nevertheless, it was a very accurate description of processes which were going on in his own society from his observation of which, although he did not fully understand them, he was prepared to propose universal laws governing all human societies everywhere.

Among those societies which could not readily be fitted into Smith's scheme of things were the slave societies of the New World. To be sure, it could be argued, and most convincingly, that giving the slave-traders and the slave-holders a free hand would encourage them to organize their affairs on a profitable basis and so contribute to the wealth of society. The difficulty with this argument was that it excluded the slaves by making them mere instruments of production, thereby invalidating the general proposition that greater freedom would inevitably lead to greater prosperity; for, if one group could be excluded, why not another? As Clarkson was delighted to note, Smith had come out strongly against slavery, but it was logic (assisted, perhaps, by his own humanitarian preferences) and not observation that led him to that position. In fact he never really considered whether the rules best suited for governing a rapidly diversifying British economy were equally appropriate for other types of society, such as colonies producing export staples by means of imported slave labour, still less what the practical effects of a general loosening of controls would be in such cases.

But, it may be asked, what connection is there between Adam Smith and the abolitionists? The most obvious one, although perhaps the least interesting, was their fondness for citing him, together with other political economists like John Millar, who belonged to the same school of thought, as evidence of the fact that slavery was impolitic. 'In his *Wealth of Nations*,' Clarkson notes, 'he showed in a forcible manner (for he appealed to the interests of those concerned) the dearness of African labour, or, the impolicy of employing slaves'.[8]

More significant, perhaps, was their own use of arguments based on the political economists' assumptions. 'It was asked', declared Buxton in June 1833, 'what, in the case of emancipation, was to make the negroes work? He would ask what made other people work? and he would say wages and free labour'.[9] Others, extrapolating more daringly, argued that freedom would be the economic saving of the West Indies. Free workers would be willing workers. They would also be potential customers for Britain's manufacturers. To all of which, not surprisingly, the West Indians replied that Parliament needed to take account of the special circumstances governing slave economies. 'They had no evidence' Hume pointed out, 'to prove what could be done by free labour in the colonies; nor had they any evidence to show that the slaves could be brought so to labour'.[10] Much of the 1833 Parliamentary debate over West Indies emancipation revolved around the basic question of whether metropolitan standards could be applied to the colonies.

This still leaves open the question as to how far the abolitionists, and those who voted with them, actually *believed* the arguments they were using. Did Buxton, or James Stephen – or James Silk Buckingham, for that matter, who was the most forceful exponent of the free-labour argument – genuinely believe that emancipation would increase production? Many grass-roots supporters plainly did, if we may judge by the letters of surprise which later flooded into the Anti-Slavery Society when it became evident that production had fallen and that Britain was thinking of turning elsewhere for her sugar.[11] But did the leaders of the movement believe it? After all, it was tempting to use one argument (that free labour was best) to counter another argument (that emancipated slaves would not work) without personally having much faith in the practical outcome, the effects of which would, fortunately, become evident only after emancipation had been accomplished.[12] Moreover, for every statement that there were good, practical grounds for wanting to get rid of the slave trade or slavery, another could be cited, often from the same source, to the effect that they should be got rid of regardless of consequences.[13] Taken at face value, these assertions would seem to support Clarkson's view that the assault on slavery was essentially a religious phenomenon, to which it is only necessary to add, by way of rounding-out the picture, that even the religious were obliged to indulge in secular polemics.

The problem with this explanation is that it makes too artificial a distinction between religious and secular thinking, and ignores the extent to which both drew their strength from a common source, namely the eighteenth-century belief in an improvable, and progressively improving, world. As an illustration of the way in which these strands came together, we may appropriately begin by noting the appearance, around the 1750s, of a new brand of social theory which maintained that the key factor in social development was the mode of subsistence. The first written expressions of this idea are to be found in France, but it was soon being developed by Scottish Enlightenment thinkers who in all probability had got it from Adam Smith's Edinburgh lectures of 1750–1. Specifically, what was being argued was that all societies tend to evolve through four consecutive stages – hunting, pasturage, agriculture and commerce – with each successive stage generating its own distinctive sets of beliefs and institutions. As later developed by Smith himself, and in even greater detail by his pupil John Millar, the idea grew into a full-blown materialist conception of history.[14]

That such an idea owed much to the actual circumstances of the times which produced it is evident. More to the point, however, is the extent to which such secular beliefs permeated the thinking of even such an avowedly religious thinker as William Wilberforce, who also saw the world as a collection of societies at different stages of development, with Britain, closely followed by the other Christian nations, in the lead. The great hope for the future, according to Wilberforce, lay in the process of cultural dissemination by means of which the civilized nations would pass on those elements of their cultures from which others, less fortunate than themselves, might best profit. If they had not yet reached the agricultural stage, they stood in need of instruction in the techniques of cultivation; if they had already reached the agricultural stage, then what they required was commerce. Above all, what they needed was an introduction to the Christian religion, which was important not only as a means of saving souls but as a vehicle for conveying Western values generally.[15]

Put in this way it may appear that such ideas might express themselves more naturally in missionary activities than in combatting slavery; and it is true that one consequence of the new belief that history was a progressive, dynamic process, and that the nations deriving their culture from Western Europe stood in the vanguard, was a dramatic increase in the scale of the efforts to bring 'civilization' to 'savages'. Many abolitionists were involved in these undertakings and for the most part subscribed to the contemporary view that cultures which differed significantly from the European norm were to be held in low esteem. Wilberforce was every bit as intolerant in his view of Hindu society as he was of the slave societies of the New World. But if what concerns us are the practical consequences of an increasinging pride in Western civilization, combined with a belief that societies were malleable and that human progress could be shared by all, it is easy to see why reformers should have been no less zealous in rooting out 'regressive,' 'immoral' or 'un-Christian' practices from their own societies than in acting as culture-bearers to remote peoples who had never had the benefit of instruction in Western values.

Whether slavery was actually regressive in an economic sense is beside the point. It is equally immaterial whether, or in what respects, Indian and African cultures were 'backward'. In each case, what impressed the proselytizers was the fact that they represented deviations from what, on the basis of their own experience, they regarded as the civilized norms. As William Robertson, the historian of India, noted in 1790, 'Men in every state of their career are so satisfied with the progress made by the community in which they are members, that it becomes a standard of perfection, and they are apt to regard people whose condition is not similar with contempt and aversion . . .'[16] This was not entirely true, for the new reformers were also intent on improving their own societies. Nevertheless, it was a point frequently noted by the defenders of the West Indian interest in the Parliamentary debates of 1833. It was the misfortune of Britain's colonists, Richard Vyvyan, M.P. for Bristol, declared, 'to be governed and controlled by the delegates of the inhabitants of the shops and factories . . . of the United Kingdom'.[17] By the same token, the planters of the American southern states were obliged to compete for control over what they saw as their own domestic affairs with the farmers and mechanics of the North.

What made the cultural trends opposing slavery so formidable, however, was not simply the conjunction of free labour and economic growth but their association with another emergent force of the period: nationalism. The fusion of nationalism with progressive history is not without logical foundations. The assumption that history is progressive, and that the direction it takes can to some degree be controlled, implies the need for an instrument capable of guiding its development, and that function is one that has been assigned principally to national governments which, in turn, have used it as a way of justifying the manner in which they have exercised their powers. Nationalism, in its modern form, is largely a creation of the later eighteenth century, and one of its distinguishing features has been a tendency towards centralization and uniformity. The effects of this have been as evident in the cultural field as in the political and economic, as national standards have emerged with regard to speech, dress, thought, and social mores. The consequences of this trend are perhaps most evident in the case of the United States, where the South's belief that Northerners were attempting to appropriate to themselves the right to define what was and what was not American and were imposing their standards on the nation at large was an important factor in the sectional hostility of the ante-bellum years. George Fitzhugh was only one of many to urge his fellow Southerners to establish their own standards and not to feel ashamed, when these differed from those of the North and of Europe, of appearing provincial.[18] For the same reason the Democratic Party appealed to Southerners (as it did to the Irish and immigrant groups generally) by virtue of its emphasis on the need to accept cultural pluralism and regional diversity, in contrast to its Whig and Republican opponents whom it saw as consolidationists, intent on strengthening the powers of the central government as a means of ensuring national uniformity. Yet although these tendencies stand out most clearly in the case of the United States, where they challenged the very existence of the nation state and were only resolved as a result of a long and bloody civil war, there is plenty of evidence that similar forces were at work within the British Empire. For just as the greater pace of northern development had the effect of making Southerners appear peculiar Americans, so the rapid expansion of the metropolitan economy made the defenders of slavery seem peculiar Englishmen by virtue of standing out against changes which their contemporaries saw as in keeping with the prevailing tendencies of the times.

If, then, it is asked why men in the late eighteenth and early nineteenth century turned against an institution which they had previously either supported or regarded with indifference we may offer an account significantly different from that given by Clarkson. First, we may begin by noting how the economic changes of the period encouraged a progressive view of history. Secondly, we may examine the way in which the social changes associated with that development helped to create a belief that there were universal laws governing human progress. Thirdly, we may observe that there was a tendency, even amongst those avowedly moved by religious notions, to link these laws to what they took to be the essential values of Western culture, and thus to believe that, potentially at least, they could be shared by all men everywhere. And, finally, we may note how these beliefs were strengthened by the advent of modern nationalism. They were, of course, arrogant beliefs, although in the case of the abolitionists this fact has gone unrecognized, mainly because of the abhorrence which slavery still inspires. Nevertheless, it is easy to see why Southern slaveholders, like Indian sepoys, should have responded violently to what they saw as a deliberate attempt to destroy their way of life by imposing on them cultural standards which they regarded as alien.

In a sense, anti-slavery marks a halfway stage between the religious struggles of earlier times and recent conflicts arising out of the opposition of more strictly secular ideologies. Not surprisingly, contemporaries interpreted it in terms of the concepts with which they were familiar, which meant putting it into a religious context. Looking back, however, it is clear that what they saw as the outcome of religious beliefs can more accurately be accounted for in cultural terms, and in particular in terms of that impulse to remake the world in its own image which characterised Western civilization during the period of its ascendency.

Notes

1 Quoted in David M. Potter and Thomas G. Manning, *Nationalism and Sectionalism in America, 1775–1877: Select Problems in Historical Interpretation* (New York, 1949), p. 1.

2 Thomas Clarkson, *The History of the Rise, Progress and Accomplishment of the Abolition of the African Slave Trade by the British Parliament* (1808), 1, 264.

3 Eric Williams, *Capitalism and Slavery* (first pub. 1944, reprinted 1964), p. 161.

4 Seymour Drescher, *Econocide: British Slavery in the Era of Abolition* (Pittsburgh, 1977). Other theories are specifically discussed in Seymour Drescher, 'Capitalism and the decline of slavery: the British case in comparative perspective', *Annals of the New York Academy of Sciences*, 292 (1977), pp. 132–42.

5 Alfred H. Conrad and John R. Meyer, *Studies in Econometric History* (1965), pp. 3–114: Robert William Fogel and Stanley L. Engermann, *Time on the Cross: The Economics of American Negro Slavery* (Boston, 1974). Although many of Fogel and Engerman's inferences have been subject to criticism, their general findings concerning the profitability and continuing viability of slavery have not been seriously challenged.

6 *Cambridge Economic History of Europe: The Industrial Revolution and After* (1965), VI, part 1, p. 1.

7 Claude Fohlen, 'The Industrial Revolution in France, 1700–1914', in Carlo Cipolla (ed.), *The Fontana Economic History of Europe: The Emergence of Industrial Societies, Part One* (1973), p. 11.

8 Clarkson, *Abolition of the Slave Trade*, 1, p. 86.

9 *Hansard's Parliamentary Debates*, 3rd series, 18 (10 June 1833), p. 517.

10 *Ibid.* (7 June 1833), p. 459.

11 Howard Temperley, *British Antislavery 1833–70* (1972), p. 147–8. For a more general discussion of the free labour versus slave labour debate, see Howard Temperley, 'Capitalism, slavery and ideology', *Past and Present*, 75 (May 1977), pp. 94–118.

12 This was a prominent theme in the Lincoln–Douglas debates of 1858;
    see, for example, Stephen Douglas's Chicago speech of 9 July in Robert
    W. Johnannsen (ed.), *The Lincoln–Douglas Debates of 1858* (New
    York, 1965), esp. pp. 29–31.

13 See, for example, *Hansard*, 18 (May–June 1833), pp. 163, 516, and
    538.

14 The best general account of this development is Ronald L. Meek, *Social
    Science and the Ignoble Savage* (Cambridge, 1975).

15 William Wilberforce, *A Letter on the Abolition of the Slave Trade*
    (1807), pp. 73–4.

16 Quoted in George D. Bearce, *British Attitudes Towards India,
    1784–1858* (Oxford, 1961), p. 27.

17 *Hansard*, 18 (30 May 1833), p. 113.

18 George Fitzhugh, *Cannibals All, or Slaves Without Masters* (1857;
    Cambridge, Mass., 1960 edn.), pp. 57–60.

17
SLAVERY AND 'PROGRESS'

by David Brion Davis

Throughout human history, slavery has been used in different ways as a symbolic test of optimism or pessimism, of faith in moral progress or despair over what Mark Twain called, in his cynical old age, 'the damned human race'. For example, in 1759 when Voltaire wrote his satirical commentary on the philosophy that 'this world of ours is the best of all possible worlds', he pictured the innocent Candide, in one of many unforgettable incidents, entering Surinam and encountering a Negro slave who is lying on the ground. The slave, who has lost both a hand and a leg, tells Candide that this is 'the price paid for the sugar you eat in Europe'. In Africa, the black recalls, he had been sold by his mother who had said, 'you have the honor to be a slave of our lords the white men and thereby you have made the fortune of your father and mother'. For eighteenth-century readers, the black's bitter remarks were an obvious parody on the philosophy of Leibniz, Jean Christian Wolff, and other theodicists who had found elaborate excuses for evil while defending God's ways to man. 'O Pangloss!' cries Candide, 'this is an abomination you had not guessed; this is too much, in the end I shall have to renounce optimism'. 'What is this optimism?' asks Cacambo, Candide's valet. 'Alas', says Candide, 'it is the mania of maintaining that all is good when all is bad'. And Candide weeps as he enters Surinam.

By the mid-eighteenth century such cynicism was becoming a fashionable response to unconvincing theodicy and religious apologetics. But as an alternative to cynicism or attempts to justify evil as part of God's design, the following century brought a remarkable upsurge of faith in historical progress, moral as well as material. Even by 1759, British and American Quakers had concluded that the atrocities of slavery were too high a price for sugar, and the Quaker initiative led to organized protest against the Atlantic slave trade. Few events in history contributed more substance to the belief in progress than the success in 1807 of both the British and American movements to outlaw their own participation in slave trade. By 1833, when Britain emancipated some 780,000 Colonial slaves, generously paying £20 million compensation to their supposed owners, the lesson seemed clear. In the Anglo–American world, excluding the Southern slave-holding states, historians, theologians, and moral philosophers increasingly cited the progressive abolition of slavery as proof of a divine purpose in history, a purpose gradually revealed and made manifest through human enlightenment.

The triumph of British abolitionism had profound implications for middle-class optimism and the idea of progress. Although liberals hailed West Indian emancipation as the culmination of a long historical process that had begun with the gradual disappearance of slavery and serfdom from Western Europe, it also differed from all previous emancipations. Most nineteenth-century historians attributed the elevation of European slaves and serfs to the beneficient influence of Christianity, though from John Millar to Comte and Marx social philosophers tended to stress impersonal social and economic forces. In either case, the progress of liberty had depended on the unfolding of some unconscious or immanent design. But the abolition of the Anglo–American slave trade and West Indian slavery were supposedly the result of a sustained agitation and an increasingly enlightened public opinion. By demonstrating the potency of ideas and of organized action to effect moral goals, the anti-slavery movement signified a new phase or dispensation in the struggle for human liberty.

This emphasis on the power of enlightened opinion led to a second, more political implication. The French Revolution had disillusioned many British and American liberals and had deepened middle-class mistrust of popular agitation. Even apart from the example of France, only a few radicals could draw comfort from the history of popular protest that ran from the English Wilkesite mobs of the 1760s and the American Liberty Boys of the 1770s to the Luddite and other quasi-revolutionary movements of the early nineteenth century. But in Britain the anti-slavery movement helped to vindicate middle-class faith in the beneficent effects of public opinion. It presented an example of contained and supposedly disinterested public influence on national policy, an example that made organized public influence seem less dangerous than before.

Even in the United States, where abolitionism raised more

explosive issues, the British demonstration of practical idealism appealed to the religious and poetic imagination. The wider meaning was perhaps best expressed by Ralph Waldo Emerson, commemorating the tenth anniversary of British West Indian emancipation, an event he described as 'singular in the history of civilization; a day of reason; of the clear light; of that which makes us better than a flock of birds and beasts: a day, which gave the immense fortification of a fact, – of gross history, – to ethical abstraction'. Emerson, it should be stressed, was not an abolitionist, but he regarded the British abolition of slavery as tangible proof of moral progress and as the dawn of a new era when the masses would awaken and insist that a clear moral standard be applied to every public question. 'The Power that built this fabric of things', Emerson said, 'has made a sign to the ages, of his will'. Like most American and British liberals, Emerson confidently acknowledged that emancipation had been encouraged by material progress and national self-interest. The British knew that 'slavery . . . does not love the whistle of the railroad; it does not love the newspaper, the mailbag, a college, a book, or a preacher who has the absurd whim of saying what he thinks'. Yet the fact remained that 'other revolutions have been the insurrection of the oppressed; this was the repentance of the tyrant'. In other words, for the first time in history the more enlightened nations were beginning to understand that morality, self-interest, and human progress were mutually interdependent and were to be achieved by the same means.

Since Emerson was expressing ideas that were gaining wide currency by the 1840s, ideas that would later affect opinion and policy not only regarding slavery but also regarding the responsibility of the progressive nations to help civilize Africa and what is now known as the Third World, it is worth underscoring two points that might easily be missed. First, the unity of morality, self-interest, and human progress became manifest only in a struggle against an institution like slavery, a product of 'gross history', which could be designated as both a reproach to Christianity and an obstacle to economic improvement. Secondly, what Emerson termed a 'repentance of the tyrant' took the form of a revolution from above, a revolution benefiting both the oppressed and oppressor, but on terms defined by the oppressor. Emerson assured his audience that the British blacks had celebrated the hour of emancipation with prayer, not with riot, feasting, dancing, or even music. The next Monday morning, 'with very few exceptions, every negro on every plantation was in the field at his work'.

Only the most bitter misanthrope could contend that the world has not benefited morally from the abolition of the African slave trade and from the eradication in most parts of the world of chattel slavery. If Emerson and the abolitionists suffered from certain naïve expectations, their expectations deserve respect as a potent historical force – a force which, like pessimistic resignation, has had tangible effects. It is worth emphasizing that when Adam Smith published *The Wealth of Nations* in 1776, slavery was a legally accepted institution in all the colonies of the New World. Although Smith sought to prove the economic benefits of free labor, he admitted that 'a small part of the West of Europe is the only portion of the globe that is free' from slavery and expressed little hope that the institution would soon disappear from the staple-producing regions of the world. And yet an African youth taken to Brazil in the 1780s, when the first anti-slavery societies were organized in England and North America, could easily have had a grandchild among the last slaves to be freed in the New World. I am not concerned here with questions of causation or with explaining why slavery was abolished within a relatively brief span of time, although I will venture the opinion that theories of economic determinism cannot supply the answer. To put the achievement in perspective we need only recall that the enslavement of Africans by Europeans had begun long before the discovery of America and that slavery itself had endured for millennia without significant moral protest.

But before rejoicing too freely over this remarkable evidence of nineteenth-century progress, we should also briefly remind ourselves of the horrors of our own century which were wholly unforeseen by nineteenth-century worshippers of progress. As late as 1933, the centennial of British slave emancipation and the year of Hitler's rise to power as Chancellor of Germany, Sir Reginald Coupland could proclaim that abolitionist principles had finally triumphed and 'that, except perhaps in remote and unsettled regions of the world beyond the present reach of civilized opinion, the final eradication of the slave-system is assured in no long space of time'. Although even the best estimates can be no more than half-blind guesses, it seems highly probable that since 1933 many more people have been subjected to new forms of political and penal slave labor than were transported as slaves, over a period of nearly four centuries, from Africa to the New World.

One can argue, of course, that inmates of modern slave-labor camps are not really slaves. No one claims to own them and their offspring as chattel property; the institution is not economic in purpose but is rather part of a penal system ensuring subjugation to the will of the state. These points have repeatedly confused debates over slavery in the United Nations and have even divided the British Anti-Slavery Society, which has concluded with wonderful conciseness that in communist societies 'slavery has been taken out of private ownership'. But to complicate matters further, one may observe that Coupland's reference to 'the slave-system' homogenized the traditional servitude of pre-modern tribesmen with the racial slavery of white planter capitalists; that true slavery has seldom played an important part in Islamic economies, long the major focus of the Anti-Slavery Society; and that forced labor has been of considerable economic importance since World War II in Russia and Eastern Europe. Moreover, the label of 'penal servitude' could be applied initially to large numbers of the African slaves sent to America, who were sold along with war captives after being convicted of crimes or trumped-up infractions of religious or political rules. I do not mean to deny significant distinctions, but if one has been working on a plantation or in a penal camp for most of one's life, it probably makes little difference whether one got there by the legal fiction of sale as a piece of property or as the result of some alleged civil or political crime that has almost faded from memory. Even the question of inherited status diminishes in importance when there is a preponderantly male population and little chance of establishing viable families, a deprivation familiar to black slaves in certain parts of the New World as well as to inmates of forced-labor camps.

That slave labor is inherently unproductive and uneconomical was a key article of faith from Adam Smith to Emerson and Coupland; it underlay much of the confidence of abolitionists and became embedded in Marxian as well as classical liberal economic theory. But during the past twenty years a school of mathematical economists, exemplified most recently by Robert Fogel and Stanley Engerman, has argued that slaves in the American South were not only profitable as an investment but that their labor was more efficient than that on Northern free-labor family farms; that slave labor contributed to a high rate of economic growth and to a relatively high per capita income; and that in 1860 Southern slavery had never been stronger or more closely tied to material progress. In a more recent study Seymour Drescher has marshalled fresh evidence to show that prior to 1814 the British slave colonies were not declining in economic importance, as commonly supposed, but were rather acquiring an increasing share of British overseas trade as well as increasing value to the British economy as a whole. The questions being raised by such economists and historians are difficult and often technical; one should be cautious in accepting even tentative answers. Nevertheless, we can no longer assume that slave systems are intrinsically unprogressive and self-destructive, or that the abolition of New World slavery was bound to occur as the result of economic forces guided by self-interest. Liberal ideology underestimated the flexibility and capacity for growth of the plantation systems of the New World, much as Communist ideology later underestimated the flexibility and capacity of innovation of the capitalist world. Western democracies have continued to underestimate the productive and scientific capabilities of totalitarian regimes, of both left and right, which have made extensive use of coerced labor. If there is any lingering confidence in the inevitability and irreversibility of universal emancipation, one might consider the possible horrors of genetic engineering which, in line with Aldous Huxley's now technologically old-fashioned *Brave New World*, might someday create the ideal natural slaves that nature has refused to create.

But my purpose here is not to engage in prophecy but rather to set the abolition of New World slavery within a wider historical perspective and to show how various perceptions of slavery have been tied, over a broad sweep of time, to notions of human progress. I realize that wide perspectives can blur one's focus, and that to leap over centuries and from one continent to another is to risk hopeless confusion. But the risk seems worth taking if I can succeed in calling attention to a curious symmetry or cycle that has characterized the history of slavery and anti-slavery over the past six centuries.

What I have in mind, if I may first briefly summarize this cycle, begins with the fact that the European exploitation of African labor was a direct outgrowth of centuries of war and trade with the more advanced Islamic world, where black slavery had long been a familiar institution. The spread of black slavery from the Mediterranean to the Atlantic Islands and finally to the West Indies and Brazil was closely tied to the expansion of European trade, technology, and religion, and hence with Europe's gradual strategic gains over the rival Islamic world. Plantation slavery, far from being an aberration bequeathed by lawless buccaneers and lazy New World adventurers, as nineteenth-century liberals often supposed, was a creation of the most progressive peoples and forces in Europe – Italian merchants; Iberian explorers; Jewish inventors and cartographers; Dutch, German, and British investors and bankers.

From the colonization of Madeira and other sugar-producing islands off the coast of West Africa to the final colonization of the New World, Negro slavery was an intrinic part of European expansion.

Indeed, given the appalling mortality of New World Indians, largely from European diseases, and the fact that Ottoman Turks had shut off the traditional sources of white slave labor from the Black Sea, it can be argued that the development of the New World as a producer of tropical staples would have been impossible without African slaves. Yet by the nineteenth century, as we have already seen, it was anti-slavery that had become intermeshed with Europe's, and especially England's, ideas of material progress and commercial expansion. And to complete the ironic cycle, the final targets of the anti-slavery movement included Spanish Cuba, independent Brazil, and Portuguese Africa, the very regions to which Europeans had first adapted Negro slavery. By the turn of our own century the remaining targets were the Islamic Middle East and Africa, the regions from which Europeans had originally derived black slavery. The persistence of various forms of bondage supposedly proved that these societies were backward and pre-modern, and thus subject to an externally imposed emancipation as a first step toward civilization and progress.

If we are to do more than simply describe this rather eerie cycle, it is important to note the problems raised by applying a term like slavery to highly diverse forms of servile labor in different cultures over many centuries. Historically, the word for slaves has been applied to captives held for ceremonial sacrifice: to household servants who were part of what the Romans called a *familia* and who, like free wives and children, were under the dominion of a *paterfamilias*; to the concubines and eunuchs of a Muslim harem; to children held as pawns for their parents' debts; to female children sold as brides; and by analogy, to subject or conquered populations; to the industrial proletariat; and to victims of racial or political tyranny. In some societies, like India, slaves have enjoyed a higher status than the lowest castes of free workers. Slaves have been given honored posts in royal courts and militias, they have been allowed to enter the arts and professions, to marry free spouses, and to travel or conduct business with minimal interference. One could also cite examples of nominally free workers who have been transported across the seas to labor in mines or on plantations; who have been segregated racially as a pariah group; who have been subject to arbitrary corporal punishment and deprived in practice of legal rights; and whose children, if technically freeborn, have had little chance of escaping their parents' status.

This confusion is itself a significant social and psychological fact. Why did Roman law place the captives who labored in Spanish silver mines within the same juridical category as the privileged urban slaves whose *peculium* allowed them to engage in business or commerce on their own and who, except for being theoretically the property of their masters, were hardly distinguishable from free merchants and shopkeepers? Why did Muslims apply the same legal definition to the elite black military and administrative officials in Iran and India that they applied to the thousands of black East Africans who labored in regimented gangs on the tidal flats of southern Iraq and who in A.D. 869 rose in mass insurrection? And quite apart from common discrepancies between the slave's legal status and his actual economic and social functions, why did religious leaders invoke the ideal of bondage to describe man's proper submission to Yaweh, Christ, or Allah?

What distinguished slavery in much of the pre-modern world was not its antithesis to free labor but its antithesis to the normal network of kinship ties of dependency, protection, obligation, and privilege, ties which easily served as a model for non-kinship forms of patronage, clientage, and voluntary servitude. The archetypal slave was an outsider, torn from his protective family matrix by capture, treacherous sale, crime, or other supposed self-alienation. The Old Testament is filled with such examples, and it is significant that in the earliest Saxon law a stranger who had no one to protect him as a family member was automatically regarded as a slave. One should quickly add that through most of history slavery has appeared as a domestic institution. Yet in a critical sense the slave did not belong to the household that claimed his service. His identity did not grow from family traditions and relationships but rather depended on his acceptance of an adventitious and existential state, and on his loyalty to authorities who were not his kin. Hence, to become a 'slave' of God or Christ was not simply to imitate the humility and subservience of a bondsman. It was also to acknowledge the transference of primal loyalties and obligations to a new and awesome power, in the hope perhaps of a new and transcendent freedom.

Deracinated from his own kinship group, the slave stood apart from the dynamics of family psychology or from what today we might loosely term the Oedipal system. By definition, he could not progress through the stages of dependency and self-assertion that would prepare him to replace his models of authority. His dependency was perpetual unless ended by physical rebellion or by the transfiguring act of manumission. This status as a dependent who is also an outsider gave slaves an added value in many patriarchal and dynastic societies. It was not accidental that Muslims extended the concept of slavery to concubines, who complemented the legal allotment of wives; or to eunuchs, whose seed could not pollute the lines of family descent.

As a kind of root or archetypal concept, slavery took on rich layers of metaphorical and allegorical meaning as Christians and Muslims adapted and added to the ancient Hebrew traditions of bondage, traditions which Jews continue to commemorate at Passover. Considering our theme of progress, the momentous verbal extensions pertained to the history of human redemption. For example, Saint Paul spoke of all creation being delivered from slavish corruption into the liberty of the children of God. Early Christians interpreted the stories of Israel's deliverance from bondage in Egypt and of Abraham's slaveborn and freeborn sons as 'prefigurations' of Christ's salvation of man. From at least as early as the Stoics, philosophers and theologians distinguished the literal application of terms like 'slavery' from the supposedly deeper and truer meanings which the terms contained. Without venturing further into historical ideas of language, it can be affirmed that virtually every vision of individual salvation or collective utopia has been conceived as a release or emancipation from a genuine but final slavery. Perfect liberty, to be sure, has been no more attainable in this world than perfect and total submission. The important point is that the symbolic associations derived from pre-modern slavery, from the example of human captives half-domesticated to an alien household, became deeply embedded in religious and secular literature. The associations survived in societies like those of Western Europe where slavery itself disappeared. Modern concepts of political, religious, economic, and even psychological liberty were originally defined in reference to some image of slavery. For the institution of bondage suggested not only deracination, submission, and alienation, but 'the state of War continued', in John Locke's phrase, between two antagonists with irreconcilable interests. As warfare sublimated, slavery could stand for an elemental struggle between exploiters and exploited; or for a necessary stage in man's individual and collective journey toward free consciousness; or as a model for converting men into commodities and for objectifying all human relationships.

This background helps to illuminate the ancient and continuing tension between slavery and religious mission. For Jews, Muslims, and Christians, all of whom believed in a mission under the guidance of a monotheistic God, religious norms proscribed the forcible enslavement of members of the same faith. Ancient Jewish law limited the duration and conditions of Jewish servitude; Muslim law expressly prohibited the enslavement of Muslims; and Christian practice, while more flexible for a time, tended to require by the late Middle Ages that slaves be of proven infidel or pagan origin. All three religions permitted the enslavement of outsiders, but usually on the assumption that such slavery was a benefit since it offered nonbelievers the chance of religious conversion, which was the earliest idea of moral progress. The critical question was not whether conversion brought immediate emancipation, which it seldom did in any society, but whether assimilation to the household's religion would bring a recognition of legitimate kinship ties and the right of natal descent. In particular, would the children of converted slaves be free or belong to their mother's owner? There is evidence that for Jews, Christians, and Muslims alike this was sometimes a difficult question to answer. For Muslims, and then Christians, the question became less difficult as slaves were increasingly recruited from alien peoples who, because of their ethnic or racial characteristics, were easily distinguishable even after religious conversion and acculturation. The relative permanence of slave status was also reinforced wherever slaves replaced the more traditional forms of conscripted, nonslave labor in such enterprises as mining, public works, and commercialized agriculture. And yet both Muslims and Christians tended to equate such uses of slave labor with the domestic and paternalistic bondage which their religions had always sanctioned. Even the final extension of slavery to the large-scale plantation was justified by the old ideal of the household as an agency of conversion and gradual assimilation.

In a sense, modern black slavery was an Islamic creation. It is true that Africans had long enslaved fellow Africans, and that Arabs were always eager to buy white slaves from markets on the Black Sea or elsewhere. From the outset, Islam was a faith to be spread by religious wars, or jihads, which made all infidels subject to enslavement. Religious mission, coupled with the paternalistic ideal of household slavery, made it seem just and natural that *Dar al-Islam*, the world where Islam ruled, should be peopled with servants from *Dar al-Harb*, the lands of infidelity. Religious warfare brought in a continuous stream of captives, at first predominately from

Europe, eventually from the Asian steppes, India, and sub-Saharan Africa. At times the very success of Muslim arms promised to exhaust the supply of infidels. Neither the female slaves in a harem nor the male slaves recruited for an Arab army were likely to reproduce their replacements. But the development of commerce with *Dar al-Harb*, supplemented later by Turkish expansion and by Mediterranean piracy, helped to fill the vacancies in Muslim harems, households, and armies. After making all these qualifications, however, the fact remains that by the late Middle Ages, when European Christians had reconquered most of the Iberian Peninsula and had begun to compete on Muslim terms for the trade of West Africa, that the lowest and most degraded Muslim slaves were almost exclusively black. The Arabic word for slave, *'abd*, was becoming a synonym for black, whereas the word *mamluk* referred only to the white slave elite.

The Arabs, like the earlier Romans and later Iberians, did not conquer empires in order to make slaves. Yet the three great periods of conquest had a decisive impact on the history of slavery. In the seventh century A.D. the Arabs and their Muslim converts conquered an area that extended from the Pyrenees to the Indus. While later losing ground in Western Europe, by the fifteenth century Muslims had encircled the head of black Africa from modern Tanzania on the east to northern Nigeria on the west, drawing slaves from distant interior regions and preparing the way for things to come. One must emphasize that the spread of Islam in Africa depended largely on dark-skinned converts who derived military and commercial power from their new religious identity. Moreover, the societies of black Africa displayed remarkable resistance, surrendering to Islamic influence only along the southern fringes of the Sahara, on the extreme northwestern border, and in a few spots along the eastern coast. On the other hand, even by the eleventh century, Arab writers were spreading all the stereotypes of Negro inferiority that would later be invoked by Christian slaveholders in the New World. Arabs cited the Biblical curse of Canaan, and held that the children of Ham had been blackened as punishment for their ancestor's sin. For Arabs, as for later Europeans, black skin suggested sin, damnation, and the devil. Arab literature is saturated with references to the nudity, paganism, cannibalism, and low intelligence of the sub-Saharan peoples. Black kings, Arabs alleged, sold their subjects without even pretext of crime of war. It would be a mistake to regard such racist beliefs as proof of a racist society. The Arabs' derogatory comments about Negroes were part of a wider contempt for non-Arab peoples. And anti-Negro prejudice was never systematized in discriminatory laws and institutions.

But because of their religious prohibition against enslaving Muslims, the Arabs were the first modern people to create a continuing demand for large numbers of foreign slaves. The demand persisted from the seventh to the twentieth century. The Arabs were also the first people to develop, on a massive scale, a long-distance carrying trade in slaves. Regardless of the humanity of Muslim law, regardless of the treatment in urban households, the slaves transported by caravan across the deserts or by small boats across the seas to the Persian Gulf, to India, or as far as China, must have suffered no less than those on the so-called Atlantic Middle Passage. A lack of statistics prevents confident estimates of the number of Africans imported into the Islamic lands of Asia or of the number who died en route. There can be little doubt, however, that the Arab slave trade became increasingly an African slave trade or that its magnitude, over more than ten centuries, equalled or exceeded that of the infamous Middle Passage to America.

As I have already suggested, Europeans adopted Arab slave-trading practices almost incidentally in what seemed to them a world-wide struggle – economic, military, and religious – with Islam. Like the later discovery of America, the Portuguese exploring ventures along the West African coast were part of a strategic move to outflank and encircle the Islamic world, breaking the Arab monopoly on trade with Asia. Black slaves were originally thought of simply as blackamoors, or black Muslims, and it was in the interest of religious conversion and of aiding the crusade against Islam that the fifteenth-century Papacy authorized the continuing shipment of African slaves to Portugal. This new religious mission happened to coincide in time with a more rapid westward expansion of sugar cultivation, an art which the original crusaders had learned from Arabs in Palestine. And by the second half of the fifteenth century, the economic and urban development of Western Europe had created a rapidly growing market for sugar, salt, pepper, and other spices that had an incalculable value to an age that knew nothing of refrigerated foods. Accordingly, when the island of Madeira experienced the kind of sugar boom that would later hit Brazil and the West Indies, a momentous change had occurred. Slaves, instead of being symbols of luxury and display, as in most of the Muslim world, were now producing the articles of luxury demanded by a new consumer class. Even before Columbus' voyages to America, most of Europe's sugar came from Portuguese

Slavery and 'Progress' 363

plantations on which the majority of workers were black. And of the nearly ten million black slaves ultimately sent to America, some 70 per cent were destined for the sugar colonies.

Before skipping to the last phase of the slavery–anti-slavery cycle, let me sum up by observing that Africa was first the victim of European religious mission activity combined with economic enterprise. Fed first by Muslim–Christian conflict and then by the rivalry for empire of Catholic and Protestant states, mission and enterprise legitimized slave-trading and slave colonies as obvious agents of progress – that is, progress toward the triumph of the true faith and toward national economic and strategic power. But by the late-nineteenth century Africa was hardly less the victim of a different combination of religious mission and economic enterprise, this time aimed, in the name of historical progress and Christian civilization, at abolishing the slave trade at its interior sources. If the European demand for slaves had helped to corrupt African societies, the influence had been indirect and had not challenged the right or capacity of black Africans for self-rule. Anti-slavery encouraged more direct intervention. Instead of justifying the annual removal of tens of thousands of slaves, supposedly for the good of their souls, anti-slavery helped to justify the subjection of entire peoples to colonial rule, supposedly for the good of their future civilization. Ironically, it was because Europeans had long associated black Africans with slavery and because they increasingly associated slavery with the primitive stages of human development, that they so easily concluded that Africans were a 'backward race' or a 'child race' needing tutelage from the world's most progressive peoples. The British, having taken the lead in repentance and in anti-slavery commitment, were by self-definition the people best equipped to assume such a burden.

By 1840, when a few British abolitionists had concluded that the slave trade in the Atlantic and Indian Oceans could be ended only by annexing African territory, Sir Robert Peel spelled out the ideology of progress that would underlie official policy in the last decades of the century. Peel (whose seeming conversion to anti-slavery was very recent) observed that while the British people had cheerfully granted £20 million at a time of great financial difficulty 'for the purpose of purifying themselves from the stain of any participation in the horrors and complicated evils of slavery', they could not 'conceal from themselves the mortifying reflection, that in having thus rescued their character . . . they had not succeeded in diminishing the sum of human suffering'. 'Until this country rescued

Christianity and the character of the white people' from the infamy
of the slave trade, Peel predicted, 'it never would be able to convince the black population of Africa of the moral superiority of their
European fellow men; scarcely could it convince them of the truths
of Christianity, which continued to tolerate such monstrous sins'.
He then called on his countrymen 'to lay the cornerstone of an
enterprise which has for its object to rescue Africa from debasing
superstitions, and to put an end to her miseries by the introduction
of the arts of civilization and peace'.

Six years later, Lord Palmerston, then Foreign Secretary, wrote
an equally revealing dispatch to Captain Hamerton, who was trying
to negotiate a treaty with the Sultan of Zanzibar to end the Arab
slave trade. Every opportunity should be taken, Palmerston wrote,

> of impressing upon these Arabs that the nations of Europe are destined
> to put an end to the African Slave Trade, and that Great Britain is the
> main instrument in the Hands of Providence for the accomplishment of
> this purpose. That it is vain for these Arabs to endeavour to resist the
> consummation of that which is written in the Book of Fate, and that they
> ought to bow to superior power, to leave off a pursuit which is doomed to
> annihilation . . . and that they should hasten to betake themselves to the
> cultivation of their soil and to lawful and innocent commerce.

It needs to be stressed that such high-handed moralism was not a
cloak for hidden economic interests. Britain's long crusade to stamp
out the oceanic slave trade was not only expensive, requiring naval
patrols and continuing bribes in the form of compensation; it was
also at odds with Britain's immediate political and economic interests, as can be seen from the strong pressures for compromise from
knowledgeable officials in the field. As Arabs were brought more
into the orbit of expanding Western markets, they were motivated
to penetrate deeper into the African interior in search of slave
labor. On the coast and islands of East Africa they also developed a
market-oriented plantation slavery that began to approximate the
earlier plantations of the New World. Britain's naval blockades
and ultimatums against the slave trade helped to retard this growth
and to undermine the political power of Britain's own Arab allies
and puppets.

The impetus behind British anti-slavery policies was mainly
religious. It was not accident that England's most famous African
explorer of the mid-nineteenth century, David Livingstone, was a
missionary willing to sacrifice his life if necessary to find the shortest
and easiest routes to the interior, so that Christianity, commerce,
and civilization could extinguish slavery in the very heart of darkness.

But these anti-slavery efforts and policies had the long-term strategic effect of establishing Britain's unquestioned moral and ideological hegemony over much of Africa and the Middle East, mainly at the expense of the Arabs who were cast in the role of civilization's delinquents. I do not mean to diminish the genuine British achievements or to blur the moral distinction between defending and abolishing slavery in the name of human progress. On the other hand, the effectiveness of anti-slave-trade rhetoric, in helping to legitimate empire, can be seen in the way it was finally taken over by France, Belgium, Germany, and other powers with African aspirations. In 1889–90 an international conference on the slave trade convened at Brussels, partly for the purpose of impressing Muslims with the united determination of Christian Europe. Although Lord Salisbury hailed it as the first convention in history assembled 'for the purpose of promoting a matter of pure humanity and goodwill', the Brussels Conference was dominated by European commercial and territorial rivalries. The Conference did, however, establish precedents for the kind of international trusteeship later institutionalized by the League of Nations. Symbolically, it also served to place the Islamic world on a kind of probationary status, suggesting that practices authorized by Islamic law and custom could have no place in the progressive and Europocentric world of the future.

As our own world has become less Europocentric, the moral distinctions between the progressive West and the so-called underdeveloped regions have become rather blurred. For a time the United Nations followed the anti-slavery precedents and policies of the older League of Nations, even giving the British Anti-Slavery Society consultative status at the Economic and Social Council. By 1970, slavery had been at least nominally outlawed in such stubborn nations as Saudi Arabia and Muscat. But at a time when the communist nations charged that capitalists sanctioned slavery, racism, and colonialism under other names, and when the so-called free world denounced slave labor camps behind the Iron Curtain, the British Anti-Slavery Society failed to arouse much public indignation over the sale of children and brides in parts of South America, the Middle East, and sub-Saharan Africa. Even in the case of numerous and obvious atrocities, the exploiters were the formerly exploited who could draw support from the Third World's hostility toward every heritage of colonialism. It is significant that Mohamed Awad, an Egyptian who headed the United Nations' investigations of slavery in the mid-1960s, ultimately focused his fire on the apartheid and colonialism of South Africa and Angola. By 1970, the United Nations had branded apartheid as the true slavery of the twentieth century.

Perhaps we have lost something from such confusion and from the dimming faith in moral progress. A public cynical over propaganda, wary of the risks of intervention, and satiated by tales of horror can hardly be sensitive to the cause of human rights. Yet the excesses and blindness of past moralism should not lead us, like Voltaire's Candide, to a resigned cultivation of our own gardens. For if the study of slavery and related forms of bondage proves nothing else, it should alert us to the precariousness of any freedom, and to the fact that enslavement has usually been seen by the enslavers as a form of human progress.

Note

I have concluded that it would be pretentious to try to 'document' this paper, which is frankly speculative and discursive and which makes no claim of furnishing new empirical knowledge. Most of the statements of fact are taken from standard sources.

INDEX

7